IT DID NOT START WITH JFK

THE DECADES OF EVENTS THAT LED TO THE ASSASSINATION OF JOHN F. KENNEDY

V O L U M E 2

WALTER HERBST

Published by Sunbury Press, Inc.
Mechanicsburg, PA USA

www.sunburypress.com

For information about special discounts for bulk purchases, please contact Sunbury Press Orders Dept. at (855) 338-8359 or orders@sunburypress.com.

To request one of our authors for speaking engagements or book signings, please contact Sunbury Press Publicity Dept. at publicity@sunburypress.com.

FIRST SUNBURY PRESS EDITION: October 2021

Set in Adobe Garamond Pro | Interior design by Crystal Devine | Cover by Lawrence Knorr | Edited by Lawrence Knorr.

Publisher's Cataloging-in-Publication Data
Names: Herbst, Walter, author.
Title: It did not start with JFK : the decades of events that led to the assassination of John F. Kenndy / Walter Herbst.
Description: First trade paperback edition. | Mechanicsburg, PA : Sunbury Press, 2021.
Summary : A right-wing movement is responsible for assassinating JFK. Understanding how this came to be is the key to unraveling the assassination riddle and can only be found by investigating the four decades before Kennedy's presidency. This final volume gets you one step closer to the truth.
Identifiers: ISBN : 978-1-62006-875-5 (softcover).
Subjects: HISTORY / United States / 20th Century | POLITICAL SCIENCE / Corruption & Misconduct | POLITICAL SCIENCE / Political Ideologies / Nationalism & Patriotism | POLITICAL SCIENCE / Intelligence & Espionage.

Product of the United States of America
0 1 1 2 3 5 8 13 21 34 55

Continue the Enlightenment!

For Julia, Emily, Ryan, and Norah, the source of my inspiration.

Contents

Acknowledgments vii

Introduction ix

Acronyms xiii

CHAPTERS

1. Fighting Communism in the Big Easy is Not Easy 1
2. There's Trouble in Paradise 26
3. One Good Revolution Deserves Another 53
4. Treason is a Deadly Business 77
5. Deadly Liaisons 103
6. No Ordinary Marine 132
7. Give Peace a Chance and Other Fairy Tales 173
8. The Defector Who Wasn't 190
9. Double Trouble from Moscow 216
10. What's Wrong With U-2? 245
11. Epilogue 271

Notes 287

Index 304

About the Author 311

Acknowledgments

Many years of research and writing passed before this book came to print, so naturally, I have many people to thank for making this possible.

First and foremost, I owe a tremendous debt of gratitude to my brother Robert, who has been there throughout the entire process. During my research, he was a sounding board off whom I could test theories and ideas and receive an unbiased reaction. While writing the manuscript, he read and edited every chapter and was a constant source of encouragement and support. His input in bringing this book to fruition was invaluable.

Thanks to David Aretha for providing professional editing services early on and helping me navigate through the book proposal submission process. David became a mentor when I needed one, and I will forever be grateful.

I also want to thank Lawrence Knorr, Marianne Babcock, Crystal Devine, Joe Walters, and the rest of the staff at Sunbury Press for all the assistance they have provided. Lawrence is a true history lover interested in the JFK assassination and was enthusiastic about publishing the book from the beginning. More importantly, he is a man of his word, and his passion and honesty made my decision to go with Sunbury Press an easy one.

My deepest thanks go to Mathew Selznick for all his hard work to ensure I professionally marketed the book. He has also become a mentor upon who I have come to rely increasingly more and more. His enthusiasm and belief in my work have far exceeded what I reasonably could have expected.

There were also countless people along the way who selflessly helped me research, write and present my manuscript for publication. They are too numerous to mention, but I am indebted to every one of them.

I would be remiss if I did not thank my family for all the support they have provided throughout the years. My parents Walter and Maria instilled a love of reading and an interest in history. My son Michael and his wife Debra, and my daughter Diana and her husband Philip, have listened to my rants about the JFK assassination conspiracy for years without complaint. They were always there for me, offering critical critique and assistance whenever I needed them, and I thank them for that.

Last but certainly not least, a most sincere thanks to my wife Margaret for the sacrifices she made, as she patiently watched me devote hours upon hours researching and writing, secreted in my study by myself. Many times, I know, she would have preferred to do something else, but she allowed me to pursue my dream of writing this book. Words cannot adequately express what that has meant to me.

Introduction

In January 1954, Lee Harvey Oswald and his mother, Marguerite, left New York and relocated to New Orleans. Their departure was a hasty one. Local authorities had told Marguerite that if her son Lee's behavior did not improve, they would take him away from her again. Two years earlier, a New York court sent Lee to Youth House, a home for troubled boys, for a psychological evaluation. It was a harsh sentence, considering Lee's only offense was truancy. Lee may have spent time at the Bordentown Reformatory in New Jersey during this period because there was a working relationship between the two facilities. If true, it would not have been good for Lee, for experiments with mind-altering drugs were done on boys at Bordentown, and Lee Harvey Oswald may have been one of their innocent victims. In any event, whether or not Marguerite was aware that doctors had subjected her son to such testing is unknown. What is known is that five days after a Big Brothers' caseworker visited the Oswalds at their home following Lee's release from Youth House, they left for New Orleans.

It was during this time in New Orleans when Oswald's political philosophy would start to develop. He showed an interest in Marxism, but he was not a Communist. On the contrary, he associated with David Ferrie, an ardent right-winger with Fascist tendencies, who would introduce the young Oswald to radical right-wing anti-Communists in New Orleans. These contacts impacted Lee, for the names of American Nazi Party members would later be found in his notebook. And for the remainder of his life, he would primarily associate with Fascists and right-wingers. But there was something about this group that must have concerned Marguerite, for after spending only eighteen months in the Big Easy, she and Lee relocate to Fort Worth, Texas. And she fled New Orleans just as quickly as she had left New York.

Lee Oswald joined the Marines on October 24, 1956, as soon as he was old enough to do so, only three months after arriving in Fort Worth. It is the point where the road to Dallas began for the future accused assassin of JFK. The Marines sent him to Atsugi, Japan, and as will be discussed in the following pages, it is at Atsugi where U.S. intelligence becomes aware of Oswald. He has contact with foreign agents, suspiciously spends extended periods in the brig and the hospital, and begins to act irrational, angry, and emotional. And the evidence indicates that he became part of a CIA program to send allegedly disenchanted service members behind the Iron Curtain. He returns to the Marine Corps Air Station El Toro in California and speaks and acts Russian. He attends a Unitarian Church led by a Communist pastor whose congregation supported Fidel Castro's turn to communism in Cuba. Fellow Marine Kerry Thornley introduced Oswald to the Church. Thornley appears to have previously known Oswald in New Orleans and would mysteriously meet Oswald in New Orleans once again during the summer of 1963. As will be shown, Unitarians would "babysit" Oswald for the rest of his life and played a role in his Russian "defection." Not only will we prove that Oswald's trip to Russia was a scam, but that it was an intelligence operation made to look like Oswald died there, and a Russian impostor took his place when Oswald returned to the United States. There was no impostor—it was the same Lee Harvey Oswald who traveled to Russia and returned home. It was all an illusion that would eventually play a significant role in the plot to assassinate JFK.

Meanwhile, while Lee Harvey Oswald began his odyssey in the mid-1950s, President Dwight Eisenhower was faced with a military that continued to get more belligerent. They repeatedly hounded the President to use nuclear weapons against their Communist rivals. Generals resigned in disgust, dissatisfied with the left-wing direction the country was leaning. Ike called it treason.

The CIA was no better. The Agency continued to pursue a foreign policy that at times undermined what the administration wanted to do. They expanded their assassination capacity, and after Castro came to power, they employed the Mafia to try and kill him. And they continued to sabotage the President to maintain the foreign policy direction they wanted. In Indonesia, they resorted to sabotage to try and force Ike into using the U.S. military in an attempted CIA-backed military coup. In Cuba, an attempted counterrevolution involving members of Castro's military and a CIA-sponsored group operating out of the U.S.Embassy in Havana was thwarted by Allen Dulles because the government that was to replace Castro leaned too far to the left. And when Eisenhower wanted to sign a nuclear test-ban treaty with the Russians, a U-2 spy plane was sabotaged so it would crash in the Soviet Union, ending any chance the treaty would be signed.

Many Americans who were part of the Havana Embassy group that tried to overthrow Castro would later become prime suspects in JFK's assassination, including June Cobb. Cobb was CIA and seemed to shadow Oswald the last year of his life. When Oswald joined the Fair Play for Cuba Committee, so did Cobb. When Oswald traveled to Mexico City, Cobb was working at the CIA station there. After the assassination, the FBI learned that the last book Oswald withdrew from the Dallas library was *The Shark and the Sardines*. It was about the United States' exploitation of Latin American countries. The person who edited the book into English was June Cobb. There are more examples of a possible connection between Cobb and Oswald, and we shall cover them all.

Finally, in the latter half of the 1950s, the discontent of the American radical right, the U.S. military, and the CIA had reached unmanageable proportions. The stakes were high, for as Eisenhower gravitated towards appeasement and coexistence with the Soviet Union, his opponents became firmer in their resolve to stop him. It was not an accident that JFK's assassination occurred a few years later when he tried to do the same thing. And after examining the events that transpired during the years leading up to Kennedy's Presidency, one can understand how such a tragedy came to be, for the evidence was already there.

Acronyms

AID	Agency for International Development
AIFLD	American Institute for Free Labor Development
AINS	Agency Identification Numbers, CIA
AMGOT	Allied Military Government
ARC	Addiction Research Center
ARPA	Advanced Research Projects Agency
AVG	American Volunteer Group
BAAC	British – American – Canadian – Corporation, S.A.
BIS	Bank for International Settlements
BOB	Bureau of the Budget
BPF	Banca Privata Fiinanziaria
BRAC	Bureau of Repression of Communist Activities
BUF	British Union of Fascists
CACC	Christian Anti-Communist Crusade
CAP	Civil Air Patrol
CAT	Civil Air Transport
CENIS	Center for International Studies at MIT
CI	Counterintelligence, CIA
CIA	Central Intelligence Agency
CIC	Counterintelligence Corp, U.S. Army
CI/R&A	Counterintelligence Research and Analysis
CISC	Committee for International Student Cooperation
CFR	Council on Foreign Relations
CID	Criminal Investigations Division US Army
CIG	Central Intelligence Group
CIP	Corp of Intelligence Police
COI	Coordinator of Information
CORE	Congress of Racial Equality
CPUSA	Communist Party USA
CRAC	Crusade of Revolutionaries Against Communism
CRBM	Continental Range Ballistic Missile
CRC	Cuban Revolutionary Council

DDP	Deputy Director of Plans. CIA
DGI	Cuban Intelligence in the United States
DOD	Department of Defense
DRE	Cuban Student Directorate
EIN	Employee Identification Number, CIA
FBI	Federal Bureau of Investigation
FBN	Federal Bureau of Narcotics
FCC	Federal Communications Commission
FLN	Front de Liberation Nationale
FOI	Field Operations Intelligence
FPCC	Fair Play for Cuba Committee
FRD	Cuban Revolutionary Front
G-2	U.S. Army Intelligence
HAMPCO	Haitian-American Meat and Products Company
HSCA	House Select Committee on Assassinations
HUAC	House Un-American Activities Committee
IARF	International Association for Religious Freedom
ICBM	Intercontinental Ballistic Missile
ILO	International Labor Office
INCA	Information Council of the Americas
INR	Intelligence and Research Bureau, State Department
INRA	Instituto Nacional de Reforma Agraria
INS	Immigration and Naturalization Service
IO	International Organizations Division, CIA
IRCA	International Railways of Central America
JIC	Joint Intelligence Committee
JIOA	Joint Intelligence Objectives Agency
JCS	Joint Chiefs of Staff
KGB	Soviet Intelligence Group
KMT	Kuomintang, Chiang Kai Shek's troops
LTV	Ling-Temco-Vought
MGB	Ministry of State Security, Soviet Union
MI	Military Intelligence
MIT	Massachusetts Institute of Technology
MK/NAOMI	CIA Mind Control Program
MK/ULTRA	CIA Drug Experimentation Program
MRR	Movement of Revolutionary Recovery
MVD	Ministry of Internal Affairs, Soviet Union
NAACP	National Association for the Advancement of Colored People
NANA	North American Newspaper Alliance

NATO	North Atlantic Treaty Organization
NCFE	National Committee for a Free Europe
NDF	National Defense Fund
NIA	National Intelligence Authority
NIS	Naval Intelligence Service
NKVD	Soviet Domestic Law Enforcement Agency
NOPD	New Orleans Police Department
NORAD	North American Air Defense Command
NSA	National Security Agency
NSA	National Students Association
NSC	National Security Council
NYPD	New York Police Department
NYSPI	New York State Psychiatric Institute
OAS	Organisation Armee Secrete
OAS	Organization of American States
OCB	Operations Coordinating Board
OCI	Overseas Consultants, Inc
ONI	Office of Naval Intelligence
OPC	Office of Policy Coordination
OS	Office of Security, CIA
OSO	Office of Special Operations
OSS	Office of Strategic Services
PB-7	Program Branch 7, Assassination branch within OPC
PCF	French Communist Party
PCG	Planning Coordination Group
PCI	Italian Communist Party
PERMINDEX	Right-wing European CIA front company
POW	Prisoner of War
PPS	Policy Planning Staff
PRC	People's Republic of China
PSB	Psychological Strategy Board
PSI	Italian Socialist Party
QJ/WIN	CIA assassin.
QKENCHANT	CIA program to recruit civilians.
RPF	Rassemblement du Peuple Francais
SAC	Special Agent in Charge, FBI
SAC	Strategic Air Command, Air Force
SACEUR	Supreme Allied Commander Europe
SCEF	Southern Conference Education Fund
SCI	OSS's Secret Counterintelligence

SDECE	Service de Documentation Exterieure ey de Contre-Espionnage
SIC	Scientific Intelligence Committee
SIG	Special Investigations Group, CIA
SIGINT	Signals Intelligence, NSA
SIOP	Single Integrated Operational Plan
SISS	Senate Internal Security Subcommittee
SNFE	Second National Front of the Escambray
SOD	Special Operations Division
SOFINDUS	Sociedad Financiera Industrial
SRS	Security Research Staff, CIA
SS	Nazi Germany's Secret Police
SSU	Strategic Services Unit
SWP	Socialist Workers Party
TSS	Technical Services Staff, CIA
U-2	CIA High-Altitude Spy Plane
UGEMA	Union Generale des Etudiants Musulmans Algeriens
UN	United Nations
UNTCOK	United Nations Temporary Commission on Korea
UPI	United Press International
USC	Unitarian Service Committee
UWF	United World Federalists
WCC	World Commerce Corporation
WFDY	World Federation of Democratic Youth
X-2	OSS's Counterintelligence Branch
ZR/ALERT	CIA Hypnosis Program
ZR/AWARD	CIA Behavior-Modification Operations
ZR/RIFLE	CIA Assassination Program
ZSP	Polish Student Union

- 1 -

Fighting Communism in the Big Easy is Not Easy

"My impression is that although he [Oswald] believed in pure Marxist theory, he did not believe in the way communism was practiced by the Russians. I was quite surprised when I learned Oswald had gone to Russia."

—James Botelho, Oswald's former Marine roommate
at Santa Ana, California, 1959

Along with the city of Dallas, New Orleans was ground zero for hate groups during the 1950s. Hatred against African Americans, hatred against Jews, and hatred against Communists. The most radical believed the civil rights movement was a Communist conspiracy financed by the Soviet Union, and there were White Nationalists dedicated to destroying this alliance. One way to do this was to infiltrate groups like the Communist Party USA, the Fair Play for Cuba Committee, and civil rights organizations with impressionable young people who shared the right-wing desire to undermine these groups. In the summer of 1963, Lee Harvey Oswald would become one of those infiltrators. His exposure to right-wing extremists with international connections would lead to his involvement in the assassination of JFK. But his relationship with these people began years before when he was a teenager living in New Orleans. And despite his Marxist views, the young Oswald shared their Fascist, racist ideology. And understanding what happened in Oswald's formative years explains how he later became involved with people who would direct him toward his date with destiny.

* * *

With third-world nationalism on the rise in the latter part of the 1950s, people worldwide responded to reports describing segregation and racial violence in America with skepticism regarding the United States' message that democracy was superior to Soviet communism. The U.S. realized it had to address its domestic race problem if it were to win over the hearts and minds of countries populated primarily by people of color. As a State Department study warned, the effect of "racial discrimination in the United States on public opinion abroad is . . . averse to our interests." The *New York Times* reported that Communist propaganda had convinced much of the world that "American Negroes live under conditions little if any different from those described in Uncle Tom's Cabin." Stories from the Soviet Union described an "increased frequency of terroristic acts against negroes [*sic*]" and that in the South, "semi-slave forms of oppression and exploitation are the rule." The U.S. Embassy in Moscow warned: "The Soviet press hammers away unceasingly on such things as 'lynch law,' segregation, racial discrimination, deprivation of political rights, etc. . . . [where] Negroes are brutally downtrodden with no hope of improving their status under the existing form of government." With stories like this reported in every corner of the world, the U.S. could not promote itself as the epitome of righteousness.[1]

Hope for change began on May 17, 1954, when the Supreme Court under Chief Justice Earl Warren, by unanimous opinion, ruled in Brown vs. Board of Education that racial segregation in public schools was unconstitutional. Then, on September 4, 1957, nine black students, called the "Little Rock Nine," under the Brown ruling, attempted to enter the all-white Little Rock Central High School, prompting Arkansas governor to call out the National Guard. A mob gathered waving Confederate flags while singing "Dixie," with many in the crowd bearings arms and looking to create an incident. "Blood will run in the streets," warned the governor. It was not until President Eisenhower sent in the 101st Airborne Division of the U.S. Army, led by Major General Edwin Walker, restored order. Walker's men used bayonets to disperse the crowd, and four platoons escorted the nine students into school. It was the start of desegregation. But it did nothing to alter the image the third-world had of the U.S. For, in the South, racial equality threatened their racist American way of life, and the events in Little Rock galvanized the region like no other issue. The hatred surpassed even what they felt about communism. Many believed it was communism that was behind the civil rights movement, which only served to energize further those opposed to desegregation.[2]

Things began to get ugly, or shall we say, uglier than usual, as soon as the Brown vs. Board of Education ruling came down in 1954. An organized resistance movement immediately sprang up throughout the South, opposed to desegregation and equal voting rights for all, led primarily by white supremacist Fascists. White Citizen Councils arose in communities throughout the South, which eventually led to a rebirth of the Ku Klux Klan. Murders and bombings of African Americans increased dramatically. Racists targeted Jews and synagogues as well. European Fascists had blamed Jews for the rise of communism in Czarist Russia, and American

Fascists now held Jews responsible for advancing communism and racial equality in the United States.[3]

In 1954 Judge Tom Brady told the White Citizens Council of Indianola, Mississippi, that Communist influences were responsible for the Supreme Court decision. Georgia's Attorney General accused the NAACP of "either knowingly or unwittingly" allowing itself "to become part and parcel of the Communist conspiracy." In 1957, the Louisiana Joint Legislative Committee to Maintain Segregation heard an ex-Communist, African American informant named Manning Johnson testify that the NAACP was "nothing more than a vehicle of the Communist Party."[4] The general belief was that desegregation was a Communist plot.

Leander Perez was a prominent judge in New Orleans' Plaquemines Parish, who became rich, illegally subleasing parish-owned land that held oil and mineral rights. Throughout the South, Perez was a leading figure in the struggle to keep segregation and connect communism to the civil rights movement. After the Brown decision, he dedicated the rest of his life fighting to preserve the Southern way of life, leaving his business dealings in the hands of his two sons. "There is a hidden hand that moves in the whole matter of race relations in the United States," Perez said, and the Zionist Jews were the "main driving force behind forced racial integration."[5]

A close friend of Leander Perez was Mississippi Senator James Eastland. A formidable power in the U.S. Senate, Eastland was Majority Leader and Chairman of the Senate Judiciary Committee and official chairman of the Senate Internal Security Subcommittee (SISS). Established on December 21, 1950, SISS was mandated to investigate domestic subversive activities within the United States. It included ". . . espionage, sabotage, and infiltration of persons who are or may be under the domination of the foreign government or organization controlling the world Communist movement or any movement seeking to overthrow the Government of the United States by force and violence."[6] As SISS Chairman, Eastland planned to prove that Communists directed and financed civil rights groups in the South.[7]

Eastland's reaction to the Brown decision was apparent. "Defeat means death," he said, "the death of Southern culture and our aspirations as an Anglo-Saxon people . . ."[8] And everyone knew that "the Negroes did not themselves instigate the agitation against segregation. They were put up to it by radical busybodies who are intent upon overthrowing American institutions." One year after Brown, he cited the "dangerous influence . . . exerted on the court by Communist-front pressure groups and other enemies of the American republic." Their ties to "the worldwide Communist conspiracy" alarmed him. He saw no reason to obey rulings set forth by "pro-Communist agitators," which he believed defined the Supreme Court.

Similarly, the U.S. military entertained the idea of a coup d'état. The CIA established foreign policy contrary to what the President desired. And the Fascist Senator Eastland urged Southern racists to ignore the Supreme Court because they were nothing more than "pro-Communist agitators."⁹ The country was sitting on a powder keg waiting to explode, and the most prominent, influential citizens throughout the South were the ones ready, willing, and able to light the fuse. And woe to those who stood in their way.

* * *

Shortly after the Brown decision, Eastland's Senate Internal Security Subcommittee held hearings regarding the Southern Conference Education Fund (SCEF), a New Orleans organization that supported desegregation. An informant, a former Communist who had spent time in the Soviet Union, testified that American Communists led the entire civil rights movement. The veracity of the informant did not matter. What was important was that the informant singled out communism as the driving force behind racial integration.

In March 1956, Eastland held similar hearings in New Orleans entitled "Scope of Soviet Activity in the United States," designed to demonstrate further that the civil rights movement was a Communist plot to create domestic unrest. "Our evidence here in New Orleans indicates very clearly that Communist leaders in Moscow . . . are reaching down into this part of the United States for agents willing to do their mischievous work," Eastland revealed. It prompted the city's mayor, de Lesseps Morrison, to order Police Superintendent Guy Banister to investigate subversive activities in New Orleans (Lee Harvey Oswald would frequent Banister's office on 544 Camp Street in the summer of 1963). Morrison called Banister "an expert in the field." Banister and Morrison subsequently met with Eastland in Mississippi to discuss how best to halt communism and desegregation. After which Morrison stated, "Mr. Banister has [a] complete liaison with the committee's staff, which was the main object of our trip."

Banister was an expert in domestic communism. In March 1957, the State of Louisiana Joint Legislative Committee held public hearings on the "Subversion in Racial Unrest; An Outline of a Strategic Weapon to Destroy the Governments of Louisiana and the United States." It stated that Banister's work at the FBI ". . . during World War II and in the Cold War . . . was largely committed to combatting subversion . . . he also devoted considerable study to Communist history, theory, strategy, and tactics." Banister would testify that "it was also my duty to develop and supervise . . . informers . . . counter spies sent in to report on the activities of the party members. That was part of my duties throughout the nearly seventeen years I served as Special Agent in Charge [at the FBI]." The point was Banister's anti-Communist resume.

Banister was no slouch at the FBI. His tenure as Special Agent in Charge was the longest ever when he retired from the Bureau. In Chicago, 500 agents, the second-largest FBI office behind New York. And using informants to infiltrate subversive groups did not end after he left the Bureau. During a February 3, 1961

FBI interview, Banister disclosed he still was "ferreting out subversive activities in the state of Louisiana," using student infiltrators "in connection with his interest and position in the Louisiana State organization known as the State Joint Legislative Committee on Un-American Activities."[10]

Hubert Badeaux had worked directly under Banister at the New Orleans Police Department and shared Banister's racist and segregationist views. After the "Subversion in Racial Unrest" hearings mentioned above, he received a letter from State Senator Willie Rainach, saying that the work of men like Badeaux, Banister, and Leander Perez "established Communism as the prime cause of racial unrest in the United States . . ."[11]

On November 14, 1960, McDonough School in New Orleans became integrated, and at a Citizens' Council Meeting that same night, 5,000 people attended to hear Perez and Rainich speak. "Don't wait for your daughters to be raped by these Congolese," Perez warned the crowd. The following year, at the National Citizens' Council meeting, Perez said Southerners had no choice but to rise and physically oppose segregation. It was not long before these groups would resort to extreme violence.[12]

Willie Rainach was an avid segregationist. He was a member of the Citizen's Council in Claiborne Parish, the Association of Citizens' Councils of Louisiana from 1955 to 1959, and the Citizens' Councils of America from 1956 to 1958.[13] They were impressive credentials, but no one was more committed to the cause than Guy Banister. A member of the John Birch Society, the Minutemen, and the Louisiana Committee on Un-American Activities, Banister published a racist publication called the *Louisiana Intelligence Digest*.[14] He was also a member of the South Louisiana Citizens' Council (Hubert Bateaux was the group's first vice president) and was involved in the Greater New Orleans Citizen's Council directed by Leander Perez and George Singelmann.

Rainach asked Banister to appear before the Special Education Committee of the Arkansas legislature on December 16-17, 1958. "Unrest Blamed on Reds" and "Half of Commy Trained Americans were of the Negro race" were how newspapers characterized Banister's testimony. That same year, Banister testified before the Joint Legislative Committee on Segregation and spoke about Communist subversion before the American Legion Un-American Committee and the Louisiana State University.

Banister was highly in demand. All these men truly believed that Communists were the driving force behind desegregation. The Soviet Union was funding Communist and civil rights groups in the U.S. to start a race war. They were hell-bent on proving that the Communist influence existed, which was why using informants to infiltrate civil rights and leftist groups was a Banister standard, right up to the assassination of JFK.

* * *

The relationship between Lee Harvey Oswald and Guy Banister in the summer of 1963 is indisputable. Several eyewitnesses confirmed that they saw the two
together in Banister's office and the restaurants around the office. When Oswald
handed out the pro-Castro pamphlet *Crime's Against Cuba* on the streets of New
Orleans, as part of his Fair Play for Cuba escapade, and had stamped Banister's
544 Camp Street office address on the inside cover, it confirmed his connection to
Banister. Banister was a hardline, devoted anti-Communist, anti-Semite, and racist.
The question is, what was Oswald doing with him? Was he a Communist, as we
have been led to believe, or was this a clever deception to make Oswald appear that
way, as Banister was known to do? And more importantly, did the two first meet in
the summer of 1963, or was there a connection between Banister and Oswald that
began with Oswald's first period in New Orleans, when he was a teenager in the
mid-1950s, right after he left New York with his mother?

After arriving in New Orleans with his mother in 1954, Oswald worked briefly
with a young man named Palmer E. McBride, who would later state that ". . . Oswald was very serious about the virtues of Communism . . . that the capitalists
were exploiting the working class . . ." Later that year, McBride took Oswald to the
home of William Eugene Wulf, the president of the Amateur Astronomy Association. Oswald spoke to Wulf about ". . . the glories of the Worker's State and . . .
that the United States was not telling the truth about Soviet Russia."[15] We should
not ignore McBride's testimony. However, other evidence contradicted what he had
to say, dispelling his assertion that Oswald was a Communist.

Oswald finished eighth and ninth grades in New Orleans, dropped out of high
school after only one month in grade ten, worked as an office clerk and messenger
for several months, and then in July 1956, he and his mother quickly left New
Orleans for Fort Worth, Texas. He once again enrolled in the tenth grade in Fort
Worth but dropped out after only one month. Oswald had no use for school. His
seventeenth birthday was less than a month away when he would be old enough to
officially enlist in the Marines, which he did on October 24, 1956. Curiously, three
weeks before that, he wrote the Socialist Party of America, asking for ". . . more
information about your Youth League. I would like to know if there is a branch in
my area, how to join, etc. I am a Marxist and have been studying Socialist principles
for well over fifteen months . . ."[16]

Why would Oswald ask if there was a Socialist Party of America group in his
area when he knew he would be in a Marine boot camp somewhere else in three
weeks? It does not make sense. Furthermore, why would someone interested in
socialism and communism want to join the Marines in the first place, the symbol of
American capitalist might? And why let McBride and Wulf know he was interested
in communism when New Orleans was a city that was solidly anti-Communist?

Did Oswald think they would react positively? Indeed, he did not. Therefore, it was more likely that this disgruntled young man, who may have previously been part of a mind control program while in a New York detention center, was purposely lying to show an interest in communism and socialism. He may already have been working with someone in New Orleans, such as Guy Banister, who used him to infiltrate leftist groups in schools and on campuses to weed out Communist youths. And Oswald broached the subject with McBride and Wulf to see how they would react. It might have been the case. Consider the testimony of Edward Voebel, "whom the Warren Commission established was Oswald's closest friend during his teenage years in New Orleans . . ." Voebel told the Commission "that reports that Oswald was already 'studying Communism' [was] a 'lot of baloney.'" And according to Voebel, "Oswald commonly read 'paperback trash.'"[17]

Aline Mosby was the first reporter to interview Oswald in Moscow after his defection. She asked him if he was a Communist. Oswald looked surprised. "Communist? I've never met a Communist. I might have seen a Communist once in New York, like the old lady who gave me a pamphlet, 'Save the Rosenbergs.'" "Segregation, I was brought up like every southern boy, to hate Negroes," Mosby recorded in her notes of the Oswald interview. "Then Socialist literature opened my eyes to reconsider reasons for hating Negroes . . . ,"[18] which explains his interest in socialism in the first place. It was not political for him, but income inequality that drew him to this philosophy. And he did not tell Mosby that his racist views had changed after he discovered socialism, just that it made him reconsider the reasons why he found himself "hating Negroes." He still felt the hatred, but why he did so had changed.

Priscilla Johnson also interviewed Oswald in Moscow after Mosby did. "I was brought up like every southern boy to hate Negroes," Oswald told Johnson. He once again claimed that socialism changed his outlook, but while discussing racism in the U.S., he casually used the term "nigger," something a committed Communist would never have done.

Thomas Beckham met Oswald in 1963 when Beckham worked for Guy Banister, and he and Oswald became "good buddies." Beckham told the House Select Committee on Assassinations: "I can't understand this Russia thing because he was always 100% American he seemed like [to me]." Oswald told him communism was Jewish because "Karl Marx was a Jew."[19] It was a typical Nazi belief, and, as described in the previous chapter, there were references to leaders of the American Nazi Party found in Oswald's notebook. Another coincidence? Maybe not, because Nazis were Socialists, and the confused young man with limited education may not have had the intellectual ability to differentiate between the two philosophies. It means his interest in socialism only began after associating with American Nazis while living in New York.

Did Oswald share the radical right view that Jews were the driving force behind communism? Consider that Oswald objected when his wife Marina wanted to name their baby Rachel, because he said it sounded too Jewish. She was named Audrey Marina Rachel Oswald. So, in all likelihood, while living in New Orleans as a youth, Oswald probably associated with Fascists who exposed him to the idea that Jews created communism and were behind desegregation, which explains the racist opinions he espoused to the reporters in Moscow.

James Botelho was Oswald's roommate at the Marine Corp Facility in Santa Ana, California, who later became a California judge. In an interview with Mark Lane, Botelho said, "Oswald was not a Communist . . . [If he were], I would have taken violent action against him, and so would many of the other Marines in the unit."[20] In a June 3, 1964 affidavit, Botelho stated that "although he [Oswald] believed in pure Marxist theory, he did not believe in the way communism was practiced by the Russians. I was quite surprised when I learned Oswald had gone to Russia."[21]

It appears that an accurate characterization is that Oswald was a racist and anti-Semite who believed in pure Marxism, perhaps because of a similarity to Nazism, but rejected the Soviet brand of communism. The difference between these two philosophies is subtle. Marxism is, "From each according to his ability, to each according to his work."Whereas communism has been described as, "From each according to his ability, to each according to his needs."[22]

In other words, under communism, people work to the level they are capable of, and they are rewarded with what they need, regardless of their productivity. With Marxism, people work according to their ability, and the state rewards them commensurate with the work they produce.

There is a similarity between Marxism and self-determination, in the sense that there are no free rides; you determine your fate by how hard you work, which was the philosophy of the radical right at that time. It was also the philosophy of Nazi Germany. Consider Oswald's racist and anti-Semitic views along with this. It equates to a eugenicist's Darwinian let the fittest survive mentality. It becomes apparent that Oswald could have misconstrued his Marxist beliefs to have coincided with those of the Fascist radical right of his era. It would explain why throughout his adult life, Oswald the Marxist spent his time almost exclusively in the company of Fascists and why he said socialism made him "reconsider the reasons" why he hated African Americans. Like most Southerners, did Oswald believe African Americans were not working hard enough to carry their weight? If true, it violated the basic tenet of Oswald's newfound Marxist belief system, and, as a result, he would believe they only had themselves to blame for what they had to endure. Suppose Oswald considered this in conjunction with the rejection of social programs that the right-wingers who were his associates abhorred. In that case, it does explain why Oswald said his Marxist/Socialist beliefs changed how he looked at race relations. Living under a system where your monetary rewards depended on the work you produced, where there were no handouts, and your skin color did not matter appealed to the young Marxist who believed that life had cheated him and his family. The bottom line is that this truant and high school dropout, who read philosophy books he was incapable of understanding, found a similarity between his belief system, fascism, and radical right self-determination, as convoluted as that sounds. It also meant that it placed Oswald in a position to be manipulated by people looking for someone just like him.

Referring to himself as a Marxist meant Oswald advocated worldwide revolution, which embodied what Leon Trotsky stood for. Trotsky had abandoned the Soviet brand of communism, which was why Stalin's henchmen assassinated him in 1940.[23] Interestingly, the Stalinists in Russia agreed with Oswald that Marxism and fascism followed the same basic principles. In 1935, the Young Communist International called "Trotsky, one of the chief organizers and ideological leader of this criminal Fascist group . . ." "Enlighten everywhere the workers, youth, especially the Socialist youth," they continued, "as to the counterrevolutionary Fascist character of the role of Trotsky and the Trotskyites." In a similar vein, the Swiss Communist Party was ordered by the Comintern to "expose Trotskyite opposition to [the] Soviet [Union], [and] explain [the] Trotskyite tendency towards fascism, [and how Trotskyites] have become direct agents of fascism in every country."[24]

After returning from the Soviet Union, Oswald contacted the Trotskyite Socialist Workers Party (SWP). In return, they sent Oswald a fifty-four-page pamphlet "as well as some other material which may be of interest to you." This other material is lost, but the circular referred to "the Stalinist degeneration [that] welled out of Moscow and began corrupting young Communist parties everywhere." Whereas the Trotskyites were ready to "save us from the capitalist barbarism and open up a new world for humanity." The day after receiving the pamphlet, Oswald airmailed them a request to send him the book, *The Teachings of Leon Trotsky*.[25]

As previously mentioned, Guy Banister had a history of using undercover informants to infiltrate Communist and leftist organizations in the United States. Banister's subordinate Sergeant Badeaux similarly wrote to fellow racist Willie Rainach in 1956 that he was grooming an individual to infiltrate leftist groups. It was around this time that Oswald first began espousing the virtues of Marxism. In another letter to Rainach dated July 10, 1958, Badeaux wrote that he was investigating the American Civil Liberties Union (ACLU) with the help of a husband-and-wife team who were former members of the Communist Party. Badeaux also referred to a book he was writing titled *Communism in Louisiana*, noting "nearly every top Red sent to Louisiana had been either a nigger or a Jew."[26]

Was it possible that Oswald was already acting as an undercover informant for Banister and Badeaux around 1956? We do know that Oswald's favorite television show at the time was *I Led Three Lives*, based on a book by Herbert Philbrick, who infiltrated Communist Party groups for the FBI. The show aired between 1953 and 1956, and Oswald never missed an episode, religiously watching it with his mother. Perhaps noteworthy is that this was the time when Oswald claimed to have become interested in Marxism. And potentially relevant is that Philbrick was a crucial witness in the 1949 trial of "the Communist Party 11." The United States had accused the group of violating the Smith Act and trying to overthrow the U.S. government.[27]

Around that time, one person in New Orleans could have been responsible for Oswald becoming a radical right-wing undercover informant. A man positioned to have introduced Oswald to Banister, who would work out of Banister's office in the years to come. A man who was rabidly anti-Communist, yet someone who Banister's secretary, Delphine Roberts, said, "Well, he had to act the part, of being what many people would call wishy-washy, one side and then the opposite side. It was important for him to be that way because he was acting like a counterspy."[28] That man was David Ferrie.

* * *

David Ferrie was born in Cleveland, Ohio. He was raised a devout Roman Catholic and spent three years at St. Charles Seminary studying to become a priest until St. Charles dismissed him in 1944 for emotional problems. He then obtained a pilot's license and began teaching aeronautics at Benedictine High School in Cleveland until he was let go for a series of infractions, including taking boys to a house of prostitution. He moved to New Orleans in 1951 and became a pilot for Eastern Airlines. That is until the police arrested him twice for having sexual relations with underage boys. In 1961, Eastern fired him.

Ferrie was heavily involved in the Civil Air Patrol (CAP), probably because it gave him direct access to the teenage boys to whom he was sexually attracted, a compulsion that would haunt him the rest of his life. He joined CAP in Ohio in 1947 and remained interested in the group after moving to New Orleans, becoming part of the Cadet Squadron at Lakefront Airport after he relocated there. Ferrie had to leave the CAP in 1954 when a cadet being training by him died in a plane crash. He then joined a smaller squadron at Moisant Airport in 1955, and it was there that fifteen-year-old Lee Harvey Oswald joined the unit that July.[29]

Multiple teenage CAP members would later confirm that Oswald and Ferrie did know each other. There is also a photograph showing a group of cadets, which includes Ferrie and Oswald. Exactly how close they were, or if Ferrie and Oswald ever had sexual relations, is unknown. What is known is that while Oswald was in Russia with his wife Marina expecting their first child, Oswald wrote on a form that if the baby were a boy, he was to be named David Lee Oswald. Ferrie was the only David that Oswald knew.[30]

There was something about young Oswald, who had begun to publicly profess an interest in Marxism, that warranted special attention from the rabid anti-Communist CAP instructor. Was it a sexual attraction? Perhaps, but recall how abruptly Marguerite Oswald left New York for New Orleans in early 1954. Lee's truancy was still a problem, and school officials warned Marguerite that they would take Lee away from her once again if things did not improve. And she could not let this happen. "Lee is his self [*sic*] again after the ordeal in New York," she wrote to John Pic after they arrived in New Orleans. "It was almost a tragedy, but a little love and patience did the trick." Was it possible that Marguerite knew Lee was involved in a drug-testing program at Bordentown Reformery and suddenly left when she feared he might be institutionalized again? Interestingly, they would leave New Orleans for Fort Worth just as abruptly in July 1956, just one year after Lee joined CAP and met David Ferrie. Was there a similar reason for their quick departure, one that involved David Ferrie, his associates, and the war they were waging against communism?[31]

David Ferrie was an extreme anti-Communist. As early as 1950, when he joined the Army Reserve, he wrote a letter to the commander of the U.S. 1st Air Force: "There is nothing I would enjoy better than blowing the hell out of every damn Russian, Communist, Red, or what-have-you . . . I want to train killers, however bad that sounds. It is what we need."[32]

When the police found Ferrie's dead body in his apartment in 1967, they discovered a note nearby. It was addressed to Al Beauboef, one of the men who had accompanied Ferrie on his mysterious late-night drive from New Orleans to Galveston on the night of the assassination. The note referenced the "Flying Baragona in the Beach," which Jim Garrison could decipher during his investigation into Ferrie's death. Beach referred to Ferrie's Beechcraft airplane, and Baragona was an American Nazi who worked out of Fort Sill, Georgia. The note meant nothing until Garrison received a letter from a Glenn Pinchback, whose job was to intercept and read mail at the same Fort Sill. Enclosed was a transcript of a letter Ferrie had sent to Baragona, which described Ferrie's dream of reunifying Germany, and a world where all the currency was in Deutschmarks. It was a new world order ruled by Germany that Ferrie wanted. In summation, Pinchback wrote that Ferrie advocated a "Neo-Nazi plot to enslave America in the name of anti-Communism" and "a neo-Nazi plot gargantuan in scope." Ferrie wanted to kill all the Kennedys and Martin Luther King, and he wrote that he was being "suffocated by the niggers and Jews . . ."[33]

We can be confident that Ferrie did not keep his radical anti-Communist and racist views hidden from those around him. And from what we know of the young Lee Oswald, what Ferrie wrote would have appealed to him and explains who introduced Oswald to fascism and how it mirrored Marxism, which Oswald already supported. No wonder the confused young Marxist was attracted to the troubled right-wing zealot.

David Ferrie was a Fascist who hated Communists, blacks, and Jews with an equal passion. He was not against resorting to extreme violence to support the causes in which he believed. But unknown to him, his strange behavior and right-wing ideology did not pass under the radar as he engaged in his private war against communism with other like-minded paramilitary types. In 1975 the Church Committee would hear testimony from Wendall Roache, who, in 1963, had headed the Immigration and Naturalization Service (INS) Border Patrol division in New Orleans. "I've been waiting twelve years to talk to someone about this," Roache told them. Most of his testimony remains classified, but what has leaked out is quite revealing.

Roache said one of INS's responsibilities was to keep an eye on Cuban exile groups in the city. It inevitably led them to the Newman Building, which housed Guy Banister's office, and where David Ferrie met with his Cuban associates to discuss ways to remove Castro from power. INS inspectors kept the building under surveillance, and they observed Oswald in 1963 going in and out of the office of David Ferrie's group, which was through a side entrance to Guy Banister's office. INS also knew about Ferrie's bizarre behavior, that Eastern Airlines had fired him, that he was gay with "perverse tendencies," and was known to "give . . . [young men all] sorts of pills at the [anti-Castro] training camp and take movies of them." In 1961 they contacted the FBI about him, and FBI documents reported that "Ferrie has a group of young boys whom he supports and controls completely . . . [and] he is keeping them doped up with narcotics, liquor, and hypnotism. Ferrie had taken pornographic pictures of the various boys in this group, which he is holding over their heads to make them cooperate with him." Ferrie also helped the boys obtain passports, indicating he intended to take them out of the country. And while INS and the FBI investigated Ferrie for morals charges, the police found an assortment of rifles, hand grenades, and ammunition in his possession, which Ferrie said were for the Cuban Revolutionary Front, an anti-Castro, Cuban exile group. And getting rid of Castro was the main pastime of those who occupied the Newman Building.[34]

Immediately after the assassination, the New Orleans Bolton Ford car dealership manager contacted the FBI, who advised that on January 20, 1961, a group of men had attempted to buy trucks from him. The American with the group identified himself as Joseph Moore. Still, he asked that the name "Oswald" be written on the purchase documents since Oswald was handling the money for his anti-Castro organization and would pay for the trucks if the deal went forward. "Friends of a Democratic Cuba" and the name "Oswald" were written on the dealership's order form and given to the FBI by the dealership manager. Receiving this information so soon after the assassination must have been unsettling for the FBI agents, for a leading figure in the Friends of a Democratic Cuba in 1961 was none other than Guy Banister.[35]

There was more. According to the Retail Merchant's Credit Association of Fort Worth, Texas, the FBI contacted them on two separate occasions within two weeks of the Bolton incident in 1961. The FBI asked if they knew of any business dealings with Oswald. At the time, Oswald was still in the Soviet Union, so why was the FBI asking about him in the Texas city where he and his mother relocated to after leaving New Orleans? And what sent the FBI to Fort Worth? We know the Bolton dealership manager did not notify the FBI until after the assassination, two years later, so something had to trigger the Fort Worth inquiry. The INS's surveillance of Ferrie and his Cuban militant associates probably led them to the Bolton dealership in 1961, and they must have informed the FBI about it when it occurred.[36]

In addition, something made the Bolton dealership manager remember, in 1963, an obscure incident from two years prior. The only explanation is that he was approached about it by INS or the FBI in 1961, making it easy to recall after the assassination. And it confirms that the FBI was investigating the Friends of a Democratic Cuba when it happened.

Another question is, if Lee Oswald were in the Soviet Union, how would the Friends of a Democratic Cuba know to use his name if Banister supposedly had not yet met Oswald when the incident took place? Ferrie already knew Oswald, so does that imply Ferrie was involved with the Friends of Democratic Cuba and Banister? Perhaps he was, but Ferrie officially said goodbye to Oswald in 1956 and only knew him for roughly one year. Does it make any sense that he would be using Oswald's name in 1961, five years later? And why would an anti-Castro organization use the name of a Marine who had defected to the Soviet Union? None of this is plausible, but they chose Oswald's name for a reason.

In May and June 1957, the Marine stationed Oswald at Keesler Air Force Base in Mississippi, where they taught him to be a radar operator. While there, he used his weekend passes to return to New Orleans, which was approximately 100 miles away from the base. His mother was in Fort Worth, and no other relatives claimed he visited them. So who Oswald saw in New Orleans during these trips remains unknown. That it was David Ferrie is a strong possibility.[37]

In summation, we know that both David Ferrie and Guy Banister were passionate anti-Communists long before JFK's assassination. In the 1950s, Banister's focus was racial segregation and proving Communists were infiltrating civil rights organizations. It is not surprising that the two men would have crossed paths after Castro came to power in 1959 when Banister became as passionate an anti-Communist as he was a racist. We also know that Oswald and Ferrie knew each other in 1955-1956, but after that, there is no known connection between them until 1963, when Oswald returned from the Soviet Union and relocated to New Orleans. He worked with Banister and Ferrie, posing as a Communist sympathizer and Castro supporter, apparently trying to infiltrate Communist groups. While Oswald was still in the Soviet Union, an anti-Castro group used Oswald's name to purchase trucks for the war against Castro. Banister and possibly Ferrie were associated with this group. If the official record is to be believed, how this could have happened is a mystery. Oswald was allegedly out of contact with the people in New Orleans for seven years, between 1956 and 1963, did not meet Banister until 1963, and only knew Ferrie for one year when he was in the CAP. If true, we are supposed to believe that Oswald just showed up in New Orleans unannounced in 1963 and started working with Banister or Ferrie, infiltrating Communist groups. It defies logic.

Meanwhile, Delphine Roberts said Ferrie was a counterspy who had to act, on occasion, like he was a Communist. And Ferrie and Banister were closely connected to Nazis and Fascist groups in New Orleans and throughout the South. At the same time, Oswald associated with American Nazi groups based on the names of neo-Nazis in his notebook, as described in Volume One. It is doubtful that this was all a coincidence. It means Ferrie must have involved Oswald in something clandestine during the brief period he was a member of the CAP in the 1950s, such as working as an infiltrator of Communist groups, which would have involved Banister, who specialized in this type of thing.

Consider there was also something about Ferrie's relationship with the CAP cadets that went beyond pedophilia, for when interviewed by the New Orleans police, many of them admitted they had traveled to Cuba with Ferrie and others after Castro came to power in 1959. One youngster, Al Landry, said, "he had been to Cuba on several occasions since the revolution . . ." Another told police that Ferrie took several boys to Honduras "to do some mining." After police searched Ferrie's home, they found a passport "taken out in the name of Albert Paul Chera-mie on August 2, 1960." It all coincided with the INS report that Ferrie obtained the necessary travel documents for the boys, but why did he need to take them out of the country? Did this possibly have something to do with drug experimentation? We know that the CIA used foreign countries like Haiti for such purposes because the government scrutiny was virtually nonexistent.[38]

Lawrence Marsh was a member of the CAP in the mid-1950s. He later spoke to the HSCA about his involvement with Ferrie. "When we would spend the week-end by Dave's for these parties," Marsh said, "he used to practice hypnosis on us and find out if it were working on us by using a compass or a pin and stick our arms. He was a fanatic about this hypnosis stuff." In *On the Trail of the JFK Assassins*, author Dick Russell described his interview with former CAP member John Irion. "The New Orleans CAP unit, at Lakefront Airport, attracted by and large a lot of underprivileged kids from broken homes," Irion told Russell. He remembered Oswald as "a recruit if I remember, but he never got much out of that stage. He would sulk and then get argumentative. I would say Oswald was there maybe six months at the most."

Regarding Ferrie, Irion said, "He fancied himself as a self-made doctor or psychologist. I personally never submitted to it because I knew better. It's possible he hypnotized other people, but back then, for kids of our age, it was more of a novelty."

Anthony Atzenhoffer, another former CAP member, told the HSCA that Ferrie "wanted the kids to participate in some . . . experiment for Tulane University. They didn't do it." Irion told Russell that Ferrie was "constantly at Tulane" during those years. Something secretive was happening at Tulane that involved these boys.[39]

And it was not just Tulane, according to a former New Orleans resident who knew two boys sexually molested by Ferrie: "The Youth Center has been a hotbed of corruption, sexual abuse, police brutality, and God only knows what else for decades . . . Ferrie used to go there posing as a doctor of some sort, some sort of sham, to recruit kids . . . He took a lot of kids to Cuba, Guatemala, and Honduras . . . He was an amateur hypnotist . . . and he practiced trance stuff on a lot of boys. [B]esides Youth Center visits, he went to the East [Louisiana] State Hospital a lot, where some of his boys were taken for treatment. . . . Ferrie was in bed, no pun intended, with one of the doctors there, who was a drug addict [and] the crazy rumor was that the hospital was treating the boys with LSD to stop them from becoming [gay] . . ."[40]

There is potential confirmation to support these allegations. In September 1975, Charles D. Ablard, General Counsel for the Army, testified before a Senate Committee. Ablard reported that: "We have learned of a 1955 contract with Tulane University which involved the administration of LSD, mescaline, and other drugs to mental patients who . . . had electrodes implanted in their brains as part of their medical treatment . . ."[41]

Dr. Robert Heath, chairman of the Tulane Medical School's Department of Neurology and Psychiatry, headed the project that performed experiments involving electrical stimulation by surgically implanting electrodes in the brains of patients. The funding for these experiments was provided, at least in part, by the CIA and the military. Heath also experimented with bulbocapnine and LSD, using unwitting prisoners at Louisiana State Penitentiary as his guinea pigs. He also practiced gay conversion therapy and claimed to have successfully converted a gay patient by implanting electrodes into the septal region of his brain, which is associated with feelings of pleasure. The patient's septal electrodes were stimulated and shown heterosexual pornographic material. He then had intercourse with a female prostitute recruited for the study, which prompted Heath to conclude he had successfully converted the patient to heterosexuality. Today, the good Dr. Heath might be considered certifiably insane.[42]

The mysterious East Louisiana State Hospital, located in Jackson, Louisiana, and what went on there must be understood if the truth about Oswald is ever to be known. As stated above, Ferrie was familiar with the hospital and brought CAP teenage boys there for treatment with mind-altering drugs. In addition, in 1960, Dr. Heath co-authored a paper with Dr. Frank Silva, published in Comprehensive Psychiatry and entitled: "Comparative Effects of the Administration of taraxein d-LSD. Mescaline, and Psilocybin to Human Volunteers." The introduction to the paper stated, "The patient donors [were] housed in a special Tulane University Research Unit at the East Louisiana State Hospital, Jackson." The Commonwealth Fund financed the project, which later was proven to be a CIA front.[43]

Dr. Silva's real name was Francisco A. Silva Clarens. Born in Cuba in 1929, he graduated from the University of Havana Medical School in 1955. He came to the U.S. and graduated from Tulane University School of Medicine in 1958, where he was an associate professor of clinical psychiatry from 1959 to 1972. The medical services director at East Louisiana State Hospital, in charge of pharmacological research, Silva was a willing participant in the drug experimentation testing conducted at the State Hospital. Doctors injected him with taraxein, LSD, Mescaline, and Psilocybin at different times. By all accounts, drug use was rampant at the hospital, but there is no proof that Silva was the drug addict doctor who was in bed with David Ferrie.[44]

Erick Crouchet was a CAP cadet under Ferrie's tutelage, and on August 21, 1961, New Orleans Juvenile detectives paid him a visit regarding Ferrie. The following day, at East Bank Juvenile Bureau headquarters of Jefferson Parish, Crouchet "made a full typewritten statement" that Ferrie had committed "acts of crimes against nature on him on two separate occasions." Subsequently, The Juvenile Bureau sent Crouchet and other boys who had all been CAP members under Ferrie to Louisiana State Hospital for a brief period.[45]

In 1968, Jim Garrison interviewed Crouchet, who revealed that in the early 1960s, he had attended a party at Dr. Heath's home. Dr. Silva was also in attendance and introduced Crouchet to Sergio Arcacha Smith, an anti-Castro Cuban closely tied to Ferrie and Guy Banister in the years leading up to the assassination of JFK. For some reason, Crouchet was returned to East Louisiana State Hospital from August 1963 through JFK's assassination in November. The timing is odd, but there is no proof that any sinister ulterior motive was behind this. It is also somewhat suspicious that Lee Harvey Oswald visited the hospital around September 1963 while Crouchet was there. Dr. Silva admitted to having a conversation with Oswald in the hospital lobby.[46] Equally suspicious is that around the same time, in Clinton, La, adjacent to Jackson, Oswald was seen by multiple eyewitnesses sitting for hours in a parked car with two men. Numerous eyewitnesses positively identified the two men. One was David Ferrie. The other was Clay Shaw, the only person ever indicted for complicity in the assassination of JFK. There was something odd about East Louisiana State Hospital, roughly 125 miles outside New Orleans, that warranted the attention of these "associates" of Oswald, two to three months before JFK would be assassinated.

East Louisiana State Hospital and Tulane University were up to no good. They were involved with drug experimentation on young boys, including CAP cadets, which may explain Oswald's involvement with Ferrie and Banister as far back as

1955. And how was it that the specter of drug experimentation continued to hover over Oswald? It existed in New York, where he may have been a victim at the Bordentown Reformatory. It was there in New Orleans when David Ferrie delivered CAP boys to East Louisiana State Hospital. As we will see, it was there while Oswald was in the Marines as well, and it was there in 1963 when Ferrie and Shaw drove Oswald to East Louisiana State for no apparent reason.

Jean Lafitte, who worked at Reily simultaneously as Oswald, used the alias' Hidell and Jack Martin. The latter worked out of Banister's office. Lafitte was associated with George White, who, as we know, was heavenly involved in drug experimentation, including what occurred at Bordentown, which may have involved Oswald.

Was this all a coincidence, or was Oswald involved in something sinister in New Orleans, unrelated to the assassination? Maybe Oswald's mother was aware that people were abusing her son most horrendously, which would explain why she hurriedly left New Orleans as rapidly as she had fled from New York.

And Jim Garrison was on the right track investigating Clay Shaw.

* * *

Clay Shaw's entry into the world of intelligence began during World War II, when he served in Europe as part of an Army Counterintelligence group called the "Special Operations Section." After the war, he returned to New Orleans and worked for Mississippi Shipping Company, a CIA front. The company's president, Theodore Brent, was instrumental in creating the International Trade Mart, whose primary purpose was to increase trade through the Port of New Orleans. The Trade Mart officially opened on July 1, 1948, with Clay Shaw as its first director.

Theodore Brent was gay and served as a mentor to young gay men in the business world. Brent's generosity impacted the young Shaw, a gay man himself. Years later, Shaw would establish a legal defense fund for young gay men in trouble in New Orleans. It was this defense fund that would connect Shaw to Oswald after the assassination.[47]

Post-war Latin America was a turbulent place, and the threat of Communist infiltration, so close to America's shores, was a constant concern. In April 1948, a Pan-American Conference took place in Bogota, Colombia. Secretary of State George Marshall headed the U.S. delegation, and the seemingly ever-present William Pawley, who had recently resigned as U.S. ambassador to Brazil, went as well. Security was tight because the CIA office in Bogota learned anti-American rebels might attempt to assassinate Marshall. There was visible unrest on display, and days before the conference began, students from several Latin American countries arrived in Colombia to hold an anti-imperialist, student-led counter-conference. One of the students was a still unknown Fidel Castro. When the local Colombian leader, who was on his way to meet with the student protesters, was shot and killed in the street (Fidel Castro was considered a suspect), riots broke out, and the local police sided with the mob. Marshall, Pawley, and the American delegation were lucky to escape with their lives. A third of Bogota was in ashes, and thousands of lives were lost. It was symbolic of the sentiment felt in much of Central and South America towards the United States because Latinos felt the imperialist empire from the north was exploiting them. The resentment remains to this day.[48]

Despite the danger south of the border, Clay Shaw planned an extensive multi-nation trip throughout Latin America from March 10 thru May 20, 1949. The trip was significant because of the connection to U.S. intelligence. On February 19, a CIA memo written by Inspector General Lyman B. Kirkpatrick instructed the CIA to brief Shaw before leaving. They also gave Shaw a list of questions to address during the trip, applicable to each country he was to visit, and the information CIA expected Shaw to submit upon his return. It was the beginning of a long relationship between Shaw and the CIA.[49]

By his admission, William Gaudet worked for the CIA from 1947 through 1969. He published the *Latin American Report,* which he issued out of his office, conveniently located in Clay Shaw's International Trade Mart. Gaudet and Shaw knew each other well. After Shaw's South American trip, he wrote a letter of introduction for Gaudet, who was about to embark on an adventure of his own in Lima, Peru, where he was to meet with Lieutenant Colonel Alfredo Tejada of the Ministry of War. The question is, why would a man of Tejada's stature meet with the publisher of a small-time Latin American newsletter? The answer is he would not unless Gaudet was representing someone else, which was undoubtedly the CIA. It means the Agency asked Shaw to write the letter of introduction, and both Gaudet and Shaw were already reliable assets for the newly formed intelligence organization.[50]

One cannot overstate the importance of a relationship between Shaw and Gaudet going back to the late 1940s. After the assassination, the FBI attempted to verify the identities of all people who had applied for entry papers into Mexico on the same day as Oswald, which was September 17, 1963. They could account for all, except one—Tourist Card No. 824084, who was a person right next to Oswald's name on the list. The FBI officially stated that "No record of FM 82084 [was] located," which turned out to be untrue, for, in 1975, the name was declassified and accidentally disclosed. William Gaudet was standing right behind Oswald, a circumstance that cannot be a mere coincidence. Gaudet was either with Oswald that day or keeping a watchful eye on him. It was likely the latter, implying that the CIA was interested in what Oswald was up to two months before the assassination.

In the 1970s, as described in *Conspiracy,* Anthony Summers interviewed Gaudet. "I do know that I saw him [Oswald] one time with a former FBI agent by the name of Guy Banister," Gaudet told Summers. "Oswald [was] discussing various things with Banister at the time, and I think Banister knew a whole lot of what was going on . . . I suppose you are looking into Ferrie. He was with Oswald . . ."

It is interesting how Gaudet phrased things. Regarding Banister, Gaudet sounded like he just happened to see Oswald talking to him. But with Ferrie, he categorically stated that Oswald and Ferrie knew each other and were together. Finally, Gaudet told Summers that "Another vital person is Sergio Arcacha Smith. I know he knew Oswald and knows more about the Kennedy affair than he ever admitted."[51]

It was the same Arcacha who CAP cadet Erick Crouchet identified as having attended a party at the home of Dr. Heath that included Dr. Silva from East Louisiana State Hospital. Arcacha was an anti-Castro Cuban exile close to Banister and Ferrie, and as Gaudet said, he knew a lot of what transpired.

In 1961, a drug addict named Rose Cherami was a patient at East Louisiana State Hospital, where David Ferrie secretly took CAP cadets. Fast-forwarding to November 20, 1963, Rose was back at East Louisiana State Hospital, experiencing heroin withdrawals. She would tell police Lieutenant Francis Fruge, the officer who drove her to the hospital, that she had been on her way to Texas with two men and they were going to kill Kennedy. What Cherami said was dismissed as the ramblings of a drug addict until the assassination happened two days later, and people began to take her seriously. She claimed that she had worked for Jack Ruby at one time, knew of Oswald, and identified a photograph of Sergio Arcacha Smith as one of the two men with whom she traveled to Dallas.

There was also an indirect connection between Cherami and George White, going back to 1954 when Cherami was the main informant for a Houston detective named Martin Billnitzer, who was investigating heroin traffickers in the region. Billnitzer was murdered by these same traffickers three days after George White arrived in Houston to assist in the investigation, and four days after Billnitzer's death, Cherami skipped town.[52]

Somehow, the same names keep popping up, connected to Oswald and potential mind-altering drugs, in ways that are difficult to explain, other than he must have been involved with Ferrie and Banister in the mid-1950s when he first arrived in New Orleans.

Returning to William Gaudet, three days after Jack Ruby killed Oswald, the FBI in New Orleans obtained a tip that in the summer of 1959, Ruby had purchased paintings while passing through their city. Ruby was in New Orleans that August, stopping there on his way to Havana, so the story has credibility. Amazingly, William Gaudet was the one who had telephoned the FBI, and it is safe to assume that his encounter with Ruby in 1959 was not by accident. Gaudet admitted he was aware of Ferrie, Banister, and Arcacha. Ruby worked with this group, for how else would Gaudet connect Ruby in 1963 to an event that occurred four years earlier in New Orleans. And considering that Oswald was involved with these men just months before the assassination, and Gaudet, as he told Anthony Summers, knew all about it, it implies that Ruby and Oswald must have known each other in

New Orleans before the assassination. And somehow, Clay Shaw happened to fit into this puzzle as well.[53]

During the 1950s, the people with CIA connections ran the Trade Mart. A "principal backer and developer," under whom Shaw served, was Trade Mart president Lloyd J. Cobb, who had received his covert security clearance from CIA in October 1953. David G. Baldwin, who handled public relations, later confirmed he was associated with the CIA. So did Baldwin's successor, Jesse Core. It was a matter of saving the Agency "shoe leather," Core would say.[54]

Lloyd Cobb's brother Alvin, one of Guy Banister's two closest friends, was cut from the same radical right-wing cloth. He was head of the Knights of the White Camellia, the Knights of the White Christians, and the Robert E. Lee Patriots, all white supremacist groups. And according to the FBI, Alvin served as the Exalted Cyclops for the United Klans of America in New Orleans. On June 14, 1955, he ran a newspaper advertisement under the heading "Knights of the White Christians," which urged citizens to protect the traditions of the South. He was said to be a "negro [sic] hater," and in a 1956 speech, he called the NAACP the "National Association for Advancement of the Communist Party."[55]

According to Jim Garrison, it is not surprising, considering the racists he worked with at the Trade Mart, that Clay Shaw was also associated with the Klan. As Donald H. Carpenter writes in *Man of a Million Fragments, The True Story of Clay Shaw*, "The issue of homosexuality cut across many strange lines. Right-wing groups like the American Nazi Party and the Ku Klux Klan were sometimes ridiculed for having [gay] members or for being among organizations that attracted 'perverts.'"[56]

It brings us back to Jack Martin, the CIA-connected associate of Oswald who worked out of Banister's office and whose name Jean Pierre Lafitte used as an alias. Like David Ferrie, whom he knew well, Martin was a religious fanatic who belonged to the same church as Ferrie did. Martin also had a past. His public record included a 1952 murder charge in Houston and a crime against nature with a gay man named "Mona Lisa." Yet somehow, Martin had connections to people in high places. He knew Louisiana Senator Russell Long, Leander Perez and had connections inside Attorney General Jack P.F. Gremillion's office.[57]

Working out of Banister's office, Jack Martin could see everything, and meet everyone, so he must have known Clay Shaw. Martin first met Banister in the 1950s when he worked for *Westbank Herald*, a right-wing paper that had intelligence ties to Latin America, and Banister was the paper's publisher. In *A Farewell to Justice*, Joan Mellen maintains that Clay Shaw recruited Banister as a CIA asset. "As managing director of the Trade Mart," Mellen wrote, "Shaw moved on to CIA operations. The use of the present tense in a 1967 document suggests he continued to be an operative with both the Domestic Contact Division and the Clandestine Services. His clandestine services number was 402897-A . . ." Mellen writes that by 1952 Shaw enjoyed the highest of six CIA security clearance categories and he became part of Project QKENCHANT. It authorized him to "recruit civilians" not officially with the Agency and to discuss "projects, activities and possible relationships." This was not under the Domestic Contact Division, but in the Agency's "operational files." "He used his clearance," Mellen wrote, "' to plan or coordinate CIA activities,' as well as to 'initiate relationships with . . . non-Agency persons or institutions.' He worked undercover."

A "Secret" CIA file uncovered many years later regarding the QKENCHANT program revealed that in August 1960, Guy Banister Associates, Inc. was of interest to the CIA. Since Shaw was the CIA QKENCHANT recruiter in New Orleans, he would have reached out to Banister.[58]

So, Shaw, Banister, and Martin were CIA assets, as was David Ferrie. And we know that Shaw and Ferrie knew each other. Benton Wilson knew Ferrie from having served at Keesler Air Force Base, where Ferrie would occasionally take CAP recruits. Wilson also worked with Jim Lewallen, who lived with his brother at a French Quarter property renovated by Shaw. Lewallen told the Wilsons that he was the lover of both Shaw and Ferrie. Ferrie wanted to borrow money to rent a plane from a CAP colleague named Herb Wagner on another occasion. It occurred during the week of the assassination. Wagner wanted someone to cosign the loan, and it was Clay Shaw who did so. During Garrison's investigation, Wagner contacted a friend of his, Roger E. Johnston Jr., the deputy marshal for the Kenner Police Department. "Here in front of my eyes," Johnston said, "was the proof." The borrower's signature read, "David Ferrie." The cosigner was "Clay Shaw."[59] Then there was Tulane psychiatrist Harold Lief. Lief treated a gay patient who claimed to have met Oswald at one of Shaw's parties. Lief knew he was telling the truth, for the patient described Shaw's house in detail, which Lief had rented himself at one time, so he knew it well.[60]

There are other examples, but the above is sufficient to make the case. In the early 1960s, Clay Shaw knew David Ferrie, Guy Banister, and Lee Oswald. It could have been unrelated to the assassination of JFK, such as infiltrating civil rights groups to prove that a connection to Communists existed. These were right-wing Fascists, one and all, connected to neo-Nazis. The important thing is they did interact for a purpose that had to be related to a right-wing cause.

With that in mind, consider another Shaw associate named Dr. Alton Ochsner, who was New Orleans' preeminent surgeon and medical researcher from the 1940s on. Ochsner worked at Tulane University before establishing the Ochsner Clinic, now known as the Ochsner Medical Center. He was president of International House while Shaw was at the Trade Mart, so the two men, who shared the same right-wing political views, worked together throughout the years on various projects. Ochsner was also a CIA contact, with a clearance rating from mid-1955 until early 1962. He was so far right that some called him a Fascist, and the timing was such that it was likely Clay Shaw who arranged for Ochsner to become a contact agent for CIA, just as Shaw had done for Guy Banister. And Ochsner must have known Banister and Ferrie as well.[61]

Ochsner became a consultant to the Army in 1955 and for the Air Force two years later. In 1957, he was cleared for a "Sensitive Position" for the US government by the FBI, and he became an official contact for the Special Agent in Charge of the New Orleans FBI office. Two years later, the FBI conducted another "Sensitive Position" investigation into Ochsner and submitted their findings to an unnamed U.S. government agency, presumably the CIA. Ochsner's relationship with the FBI was terminated several days later, on October 21, 1959, and he accepted an assignment from the other agency whose name remains hidden.[62]

More than anything else, what defined Ochsner was his passionate anti-Communist beliefs. "He was like a fundamentalist preacher," recalled one associate, "in the sense that the fight against Communism was the only subject that he would talk about." Edward T. Haslam is the author of *Dr. Mary's Monkey*. His father was a surgeon who knew Ochsner and heard a rumor that "Ochsner was part of an international fascist group and had been very close to Nazi scientists who fled to South America at the end of World War II, particularly in Paraguay . . ." Ochsner was also a segregationist and proponent of eugenics, who hated President Kennedy and his liberal policies, as demonstrated by a letter Ochsner wrote in the early 1960s to the U.S. Senator from Louisiana, Allen Ellender: "I sincerely hope that the Civil Rights Bill can also be defeated, because if it . . . passed, it would certainly mean virtual dictatorship by the President and the Attorney General, a thing I am sure they both want."[63]

Ochsner's right-wing fascism put him in close contact with numerous Latin American dictators. Nicaragua's Anastasio Somoza was one to whom Ochsner was particularly close, which may be why Somoza's physician, Dr. Henri De Bayle, sat on the Board of Directors of Guy Banister's Anti-Communist League of the Caribbean. Juan Peron of Argentina was another.

There was also a connection to oilman Clint Murchison who, while a patient of Ochsner's, donated $750,00 to the Alton Ochsner Medical Foundation. Meanwhile, Murchison purchased 30,000 acres of Louisiana swampland and developed the property, which now covers one-third of New Orleans. There was speculation that the land was sold to Murchison by Lady Bird Johnson.

As described in Volume One, the right-wing Murchison was a member of the Suite 8F Group. Some Suite8F members had questionable dealings with Bobby Baker in Haiti, employed Guy Banister, and associated with George de Mohrenschildt. Others worked with Jimmy Hoffa, Lyndon Johnson, Irv Davidson, Ed Levinson, and organized crime figures such as Carlos Marcello and Vito Genovese. William Pawley and Jack Crichton were Suite 8F members who had dealings in Spain when it was the center of international fascism. Therefore, a relationship between Ochsner and Murchison established the New Orleans doctor's right-wing credentials far beyond the Big Easy.

With the financial help of Murchison, Ochsner helped found the Information Council of the Americas (INCA), a far-right anti-Communist organization whose goal was to keep communism out of the Western Hemisphere. INCA's offices were in the International Trade Mart, as were the offices of the Civil Air Patrol. Ochsner also financed the newsletter published by William Gaudet, whose offices were also in the Trade Mart. There was a lot of right-wing activity going on at Clay Shaw's place of business. It was the perfect cover for such groups, especially those interested in connecting with right-wing organizations worldwide.[64]

In 1960, Clay Shaw was the Program Chairman for the Foreign Policy Association of New Orleans. At the same time, Dr. Ochsner belonged to the National Foreign Policy Association. The two organizations were affiliated and were anti-Communist. The head of the Public Relations Committee of the Foreign Policy Association of New Orleans was Jesse Core, who was married to Lucy Ruggles, the daughter of the publisher of the *Dallas Morning News*. This connection gave the organization ties to some of the most prominent people in Dallas and further connected the right-wing elements of the two cities.[65]

Perhaps Shaw provided a clue to what transpired with Oswald nearly five years after his trial ended. He was a patient at the Ochsner Foundation Hospital, and a longtime acquaintance, George Dureau, visited him. As Dureau later recalled, Shaw said, "You know, I wasn't guilty of what Garrison charged . . . But Garrison had the right idea . . . Someone like me, with a background in army intelligence and with post-war intelligence connections, very well might have been asked to meet with someone like Oswald or Ferrie, to give them a package or some money or whatever, and I would have faithfully done it without ever asking what I was doing it for."[66]

* * *

Clay Shaw's intelligence connections remained secure throughout the Cold War. In the mid-1950s, he was involved in international spying on behalf of the CIA. In 1955 he traveled to Czechoslovakia as "a CIA observer." The following year he was in Spain and Italy, also on the Agency's behalf. It was around that time that Shaw purchased an apartment in Madrid. As we have already seen, Spain was where many Fascists gathered, including those who supported the Donovan/Dulles stay-behind armies, Charles Willoughby, and the OAS rebelling against France. Undoubtedly, Shaw was in Madrid for the same reason.[67]

Victor Marchetti claimed his CIA superiors told him that Shaw was a CIA contact who monitored businessmen going behind the Iron Curtain, "To try and find out so-and-so was going to a denied-access area." The CIA would then debrief the businessmen after they returned.[68]

In 1958, Shaw became affiliated with PERMINDEX, a right-wing organization in Europe allegedly founded to promote worldwide trade that was a CIA front. The same was true about the Centro Mondiale Commerciale (World Trade Center), PERMINDEX's sister company. The CIA created both organizations to launder money from the Mafia and other U.S. interests through the Vatican. The point was to put money into the coffers of European political parties and right-wing organizations the Agency approved of, including the OAS. Shaw was on the PERMINDEX Board of Directors, referenced in his "Who's Who in the South and the Southeast" biographical listing. The Department of Commerce referred to it as "this shadowy organization." Their reputation was already well known.[69]

In 1962, for engaging in subversive intelligence activity, the Centro Mondiale Commerciale and Permindex were expelled from Italy. According to the Italian newspaper *Paesa Sera*, the Centro was "the point of contact for a number of persons who, in certain respects, have somewhat equivocal ties whose common denominator is anti-Communism so strong that it would swallow up all those in the world who have fought for decent relations between East and West, including Kennedy." According to the paper, the Centro was ". . . set up as a cover for the transfer of CIA . . . funds in Italy for illegal political – espionage activities." Italian and French newspapers said Permindex had secretly financed the OAS and their attempts to assassinate de Gaulle.[70]

The Board of Directors of the Centro read like a Who's Who of Fascism. Gutierrez di Spadaforo, an Italian prince and former Mussolini undersecretary, was related through his daughter-in-law to Hjalmar Schacht. Frank Wisner's contact was Ferenc Nagy, a supporter of European Fascist movements and a former premier of Hungary, who headed an anti-Communist party. Also on the Board was Giuseppi Zigiotti, the president of the Fascist National Association for Militia Arms.

Shaw's address book contained the names of several European Fascists, including Herman Bochelman (who admired the Nazi Waffen-SS) and John DeCourcy (imprisoned in England for Fascist sedition).[71] There is no doubt that Clay Shaw was on good terms with Fascists worldwide, including the United States, and it may have been through him that others in New Orleans got involved in the Fascist movement. Recall that Maurice Gatlin, who worked out of Banister's office, provided financing to the OAS.

There is also the story of ex-CIA agent Robert Morrow. Morrow claimed that during the Bay of Pigs invasion, he was flown by David Ferrie into Cuba's Camaguey Mountains, searching for missiles that both men were part of a group headed by Tracy Barnes. Later in 1961, Morrow met Ferrie again, in Athens, Greece, regarding a CIA weapons shipment for a Cuban exile group. After this, it was onto Madrid, where Ferrie received instructions to go to the offices of PERMINDEX, which connected Ferrie to the international Fascist network.[72]

The group in New Orleans supported this international Fascist group. However, the removal of Communists from the U.S. government, specifically JFK, interested them first and foremost. The radical right-wing in Dallas and Houston, so closely affiliated with their counterpart in New Orleans, felt the same way. And it was likely elements of these groups that were involved in JFK's murder.

One final word about this. A 1967 CIA memo, confirmed by the CIA in 1998, connected Clay Shaw to the previously mentioned QKENCHANT. The person at CIA who wrote the 1967 memo was Marguerite Stevens of the Office of Security. In 1960, Stevens provided James Angleton's Counterintelligence Division information on American defectors to the Soviet Union, including Oswald. Chapter Six will discuss the CIA program that sent Americans behind the Iron Curtain in greater detail. It is mentioned here before of a possible connection to Shaw and his right-wing associates in New Orleans. [73]

Does this mean that Oswald was a CIA asset brought into the program by the person in charge of QKENCHANT in New Orleans, Clay Shaw? And did Marguerite Stevens investigate both Oswald and Shaw because there was a connection between the goings-on in New Orleans and Oswald's defection? If so, this connection to the CIA must have occurred before Oswald joined the Marines, which would have been while Oswald was part of the Civil Air Patrol. It would explain why David Ferrie was so anxious to have Oswald enlist a year before he was legally old enough to do so because there was something significant about getting Oswald into the Marines as soon as possible. And it clarifies why Guy Banister's Friends of a Democratic Cuba knew about Oswald when they attempted to purchase the trucks from the Bolton dealership because the New Orleans connection to Oswald included Shaw, Ferrie, and Banister, dating back to the mid-1950s when they first became aware of him. And if this is all true, Oswald did not just appear unannounced in New Orleans after leaving George de Mohrenschildt in Fort Worth, Texas, in 1963. He just went back to the people who had been directing him from the start, for they most likely needed his services again. The question is, was the assassination of JFK what the New Orleans group had in mind when they got together again in 1963 with Oswald or was this just a continuation of a previous operation that began so many years before. Were right-wing Fascists in New Orleans part of the group that assassinated JFK? Or were they innocent and became suspects because of their close relationship with Oswald. Was it a relationship that involved something else? We shall revisit this, but first, an investigation in Cuba may provide some clues.

- 2 -

There's Trouble in Paradise

"Now they're going to find out about Cuba; they're going to find
out about the guns, find out about New Orleans, find out about
everything."
—Jack Ruby to his attorney during his trial for murdering Oswald

*The struggle for power in Cuba played a role in the assassination of JFK, as Cuban
exiles, American paramilitary types, organized crime figures, CIA, military people, and
a host of others were all drawn to the tiny Caribbean island. Jack Ruby was one, as he
attempted to sell guns to any side willing to pay the price. So was June Cobb, an attractive young woman who found herself working for Castro after editing his manifesto into
English. Cobb worked for the Federal Bureau of Narcotics and CIA, and in Havana,
was part of a group that tried to overthrow Castro in the late 1950s. It is also possible
that she was a connection to Lee Harvey Oswald. Both were involved with the Fair Play
for Cuba Committee and the Civil Air Patrol. Cobb was from Norman, Oklahoma,
and an address from that city was found in Oswald's address book after the assassination,
even though there is no evidence he ever visited there. She seemed to have shadowed
Oswald to Mexico City two months before Kennedy's murder. And at the time of the
assassination, Oswald withdrew from the Dallas library a book entitled The Shark and
the Sardines about a shark (the United States) that devoured sardines (Latin American
countries). June Cobb was the one who had translated the book into English. And if she
were involved with Oswald, it meant the CIA was as well, which would have included
the group in Havana of which she was a part.*

* * *

Long before Castro came to power on January 1, 1959, Cuba had a history of
corruption. Federal Bureau of Narcotics agent Claude Flomer blamed the island's
troubles on the Cuban police: "As a result of inefficiency and corruption, past and

present, in the national police, all of the vices known to modern civilization have prospered for many years in Cuba. At present, just as in the recent past, the major criminal conduct in Cuba revolves around assassination[s], gambling, prostitution, and an [sic] extensive traffic in marijuana and narcotics drugs." British diplomats in Washington D.C. during World War II reported home that, "Both the State Department and the American ambassador are very worried about the corruption existing in the Cuban government, a corruption which, though endemic, apparently now exceeds anything which had gone on previously . . ."[1]

Carlos Prio served as President of Cuba from 1948 until 1952, until a military coup by Fulgencio Batista sent him into exile in Miami. As president, Prio amassed a small fortune, estimated to be as high as $100 million. He stole vast sums of money from the Cuban economy, which he invested in Miami real estate, primarily in partnership with Meyer Lansky. He revitalized the Cuban narcotics trade and developed a close relationship with American gangsters in the process. It was a disaster for the Cuban economy, for as Prio's wealth increased, so did the suffering of the Cuban people. Under his leadership, the separation between the haves and have-nots, which had plagued Cuba seemingly forever, reached a new level.[2]

Fidel Castro was born into wealth, but he rejected his privileged background and embraced the revolutionary movement growing within Cuba. As early as 1951, he became a thorn in the side of President Carlos Prio, and like most Cubans, Castro found it intolerable that Prio became wealthy while most people struggled to survive. A typical example of Prio's abuse was his two-thousand-acre farm in the heart of tobacco country, where farmhands worked under slave-like conditions. At the same time, the Cuban military managed the farm in violation of Cuban law.[3]

By February 1952, Castro was chastising Prio on Cuban radio for his close relationship with American gangsters. He called for Prio's removal while simultaneously developing a solid following of his own. Unfortunately for both Prio and Castro, the Batista coup a month later resulted in a change of plans for both men.

After Batista came to power, Castro's revolutionary movement began to grow. His first attempt at armed resistance came on July 26, 1953, when Castro and his followers attacked Batista's Moncada Barracks. It was a disaster, and half of Castro's force was captured, tortured, or killed. Arrested and put on trial, Castro told the courtroom: "Condemn me. It does not matter. History will absolve me." He was sentenced to fifteen years in prison but served only twenty-two months. He could not remain in Cuba safely, so he relocated to Mexico to prepare for his return and the revolution he was sure would topple Batista.[4]

Meanwhile, living in Miami and desperate to return to power, Carlos Prio personally funded various Cuban exile groups and individuals who shared his passion for removing the tyrant Batista from power. Antonio Echeverria was the head of the Cuban Student Directorate (DRE), a Havana-based paramilitary organization, and it was the DRE and Echeverria who caught Prio's attention.

In August 1956, Echeverria met with the recently released Castro in Mexico City. On September 1, they held a joint press conference demanding that Batista have legitimate elections and restore the Cuban constitution. The move attracted Castro to Cuban students and linked his guerilla movement with the urban resistance of the DRE. It was a step in the right direction for Castro.

The importance of press conferences notwithstanding, the DRE relied on violence to achieve its objectives. They attempted to assassinate Batista in 1956, the same year they aligned themselves with Castro, but were unsuccessful. One DRE member, Rolando Cubela, did manage to shoot and kill the head of the Cuban police, which forced Cubela to flee Cuba and find sanctuary in the United States. He later returned and became a colonel in Castro's army. After the revolution, he was named head of Cuba's student union, and *Time* magazine called him "Castro's gun-toting bully boy." Cubela would become a critical figure in the JFK assassination saga, for he would eventually approach the CIA, claiming he wanted to defect. On the day of JFK's assassination, he met with the CIA's Desmond FitzGerald in Paris to discuss the possibility of killing Castro. Whether Cubela was a legitimate defector, or a Cuban double agent infiltrating U.S. intelligence, was never determined. However, the timing of his meeting with FitzGerald may not have been a coincidence.

Undaunted, on March 13, 1957, the DRE attempted to assassinate Batista a second time, but the Cuban leader once again escaped unharmed. More importantly, the encounter was a disaster for the DRE. The police cornered the students just blocks from the University of Havana, and Echeverria and four others were shot and killed. Other members of the DRE were tracked down and murdered, crippling the DRE student movement. It proved advantageous for Castro, for his revolution became the primary option to remove Batista from power.[5]

The U.S. government began to take notice, and that same year CIA inspector general Lyman Kirkpatrick traveled to Havana to meet with U.S. ambassador Arthur Gardner, a strong Batista supporter. Sensing the rebel movement was gaining strength, Kirkpatrick instructed Gardner to continue supporting Batista while developing a relationship with the rebels. It was a change in philosophy, as the U.S. State Department increasingly began to look for an alternative to Batista, the Cuban dictator.

Support for Castro was growing in the United States, especially on American campuses. An Indiana group founded American Students for a Free Cuba, which supported Castro. In May 1958, students at the University of Colorado hanged Batista in effigy, and Eisenhower had to halt the sale of arms to Batista in the face of strong opposition. The National Student Association (NSA) proclaimed that "any imperialist attempt to dominate a country economically and politically is contrary to the development of higher education and national culture." The NSA statement intended to point an accusatory finger at the United States.[6]

Meanwhile, Carlos Prio was still in Miami, continuing to finance various anti-Batista groups, including remnants of the DRE who had managed to flee to America. Castro, recognizing he was running out of time if his revolution would be successful and desperately in need of financial assistance, turned for help to the man he had once despised—Carlos Prio. Initially, Prio rejected the rebel leader, but he was not one to burn bridges. After the two men secretly met, Prio pledged $50,000 in support of Castro. He was motivated by a belief that, if Castro were successful, he would be too inexperienced to take over the Cuban government. Castro would have no choice but to make Prio the new president. However, when Castro finally did come to power in 1959, there was no room for Prio in the new government. He would spend the remaining days of his life unsuccessfully trying to overthrow the Communist leader.[7]

With the help of Prio's donation, Castro returned to Cuba on December 2, 1956, with eighty-one followers aboard the American yacht, Granma. Unfortunately for the rebels, Batista's army was waiting, and fewer than twenty of Castro's followers survived the confrontation. Those that did took refuge in the Sierra Maestra mountains. Here, living under Spartan-like conditions, Castro began to gain popularity among American adventurers and mercenaries who saw in Castro's fight for freedom a similarity to the American revolution.[8]

Despite his difficulties, Castro was sure that most Cubans supported him and his rebels. By the time he had to find refuge in the Sierra Maestras, Batista, his relatives, friends, and influential associates had stolen almost half a billion dollars from the Cuban economy. American business exacerbated the problem by removing large sums of money from Cuba, which drained the Cuban economy. According to a U.S. Department of Commerce report from that period, "American participation [in Cuba] exceeds 90 percent in the telephone and electric services, [ ] about 50 percent in public service railways, and roughly 40 percent in raw sugar production . . ." It was clear that with Batista in power, the influence of American business was not going to diminish, and the oppression of the Cuban people would continue.[9]

Meanwhile, Carlos Prio, who had been illegally shipping arms to Castro, was closely monitored by the FBI. On February 13, 1958, the Justice Department indicted Prio for violating the Neutrality Act, which prohibited American involvement in the affairs of foreign nations. Arrested along with Prio were several Houston men, including gun smuggler Robert Ray McKeown, whose daughter was said to be Prio's girlfriend. Prio had provided McKeown with financing to purchase a safe house near Houston for storing arms destined for shipment to Castro's forces. McKeown had no choice but to plead guilty, for which he received an eighteen-month suspended sentence in October 1958. Interviewed by the *Houston Post*, McKeown said that Prio had promised him fifty percent ownership of the Biltmore hotel in Havana were their efforts successful. There was extensive press coverage of

McKeown's story, and as we will see, one person who would become particularly interested in McKeown's expertise was Jack Ruby.

McKeown owned a manufacturing plant in Cuba during the 1950s but left in 1957 when he failed to pay kickbacks to Batista. He eventually got to know Castro well and claimed to have been promised "a government position in Cuba or perhaps . . . some franchises or concessions . . ." but nothing came of this once Castro came to power.[10]

While McKeown was busy supplying the rebel Castro with weapons, the U.S. arms embargo against Cuba was in place. Batista needed assistance, which attracted Irv Davidson, the Washington public relations man and arms supplier to foreign governments discussed in Volume One. In November 1958, when he was already working with Jimmy Hoffa, the FBI learned that Davidson had received a $260,000 letter of credit from the Cuban government to purchase arms from Israel, bypassing the American embargo.[11] Recall that Davidson was also involved with Clint Murchison and Bobby Baker in a Haitian operation and that Davidson was close to Carlos Marcello. The Cuban revolution attracted anyone interested in making some quick money, including people connected to organized crime.

By 1958 it was clear that the removal of Batista was inevitable. The police force in Havana had grown to eight thousand strong, and the presidential palace essentially became a fortress protected by machine-gun-toting guards. Student protests were so rampant that the University of Havana had already been closed for two years. Around this time, a seemingly innocent event occurred, which would prove to have enormous ramifications in the future as Castro's prominence grew. The Cuban Communists, recognizing the growing strength of the revolution, decided to back Castro. They were a relatively weak movement of 20,000 people in a country of roughly 6.5 million. Years later, Castro would recollect: "If you asked me whether I considered myself a revolutionary at the time I was in the mountains, I would answer yes. If you asked me, did I consider myself a Marxist-Leninist, I would say no."[12] In the U.S., whether Castro was a Communist or a Marxist-Leninist needed to be known.

* * *

June Cobb was a CIA and FBN asset who had a connection, either directly or indirectly, to Lee Harvey Oswald and the assassination of JFK. In the years after JFK's assassination, she was sufficiently important that the CIA conducted an extensive review of her 2,500-page Agency file and labeled "secret" all documents about her work with the FBN. However, other papers have leaked, and these, coupled with two CIA Office of Security interviews with Cobb, have allowed researchers to establish who she was involved with and what she was doing.[13]

Her story began in 1948 when she met and allegedly fell in love with Rafael Herran Olozaga. Herran was from a prominent Colombian family whose grandfather and great-great-grandfather each served as the nation's president. That same year, Rafael, his twin brother Tomas, and Cobb began processing and trafficking opium within Colombia, a departure from the legacy handed down to the two brothers by their ancestors. In 1950, Cobb returned to the U.S. to spend time with her father in Oklahoma, but she was back in Colombia ten months later. However, by 1951 a rare blood disorder forced her to leave the Herran brothers once again. Cobb returned to the U.S. and was a patient for several months at Mount Sinai Hospital in New York City.[14]

Several months in a hospital was quite extensive, even for a blood disorder contracted in South America. And considering what we know about Cobb, there is reason to view this with suspicion, especially when we think about what else went on at Mount Sinai during that same period. Recall that Dr. Harold A. Abramson experimented with LSD on adolescent patients at Mt. Sinai, and the CIA funded it. "We ran experiments on students out of an old, unused space in Mount Sinai Hospital," reported Dr. Margaret Furguson, who worked with Abramson. "We did some experiments out on Long Island where [Abramson] had another office. Once there was a student who came back over the weekend from a Friday experiment. He was shaking, terribly frightened, and vomiting . . . I took care of him myself. . . . There were a lot of doctors from the military that came to see him."[15]

Drug experimentation on innocent people during the 1950s, without their consent, was a dark period in American history that cannot be justified. And that so many people spent extended periods in institutions while they were tested and probed, which may have included Lee Harvey Oswald, only serves to exacerbate one's disgust for what went on. Perhaps June Cobb was also one of those people, which would explain her extended hospital stay.

Also of note is that when someone pushed Frank Olson through a window in his room at the Statler Hotel in New York City, his roommate phoned Dr. Abramson. It confirmed that Abramson was involved in LSD experimentation at Camp Detrick, as well as Mount Sinai.[16]

After her release from the hospital, Cobb remained in New York City and worked as an administrative assistant at Mount Sinai. It was somewhat odd that Cobb would immediately start working at the same hospital where she had been a patient for months. Cobb then joined *Time* magazine in the letters department during the summer of 1952. The following year she was employed by Chicago's Cook County Hospital as a secretary to the director of medical education, the same physician she had worked for at Mount Sinai in New York. Was this all innocent, or was someone keeping watch over her? She returned to New York later that same year and worked as a translator and interpreter for clients referred to her by "a good friend" named Warren Broglie, the manager of the Waldorf Astoria hotel. Broglie's relevance is that he also served undercover as an asset and confidential informant for the FBI, FBN, and CIA, which is undoubtedly how he and Cobb became acquainted. For how else would a woman who spent several months in a hospital, worked at low-level jobs, and relocated to Chicago for a while, then get to be friends with the manager of one of the most prestigious hotels in New York City? And according to his CIA file, for over twenty years, beginning in mid-1952, Broglie was considered a "most reliable asset whose loyalties are unquestioned."

To understand Broglie's importance to the Agency, consider that he was sent to Egypt in 1955 to become the general manager of the Nile Hilton in Cairo, which was when Nasser nationalized the Suez Canal. It is also worth noting that Broglie, Allen Dulles, and Conrad Hilton, whom Dulles knew well, were all Knights of Malta. Recall this was the Roman Catholic organization to which many high-ranking CIA operatives, military officers, and international men of means and influence belonged. Supporting the Vatican in the war against communism seemed to be the only prerequisite for becoming a knight. Undoubtedly, Broglie's excursion to Egypt was for the same reason, making his long association with June Cobb that much more relevant.[17]

June Cobb would meet the Herran brothers once again in 1955 when she was in Colombia working for the Colombian-American Culture Foundation. She remained for a while and taught briefly at an American school. Perhaps this was legitimate, and there is no proof that it was not, but it sounds more like she was on assignment for U.S. intelligence. Teaching was a means of placing agents in third-world countries with an adequate cover, as Oswald's cousin, Marilyn Dorothea Murret, could do.

Cobb then traveled to Havana with the Herran brothers in December 1956 to sell heroin and cocaine. Fortunately for her, she left Cuba for Coral Gables, Florida, the day before Cuban law enforcement and FBN agents from New York arrested both brothers. Cobb's timely departure was not an accident, for she was likely the person who notified the FBN about the Herrans. The brothers were released but re-arrested the following year "when a woman with CIA connections," who had dealt with the FBN's George Hunter White and Harry Williams in Cuba months before, contacted the FBN in New Orleans and told them about the laboratory operated by the two brothers. Once again, the woman who spilled the beans was June Cobb.

In *A Secret Order*, H.P Albarelli, Jr. writes that June Cobb worked undercover for the FBN. She did her job well, associating with leading Mafia figures and other questionable characters in the execution of her assignment. The list included Santos Trafficante, Jr., Carlos Marcello, Jack Ruby, and Sam Giancana. Ruby associates John Roland Jones and Lewis McWillie. Also, "Ronald Dante, better known as Dr. Dante, a hypnotist . . . and frequent visitor to Mexico City and Cuba . . . Henry Saavedra, who worked for Trafficante at his Capri Casino in Havana and who was known to have associated with Sylvia Duran [who worked at the Cuban embassy in Mexico City and allegedly had an affair with Oswald in September 1963]. Saavedra also sometimes worked with John Roland Jones, who with Maurice Melton, a Chicago-based trafficker, and Jack Ruby occasionally smuggled a load of opium from Mexico to Dallas, Houston, and Chicago."[18]

The names provide a treasure trove of information. We know mob bosses Trafficante and Marcello were involved in delivering drugs to the U.S. through Cuba as part of the Dulles/ Donovan/WCC/Corsican operation, and that Trafficante and Giancana were involved in the CIA/Mafia plots to assassinate Castro. Jack Ruby was already involved in drug dealings in Texas, working for Joseph Civello, who ran the Texas operation for the Marcello crime family. Ruby will travel to Cuba to get Trafficante out of prison in two years, summoned by Lewis McWillie. John Roland Jones was probably Paul Roland Jones, the man who tried to bribe officials in Dallas when Ruby first moved there from Chicago. He would also visit Ruby in Dallas just two weeks before Kennedy's assassination. FBI memorandums connect Saavedra to Trafficante in Havana, right after Cuban authorities released Trafficante from prison. That June Cobb was involved with all these men by 1957 means she was very well-connected regarding drug trafficking from Cuba to the U.S., making her a significant person of interest.

Cobb and the Herran brothers also encountered representatives of Corsican drug trafficker Paul Mondoloni, whose name repeatedly appears related to the drug operation funding the Dulles/Donovan stay-behind armies in Europe. For almost a decade, Mondoloni was a leading drug trafficker and primarily used Cuba as the intermediate point for delivering drugs to the United States. The bottom line is that Cobb destroyed the drug operation of the Herran brothers, and the reason may have been to ensure that the lion's share of drugs delivered into the United States came from the Corsican operation, which included Trafficante and other mobsters working under Lucky Luciano. Meanwhile, Cobb's good friend Broglie was CIA and a member of the Knights of Malta, which meant he was a warrior in the Vatican's effort to rid the world of communism. It most likely connected him to the Dulles/Donovan operation, including the Corsican and Luciano Mafia and the WCC, which involved all the Fascist characters in Madrid associated with this group. It was no wonder that the struggle for power in Cuba was being watched closely in the U.S. The connection of FBN agent June Cobb to mobsters, CIA agents, and paramilitary types moving drugs through Cuba that provided the lion's share of the information. It became even more critical as the chances increased that Castro's revolution would succeed, potentially placing the U.S. intelligence drug operation run by mobsters and Corsicans in jeopardy.

* * *

By the mid-1950s, as Castro's popularity continued to grow, there was concern among the right-wing in the United States. Communists were part of his revolutionary movement, which meant steps were needed to prevent them from taking control of Cuba. The State Department, motivated by a desire to have the dictator

Batista removed at any cost, rejected the idea and claimed they "had no conclusive evidence that the [Castro] movement was Communist-inspired or Communist-dominated." However, Allen Dulles was not so sure. During the Easter weekend of 1955, he secretly traveled to Havana to provide Batista with funding for a new agency to fight communism, the Bureau of Repression of Communist Activities (BRAC). But Batista could not be trusted. Before long, BRAC became symbolic of the regime's brutality, as it did not hesitate to arrest, torture, or murder those who opposed the Cuban leader, driving the wedge deeper between himself and the Cuban people.[19]

It was not just BRAC that terrorized Cuba. In Oriente province, Rolando Masferrer, better known as El Tigre, handled the government-sanctioned brutality. Since the late 1940s, when he arrived on the scene as a student from the University of Havana and an enemy of Fidel Castro, Masferrer associated with the Havana Mob and cast a dark cloud over Cuban politics. His gang of cutthroats would publicly display the bodies of their murdered victims, as was the case when they murdered four youths suspected of involvement in civil resistance. Their bodies strung up on telephone poles outside Santiago. But what Masferrer and his minions engaged in proved counterproductive because, for every four youths killed by the Batista regime, ten more would join the revolution.[20]

Because the CIA had created BRAC, Inspector General Lyman Kirkpatrick was sent to Cuba in 1958 to get a first-hand look at the atrocities family victims accused the group of perpetrating. "The horrible wounds on the woman's body were convincing," read Kirkpatrick's account of what he had seen. "As were the reports of case after case of the sons of prominent Cuban families who had joined either the students' organization or . . . [Castro's] July 26 movement and had been arrested and killed." The head of BRAC, Colonel Mariano Paget, ignored Kirkpatrick's protests, and BRAC continued its tortuous ways, undaunted. As a result, sensing the widening gap between Batista and the Cuban people of all classes, Kirkpatrick cabled Washington that, in his opinion, Batista would not survive the year.[21]

BRAC and El Tigres made it difficult for the U.S. to continue to support Batista. Then in March 1958, it became almost impossible, as Batista suspended constitutional guarantees and essentially staged a mock election for president in November, in which a small turnout of voters cast their ballots for his hand-picked candidate. Meanwhile, the support for Castro continued to grow, and in a show of strength, Raul Castro kidnapped Americans and held them for a month. On June 26, the Cubans took hostage eleven U.S. civilians working for a mining company. The Cuban revolutionaries then brazenly captured twenty-four U.S. Navy enlisted men the next day.

The rebels promised to release the hostages only if the U.S. stopped furnishing Batista with weapons and ceased using the American base at Guantanamo as a staging ground for counterinsurgency operations.[22]

To make things even worse, by the second half of 1958, the American ambassador to Cuba, Earl Smith, concluded that Castro was a Communist. However, the United States, while continuing to make arrests of arms dealers supplying Batista, did not have a plan for thwarting the rebel leader's continued popularity.[23] Anti-Batista Cubans who supported Castro insisted he was not a Communist, telling American officials that democracy would return to Cuba once Castro's revolution removed Batista from power. It was a matter of extreme importance, for Batista could not remain without American support.

There was obvious concern at the White House, and Ambassador Smith was summoned to Washington to offer his insight into the proper American course of action. William Wieland, the State Department's Director of Caribbean and Mexican Affairs, and the right-wing William Pawley, who was always willing to answer the call when needed, met with Smith. Pawley was close to Carlos Prio, Batista, and the Dominican Republic's Rafael Trujillo, another Caribbean dictator who ruled with an iron fist, so it was clear where Pawley's allegiances lay. By this time, Pawley had also served as American ambassador to Brazil and Peru under Eisenhower and was friends with Allen Dulles. Pawley was an important figure who had helped change the Flying Tigers into one of the CIA's first airlines, Civil Air Transport, and helped establish a front company for the airline called the Pacific Corporation. He was also involved in the overthrow of Arbenz in Guatemala, which meant he was close to those in the CIA who would attempt to overthrow Castro after he came to power. It was why Pawley was considered dangerous by those at the State Department who opposed Batista.[24]

Pawley's main advantage was that he was close to the President. "In four or five meetings with Eisenhower during those years," Pawley recalled, ". . . I warned him of a Communist takeover if Castro ever came to power." However, Batista's heavy-handed tactics made it impossible for the United States to continue to support him. Pawley adamantly implored Eisenhower that if he was unwilling to support Batista, he should at least consider replacing him with a U.S.-backed military junta. For Pawley, anyone was acceptable in place of Castro.[25]

Pawley met with Ambassador Smith and William Wieland, but it was clear that Wieland and Pawley had different ideas regarding what to do in Cuba. Wieland was far to the left and believed Pawley did not understand the problems of Latin America and the people's struggle to fight oppression. It was a strange duo to bring together to determine the future of Cuba, but unknown to Wieland, Pawley already had a plan that had the backing of the CIA Director and Eisenhower. It involved Pawley traveling to Cuba and telling Batista to go into exile, for the U.S. could no longer support him. It was only a matter of time before the revolutionaries would forcibly remove him. A military junta would take charge until they were ready for fair elections. The U.S. could then control who the next leader of Cuba would be, and concerns over the possibility of Castro being a Communist would become irrelevant.[26]

The U.S. decided to go ahead with Pawley's proposed plan. However, he arrived in Havana as a private citizen without the blessing of the President. The State Department had caused this last-minute change, believing it was politically safer to isolate Ike from direct involvement in removing a foreign leader. It was inevitable that, under such an arrangement, Batista rejected Pawley's demand that he hand over the government to someone else. He remained in power, and William Pawley returned to the United States, unsuccessful in accomplishing what he had set out to do.[27]

With Pawley's failed attempt to convince Batista to step down, the Cuban leader's reign of power was in jeopardy. In the latter part of 1958, a group of Castro's men, led by Che Guevara, captured the provincial capital of Santa Clara in Central Cuba. Sensing the end was near, Batista fled Cuba for the Dominican Republic, and on January 1, 1959, Fidel Castro triumphantly entered the city of Havana. Castro maintained he was not a Communist but the leader of a Socialist revolution in Cuba and throughout South America. A distinction that did not fall on deaf ears among the right-wing in the United States, who began to realize that Castro was a formidable enemy that they had to remove. Organized crime felt the same way, for, between the Mafia and CIA, the pipeline of drugs between Havana and the U.S. had to continue, regardless of the cost.

* * *

By the mid-1950s, organized crime began to hedge its bets by supplying arms to Castro's rebel army if his revolution successfully overthrew Batista. As Santo Trafficante told his attorney, Frank Ragano, whoever followed Batista would still need the casinos to fund the national economy. He hinted that he had already begun planning for the eventuality that Castro would be victorious. Ragano took this to mean that Trafficante was secretly supplying the rebels in the Sierra Maestra Mountains. After the revolution, Castro did not concern Trafficante, and the mobster remained in Cuba. "Castro is a complete nut! He's not going to be in power or office for long," Trafficante told Ragano. "Either Batista will return, or someone else will replace this guy because there's no way the economy can continue without tourists, and this guy is closing all the hotels and casinos. [It] is a temporary storm. It'll blow over."[28]

Norman Rothman partnered with Meyer Lansky and brothers Gabriel and Sam Mannarino in both the Sans Souci and Tropicana casinos, where they shared a portion of the profits with Batista. Like Trafficante, Rothman would support whoever ultimately came to power, and proactively, along with the Mannarino brothers, he established contact with the 26th of July Movement early on. Most likely, Trafficante was aware of what Rothman was doing.[29]

The Mannarino brothers told Rothman about a cache of weapons stolen from a National Guard armory in Canton, Ohio, on October 15, 1958. Rothman was interested and rented a plane for six thousand dollars to run the guns to Cuba, which he intended to pay for with stolen securities as collateral for a loan. At first, everything went well, but while being shipped, the U.S. border patrol confiscated the weapons, and most of the conspirators were indicted, including Rothman and the Mannarinos. In 1960 Carl Noll, an ex–New Orleans mobster turned government informant, told the FBI that Carlos Marcello was also deeply involved in the arms deal. The *Chicago Sun-Times* reported that the arms were for Castro's rebels.[30]

In a separate incident, Rothman and Salvatore Mannarino were indicted, along with mobster Pepe Cotroni, for receiving stolen bonds from a 1958 bank robbery in Canada, which were to be used to pay for Castro's guns. But the CIA had no choice but to ensure they set the gangsters free, for the mobsters could expose the Agency's involvement with the Mafia if they were ever brought to trial and disclosed what was going on. According to researcher Peter Dale Scott, "In 1978, Rothman told a CBS television interviewer that he had avoided conviction because of the CIA's interest in his gunrunning activities." It was not the end of the CIA's interest in Rothman, nor the last time they would intervene so that mobsters would not have to stand trial.[31]

Pepe Cotroni managed the family's narcotics business, with New York Mafioso Carmine Galante and their contact in Montreal, Lucian Rivard. In 1956 Rivard relocated to Havana. Along with Corsicans Paul Mondoloni and Jean Croce, they moved narcotics through several nightclubs they operated while paying Batista approximately $20,000 per week for the privilege to conduct their illicit business. The following year, Cotroni agreed to buy heroin from Jean Dominick Venturi, a Mondoloni associate in France. By the end of the year, Cotroni and Galante, whose trucking company did business in Montreal, supplied fifty kilograms of heroin per month to the five biggest Italian wholesalers in New York.

On November 24, 1958, FBN Atlanta District Supervisor Jack Cusack, whose jurisdiction included Cuba, sent a memo to FBN Director Anslinger. It stated that Mondoloni sold between fifty and one-hundred-fifty kilos of heroin every three to six months to Rothman and "almost all important Italian-American suspects visiting Havana." Cusack said that Mondoloni's operation in Cuba had started in 1955 with Rothman and Trafficante and "poses a most serious threat to the suppression of the illicit heroin traffic . . ."[32]

Mondoloni was also a contact of Jean-Pierre Lafitte (and an alias which Lafitte used). Along with fellow Corsican Jean Jehan, he was behind the French Connection drug operation, part of the Dulles/Donovan operation to finance stay-behind armies in Europe. Mondoloni had connections. He was arrested in Havana in December 1956 and extradited to Paris two months later. Still, he fought his deportation any way he could, reportedly having the Cuban Minister of the Interior intercede on his behalf, bribing officials, and marrying a Cuban woman. However, the French ambassador was determined to have him deported to France. Colonel

Orlando Piedra, the chief of the Bureau of Investigations and director of the Cuban secret police, hand-delivered the deportation documents to Batista. In the end, Mondoloni received only a two-year prison sentence from a French court for armed robbery, and in five months, he was back on the street. He was too important and knew too much to have been treated any harsher. And as described above, June Cobb and the Herran brothers were familiar with numerous Mondoloni underlings.[33]

Mondoloni was not the only one who authorities protected. After U.S. authorities arrested Rothman, McKeown, and Carlos Prio for sending arms to Castro, the CIA made sure they were released. The Agency was supporting all these gunrunning activities, and the mob had nothing to fear. So, from Lucky Luciano's involvement with OSS during World War II, U.S. intelligence was in bed with organized crime, and the relationship was not going to end anytime soon.[34]

Recall that Jean Jehan was the building owner in New York City, where George Hunter White rented an apartment to conduct drug experiments on unsuspecting civilians for the CIA. And along with the names Hidell, Mertz, and Jack Martin, Mondoloni and Jehan were two aliases used by Lafitte. Mondoloni's Corsican heroin network partnered with Michael Mertz, while Mertz was simultaneously involved in the Fort Benning drug bust that included Santo Trafficante and Carlos Marcello. Lafitte and George White had also known Jack Ruby since 1947. The same names kept popping up, which meant their relationships grew stronger as the years passed. In addition to their involvement in an international drug operation supporting the CIA, there was also a connection to running guns to Castro's rebel army. And it was intriguing that Jack Ruby was connected to Norman Rothman and gunrunning himself and was part of the overall operation.

In *The Hidden History of the JFK Assassination*, author Lamar Waldron writes: "Also in the late 1950s, FBI files—most provided to the Warren Commission— show that Ruby became involved in gunrunning to Cuba with several associates of Trafficante, among them Norman Rothman and Dominick Bartone, as well as Carlos Prio. LA mobster Mickey Cohen was also running guns to Cuba at that time, and 'Ruby told one of his business partners . . . he was a close friend of Mickey Cohen.' The FBI documented numerous ties between Ruby and Cohen's girlfriend Candy Barr. Ruby also knew Hoffa, according to Hoffa's son . . . ," and Hoffa was also involved in running guns to Cuba.[35]

Hoffa was involved in drug smuggling as early as the 1940s, when the FBN "revealed [that] Detroit drug smugglers were receiving narcotics from Santo Trafficante in Tampa, via New Orleans," which involved Carlos Marcello, Frank Costello, and Meyer Lansky. "The Teamsters facilitated the Mafia's national drug distribution system, for after being received from overseas sources, narcotics were transported to Joe Civello in Dallas" by a trucking company.[36]

As previously discussed, former Teamster vice president Allen Friedman connected Jimmy Hoffa to French Connection drug runners. Friedman also claimed that Hoffa was "aware of the Cuban revolution and the need for arms by both sides" and that "military surplus weapons were readily available through both legitimate and illegal sources." He "decided to support both sides . . . making the most money possible," using Trafficante's Florida empire as a "shipping base" for the "guns and a few army surplus planes." "Hoffa wanted to continue gun-running after Castro took control of Cuba," Friedman said, and "wanted to utilize Teamster money . . . to aid friends involved with gun-running." It "was Hoffa's way of trying to help organized crime figures . . . Hoffa's main interest was in helping Santo Trafficante," whose "Miami office was in Teamster Local 320."[37]

One of Hoffa's "most trusted lieutenants," Joe Franco, confirmed that Hoffa "started handing over money to buy arms" for Castro. "And for a long time, he continued to give money for arms for Castro . . . and there was [sic] a few times when Jimmy asked that Castro send people over here to do little jobs for him."[38]

"I think my dad knew Jack Ruby . . . so what," said Hoffa's son. Considering the same circles Hoffa and Ruby traveled in, dealing arms and narcotics, it was not "so what." It was a big deal and further confirmed how closely connected all these people were to Ruby.

Like his Mafia friends, Hoffa furnished arms to both sides in Cuba, hoping to ingratiate himself with whoever proved victorious. In 1957 a Hoffa-connected arms dealer, Dominick Bartone, who may have also had dealings with Jack Ruby, formed a company named Akros Dynamics to provide $1.5 million in financing for eleven C-74 Globemaster aircraft from the U.S. government to sell to Batista. Over the next two years, Bartone and other associates tried to arrange a loan from the Teamsters to finance the deal, but Castro's revolution put an end to it. [39]

Once Castro took over the government, Akros Dynamics attempted to sell the planes to him, with the idea that Castro would then let the mob return to Cuba. Bartone and some of his partners made trips to Cuba to make it happen, including Jimmy Hoffa. Edward Partin, a Louisiana Teamster who became the government's key informant against Hoffa in 1962, commented years later that, "The whole thing was purely and simply Hoffa's way of helping some of his mob buddies who were afraid of losing their businesses in Cuba. . . . They were trying to score points with Castro right after he moved in."[40]

There is no doubt that Jack Ruby was involved with the mob in arms smuggling to Castro, which Ruby's statements support. After he killed Oswald, a psychiatrist who visited him in jail reported that Ruby was distraught over having helped Castro come to power. In another incident, in a letter smuggled out of jail, Ruby wrote: "I had sent guns to Cuba. . . ." Finally, Ruby told his lawyers, "now they're going to find out about Cuba, they're going to find out about the guns, find out about New Orleans, find out about everything."[41] Ruby's reference to New Orleans is revealing and provides an insight into with whom he was involved. Recall from the previous chapter that CIA asset William Gaudet claimed to have seen Ruby in New Orleans buying paintings in 1959, which, in addition to Carlos Marcello, connected Ruby to Guy Banister, David Ferrie, Clay Shaw, and Sergio Arcacha Smith. It was not a coincidence that G. Wray Gill was the attorney for both Marcello and David Ferrie.

An FBI report stated that "a former Oklahoma law officer . . . says that an incident in 1958 . . . linked . . . Jack Ruby to gun running. The guns and ammunition were [ ] taken to Cuba." That "an investigation by the Texas Department of Public Safety and the FBI revealed [the] involvement of Jack Ruby, owner of the Carousel Club in Dallas, in the gunrunning incident," which included "a car loaded with guns and ammunition."

In an interview with the FBI on December 21, 1963, Ruby reported that "at a time when Cuba was popular," he had contacted a well-known gun smuggler in the Houston area, who turned out to be Robert McKeown, who we know was already well known to the FBI. McKeown confirmed to FBI agents that Ruby had contacted him to sell jeeps to Castro. In a letter to Lee Rankin, the General Counsel for the Warren Commission, J. Edgar Hoover wrote that their "investigation related primarily to the activities of Carlos Prio Socarras who, with a number of others, including McKeown, was involved in a conspiracy to ship arms, munitions, and other war materials to Fidel Castro to assist him in his efforts to overthrow the Batista regime in Cuba."[42]

In addition, a CIA file kept secret for thirty years reported that "[Norman] Rothman has a long history of . . . illegal arms dealing" and "is known to CIA as a hoodlum with ties to pre-Castro Cuba." The CIA file also said "Rothman" knew "Frank Fiorini [aka Sturgis]" and that "Rothman first came to CIA's attention in 1958 when he was residing in Dallas, Texas." Another CIA memo claimed that "Rothman has engaged in many exploits and deals with Masferrer" and that "Rothman . . . claims to know Prio . . ."[43]

The connection between Rothman, Prio, and Dallas, Texas, makes sense, for the timing of the second memo coincided with the 1958 indictment of Rothman, Prio, and Robert McKeown for trying to send guns to Castro, as cited previously in this chapter. In January 1959, Ruby contacted McKeown suggests he was probably connected to Rothman and Prio as well.

Ruby's first known involvement in gun smuggling was reported to the FBI by an informant named Blaney Mack Johnson. He was a pilot who had mob connections in Florida and was similarly engaged in helping Castro if he could turn a profit. According to Johnson, Ruby was part owner with numerous organized crime figures of a gambling house in Hallandale, Florida, The Colonial Inn. The FBI report quoted Johnson saying Ruby "was active in arranging illegal flights of weapons from Miami to the Castro organization in Cuba." A collaborator with Ruby was the well-known gunrunner Eddie Browder, and together they ran their operation out of the Florida Keys.[44]

Then there was the story told by Mary Thompson, who, after the assassination, contacted the FBI to report that she also had an encounter with Jack Ruby. Along with her daughter and son-in-law, in 1958 (the year McKeown, Rothman, Prio, and Mondoloni were all indicted), they visited her brother, ex-Dallas policeman James Woodward, at his cottage in the Florida Keys. While there, Woodward introduced them to Jack, a friend who owned a house nearby. After seeing Ruby's picture on television as Oswald's killer, both Thompson and her daughter knew he was the man they had previously met. Thompson's brother was a Dallas policeman who had known Ruby, as did every cop in the city. Mary learned that Jack was originally from Chicago, owned a drinking place in Dallas, and had organized crime connections. She also noticed that his car had Texas plates.

One night, Woodward got drunk and told his sister that Ruby was running guns to Cuba. Woodward's wife added that "Jack had a trunkful of guns and inferred that Jack was going to supply them to the Cubans . . . [It] was at the time of the revolution in Cuba." He also gave his sister a warning which was consistent with Ruby's violent nature. "Get Dolores [Thompson's daughter] out of Jack's house," he said, "because Jack might try to rape her."

The FBI was unable to locate Woodward after the assassination to verify if Thompson's story was true. However, they did uncover some interesting information about Woodward, courtesy of the Knoxville, Tennessee FBI. Knoxville had interviewed Woodward in September 1963 and reported that Woodward "alleged he had participated in an invasion of Cuba before the Castro regime; [and] furnished ammunition and dynamite to both Castro and Cuban exile forces." In October, Woodward was questioned again by the Knoxville FBI, at which time he claimed that the dynamite was being stored "by Cubans to be used by Cuban exile forces against the Castro regime."[45]

The independent reports of Blaney Mack Johnson and Mary Thompson are credible and confirm that Ruby was involved in gunrunning activities. Johnson also told the FBI about an association between Ruby and Carlos Prio, that Ruby had "purchased a substantial share in a Havana gaming house in which one Collis [phonetic] Prio was [the] principal owner." Johnson continued "that Collis Prio was within favor of former Cuban leader Batista but was instrumental in financing and managing accumulation of arms by pro-Castro forces."[46]

Exactly how much Prio was in favor of Batista is questionable, considering Batista was the man who overthrew him. Maybe Prio was also playing both sides by supporting Batista and the rebels at the same time. Regardless, what is essential is that one of Prio's most trusted and reliable underlings involved in running guns to Castro was Frank Sturgis. The CIA memo mentioned above included Sturgis' name along with Norman Rothman's. And according to Andrew St. George, the supersleuth reporter who was close to the Cuban exile community: "In 1955, Frank [Sturgis] began to run clandestine night flights into Cuba for former President Carlos Prio . . . , sometimes delivering passengers (agents, contact men, underground organizers) sometimes cargo (tommy guns, hand grenades, plastic explosives) to be employed, in some manner or another, against Batista."[47] Considering that both Sturgis and Ruby were closely associated with Prio and Rothman, it stands to reason that Ruby and Sturgis must have known each other as well during this period.

Thirty-four-year-old future Watergate burglar Frank Sturgis (aka Fiorini) was a World War II veteran and former nightclub manager from Virginia Beach. He became a soldier of fortune and developed a relationship with Castro's 26th of July Movement. In 1975, Sturgis told a reporter for the *New York Daily News* that a family connection introduced him to Carlos Prio and was likely how Sturgis became involved with Castro's rebels. He began working for Prio in 1958, buying cars in Miami, loading them with arms, and shipping them to Cuba. Sturgis traveled extensively throughout the U.S., Mexico, and South America, smuggling guns to Castro. In July 1958, he was apprehended in Cuba for gun trafficking and deported to the United States, which prompted an investigation by U.S. Customs officials. A raid of his Miami house netted over 250 guns and 50,000 rounds of ammunition, resulting in his arrest on July 30 for Neutrality Act violations. As might be expected, nothing came of it.

In September, Sturgis told an FBI informant that he was looking for gangsters willing to provide arms to Castro's rebels. It was probably at that time, most likely through Carlos Prio, that Sturgis began working with Norman Rothman. "Norm also helped out with his own contributions," Sturgis would later say, "and by putting me in touch with well-heeled Cuban friends." Both Sturgis and Rothman eventually became middlemen between the mob and CIA.[48]

Despite the FBI's interest in him, in November, Sturgis and Pedro Diaz Lanz, a Cuban exile with whom he worked closely, traveled to California, Arizona, and Venezuela in November. The Mexican police arrested them carrying a huge cache of arms south of the border, but they contacted the local CIA and were quickly released. The U.S. government continued to turn a blind eye to the arms trafficking of organized crime, paramilitary types, and Cuban exiles who were supporting Castro. In early 1959, after Castro came to power, Sturgis claimed to have been his chief arms buyer in Miami.[49]

What remained consistent was that Carlos Prio, Frank Sturgis, and Norman Rothman worked closely together, and Jack Ruby knew all three. Rothman was also in league with Eddie Browder, whom Blaney Mack Johnson claimed work with Ruby. He was close to Santo Trafficante, the principal owner of the Sans Souci in Havana, where Rothman was the manager. This relationship with Trafficante would later create for Jack Ruby an opportunity to involve himself deeper into the affairs of Cuba.

* * *

June Cobb appeared before a U.S. subcommittee on March 30, 1962. She testified that "In February of 1959, [one month after Castro came to power] I had made a brief visit to Havana out of curiosity, to see if the advertised changes there were taking place . . . I spoke with Fidel Castro's Minister of Health about cooperation between the revolutionary government and certain Peruvian, Bolivian, and Colombian doctors who were interested in combating the use of coca leaves and, therefore, the use of cocaine, as part of their declared campaign against vice."[50]

Interestingly, Cobb was now acting as an intermediary interested in cracking down on illegal drug use under Castro when she previously was involved with the Herran brothers processing and trafficking opium. And the brothers were arrested after Cobb told the FBN about their drug operation. We also know the brothers were involved with Paul Mondoloni when the French drug trafficker worked with Norman Rothman and Carlos Prio. They were all eventually arrested by authorities for drug and gun smuggling related to Cuba as well. The other names Cobb associated with included Santos Trafficante, Jr., Carlos Marcello, Jack Ruby, and Sam Giancana, and they were all involved in smuggling drugs into the United States. It all confirms that June Cobb was working undercover for the FBN at the time.

She also told the Senate subcommittee, "In 1959, I was employed [doing] some editing with the same doctor for whom I had worked a few years before, editing of medical textbooks."[51] It seemed to be a casual reference, almost in passing, to the same doctor she had worked with at Mount Sinai and Chicago around 1952, seven years prior, around the time of her prolonged hospital stay. It is hard not to view this relationship with suspicion, considering Cobb's connection to the FBN and the CIA and how often she seemed to gravitate to this man whenever she returned to the United States. He may have been her handler for either agency.

It is here where her story begins to get interesting. Early in 1959, while still in New York and working for her suspicious doctor friend, Cobb claimed that she took it upon herself to translate into English and have published "an edition of Fidel Castro's defense plea after the Moncada attack, and certain other activities with the 26th of July." It was a copy of Castro's *History Will Absolve Me* speech. Then, when Castro visited the United States in April, she was introduced to him at the Statler Hotel in New York (coincidently, the same hotel where someone pushed Frank Olson through the window). She showed the Cuban leader her translated version of his speech, which pleased him greatly, and he ordered that one thousand copies be printed and distributed in New York. Cobb also met with Castro's private secretary Celia Sánchez, who invited her to Havana to work in the Ministry Office. Undoubtedly, her attractive looks had something to do with the invitation, which she accepted. Cobb traveled to Havana almost immediately, in the spring of 1959, "where I was put in charge of English publications of the Prime Minister's office on behalf of the revolutionary government," until returning to the U.S. in October 1960. She left Cuba because she had become disillusioned with Castro's turn to communism, so she claimed, but there may have been another reason.[52]

Marita Lorenz first met Fidel Castro in Havana in 1959 when a cruise ship captained by her father docked at the Cuban capital. Offered a job as Castro's secretary, she declined, only to become his translator two weeks later. Shortly after that, Marita became Castro's mistress, but as rumors of the affair circulated throughout Havana, Lorenz found herself a virtual prisoner in her room on the 24th floor of the Havana Hilton. She became pregnant, supposedly with Castro's child. However, in *Oswald and the CIA*, John Newman wrote that he was told by June Cobb directly that the father was not Castro, but his military aide, Captain Jesus Yanez Pelletier.

It tells us that, at the very least, June Cobb was closely involved in the Marita Lorenz story.[53]

Long before she was pregnant, Lorenz had become disenchanted with the life of isolation she had to endure. Then she met Frank Fiorini (Sturgis), the new Chief of Security and Intelligence for the Cuban Air Force, and Minister of Games and Chance, a reward for his help in bringing Castro to power. Unknown to the Cubans, Sturgis was working undercover for the CIA. He agreed to get Lorenz out of Cuba in exchange for information she could provide that would be valuable to U.S. intelligence. Lorenz agreed, furnishing Sturgis with many documents and files that Castro had left strewn around her room.[54]

Marita had an abortion in Cuba and became ill while she recuperated, and it was then that Sturgis helped her escape. The CIA arranged to have her admitted into Roosevelt Hospital in New York City, where American soldier of fortune Alexander Rorke befriended her. He wanted to involve her in an assassination attempt against Castro. After Marita recovered, she was flown to Miami and placed in a safe house where Rorke and Sturgis tried to talk her into helping them. She finally agreed, and in early January 1960, she returned to Cuba with two poison capsules destined for Fidel. To her relief, Castro warmly welcomed her. However, she had placed the capsules in a jar of cold cream to pass through customs undetected and found they had melted when she later tried to retrieve them.[55]

"I owe Frank Fiorini and Alex Rorke . . . my life," Lorenz wrote, "after my close, personal involvement with Dr. Fidel Castro Ruz. I was active in Miami towards the end of 1959[. I] became a member of the International Anti-Communist Brigade [founded by Fiorini] and took a blood oath to join Frank Fiorini's secret assassination group in early 1960."[56]

Alexander Rorke was active in the war against Castro. That is until his plane disappeared somewhere over the Caribbean in September 1963. An FBI reported dated November 13, 1963, stated he was on a mission to bomb Havana. Following his disappearance, a report from the New York office of the CIA's Domestic Contact Division, which Tracy Barnes ran, stated, "The name of June Cobb as a double agent appears in the Rorke papers. . . ."[57] Cobb was already working for the CIA by this time, but some were concerned that she worked undercover for Castro.

Cobb had been brought into CIA by agent Harry Hermsdorf, who was acting undercover himself as a European journalist in Havana, using the alias Heinrich

Heubner. They first met in the Havana Hilton's hotel coffee shop, and from May 24–26, 1960, they would meet again at various times at Cobb's hotel. Hermsdorf never mentioned the CIA in their discussions, but he offered her a long-term employment opportunity. Cobb was interested. They met again in the United States, where she was subjected to intense questioning and a polygraph test while CIA technicians stayed in an adjoining hotel room recording what she had to say. On one visit to New York in October 1960, the surveillance log showed that Cobb phoned the number of Alexander Rorke. The question is, how did she already know his number? Was it because Cobb was involved with Sturgis in the escape of Marita Lorenz from Cuba? Cobb knew Lorenz, so there is no other logical explanation. It also suggests Sturgis initiated the CIA's interest in Cobb, which is feasible since he already knew her when she met Hermsdorf.[58]

Consider an FBI report dated April 15, 1960, a month before Hermsdorf first contacted Cobb, which stated she was also a confidential informant for ardent anti-Communist Jon Speller, whose father owned a right-wing publishing company. Speller knew Rorke, Hemming, Sturgis and William Morgan, another former U.S. Marine turned soldier of fortune involved in Cuba. The report stated that the previous month, Speller learned from three sources that "there is a cell of seven American communists in our [Cuban] Embassy." One of the sources who furnished this information was June Cobb, described in the FBI report as a "translator" who worked "in Castro's office." The report also said Cobb had been ". . . interviewed by [the New York City FBI office] on December 2, 1959 . . . [and] expressed admiration for Castro, sympathy for aims of [the] Cuban revolution, and conviction there is no communist influence in Castro regime . . . Speller claimed Cobb has now become concerned about Communist influence in Cuba and has organized a network of anti-communist Cubans in that country . . . Cobb feels State Department is pro-Castro, and she has not furnished information to State since she fears it would get back to Castro and jeopardize her life."[59]

If Cobb "organized a network of anti-Communist Cubans" to undermine Castro, she was much more than your average informant working undercover. And these Cubans were likely part of Castro's government or military, who had become disenchanted with the Cuban leader because that is where Cobb worked, so she had access to such people. The plan must have included the assassination of Castro, for how else could they have removed him from power? And since this was around the time that Rorke and Sturgis were trying to involve Marita Lorenz in an assassination attempt against Castro, and Cobb already knew Rorke and Sturgis, it stands to reason that she was involved in the same effort to kill Castro.

After the CIA officially hired Cobb, she returned to Havana on June 7, 1960. Hermsdorf's report that month stated: "If Miss Cobb can be controlled and accepts steering, it would perhaps be desirable to mold her into a long-range asset by having her become very cozy with the communist leaders and become, overtly, even more 'rabid' about the revolutionary movement. Later she could perhaps be used elsewhere in Latin America, probably among the rabid left-wing youth groups that are becoming increasingly anti-American . . ."[60]

In other words, Hermsdorf intended to make June Cobb appear to be ardently pro-Castro, and since she was a beautiful woman, she would have no trouble infiltrating Communist and left-wing groups. She returned to the U.S. in the latter part of 1960 because she felt Castro was on to her and it was too dangerous to stay in Cuba. And infiltrating left-wing groups is what June Cobb began to do. On behalf of the CIA and pretending to be a pro-Castro Communist, she infiltrated the Fair Play for Cuba Committee (FPCC), the same organization Lee Harvey Oswald claimed to belong to when he opened a fake FPCC chapter in New Orleans in the summer of 1963. The CIA was interested in the head of the FPCC's New York chapter, Richard Gibson, an African American involved with Patrice Lumumba of the Congo, a pro-Soviet Communist who was causing the Agency great concern. Cobb managed to connect with Gibson and CIA technicians eavesdropping in the adjoining hotel room next to Cobb's recorded their discussion. A follow-up report stated that "On the 27th [October 1960], Richard Gibson of the Fair Play for Cuba Committee (FPCC), spent the evening with Cobb . . . and talked rather freely about the [FPCC] Committee. Said they 'want to destroy the world.'" Cuba provided the FPCC with financing, and ". . . FPCC is working . . . with the Lumumba faction. Roa [Cuba] wants to send Gibson to Africa since money from Cuba promotes 'the thing' in Africa. FPCC is also involved in the Algerian situation . . . He has been to Russia and to Ghana. Robert F. Williams [of the NAACP] is also apparently instrumental in stirring up trouble (in the US over racial issues?). Gibson has no love in his heart for the US. The FPCC is stirring up the Negroes in the South—says their plans have lots of loopholes, and they expect to be arrested, but they intend to carry on war against the US."[61]

As described in the previous chapter, the greatest fear of Senator Eastland, Leander Perez, Guy Banister, and their Fascist associates, which likely included Lee Harvey Oswald, was that Fidel Castro was financing the FPCC and civil rights organizations. Cobb's work infiltrating the FPCC seemed to confirm that this was true.

The evidence is convincing that June Cobb was not a double agent but was posing as a Castro sympathizer to ingratiate herself with pro-Castro and Communist groups. Her importance within the U.S. intelligence network had grown by all appearances, making her relevance to our narrative that much more critical. The evidence also shows that a relationship between Cobb and Oswald may have existed after Oswald returned from the Soviet Union, which went beyond a mutual interest in the Fair Play for Cuba Committee.

Even the FBI was interested in what she had to say. A letter to Jane Roman, a liaison with Angleton's counterintelligence staff, stated: "As you know, the FBI has expressed an interest in such information that Subject [June Cobb] can provide concerning the Fair Play Committee [sic]." The letter was from a CIA counterintelligence officer in the Western Hemisphere division. June Cobb was starting to develop quite a reputation.[62]

Consider that June Cobb was also a member of the Civil Air Patrol in Norman, Oklahoma, attaining the rank of 2nd class Lieutenant. It was the same organization that Lee Harvey Oswald served under David Ferrie while living in New Orleans. Meanwhile, David Harold Byrd, the wealthy Texas oilman who owned the Texas School Book Depository building, was one of the founders of the Civil Air Patrol. After World War II, Byrd helped incorporate CAP, and the government designated it as an Auxiliary of the Air Force. In 1948, the CAP made Byrd Coordinator for the Southwest Region, including Texas, Oklahoma, and Louisiana. He was also made Vice Chairman of the National CAP Board and took over as Chairman in 1959.[63]

It would be reasonable to argue that this was all a coincidence were it not that the notation "Norman, Oklahoma" was written in Oswald's notebook, which was authorities found after the assassination. Oswald did not know anyone in Norman and had no known reason to go there. Oswald also wrote a street address below the Norman reference in the notebook, 1318 ½ Garfield. The property owner from 1961 to 1967, Mae Logan, said several white teenagers and one black teenager had lived there between 1962 and 1963. However, they got involved with drugs, stopped paying rent, and the police arrested them in Phoenix, Arizona. The woman who lived there, before the teenagers, developed cancer and was hospitalized. Two years before that, the woman's parents both died from cancer.[64]

There was something else about Norman, Oklahoma, that may be significant. In 1977, the University of Oklahoma admitted that during the 1950s and 1960s, the university was part of the CIA's MKULTRA program. Researchers conducted tests on animals and humans at the mental hospital in Norman. Dr. Louis West was involved in these experiments. In the early 1950s, West, then an Air Force doctor, was part of a panel asked to investigate why 36 of 59 airmen captured in the Korean War had cooperated with the Chinese, who at the time were accusing the United States of having committed war crimes. A recovered CIA document that listed different MKULTRA subprojects showed that Subproject 43 was associated with West and occurred at the University of Oklahoma in 1955 and 1956. It involved experimentation with LSD provided by the Geschickter Foundation for Medical Research.[65]

There was more to Dr. West's story, for inexplicably, he was the doctor asked to interview and do a psychiatric evaluation on Jack Ruby during his trial for killing Oswald. West found Ruby insane, which saved him from the death penalty. One might think that if the CIA were directing West, an insanity evaluation might have been counter to what the Agency would have wanted, but the opposite was the case. For if the court had sentenced Ruby to die, he might have revealed what he knew about the assassination plot, having nothing left to lose. Letting him serve time in prison while he appealed his conviction was the right thing to do if you wanted to keep him quiet. It is why it was suspicious that on October 25, 1966, when a judge finally granted Ruby a retrial after ruling that his original trial was unfair, a doctor visited Ruby in prison and gave him an injection. Ruby would die of lung cancer on January 3, 1967, just one month after doctors discovered tumors in his lung. It was a little over two months after Ruby was granted a retrial. Some believe Ruby was murdered, including the victim himself. According to Dallas Deputy Sheriff Al Maddox, "He [Ruby] said, 'Well, they injected me for a cold.' He said it was cancer cells. That's what he told me, Ruby did. I said, 'You don't believe that bullshit.' He said, 'I damn sure do!' Ruby shook hands with me, and I could feel a piece of paper in his palm . . . he said it was a conspiracy, and he said, . . . if you will keep your eyes open and your mouth shut, you're gonna learn a lot."[66]

Dr. West's connection to Norman is perhaps relevant to a possible Cobb/Oswald connection. Consider also that according to Albarelli, Thomas Eli Davis and another soldier-of-fortune named Loran Hall also spent time in Norman, Oklahoma. Recall that Davis ran guns with Jack Ruby, was CIA-connected, and in 1963 Davis tried to organize a paramilitary force to invade Haiti. Of interest is that from July 16 to October 1, 1958, a physician admitted Davis for psychiatric treatment at Detroit, Michigan's Lafayette Clinic. An FBI report stated his physicians believed he "displayed tendencies and symptoms of a 'scizo-phrenic' [sic] mental condition." We know that, like Oswald, Davis had an overbearing mother. His father was passive and a heavy drinker. And as one might now expect, beginning in 1954, the Lafayette Clinic was being used by the CIA to conduct MKULTRA mind-control experiments. Could Davis have been one of Lafayette's subjects, like Oswald was at the Bordentown Reformatory? Recall the Davis was an FBN informant who knew both Charles Siragusa and George Hunter White. Adding to the intrigue is that Dr. West also visited Lafayette Clinic, and one wonders if Davis' and Oswald's connection to Norman, Oklahoma was the drug experimentation West conducted there.

Like Davis, June Cobb was also an FBN informant and an associate of Thomas G. Proctor. As described in Volume One, Proctor was an associate of Victor Oswald in Madrid. Davis was arrested in Morocco because he had a letter of introduction that was to be sent by Victor Oswald to Proctor, and Davis was released from prison by QJ/WIN, who was part of ZR/RIFLE, the CIA assassination group operated by Bill Harvey. As previously mentioned, Harvey worked with George Hunter White and Jean Lafitte and was interested in mind-altering drugs and their possible application in assassination operations. Meanwhile, there was a plan to assassinate Duvalier in Haiti while Davis organized an army to invade that country and Cobb's potential involvement with an assassination team herself. The connections to this group are considerable, including Jack Ruby through Davis, Jean Lafitte, George White, and many others associated with the WCC and the Dulles/Donovan stay-behind armies.

Additionally, how was it that June Cobb spent months in a New York hospital where the CIA performed mind-altering drug experiments? She then returned repeatedly to Norman, Oklahoma, as did Thomas Davis and Loran Hall, where CIA performed mind-altering drug experiments as well? Was this a coincidence, or were they all guinea pigs in mind-altering drug experiments, and was that the common thread that joined these people?

Loran Hall was a central figure in the effort to remove Castro from power. After the assassination, J. Edgar Hoover would use his name to dispel claims that Oswald seemed to be in two places at once, a critical open item that the FBI had to explain if Oswald was the lone assassin. Hall served in the Army in Germany from 1947 to 1952, followed by several difficult years in Wichita, Kansas, including a broken marriage. He was arrested for passing bad checks and became a police informant regarding local gambling operations. Most importantly, as it pertains to our discussion here, is that in 1957 he suffered a mental breakdown, and he spent six months in a VA hospital as a result. Then in March 1959, he went straight to Cuba without warning and was introduced soon after to Frank Sturgis. He became involved in the training of troops for a planned Cuban invasion of Nicaragua to overthrow Somoza. However, the Cubans arrested Hall on suspicion of being an American agent, and three months later, he was released and returned to the United States. But while he was in the Cuba prison, he served time with Santo Trafficante. The mob boss also was suspected of being a Castro agent when he was allowed to leave prison and returned to the U.S.

Something does not seem right as we try and put the pieces together. Various characters connected to Norman, Oklahoma, had extended hospital stays, some in mental institutions. There was a belief that they were all supporters of Fidel Castro, which included Oswald, June Cobb, Thomas Davis, and Loran Hall. In actuality, the evidence strongly suggests they opposed Castro. Like Jack Martin and Richard Nagell, others wound up with extended hospital stays related to mental issues at convenient times. Is it too far-fetched, or was there a CIA mind-control program in existence at that time that had for many years treated people who would be connected to the JFK assassination, either directly or indirectly?

In June 1963, the FBI investigated Thomas Eli Davis because of the attempted invasion of Haiti he was putting together. FBI agents visited the Lafayette Clinic as part of their investigation. They met with Dr. Elliot D. Luby, who, it is known, carried out extensive experiments with LSD and other mind-altering drugs. Luby also had a connection to Dr. Louis West.[67] Another associate of Dr. West was a CIA psychologist named John Gittinger, who, during a 1980 legal deposition, reported that "projects involving hypnotism carried out in Panama" were "mostly of an experimental nature," while those in Mexico City were "nearly always of an operational nature." "In Mexico City," Gittinger continued, "there was more emphasis on the esoteric elements of behavior manipulation, on things like hypnosis and other such matters left outside the MK/ULTRA sphere."[68]

Hypnosis was something David Ferrie dabbled in, as did "Ronald Dante, better known as Dr. Dante, a hypnotist, stage magician and frequent visitor to Mexico City and Cuba," and an associate of June Cobb, as previously described. And a connection to Mexico City is relevant because of Oswald's trip to that city two months before the assassination and his possible connection to June Cobb. In the second half of 1963, the CIA transferred Cobb to Mexico City with the cryptonym LICOOKY-1.[69] She became a CIA asset for the Mexico City station, reporting to David Atlee Phillips, an important assassination figure covered in the next chapter. And at the time, Cobb's good friend Warren Broglie was conveniently managing the Hotel Luma in Mexico City, where Oswald was said to have visited.

Through a friend, Cobb rented a room at the home of Elano Garro, who, as described in Volume One, was the woman who claimed to have attended a twist party with Oswald in Mexico City. This event prompted the State Department's Charles William Thomas to write Secretary of State Dean Rusk, suggesting that the U.S. government reinvestigate Kennedy's assassination. While living at the Garro home, Cobb claimed she overheard a conversation between Garo, her daughter Helena, and Garro's sister, Deva Guerrero, regarding the twist party. The three women were all related to Sylvia Duran, the Cuban Embassy employee at the party. Duran allegedly had an affair with Oswald in Mexico and was close to Henry Saavedra, the Trafficante associate who knew June Cobb. It was not a coincidence that Cobb rented a room from the woman who claimed she attended the suspicious party, but precisely what prompted Cobb to seek her out?[70]

Most likely, Cobb did so to discredit Garro, for Cobb was the one who notified the CIA of Garro's story shortly after the Warren Commission Report was released. She gave ambiguous reports of what she was told by Garro, placing her credibility in question. Perhaps Cobb wanted to create doubt about Oswald having contact with Cuban Communists in Mexico City or direct attention away from something else, such as the mind-altering drug experiments in Mexico, Panama, and Haiti, as Charles Thomas uncovered. On the other hand, maybe Cobb was at the twist party herself, considering she had been infiltrating the FPCC and would have been a welcome attendee. Cobb created doubt in Garro's story to keep hidden her relationship with Oswald. Whatever the truth, Garro eventually threw Cobb out of her house, recognizing this was a dangerous woman who could only cause her harm.

Finally, after Oswald left Mexico City, he traveled to Dallas and his eventual date with destiny. The FBI would discover after the assassination that he withdrew only one book from the Dallas Public Library during this period, *The Shark and the Sardines*. The book was missing when Oswald's possessions were examined after his arrest and was mysteriously returned to the library many years later.

The Shark and the Sardines, written by Juan Jose Arevalo, a former president of Guatemala, is a metaphor about a shark, the United States, which devours sardines,

Latin American countries, with the help of Wall Street and other American mon-
ied interests. *Kirkus*, an American book review magazine, summarized the book as
follows:

> "Page after page 'demonstrates' that the Yankees became great while
> progress in Latin America halted under a multi-faceted exploitation
> financed by the Machiavellian coalition of the White House with Wall
> Street . . ." It culminated in an "'international scandal' when Dulles,
> Eisenhower, and the CIA backed counter-revolutionaries who ousted
> Dr. [Arevalo's] pro-Communist government. It is the latter's contention
> that the philosophy of the 'cadaverous Rockefellers' equals Al Capone's;
> that imperialism is embodied in the United Fruit Company, the rape
> of Chilean copper, the dastardly treaties with Nicaragua, Uruguay, and
> Brazil, the Pan-American looting of minerals, the NAM, the nefari-
> ous Marshall Plan, the 'secret revelations' of General Motors' pro-Nazi
> entanglements, the camouflaging of Russia as the common enemy, and
> that 'brink of war' is either capitalism's pathologic phase or the jugglings
> of New York's Carthaginian circus. And to top it off, he [Arevalo] drags
> in the 'confession' of a Marine general who was reputedly offered [$] 3
> million by Stock Exchange 'agents' to deliver the US into their hands.
> This attempted coup, according to Dr. Arevalo, was never made public in
> any manner, shape, or form anywhere in America . . ." However, Dr. Are-
> valo's own agents found out (at the movies). The *Shark and the Sardines*
> is not a book but a tract, a Party line announcement that peace is bad for
> business and that campaigns like Korea result [from this policy]."[71]

Everything mentioned in the above review, including American imperialism,
the perpetual war machine, a military takeover of the U.S. government, and the
exploitation of so-called "subhuman" nations and people, can be supported by facts
already discussed in this book. Oswald was reading it at the time of the assassination, which could suggest he was being influenced by those genuinely responsible
for Kennedy's murder. And considering the CIA combined brainwashing with
mind-altering drugs, it should come as no surprise. And it is somewhat alarming that the person who translated *The Shark and the Sardines* from Spanish into
English was June Cobb. And the book was signed out from the library in Dallas
by Oswald on November 6, 1963, roughly four weeks after returning from Mexico
City. Does this prove that Oswald and Cobb met while they were both south of the
border, or was his decision to read *The Shark and the Sardines* so soon after returning
from Mexico just another coincidence? In this author's opinion, to believe this was
a random occurrence, one would have to be completely delusional. Considering the
other evidence cited above, these two must have met while in Mexico City, and they
already probably knew each other before that. The question is, was a relationship
between Cobb and Oswald related to JFK's assassination? Or were they involved in

something unrelated to the assassination that had to be covered up after Kennedy's murder because disclosure could have destroyed the CIA and done irreparable harm to the U.S. government?

Interestingly, the FBI immediately learned that Oswald had withdrawn *The Shark and the Sardines* from the library. Why was this information not disclosed at that time? It is hard to understand, for it would have provided a motive for why the alleged pro-Castro Oswald killed Kennedy. The Warren Commission could have argued that Oswald assassinated JFK because he was upset over American imperialism in Latin America. But this was never presented to the American public. Perhaps it was more important at the time to disassociate Oswald from the name June Cobb, who may be the key to unraveling the Oswald mystery. It means delving deeper into what occurred in Cuba in the year after Castro came to power is essential, which we will do in the next chapter.

- 3 -

One Good Revolution Deserves Another

"[David] Morales was a hitman for the CIA. He was a killer. He
said it himself. . . . he had killed people for the CIA in Vietnam, in
Venezuela, in Uruguay, and other places. These were not murders
in the heat of combat . . . these were assassinations of individuals or
groups selected for annihilation."

—Gaeton Fonzi of the House Selection Committee on Assassinations

*There was an attempted coup in Cuba in 1959, before the failed Bay of Pigs invasion,
orchestrated by the CIA and their minions in Cuba. It included Fidel Castro's assassination. The plotters formed an alliance with a group within the Cuban military that did
not want Cuba to be a Communist country but still wanted a leftist leader. Meanwhile,
the radical right in the United States envisioned a pro-business right-wing Cuban who
did not care about the welfare of the Cuban people as Castro's replacement. However,
none of this came to be because CIA's Allen Dulles exposed the plot to Castro's supporters, and those behind the coup were arrested and executed. The Bay of Pigs invasion
would later be sabotaged by the CIA as well. And it was not an accident that numerous
Americans involved in these two thwarted plots to overthrow the Cuban government
would feel betrayed and are prime suspects in the assassination of JFK, for the road to
Dallas started in Havana.*

* * *

On January 7, 1959, the United States formally recognized Castro's new
government, less than one week after Castro marched triumphantly into Havana.
Eisenhower did so reluctantly, aware of the rumors circulating that Castro was a
Communist. Still, he had also received intelligence that there was a growing anti-
Castro movement within Cuba, and he wanted to give that a chance to develop. He

reserved the right to take a hard line against the Cuban government in the future if circumstances dictated that this was necessary.[1]

Three days later, the front page of the *Havana Post* contained a message from Fidel Castro. The Cuban leader invited "American tourists and . . . American businessmen to come back to Cuba . . . We are back to normal in Cuba . . . where there is liberty, peace, and order; a beautiful land of happy people . . ."

Despite Castro's spin that everything was rosy in Cuba, there were signs of discontent. And things were changing. Cuba's new president Manual Urrutia told reporters that the Communist leadership forbade all types of gambling on the island. On January 16, the new Cuban Prime Minister, Jose Miro Cardona, supported Urrutia, publicly declaring that "the government stands . . . opposed to the reestablishment of gambling in any of its forms . . ." But as Santo Trafficante had predicted, Cuba needed the revenue generated by the casinos, so Castro overruled Urrutia and Cardona, and the casinos stayed open. The most dedicated revolutionaries disapproved, but they had no choice but to work with American Mafioso, who owned and operated the casinos, at least for the time being.[2]

Tourists were reluctant to visit Cuba because of the reported execution of five hundred twenty-one former Batista officials following war crime trials conducted without due process. Before long, it became clear that anyone who opposed Castro would probably face a similar fate. In one instance, seventy-one prisoners were shot and thrown into a common grave, while Che Guevara signed fifty other death sentences. One survey found that ninety-one percent of the Cuban people supported executions, which Cuban television sometimes broadcast. Magazines showed graphic photos of bloody corpses, so there was no denying what was occurring. The people wanted blood, Castro said, and he gave it to them.[3]

The mass killings raised questions about the democratic ideals Castro claimed to possess, so to diffuse the animosity building in America, in April, the Cuban leader traveled to the United States as part of what was called "Operation Truth." But he had been invited by the American Society of Newspaper Editors, not the U.S. government. Eisenhower refused to see him and asked Vice President Richard Nixon and Acting Secretary of State Christian Herter to spend a couple of hours with Castro to appease him and his supporters. Castro wore his trademark green military fatigues wherever he went. He placed a wreath on George Washington's grave, toured the Bronx Zoo, ate hot dogs and hamburgers at Yankee Stadium, and generally delighted Americans, who were to a large extent enamored with the revolutionary leader. However, as Castro told the Council on Foreign Relations, Cuba would not beg the U.S. for economic assistance. There was tension, and he stormed out of their meeting when he disapproved of the questions they were asking.[4]

But the purpose of the trip was to promote tourism, so at a New York City press conference, Castro stated the goal was to make this Cuba's primary industry. They intended to spend $200 million to attract two to three million vacationers per year. Despite apprehensions, the American Society of Travel Agents agreed not to cancel their next annual conference, which was to take place in Havana in October 1959. Two thousand agents made the trip, and Castro spent an hour frolicking with them at a dinner held in the capitol building while U.S. ambassador Philip Bonsal sat at a table with Raul Castro. Everything went according to plan until Cuban anti-aircraft guns fired at planes, dropping anti-Castro leaflets upon the city, and those who no longer supported the revolution threw grenades at moving cars. Any chance that the travel agents would promote Cuban tourism upon their return to the United States effectively disappeared.[5]

Meanwhile, the FBN asked the Cuban government to deport the Mafia bosses who owned and ran casinos. Castro was reluctant, claiming that the ex-Batista supporters who had escaped to the United States were "war criminals" and should be returned to Cuba to stand trial for their crimes. Still, he asked for a list of the drug smugglers the U.S. was interested in and even threatened to execute the gangsters in Cuba to save everyone the trouble of handing them over. Things began to move forward when Cuban attorney general Mario Fernandez y Fernandez introduced a campaign to eliminate drug trafficking and deport the Mafioso to the U.S. On May 6, 1959, Cuban police arrested Jake Lansky and Dino Cellini, the manager and personnel director of the casino at Havana's Hotel Riviera. Also detained around the same time were Lucien Rivard, the gangster Paul Mondoloni relocated from Montreal to Havana, Charles Tourine, Jr., and Giuseppe Di Giorgio. But when the Cubans learned no drug charges were pending in the U.S. against these men, they were released. It only served to alienate the government from the north even more.

* * *

In July 1958, roughly five months before Castro ousted Batista from power, Santo Trafficante and Meyer Lansky were privately flown from Cuba to the Dominican Republic to meet with the Dominican dictator, Rafael Trujillo. They discussed building casinos there, either as an addition to what the Mafia already had in Havana or possibly as replacement should the casinos in Cuba be closed after Castro came to power. By February 1959, the CIA was also in contact with Trujillo. It may have had something to do with the Trafficante and Lasky meeting the previous July, but it had nothing to do with building casinos. It involved the removal of Castro from power, which both the mob and CIA wanted. The former head of Cuban State Security later claimed that the CIA began plotting a coup to overthrow Castro that same month when a "CIA representative . . . met with Trujillo and his chief of intelligence Colonel Johnny Abbes." The Cuban said the CIA "didn't have to give its public consent" to the operation they were planning. The Agency "only had to look the other way and then, once the deed was done, pretend that it had just heard about it," and they could then "plausibly deny it." If this is true, it means

Trujillo and the Mafia were conspiring to assassinate Castro. They made the CIA aware of it but did not need their help.[6]

Trujillo was not new to the struggle for power in Cuba. In the mid-1950s, he had supplied weapons to Carlos Prio, but when Prio aligned himself with Castro, the guns fell into Castro's rebels' hands, which did not sit well with the Dominican dictator. And as Castro's prospects for victory began to improve in 1956, Trujillo threw his financial and military support behind Batista, which proved to be a mistake, for after coming to power, Castro intended to exact revenge against the man who had plotted against him. A Cuban invasion of the Dominican Republic occurred on June 14, 1959, but was unsuccessful. A second attempt one week later also failed. The invaders were hunted down and captured. The leaders pushed out of an airplane in midflight to their death.

In the spring of 1959, dissension in Castro's ranks began to appear. Eloy Gutierrez Menoyo was the Second National Front of the Escambray (SNFE) leader, a guerilla force fighting alongside Castro against Batista. A CIA document dated March 3, 1959, said Gutierrez was "disturbed with Fidel Castro . . . he is taking all of the honors of the revolution, rather than sharing them with any of the other revolutionary leaders." Jealousy, combined with Castro's turn to communism, prompted Gutierrez to escape to the U.S. in January 1961 and fight against Castro with other Cuban exiles. But not before trying to oust Castro from power before he left.[7]

Maurice Gatlin, the Guy Banister associate who was general counsel of the Anti-Communist League of the Caribbean, who had sent money to the OAS for the assassination of Charles de Gaulle, on March 30, 1959, sent the following report to the FBI after returning from Havana: "We also learned, through sources that I have found to be reliable, that [Che] Guevara . . . intend[s] to liquidate their communist frontman, Fidel Castro, around June or July, arranging his death so it will be attributed . . . to a 'gringo' for propaganda purposes."[8]

Clearly, by the spring of 1959, the frustration with Castro had grown to where the assassination of the Cuban leader was a real possibility, and an American was to be the fall guy and take the blame. If true, it mirrored what happened in Guatemala and was right out of the Agency's assassination handbook. But how did Gatlin know that Guevara wanted to kill Castro? Was Che working with American mercenaries who had also turned against Castro, or was there someone inside keeping the Americans apprised of what was going on within Castro's inner circle? Recall from the previous chapter the FBI report that June Cobb had "organized a network of anti-communist Cubans" to overthrow Castro, probably including Frank Sturgis and Alexander Rorke. The logical conclusion is that Cubans and American mercenaries worked together to kill Castro, and June Cobb was in the middle of it all.

Frank Sturgis testified before the Rockefeller Commission in 1975. The New York Daily News then interviewed him. He recounted how CIA agent Park F. Woolam recruited him in Santiago de Cuba just before Castro's takeover. Sturgis began working with Colonel Nichols, the military attaché in Havana, whom Sturgis believed was also CIA. According to Sturgis, as early as 1959, he started recruiting agents in a plot to assassinate Castro and his top men, which would have included Raul Castro and Che Guevarra but was told by Nichols not to proceed. An order Sturgis most likely chose to ignore.

As we have discussed, one person Sturgis was particularly close to was Norman Rothman. Rothman allegedly tried to enlist Castro's bodyguards in an assassination attempt against the Cuban leader, coinciding with Castro's disciple's discontent. According to sources, Rothman and Sturgis were the "go-betweens" for the CIA, as the two men did what they could to try and stay out of prison in the U.S. for their gunrunning activities. "Rothman was in touch with several CIA agents," according to a former CIA official. "They had many meetings concerning assassination plots against Castro." According to this agent, Rothman tried to enlist fellow mobsters Santo Trafficante, the Mannarinos, Sal Granello and Charles Tourine of New York, and Johnny Roselli.[9]

These were all the same mobsters who were in bed with Sturgis and other American mercenaries running guns to Castro while Batista was still in power, all done under the watchful eye of·CIA, with the Agency's approval. As described above, Trafficante and Lansky had met with Trujillo the previous year to get rid of Castro. After Castro came to power, it is not surprising that these players would try to assassinate him again.

Opposition to Castro became more intense as it became clear he was a Communist. On May 17, 1959, the Agrarian Reform Law was enacted in Cuba, limiting the size of farms and real estate, and anything over the limit was confiscated and redistributed to peasants. The law also stated that foreigners could not own sugar plantations. The Cuban government cut rents for the poor in half, and as Raul Castro and Che Guevara's roles in the new government increased, the writing was on the wall, and one-time supporters of Castro turned against him. One of those was June Cobb, who, as we know, was probably already working for the CIA as an invaluable informant, considering her closeness to Castro's inner circle. And perhaps through Cobb Gatlin and the Agency learned about Che Guevara's desire to eliminate Castro. However, Cobb's connections within the U.S. Embassy in Havana were more important, including David Morales, an ex-Army veteran who joined CIA in 1951, and became a top assassin for the Agency. In later years admitted to having been involved in the JFK assassination.

Gaeton Fonzi was part of the House Select Committee on Assassinations in 1977. In his book, *The Last Investigation*, Fonzi describes how Morales' career began as an enlisted man stationed in Munich during World War II. He joined the CIA after the war. In 1954, he worked with David Phillips in the Guatemalan coup that ousted Arbenz. Howard Hunt, Tracy Barnes, Johnny Roselli, and William Pawley were part of this operation also. Morales stayed with Phillips after Guatemala. He worked with him in Cuba in 1959 and again during the Bay of Pigs. In later years in Vietnam, a Marine officer who knew him then told Fonzi Morales was "a fairly heavy drinker when I met him. He was a 'macho' kind of guy, strongly opinionated, an enforcer type . . . I got the impression he was always able to control everyone who worked for him. I wouldn't want to cross him."

Fonzi also learned that "Morales was a hitman for the CIA. He was a killer. He said it himself. . . . he had killed people for the CIA in Vietnam, in Venezuela, in Uruguay, and other places. These were not murders in the heat of combat . . . these were assassinations of individuals or groups selected for annihilation." Much of the information Fonzi received about Morales came from Ruben Carbajal, a boyhood friend. Carbajal remained like a brother to Morales until he died in 1978 by "natural causes." Carbajal doubted this was so, for Morales once told him, "they are the most ruthless motherfuckers there is and if they want to get somebody, they will. They will do their own people up."[10]

If the assassination of Castro were being contemplated in 1959 while Morales was in Havana, he certainly would have been involved. There is also relevance to the Kennedy assassination, based on what Carbajal told Fonzi. He had made a trip to Washington to see Morales years after Kennedy's assassination, accompanied by his friend Bob Walton. After dinner one evening, they returned to Walton's hotel room, where the drinking got heavy. Morales boasted of his past CIA exploits, including some of the assassinations he had performed. Morales queried Walton, whom he did not know, about his background. The Harvard Law School graduate said that, among other things, he had done volunteer work for John Kennedy's Senatorial campaign and that at Harvard, he was part of a group that had invited Kennedy to come and speak. The mere mention of Kennedy's name threw Morales into a rage. "I remember he was lying down, and he jumped up screaming," Walton said. " 'That no-good son of a bitch motherfucker!' He started yelling about what a wimp Kennedy was and talking about how he had worked on the Bay of Pigs and how he had to watch all the men he had recruited and trained get wiped out because of Kennedy." Morales added a postscript to his tirade. "Well," he said, "We took care of that son of a bitch, didn't we?" Carbajal confirmed that the story was true.[11]

According to several researchers who investigated Morales, he became the CIA's top assassin in Latin America in Caracas, Venezuela. In 1958 the CIA moved him to Havana, where he ran Agency operations out of the U.S. Embassy. He met with David Phillips once again, already in Cuba posing as a businessman undercover as David A. Phillips Associates. Morales also sometimes worked with Tony Sforza, whom he had met in Venezuela. Sforza was associated with the Mafia, Corsican

Brotherhood, French assassins, drug traffickers, and drug smugglers. Sforza may also have been in Havana.

Assassinating Castro was serious business, and plausible deniability had to be maintained. It was why before June Cobb testified in front of the U.S. Senate Subcommittee in 1962; the CIA was concerned about what she might disclose. A CIA memorandum entitled "June Sharp Cobb (201-278,841)" was written by her Agency handler, Jean T. Pierson, an "intelligence researcher" for Task Force W, which was CIA's name for their involvement in the secret war against Castro. It included ZR/RIFLE, the assassination program, and it was all run by William Harvey. "Lt. Col. Davies" was a military officer assigned to Task Force W. Pierson told him about Cobb's upcoming testimony. Davies then "advise[d] Mr. [William] Harvey, C/TFW, of the situation." Davies, Harvey, and Morales created aliases and false information for Cobb and others, including Anthony Sforza, Frank J. Belsito, and Rene E. Dubois. All were deeply enmeshed in the CIA's more unsavory operations. These agents were involved in "wet affairs," i.e., assassinations, and their involvement with Cobb must have begun in Cuba in 1959. It was serious business, and the CIA had to keep that information out of the hands of the U.S. Senate. June Cobb was no stranger to assassination operations. And the interest Harvey and Morales displayed in protecting her from Senate investigators speaks volumes about what her role was at the CIA and that the assassination group ZR/RIFLE was where she worked. [12]

Gerry Patrick Hemming, the American mercenary close to Sturgis, said he was approached in Havana in 1959 by Colonel Samuel G. Kail. Kail was Sturgis' contact inside the U.S. Embassy. As described by CIA's Justin Gleichauf: "My deputy, Col. Samuel G. Kail, former Army attaché in Havana . . . handled military administrative matters. The arrangement worked well; we never had a case of dissension between military and civilian personnel or rivalry among services . . ."

Kail also may have worked closely with Frank Brandsetter, an undercover Army Intelligence agent, who managed the Havana Hilton when Castro ousted Batista. Brandsetter was Morales' connection to mobsters in Cuba. He knew David Phillips, June Cobb, and Geraldine Shamma, an American married to Alfred Suarez, the heir to a Cuban tobacco fortune worth $22 million when he died in 1952. Despite her wealth, she became part of the anti-Batista underground during the 1950s and worked against Castro when he came to power, believing Cuba had just replaced a right-wing dictator with a leftist one. Through Sturgis, she became part of the resistance, working for the CIA via the American consulate, helping anti-Castro political and military leaders get out of the country, which she did with the help of a high-ranking Cuban intelligence officer. Eventually, the Cuban government arrested her for counterrevolutionary activities. [13]

John Martino was another person involved with Morales in Havana. Closely connected to Trafficante, an FBI memo sent to J. Edgar Hoover in late July 1959 reported that "Martino has made twelve to fourteen visits to Cuba since January 1, 1959." Years later, Martino would reveal that he was smuggling money out of Cuba. He was arrested in Havana on July 23 for flying into the country illegally with his twelve-year-old son, charged with helping counterrevolutionaries to leave the country, which he must have done in conjunction with Geraldine Shamma.[14]

In his 1963 book *I Was Castro's Prisoner*, published before the JFK assassination, Martino confirmed that he knew Morales in Cuba and was familiar with CIA personnel. He wrote that Morales replaced CIA's Earl Williamson in the U.S. Embassy after Williamson was "quietly withdrawn" for promising to provide official recognition to Castro's rebels, which was against what the Agency intended. Martino described Morales as "an American of Mexican descent and an intelligent and patriotic public servant. Morales sent voluminous reports to Washington concerning the communist affiliations of Fidel Castro and his henchman . . ."[15]

Martino worked for Trafficante, and his name was in George Hunter White's address book and Jean Lafitte's notes concerning his trips to Florida and Cuba. Martino was also one of the many aliases Lafitte used. Lafitte visited Martino in prison in Havana, as did Charles Siragusa of the FBN. And like Morales, years later, John Martino claimed to have been involved in the assassination of JFK.

Future Watergate burglar Bernard Barker was part of Batista's police force before Castro came to power. Somehow he managed to survive the transition and was recruited by the CIA in Havana in 1959 and "provided Havana Station information on police and political matters. He was also used to transport our agents to the harbor(s) for exfiltration." He would be smuggled out of Cuba later that year and landed in Tampa, working with Cuban exiles in the war against Castro. Fellow Watergate burglar Howard Hunt would be named his CIA case officer.[16]

Morales worked with Barker while he was in Havana, and Barker was a "support agent" for "Woodrow C. Lien" (real name Henry Hecksher) of the CIA. Hecksher was an OSS veteran who joined the CIA early on. He was stationed in Berlin during the mid-1950s and was also involved in the Guatemala operation that overthrew Arbenz in 1954, where he first worked with Phillips, Hunt, and Morales. He also served in the Far East, but the official record is ambiguous regarding where and when he served. Hong Kong, Laos, and Japan are all possibilities, and he likely spent time in all three places. Oddly, his obituary did not mention Cuba, and his official record neglected it as well, but he did serve there.[17]

According to files declassified by CIA years later, Hecksher's signature appeared on numerous reports relating to Project AM/WORLD, Manuel Artime, and anti-Castro operations. AM/WORLD was CIA's cryptonym for the OMEGA Plan, a second massive invasion of Cuba by the U.S. to oust Castro in December 1963 with the help of a general within Castro's army named Juan Almeida, one month after JFK's assassination. There was a great deal of secrecy surrounding Hecksher's Cuban operations. Why was it necessary to purge his Cuban experiences from the official record to appear as if he was never in Cuba? And what happened in Cuba that was so potentially dangerous that it had to remain hidden? Was it the JFK assassination that created the need for such secrecy, or was it something else?

One thing we know about Hecksher is that he was an avid anti-Communist. As Peter Sichel, Herksher's CIA superior in Berlin, recalled: "Unfortunately Henry became, as he got older, extremely right-wing. He became an absolutist, and I think he got retired a little too late. That should have happened a little early, [sic] before he got involved in this whole mess in Cuba and what-have-yous."

What does that mean, "he got involved in the whole mess in Cuba . . ."? There were numerous intelligence agents and military personnel involved in Cuban operations, but this did not describe who they were. But Hecksher's Cuban experience defined him and in a negative way. "My intelligence specialty is political action," Hecksher wrote, "but not to the exclusion of related pursuits, such as counterintelligence [which was James Angleton's domain]. The dominant focus of my professional interests has at all times been the Soviet Union, its satellites, and its surrogates . . . I always considered myself targeted against the KGB (active measures) and the International Department of the Central Committee of the CPSU." So, it was a deep hatred for communism, particularly the Soviet Union, that drove Hecksher. The question is, was there a limit to what he might do to contain the spread of communism, especially into the Western Hemisphere? It is a question that one could have asked all those associated with the U.S. Embassy in Havana in 1959.

Regarding AM/WORLD, Hecksher described a meeting between November 7 and 10, 1963, where a leading advisor for Manuel Artime, a top Cuban exile figure, said the U.S. could not defeat Castro while JFK was President. Similarly, a close associate of Artime's named Rafael "Chi" Quintero said that Hecksher did not believe AMWORLD was going to work. If it was not going to work, why was it allowed to continue? And if stopping it was out of the question, what else might they have done to ensure it would succeed? More about this in the next book. But considering the timing in conjunction with JFK's assassination, this is indeed troubling. It is also pertinent to our narrative here because the same people seemingly involved in AM/WORLD had previously worked together out of Havana, attempting to overthrow the Cuban government and kill Castro in the process. [18]

Martin Fox was the owner of the Tropicana in Havana, whose Santo Trafficante ran the casino. In September 1958, Fox brought a blackjack dealer from Las Vegas to Havana, supposedly to become a pit boss and credit manager. The man's name was Lawrence McWillie, a gangster from Dallas who knew Jack Ruby well. Testifying before the HSCA in 1978, McWillie said, "I managed the Tropicana some, and then the government took it over, and I was sent to the Hotel Capri [also run by Trafficante] by Martin, who said you could get a job there, so go there." It sounded innocent enough, but then McWillie described his actual function after Castro took over: "They would ask me to go . . . to Miami and deposit some money for them, and I would do it . . ."

John Martino also knew McWillie, not surprising since Martino also traveled back and forth to Miami, transferring money from Cuba to the United States. Norman Rothman knew McWilllie as well, which is understandable, considering Rothman's ties to Trafficante. McWillie knew Sturgis through his connection to Rothman and that as Minister of Games and Chance under Castro, Sturgis would encounter McWillie as part of his job.[19]

There was a great deal of resistance to Castro in 1959. The mob sensed that the casinos would inevitably be closed (which happened in October 1960), and CIA and American mercenaries realized that Castro was a Communist. Cubans who had supported him because they wanted Batista gone began to flee to the United States, wanting nothing more to do with a dictator who embraced communism. Meanwhile, turmoil within the new Cuban government grew as the relationship with the United States continued to deteriorate, resulting in Castro's resignation as prime minister on July 17. He could not work with President Urrutia, who, he said, was a traitor. The people revolted, which was Castro's intent, resulting in Urrutia's arrest, but Castro's ability to govern remained insecure. The Cuban economy was in tatters, with high unemployment and private investment nonexistent. The situation was exacerbated by falling sugar and tobacco prices. Defections occurred with regularity, including the chief of Castro's Air Force, Maj. Pedro Luis Díaz Lanz, Sturgis' compadre, who fled to the U.S. in late June. It all set the stage for a possible coup attempt in the summer of 1959.

* * *

It was not a secret that Castro was a marked man. In July 1959, Dorothy Kilgallen was the first reporter to write about the alliance between CIA, the Mafia, one-time Batista supporters, and ex-Castroites, who all wanted to overthrow the Cuban government. It was very early on, and how Kilgallen received her information was never revealed. She wrote in her newspaper column: "If our state department heads in Washington deny they're gravely worried over the explosive situation in Cuba and nearby Latin American countries, they're either giving out false information for reasons of their own or playing ostrich, which might prove to be a dangerous game.

"US intelligence is virtually nonexistent if the government isn't aware that Russia already has bases in Cuba, and Russian pilots in uniform are strutting openly in Havana. Fidel Castro is the target for so many assassins, they're apt to fall over each other in their efforts to get him.

"The Mafia want to knock him off. So do the Batista sympathizers, of course, and then there are his own disillusioned rebels, just for starters. He has machine guns and other ammunition mounted on every key rooftop near his base of operations, but the smart money doubts if any amount of precaution can change his status as a clay pigeon."[20]

As described previously, in February 1959 Frank Sturgis claimed he first became involved in a plan to assassinate Fidel Castro. It began with Eloy Gutierrez
Menoyo, a fellow rebel and head of the SNFE, who became disenchanted with the
Cuban leader and thought of overthrowing him. Later that month, an American
soldier-of-fortune named William Morgan, closely associated with Gutierrez, received a phone call from an American mafioso acting as a messenger for Trujillo. A
meeting then took place in a room in Havana's Hotel Capri," which was operated
by Santo Trafficante, who, along with Meyer Lansky, had met with Trujillo just
months before. The plan was to orchestrate a coup in Cuba and assassinate Fidel
Castro. Morgan replied that "for a million dollars he would turn the SNFE against
the revolution and 'bounce Fidel Castro from power.'" At the time, Morgan was
still serving in Castro's army and was aware of Gutierrez's displeasure with Castro's
turn toward communism. The Mafia contact would later tell Morgan that Trujillo
agreed to pay what Morgan had requested.[21]

A CIA memo reported that on "March 26, 1959," a reliable informant said,
"he had been in Cuba about a week before," and that "Morgan claims 2,000 of his
former troops are now in the Cuban Army and still loyal to him. The memo continued that "Morgan then came to Havana and met an American from Cleveland, [the
aforementioned] Dominick Bartone, who is . . . trying to sell some Globemaster
[planes] to Fidel Castro."

The sale of the planes now shifted from Castro to Morgan, which also involved
Jack Ruby. Eyewitness testimony provided to the HSCA in the late 1970s, but
was not revealed publicly until the 1990s, confirmed that this was true. A meeting
took place at Morgan's Havana home in June, which included Lawrence McWillie
accompanied Ruby. There are several days in June where investigators could not
account for Ruby's whereabouts. So, accounts that he was at the meeting in Havana
cannot be disproven. Events we will discuss shortly suggest he was likely there.

Morgan associate, and fellow soldier-of-fortune Gerry Patrick Hemming, told
authors Lamar Waldron and Thom Hartmann that he was also present at the meeting. Interestingly, before going to Cuba, Ruby was in contact with the FBI, and
he met with his FBI contact on June 5, which suggests the meeting with Morgan
occurred shortly after that. We know that an acquaintance of Ruby's who worked
at the airport "overheard Ruby talking on the telephone instructing one of his employees not to disclose his whereabouts 'unless it were to the police or some other
official agency.'" Author Anthony Summers uncovered this testimony and correctly
pointed out that the FBI was the only official agency to contact Ruby, suggesting
that Ruby was the informant providing information to the FBI regarding Morgan's
operation.[22]

Meanwhile, according to the former head of Cuban State Security, an April
meeting was held in Miami, where Morgan met with several others who had
agreed to become involved in the operation, including a former "general in Batista's army." Morgan had said at the same meeting that the "SNFE and the White

Rose counterrevolutionary group would carry out the task. The White Rose was composed . . . mainly [of] ex-soldiers of the Batista regime." They were scattered throughout Cuba in small cells, like the Dulles/Donovan stay-behind armies in Europe. Morgan said Gutierrez agreed to be part of the operation, "but only on the condition that the US government supported it." In Miami, the Dominican Consul told Morgan the project was being "coordinated at the highest levels of [the US] government."[23]

Sometime that spring, Morgan and Gutierrez appeared at the U.S. Embassy in Havana, according to Paul Bethel, the Press Officer at the embassy who was a friend of David Phillips and also connected to CIA, with an offer to provide "details regarding the early Communist takeover of the Cuban government." They were there to look for embassy assistance for the intended coup they had in mind, which was still in the development stage. David Phillips would later admit that he became part of the plot. Morgan confirmed that Gutierrez's "SNFE was still intact, an entity apart from the Castro government," and they were "being quietly organized into a political party." The CIA told Bethel to keep tabs on what these two mercenaries were doing.

Paul Bethel was an interesting character in his own right. In the early 1960s, he was the founder and director of the anti-Castro group, Citizens Committee to Free Cuba. It was a similar name to the Free Cuba Committee, which Henry Wade said Oswald belonged to on the night of the assassination, only to be corrected by Jack Ruby. Perhaps Wade was right, and Oswald had a connection to Bechtel's group. Bethel was an ardent right-winger who wrote a book in 1969 entitled *The Losers*, which portrayed John Kennedy, his Cabinet, Robert Kennedy, and Martin Luther King as Communists. Bethel's background was in the military, but his connections were to the intelligence community. He served in Germany when William Harvey was CIA station chief there, which means he already knew the CIA's head of assassinations when the Agency was trying to kill Castro. Bechtel was also in Tokyo as a press officer when Oswald was at Atsugi, which does not prove they were involved together, but it is suspicious, nonetheless. When JFK was assassinated, Bethel was close to two Cuban exile groups, the DRE and Alpha 66. So were Carlos Prio, William Pawley, and David Phillips. Without question, like so many others, Paul Bechtel was a person of interest in the JFK assassination.[24]

The FBI was also aware of what was happening in Havana, probably through information obtained from Jack Ruby. The FBI reported that on May 1, 1959, they were advised: "of funds [ ] funneled to William Morgan . . . [who] reportedly agreed to establish a new revolutionary anti-Castro front in the Escambray area [and] Carlos Prio . . . and the Dominican Republic are supplying the other arms and equipment."

In addition to Ruby, FBI headquarters learned about the proposed coup in Cuba from several sources, including General Manuel Benitez, a former Cuban legislator and head of the National Police, and lobbyist Irving Davidson.[25] As previously discussed, Davidson had worked with Jimmy Hoffa the previous year selling guns to Castro, was involved with Clint Murchison and Bobby Baker in Haiti, and was also closely connected to Carlos Marcello. The involvement of these men in a coup to topple Castro in 1959 was not out of the question. H

Davidson met with FBI assistant director August Belmont on behalf of Cuban millionaire banker and sugar magnate Julio Lobo by the end of June. Lobo's conservative exiles, the Crusade of Revolutionaries Against Communism (CRAC), also had designs on getting rid of Castro. Davidson advised the FBI that unless CRAC received backing from the United States, they would join Morgan's group and become part of their invasion from the Dominican Republic.

The State Department also learned about the plan in June. They subsequently warned all Latin American embassies of a possible invasion of Cuba from the Dominican Republic by pro-Batista forces. On July 30, an informant told the FBI in Havana that he had seen the Dominican consul general give Morgan $20,000 and knew Morgan was planning Castro's assassination in conjunction with the pending invasion.

Paul Bethel would later write that Morgan told him: "I have five thousand men. Willing and able to fight against Communism . . . Sure, [Gutierrez] Menoyo is the leader, but the boys follow me. Menoyo is also with us, though." Bethel "went immediately to the Embassy, wrote a long memorandum . . . and gave it to the Deputy Chief of the CIA."[26]

Look magazine editor William Attwood was in Havana in July 1959 and attended a party at an upscale home (Geraldine Shamma's, perhaps). He heard several Americans openly discussing the imminent assassination of Castro. "As a matter of fact," he said, "I was introduced to two alleged assassins, people who had been selected to do the job, which actually dumbfounded me." Attwood also heard from Julio Lobo that "there was a contract out" on Castro and that he "would not live out the year." Other partygoers said the talkative Americans were CIA.[27]

The story now shifts to Robert J. Kleberg, Jr., a wealthy cattle rancher and oilman from Texas, associated with people like Allen Dulles, J. Edgar Hoover, Lyndon Johnson, and Nelson Rockefeller. Kleberg owned other ranches around the world, including *Becerra* in Cuba.

Jack Malone was a long-time CIA asset and another Knight of Malta, who worked for George and Ronny Braga, wealthy Americans who had made their money at the expense of the Cuban people through their company, Czarnikow-Rionda. George knew Allen Dulles well, having served on the J. Henry Schroder Bank & Trust Company board of directors. Malone had also worked with Cardinal Spellman, the right-wing cleric who would send priests throughout Latin America acting as spies for the CIA. In 1951 Kleberg's King Ranch and Czarnikow-Rionda, which included Manati Sugar Company, merged into a single Cuban company,

Compania Ganadera Becerra. Jack Malone was named its president. Malone was well connected at the CIA and was good friends with David Phillips. Fellow Texans Kleberg and Phillips were also close enough to be on a first-name basis.

Gustavo de los Reyes was the owner of the ranch closest to *Becerra*, a sugar plantation called *La Caridad.* Kleberg also knew Alberto Fernandez, a thirty-four-year-old Cuban who owned five cattle ranches on the island. By the summer of 1959, with their properties in Cuba soon to be confiscated and their fortunes on the verge of disappearing, Gustavo de los Reyes and other ranch owners attempted to build a groundswell of public support that would lead to the removal of Castro. They became part of the William Morgan counterrevolution, and the person who brought the cattlemen into the fold was David Phillips. He was initially introduced to de los Reyes by Malone. Around the beginning of August, de los Reyes traveled to Washington looking for the U.S. support needed to return Cuba to the pre-Castro days. It led to a meeting with Allen Dulles, who surprised the Cuban by objecting to what they were trying to accomplish in Cuba. "We're on good terms with Russia. Castro is their ally. We don't want trouble with Russia, and so we cannot back efforts against Castro," Dulles reportedly said. It is also interesting that, around the same time, Geraldine Shamma had an opportunity to meet Eisenhower in the White House, where she hand-delivered him proof that Fidel and Raul Castro were Communists. "Unfortunately, we can't do anything about it at this time," Ike said. "We can't do anything to antagonize the government of Fidel Castro. There are too many people supporting him."[28]

What motivated Dulles and Eisenhower to object so vehemently when they could have Maintained plausible deniability very easily? One of two reasons. First, we must consider what else was going on in the world simultaneously, involving the Soviet Union. Since 1956, when Khrushchev thought the Suez Crisis ended because he had threatened to use nuclear weapons, his bluster increased exponentially. In November 1958, the Soviet leader threatened the West again, demanding that France, Britain, and the United States abandon Berlin, a "free city" according to the Potsdam Agreement. At that time, the western allies controlled West Berlin, while the Soviets controlled the eastern half of the city, but the entire city lay within Soviet control, which did not sit well with the Soviets. The Soviet foreign ministry announced that the Allies had violated the terms agreed to at Potsdam and ordered them to evacuate West Berlin, which would have left the entire city in the hands of the Soviets. Known as the Berlin Ultimatum, Khrushchev told the western allies they had to leave Berlin by May 27, 1959.

The reaction in the United States was what one might have expected. At an NSC meeting on January 29, 1959, John Foster Dulles called it a test of America's "moral courage." His position was that the U.S. should force the issue and provoke a military conflict with East Germany. The Joint Chiefs went even further, planning a full-scale nuclear war for May 27 if the Soviets attempted to remove Allied forces from West Berlin forcibly. General Norstad, the Supreme Allied Commander Europe, wanted to send an armored column down the autobahn. Joint Chiefs chairman Nathan Twining told NATO: "We must ignore the fear of general war. It is coming anyway. Therefore, we should force the issue on a point we think is right and stand on it. Khrushchev is trying to scare people. If he succeeds, we are through."

Eisenhower remained level-headed through all this and emphasized that if hostilities were unavoidable, the only option the United States would entertain was a full-scale nuclear war. As a result, the May 27 deadline passed without incident, but Khrushchev remained aggressive. In a meeting in Moscow, Khrushchev warned Averil Harriman that one bomb would destroy Bonn, and three to five would take care of France, Britain, Spain, and Italy. "If you start a war, we may die, but the rockets will fly automatically. We are determined," he said, "to liquidate our rights in Western Berlin. What good does it do you to have eleven thousand [American] troops in Berlin? If it came to war, we would swallow them in one gulp . . . Your generals talk of tanks and guns defending your Berlin position. They would burn."[29]

Allen Dulles likely understood that the retaliation against Berlin would be harsh if a successful coup against Cuba assassinated Fidel Castro. And the German companies connected to Dulles would be lost if the Soviets overran West Berlin. So, this may have been why Dulles rejected de los Reyes' request for U.S. assistance in executing the coup.

The second possibility for not supporting de los Reyes was that, even though the group involved in the coup consisted primarily of one-time supporters of Batista, the driving forces behind the operation were Morgan and Gutierrez, who had fought alongside Castro. These men continued to serve Castro after he came to power and only turned against him when he became a Communist. It was not who the right-wing Fascists in the U.S. wanted in charge when replacing Castro. The Cuban exile Batistaites had a name for this—Fidelismo sin Fidel. In other words, Fidel Castro would be gone, but nothing would change, which was unacceptable. To satisfy the right-wing in the U.S., the new government would allow American businesses to resume their lucrative operations in Cuba and permit the Mafia to return to their glory days reliant upon casinos and gambling. And we can assume that Dulles wanted to reestablish the Corsican drug network that financed operations conducted without Congressional approval.

Consider that Howard Hunt referred to Gutierrez as a pro "Castro fanatic . . ."[30] In addition, during their meeting, Dulles told de los Reyes that ". . . Morgan is a crook!" It is important to note that Hunt and Dulles were close. After the Bay of Pigs, Dulles reassigned Hunt to be Executive Assistant to Director of Central Intelligence.[31] Before that, Hunt had helped Dulles write his book, *The Craft of Intelligence*. So, it appears that another possible reason that Dulles was unwilling to support the coup was that the leaders were one-time supporters of Castro. What happened next seems to support this scenario.

Dulles promised to keep the details of his meeting with de los Reyes confidential. However, he wasted no time in contacting the State Department. A telegram dated August 2nd was sent to Ambassador Philip Bonsal in Cuba, telling him what they discussed at the meeting and the people involved in the coup. It was an apparent attempt to undermine what the plotter had planned in Cuba. And Dulles knew that Bonsal, who had actively cultivated relationships within Castro's government, would want to warn the Cubans, which he did by sending a telegram to Castro's foreign minister, Raul Roa. "There is a conspiracy in your Army to betray you," Bonsal wrote, naming William Morgan as the leader of the group.

The result was the arrest of Morgan, who the Cubans would eventually execute. There is also speculation that Gutierrez learned someone had betrayed them, and to protect himself, he told Castro's people about the coup and who was responsible. Castro's army arrested several thousand Cubans involved in the coup, and the plot to remove Castro from power ended. And it was all due to Allen Dulles' betrayal of the plotters by releasing details of the coup after promising he would do nothing of the sort. Others in the future would also learn the hard way not to trust Allen Dulles.[32]

It was not the end of local resistance in Cuba, however. Another coup took place in late 1959, which involved Manuel Artime, who was second in command of Castro's Instituto Nacional de Reforma Agraria (INRA), Carlos Prio, Tony Varona, who had served in Prio's government, Bernard Barker and Frank Sturgis. Sturgis' involvement suggests the inclusion of his Havana associates, which would be June Cobb, David Phillips, David Morales, Geraldine Shamma, Pedro Diaz Lanz, Henry Hecksher, and probably others, including Mafia figures. And at the time, Sturgis, Cobb, and Shamma were still part of Castro's government. Cuba's account of the attempted coup stated, "The US Embassy pulled the strings of the conspiracy . . . the link with Artime was Bernard Barker, an old police official of the Batista dictatorship . . . Through this conduit, Artime kept the Embassy informed about developments."[33]

According to the Cubans, "Artime elaborated a plan, with the support of Prio" and "Varona . . . to organize subversion in the eastern part of the country . . . they planned an uprising . . . under Artime's command; which they expected to . . . spread to the rest of the country."

The second attempted coup began on October 19, 1959, but was not well coordinated. Three bombs thrown at Castro failed to kill him. Two days later, Sturgis and a pilot, probably Pedro Diaz Lanz, "scattered thousands of leaflets over the city of Havana, exhorting the population to rise against the revolution." The coup was unsuccessful, and Artime and others quickly made their way to the United States to continue their war against Castro's regime from afar.[34] It was clear that anything other than an uprising orchestrated by ex-Batista supporters was unacceptable to the radical right in America. But it was not the end of mysterious activity within Cuba.

* * *

William Morgan and his compadres were not the only ones arrested in the summer of 1959. The Cubans apprehended John Martino on July 23, around the first coup attempt, accused of funneling money from Cuba to the United States. It is unlikely that Castro's people thought he was involved in the coup, for he survived the ordeal and eventually was released. Still, he spent forty months behind bars, a considerable amount of time.[35]

Loran Hall, the ex-military man described in the previous chapter, connected to Norman, Oklahoma, inexplicably turned up in Cuba during 1959 and was introduced to Frank Sturgis shortly after that. Castro's people employed him to train military troops for an invasion of Nicaragua in the planning stages. Despite this, the Cubans arrested Hall in April on suspicion of being an American agent. Perhaps the Cubans believed he was involved in the attempted coup. He was released from prison after serving only three months, but not before meeting Santo Trafficante at the Triscornia detention camp. The mobster had been in jail since Raul Castro had him arrested in June. Hall returned to the United States shortly after his release from prison.[36]

The time Trafficante spent behind bars was not a taxing ordeal, for those who saw him there said he lived in the virtual lap of luxury. For example, while incarcerated, his daughter was married at the Hilton Hotel in Havana, and Castro allowed Trafficante to leave the prison and attend the wedding. Not your typical prisoner, it appeared the Cubans bent over backward to appease him. They released him on the same day as Loran Hall, which may have been coincidental, but it is still suspicious.

There are many questions about why the Cubans imprisoned Trafficante. Did they do so, knowing he would be willing to buy his freedom? Was he jailed to disassociate him from the coup that was happening simultaneously so the mob boss would not have to get involved? Was Trafficante working with Castro, as the facts seem to demonstrate, and was his arrest was a ruse? And with that in mind, was his prison stay a necessary measure until it was safe for him to return to the United States?

Trafficante, who had controlled five casinos or hotels in Cuba, was unable to leave for fear of being subpoenaed in New York for the 1957 murder of Albert Anastasia. He had tried to open a competing casino in Havana, which prompted Trafficante to arrange a friendly meeting with him in New York. An hour after Trafficante checked out of the Park-Sheraton Hotel, three gunmen murdered Anastasia in the hotel barbershop. Naturally, Trafficante was considered the one responsible. He also wanted to avoid questions about the Appalachin meeting of mob bosses, which occurred one month after Anastasia's murder. He went into hiding after the Cuban police arrested casino owners Jake Lansky and Dino Cellini for narcotics trafficking on May 6, 1959, but Castro's Cubans eventually apprehended him.

Meanwhile, back in the U.S., the murder case against Trafficante was dropped for no justifiable reason, other than that CIA requested it, as they had done in other past mob cases involving gunrunners and drug traffickers. As a result, Trafficante returned to Tampa without fear after the Cubans eventually released him. [37]

It is suspicious that Trafficante met with Raul Castro while he was still incarcerated and was released shortly after that. Trafficante never explained what happened, but his lawyer Frank Ragano believed he bribed his way out. "Either Santo used his own money that he had hidden in Cuba," said Ragano, or ". . . one of his wealthy Cuban friends reached someone in Castro's government."[38] It is all speculation. The only thing we know for sure is there were friends of Trafficante on the outside trying to extricate the mob boss from prison.

Jack Ruby was a small-time hood whose criminal activity was restricted to bullying patrons and dancers, dabbling in local prostitution, illegal gambling, drug trafficking, and the like. However, we know he was involved in running guns to Castro's rebels, the first coup attempt against Castro, and the attempted sale of planes with Bartone and Hoffa, first to Castro and then Trujillo. And this exposure to illicit Cuban affairs explains how in the summer of 1959, Ruby became involved in an operation that far exceeded anything he had previously done. He was summoned to Havana by Lewis McWillie, and the evidence is strong that while there, he visited Trafficante in the Cuban prison where he was a captive. We know that Ruby had made at least one trip to Cuba related to the coup and the sale of planes to Morgan, but did this also involve trying to get Trafficante out of prison, or were these two events not connected in any way? Whatever the answer, Ruby now placed himself in potential jeopardy, for if something went wrong, there was a strong possibility that Jack Ruby would have found himself behind bars in a Cuban jail cell alongside Santo Trafficante.

As previously mentioned, before going to Cuba, Ruby contacted the FBI, who promptly opened a "potential criminal informant file" on him. Immediately after his initial meeting with his FBI handler, Ruby purchased a wristwatch with a built-in microphone, a telephone bug, a wired tie clip, and a bugged attaché case. The following month he opened a safe deposit box for the first and only time while living in Dallas. It appears he was involved in something over his head, and he was extremely nervous about the potential consequences. For Ruby, the FBI was an insurance policy if things went wrong. However, the FBI eventually closed their file on Ruby after nine meetings claiming the Bureau received nothing of substance from him. Despite this, critics have correctly argued that the FBI would not have met with Ruby on so many occasions unless he provided them with something of value. Ruby was likely the informant who provided the FBI with information regarding what was going on in Cuba. And perhaps the safe deposit box was a place to store this equipment when he did not need it. The truth is, Jack Ruby was involved in something meaningful. And those who were directing him, be they mobsters,

CIA agents, American mercenaries, anti-Castro Cuban exiles, or a combination of all the above, trusted Jack Ruby with sensitive work in a situation where the stakes were extremely high.

But more likely, someone expendable was needed for a dangerous assignment, and Ruby fit the bill. In short, the Mafia, the FBI, and possibly others used Jack Ruby. It would not be the last time.

Ruby's initial involvement in the Trafficante affair occurred in 1959 when a friend named Elaine Mynier traveled to Havana with a message for McWillie from Ruby. It was a brief coded message, "consisting of letters and numbers, including the word 'arriving,'" Mynier said. Ruby did not want anyone to know he was going to Havana. Mynier worked at the Dallas airport and "frequently saw Ruby and McWillie . . . coming and going on their frequent trips."[39]

Around the end of July, Ruby had dinner at a restaurant at Love Field in Dallas with Pedro and Martin Fox, the owners of the Tropicana, and according to what Trafficante would later say, the Fox brothers were trying "their best to get me out [of prison]." In addition to gambling, the Fox brothers were heavily into drug trafficking. Ruby later said they were in Dallas to "collect a debt," which implies that Ruby was indebted to them for some unexplained reason. Perhaps they viewed Ruby's involvement in Cuban affairs, specifically the attempted coup, as the reason for Trafficante's predicament. Whatever it was, Ruby was indebted to them, could not say no, which explains the eavesdropping equipment he felt compelled to purchase. He was scared.

On August 8, Ruby flew to Havana. Both he and McWillie later claimed that he stayed for only a week, but a Cuban exit card indicated he remained until September 11, over a month later, which contradicted this. There is also evidence that Ruby shuttled back and forth between Cuba and the U.S. during this period. On August 10, two days after arriving in Havana, records show that the police in Dallas interviewed Ruby for traffic violations. On August 21, he entered his safe deposit box, and on the 31st, he met with agent Flynn of the FBI. On September 4, he reaccessed his safe deposit box.[40]

Around that time, another friend of Ruby's, Meyer Panitz, was called by McWillie from Havana, telling him Ruby was in Miami. Panitz found Ruby at a Miami restaurant, a place where Trafficante was a regular customer. It is safe to assume this was all somehow related to Ruby's multiple trips to Cuba.

During the Labor Day holiday, September 5-7, Ruby was back in Havana. After the assassination, three American tourists reported they had talked with Ruby at the Tropicana, who said he was from Chicago and ran a nightclub in Dallas. However, Ruby was still in Cuba on the 8th, based on a postcard received by another friend in Dallas, Alice Nichols. On September 11, he officially left Cuba for the United States and returned to Havana the following day on a flight from Miami. He stayed for one day only, returning to New Orleans on the 13th.

Ruby's shuttling back and forth seemed to contradict his and McWillie's claim that he had gone to Cuba for leisure. That eyewitnesses saw him in the United States while he was supposed to be in Cuba confirms he undoubtedly was involved in criminal activity. In a deposition, McWillie later claimed that one of his duties for the Fox brothers was to take money from the Tropicana and deposit it in the Pan American Bank in Miami. Was this a clue to the role Ruby played? The Assassinations Committee concluded that Ruby "most likely was serving as a courier for gambling interests," but his exact reason for shuttling back and forth remains a mystery.[41]

Possible evidence that Ruby was trying to get Trafficante out of jail came four days after the assassination. A British journalist named John Wilson, also known as Wilson-Hudson, contacted the American Embassy, claiming that while working in Cuba during 1959, he came across an "American gangster type named Ruby." Wilson, who was in prison in Cuba while awaiting deportation, claimed he met an American gangster named Santo living under luxurious conditions inside the same jail. He also witnessed Jack Ruby visit Santo, something both Ruby and Trafficante vehemently denied after Ruby shot Oswald. Still, considering the circumstances, it would be foolhardy to have expected them to say anything else.

According to the records of the U.S. embassy in London, Wilson was a freelance journalist who spent most of the 1940s and 1950s living in Chile. He told embassy officials that Castro had imprisoned him because he had worked for Batista at one time. However, there was more to John Wilson than what he let on.

In 1976, assassination researcher Bernard Fensterwald, Jr. uncovered documents related to Wilson through the Freedom of Information Act. According to a confidential memo from Richard Helms to the FBI dated November 28, 1963, the CIA had maintained a file on Wilson dating back to 1951. He "was a contact of one Bert Sucharov, a suspected Soviet agent in Santiago, Chile." In addition, British authorities had tried to have Wilson expelled from Chile because he had impersonated a British Royal Air Force officer. A CIA source in Chile said he was "very probably an intelligence agent." Everything about this man pointed in that direction. His reason for turning up in a Cuban jail was a foiled plot between Wilson and three Americans. They had tried to launch an aerial bombing raid on Nicaragua, probably the same operation that got Loran Hall arrested. One wonders, was this attack on Nicaragua orchestrated by the CIA and blamed on Castro so that other Latin countries would be motivated to get involved in the plot to oust Castro from power?

Wilson came forward with his story that tied Ruby to Trafficante just two days after Ruby shot Oswald. His motive must have been to establish, for the record, a link between Ruby and the mob boss, which could tie Trafficante to the JFK assassination. Perhaps he intended to connect Ruby to organized crime as a whole while deflecting attention away from the CIA. For revelations about a Trafficante involvement in the assassination were not even considered in 1963. Regardless, Wilson brought this up so soon after the assassination, making one believe his story was true. The question is, was the CIA setting up the mob to take the fall for JFK's assassination, and did the Mafia order Ruby to silence Oswald to prevent this from happening?[42]

We also know that the CIA monitored Ruby as he traveled back and forth to Cuba. On November 27, 1963, the CIA-connected William Gaudet contacted the New Orleans FBI to "advise that he had heard Jack Ruby from Dallas, Texas, had purchased paintings from one Lorenzo Borenstein." The FBI contacted Borenstein, who confirmed that he knew Ruby and had sold paintings to him in the summer of 1959, when all the activity in Cuba took place.[43]

Gaudet's domain was New Orleans and the Cuban exile community. Therefore, we can assume that Ruby was already part of that world in the summer of 1959. And Ruby's New Orleans contacts were part of the operations occurring in Cuba. It likely included Carlos Marcello.

Gerry Patrick Hemming served under Castro when Trafficante was detained in prison and confirmed Ruby was in Cuba. Mobster John Roselli reportedly told a friend that "Ruby was hooked up with Trafficante in the rackets in Havana." Finally, a confidential HSCA memo stated that "Lewis J. McWillie, a close friend with Jack Ruby and a man with many contacts among organized crime figures, indicates that in 1959 Jack Ruby traveled to Cuba and visited Santos Trafficante in jail." There was little doubt that Ruby was actively involved in trying to get Santo Trafficante out of prison.[44] However, if Ruby believed his association with some of the leading mobsters in Cuba would raise his standing in the organized crime hierarchy, he was sadly mistaken. After the release of Trafficante in the late summer of 1959, Ruby returned to Dallas and continued his small-time operations, with no appreciable improvement in his life from what it was before when he received the phone call from McWillie summoning him to Cuba. As always, he continued to dabble in gunrunning, only now the guns were not destined for Castro, but the Cuban exiles who opposed him.

* * *

There was also an incident in 1963 that is worth mentioning because it was related to the JFK assassination, told by Marita Lorenz, and is relevant to the events that transpired in Havana in 1959. It is relevant because of the people she claimed were involved. According to Lorenz, about a month before the assassination, she joined Frank Sturgis at the Miami home of Orlando Bosch, one of the more violent anti-Castro Cuban exiles during the early 1960s. It was a highly secretive meeting, with the topic of discussion centering on the streets of Dallas. Lorenz thought they were planning to "take another armory" to steal weapons from the U.S. government that would be given to Cuban exiles fighting against Castro. It was something they had done before. Also present at this meeting, Lorenz claimed, was Lee Harvey Oswald.

Just before the assassination, there was a second meeting at the home of Orlando Bosch. Shortly after that, Lorenz, Sturgis, and others, including Gerry Patrick Hemming, two Cuban brothers named Novis (likely the violence-prone Novo brothers), and Pedro Diaz Lanz, traveled from Miami to Dallas in two cars. The car Lorenz traveled in had a high-powered rifle, outfitted with a scope and silencer, hidden in the trunk. A cache of guns was in the second car—machine guns, rifles, thirty-eights, and forty-fives. It was not an unusual circumstance, for transporting guns for Cuban exiles was a typical operation.

Arriving in Dallas, the group settled into a motel on the outskirts of town. They were met at the motel by Howard Hunt, the ultra-conservative CIA intelligence officer. He had been a liaison to the Cuban exile community ever since the Bay of Pigs. Lorenz would testify under oath that Hunt was the paymaster for the group and had similarly paid Sturgis to transport weapons in the past. On this occasion, Hunt hand-delivered money for the pending operation. Sturgis told Lorenz that her only function was to serve as a decoy, but precisely what she was to do was never adequately explained. Lee Harvey Oswald and Jack Ruby were also at the motel, and the latter was someone Lorenz had never met before.

Lorenz began to ask questions about the operation she knew little about, making Sturgis nervous. She flew back to Miami that evening, which was the night before the assassination. She only became aware of what she believed was the real reason for the group's presence in Dallas after hearing news reports that someone had killed the President.[45]

The source of the above account was Lorenz's notebook describing the incident (which the House Select Committee on Assassinations knew about). As well as the testimony she gave under oath in the trial of Hunt vs. Liberty Lobby. The latter was a defamation case brought by Howard Hunt against publisher Liberty Lobby, who had written that Hunt might have been in Dallas the day of the assassination and a participant in the crime. The jury would rule against Hunt in that case.

Gaeton Fonzi, who investigated Lorenz for the HSCA, found her story regarding the pre-assassination caravan hard to believe, despite considering her a credible witness in other matters. Regardless, her story is compelling nonetheless. And suppose Lorenz was telling the truth, that a caravan of American mercenaries and anti-Castro Cuban exiles traveled to Dallas the day before the assassination and met there with Lee Harvey Oswald, Jack Ruby, and Howard Hunt. In that case, the apparent conclusion to be drawn is that they were part of the assassination plot, but this is not necessarily the case. Perhaps they were involved in something unrelated to JFK's assassination, such as gunrunning arms to Cuba. Or maybe they were set up to take the blame for JFK's assassination and told to be in Dallas on the day. Allen Dulles had sabotaged the coup in Havana. Maybe the CIA sabotaged this group once again. We know that these people hated Castro for hijacking Cuba and hated JFK for betraying their cause. Nevertheless, some of those involved in the Lorenz caravan, and others, were significant figures in the war against Castro since 1959 and are prime suspects in JFK's assassination.

Consider the following:

- Frank Sturgis, Howard Hunt, and Bernard Barker would have a long working relationship. All three would take part in the Watergate burglary that led to the downfall of Richard Nixon.

- According to his son, St. Jean Hunt, on his death bed, Howard Hunt confessed to being involved in the assassination of JFK and that David Morales, Lyndon Johnson, Cord Meyer, and William Harvey were also involved.

- As previously mentioned, David Morales confirmed to friends that he did take part in the JFK assassination.

- Antonio Veciana, the head of the notorious anti-Castro group Alpha 66, met with David Phillips sometime during the summer of 1963. Phillips used the alias Maurice Bishop, and according to Veciana, Lee Harvey Oswald was there with Phillips.

- In September/October 1963, Phillips worked at the CIA Mexico City station when Oswald visited that city. At the time, June Cobb worked for Phillips out of the same Mexico City station. As we have discussed, multiple examples point toward a possible relationship between Cobb and Oswald just before the assassination.

- David Phillips, Howard Hunt, David Morales, Henry Hecksher, and Tracy Barnes worked together in 1954 to remove Arbenz from Guatemala.

- John Martino would claim after the assassination that he played a role in Kennedy's death.

- Martino was close to Trafficante. According to an informant, Santo Trafficante, Carlos Marcello, and Jimmy Hoffa all predicted the assassination of JFK long before it happened.

There is a strong possibility that those trying to remove Castro from power in 1959 were part of, either directly or indirectly, the assassination of JFK. But regarding the Cuban exiles, it is essential to differentiate between the Cubans who supported Batista and those who supported Castro's revolution. They had different visions for the future of Cuba and despised each other. CIA supported the former, while the U.S. State Department supported the latter. The AM/WORLD operation, the invasion of Cuba that was to occur in December 1963, was subsequently canceled. Robert Kennedy was in charge of the CIA war against Castro at that time.

The new government established in Cuba was to be run by ex-Castro supporters who had turned against him after Castro embraced communism. It was not what the international right-wing, Fascist consortium wanted. The right-wing at the CIA, the military, Texas oilmen, conservative industrialists, paramilitary groups, and the Mafia were against it. This group wanted to install an ex-supporter of Batista and return Cuba to what it was like before Castro came to power. It raises the question, was Kennedy killed to prevent AM/WORLD from happening? The answer is probably yes, for the Kennedy administration similarly turned its back on ex-Batistaites during the Bay of Pigs, intending to fill the new Cuban government with ex-Castro supporters if the invasion was successful. CIA knew this and proceeded anyway with an operation that had no chance of succeeding because they wanted it to fail. It was sabotage, just as Dulles had betrayed the coup against Castro in 1959. And to understand why Kennedy had to die, just follow the history of sabotage starting with the Korean War, the downing with the U-2 flight over Russia, the Dulles sabotage of the coup to oust Castro, and the sabotage of the Bay of Pigs invasion, and see who was behind it. The radical right was willing to do anything to ensure that their plan of eliminating communism would occur. Even assassinate a President.

- 4 -

Treason is a Deadly Business

"Killing people is wrong, but it happens, and if someone had polished off Idi Amin, it would have saved a lot of people a lot of grief. But at the same time, it must be a decision in the hands of people you can trust and who will not take such a decision lightly."
—Richard Bissell: CIA Deputy Director for Plans

As Eisenhower's second term neared its end, military spending was out of control, as official U.S. policy maintained an overwhelming nuclear superiority over the Soviets. A conventional war was not an option because it might escalate into a nuclear exchange, so the CIA's covert operations became even more critical. It included assassinations, and they targeted the leadership in Cuba more than anyone else. Not everyone agreed with this, and military generals resigned in protest and publicly questioned the President's ability to lead. There was talk that the military might instigate a coup, which the radical right welcomed, for a nuclear showdown with the Soviets was still what they wanted. By the time Kennedy took office, they would be willing to assassinate JFK to achieve this. A full-blown military invasion of a foreign country like Cuba was what the hawks wanted. And done correctly, there would be no ramifications. They had not yet reached that point under Eisenhower, but the first signs of treason, indicating that a takeover of the U.S. government could occur, were visible during his Presidency. Meanwhile, the radical right within the CIA created an assassination group, Operation 40, to ensure a new right-wing Cuban government would replace Castro once the CIA eliminated him. Operation 40 intended to accomplish this by assassinating the leftist Cuban exile government waiting in the U.S., which the State Department and the liberal element at the CIA had selected.

Assassinations were always an acceptable option.

* * *

From April 1954 to May 1955, a special United Nations subcommittee on dis-armament, consisting of the United States, the Soviet Union, the United Kingdom, France, and Canada, gathered to discuss the possibility of halting the arms race. The West's call for disarmament included an inspection to ensure that what they agreed to do was carried out. The Soviets insisted they would not accept on-site reviews by Western inspectors, for unknown to the West, the Russians were severely behind in the number of nuclear weapons and did not want to reveal that this was the case. It was unacceptable to the West, as were other Soviet demands, such as a total ban on nuclear weapons, equivalent reduction of conventional forces, and elimination of military bases on the territories of foreign countries. However, on May 10, 1955, the head of the Soviet delegation, Jacob Malik, offered a new proposal that, accord-ing to Soviet specialist James Richter, "brought the two sides closer to nuclear and conventional disarmament than . . . at any other time during the 1950s."

Malik said the Soviets were willing to accept surveillance posts on Russian territory, and they would be open to an international disarmament agency to verify compliance. They were also ready to cut conventional force levels, which they enjoyed over their opponents. They still wanted to shut down military bases on foreign territory. However, they were willing to comply with what the United States and its allies were looking to obtain for the most part.

Despite an apparent olive branch by the Russians, the U.S. rejected the offer because they never intended to settle with the Soviets. The consensus American opinion was that they could not trust Communists, and what the Soviets proposed was just propaganda to cast themselves in a positive light around the world. Op-ponents said the USSR wanted to free up money they could transfer from defense spending to the economy, which was in desperate need of bolstering. John Foster Dulles knew the Russians needed "to deal more effectively with their severe internal problems," but he remained unmoved by their plight. Coexistence was not an op-tion. The American position remained the same—continue military spending at a breakneck pace, inevitably destroying the Soviet economy.[1]

By 1956, however, concerns about Eisenhower's "massive retaliation" policy began to surface, as critics questioned the intelligence of maintaining such a hard-line approach. The Russian nuclear arsenal continued to grow. As they developed a means to deliver nuclear missiles over a longer distance, it became clear that Ike could never use nuclear weapons unless it were in extreme circumstances, such as resisting an all-out invasion of Western Europe by the Soviets. Still, Eisenhower did not waver and maintained that he was willing to use nuclear weapons in any confrontation, wherever and whenever the need arose. General Andrew Goodpaster quoted him saying: "Massive retaliation . . . is likely to be the key to survival. He reiterated that planning should go-ahead for the use of tactical atomic weapons against military targets in any small war in which the US might get involved." Ike was willing to use nuclear weapons without any restrictions.[2]

The following year, Eisenhower began to have concerns of his own, so he asked the NSC to appoint a group to investigate how best to protect the American people in the event of an all-out nuclear war. H. Rowan Gaither, a co-founder of the think tank, the Rand Corporation, was chosen to chair the new committee. Officials from NORAD (North American Air Defense Command), the Strategic Air Command, the office of the Secretary of Defense, the Federal Civil Defense Administration, the Weapons Systems Engineering Group, and the CIA made up the rest of the panel. Defense contractors were also well represented.

The committee's conclusion was dire indeed, for they determined there was no way to protect the American people from a major nuclear attack. Soviet Intercontinental Ballistic Missiles (ICBMs) were a significant concern, for, by this time, they had successfully fired ICBMs over 3,000 miles. Herb York, the scientific director of the Livermore Laboratory, and Jerome Wiesner, a presidential scientific advisor and MIT engineering professor, were mandated to investigate the magnitude of the ICBM threat to the United States.

There was no means of definitively determining how many missiles the Russians had. So according to York, they "took the best data there were on the Soviet rocket development program . . . [and combined it with what they knew] about the availability of factory floor space [in Russia] . . . and concluded that they would produce thousands [of ICBMs] in the next few years."

But their assumptions were way off, for the Soviets had nowhere near the number of missiles they assumed they did. However, no one could dispute their findings. It served as a wake-up call for Eisenhower and those who supported massive retaliation, for if what York and Wiesner said was correct, and the Soviet did plan to produce a thousand ICBMs in only a few years, that could only mean one thing. They were preparing for a total nuclear war.[3]

There was also a limit that the U.S. could spend on defense. And what concerned Eisenhower were the hardliners in the military who did not recognize this. He said that "national security and national solvency are mutually dependent . . ." and the "permanent maintenance of a crushing weight of military power would eventually produce dictatorship [in the U.S.]." And any person who did not understand this "should not be entrusted with any . . . responsibility in our country." He was already thinking of the military-industrial complex and was alarmed by the potential for catastrophe that it posed. Advertisements he had seen placed by defense contractors in *Aviation Week* and the "selfish" demands, especially Air Force generals, disgusted him.[4]

During the 1950s, Representative F. Edward Hebert of Louisiana "found that there were . . . swarms of retired officers working for defense contractors—92 for North American Aviation. . . . A bill to regulate the activities of retired officers passed the House. In the Senate, [Lyndon] Johnson, giving the military establishment the last year [1960] of his allegiance as Majority Leader, saw that the bill was properly laid to rest without . . . action."[5]

Privately, Ike grumbled about munitions makers and "fat cats" trying to make money off something as serious as military spending and nuclear missiles. Regarding congressional leaders, he wondered how they had suddenly become "military experts" and accused them of having "fallen victim" to the "salesmanship" of the arms industry.[6]

As the end of Ike's presidency drew near, nothing had changed. They continued to spend recklessly. Military officers were given jobs with defense contractors they were not qualified to hold, and defense executives received positions in government for which they were equally untrained. Meanwhile, Congressional leaders, military generals, and defense contractors were in bed with each other, creating a weapons industry not based on necessity but on pushing the spending envelope as far as it would go.

As far as military generals were concerned, Eisenhower lamented that "habitually, when with me, [they] give the impression that they are going to work out arrangements that will keep the military appropriations within manageable proportions . . . Yet, when each Service puts down its minimum requirements for its military budget for the following year, and I add up the total, I find that they mount at a fantastic rate. There is seemingly no end to all of this."[7]

Eisenhower was frustrated with the military and its uncontrollable spending. "He knew too much about the military to be fooled [by them]," Ike said, but this might not be true of his successors. "Someday, there is going to be a man sitting in my present chair who has not been raised in the military services and who will have little understanding of where the slashes in their estimates can be made with little or no damage," Ike wrote. "If that should happen while we still have a state of tension that now exists in the world, I shudder to think what could happen in this country."[8] Little did Ike know that the President he described would be his successor.

Interservice rivalries might have been what angered Eisenhower the most, for it resulted in unnecessary, wasteful spending. "The Army and Air Force 'race' to build almost duplicate CRBMs [Continental Range Ballistic Missiles] incensed him," wrote historian Sherman Adams.

As a result, based on the findings of the York and Wiesner committee, on January 7, 1958, Eisenhower advised Congress to allocate $10 million "for the Advanced Research Projects Agency (ARPA)," and two nights later, he publicly announced the creation of this new agency in his State of the Union address. "Some of the important new weapons which technology has produced do not fit into any existing service pattern," Ike explained. These new weapons should "transcend all services, at every stage from development to operation." As weapons technology increased and made old ones obsolete, instead of working together, the different military branches became involved in "jurisdictional disputes" that "bewilder and confuse the public . . ." He created ARPA, Ike said, in "recognition of the need for single control in some of our most advanced development projects." It was a public tongue lashing directed at the Joint Chiefs.[9]

No one could argue that having all military branches working together was more cost-effective. Still, there remained a disagreement regarding whether or not it was acceptable to use nuclear weapons for all conflicts, regardless of how localized and contained an act of aggression might be. In 1958, the U.S. government issued a "Basic National Security Policy" statement, which said: "It is the policy of the United States to place main, but not sole, reliance on nuclear weapons . . ." However, if "local aggression" occurred in "less developed areas," the U.S. reserved the right to deploy forces without nuclear weapons. So, by 1959, the assumption was limited warfare did not require nuclear weapons. And even Ike realized that "the more the services depend on nuclear weapons . . . ,[the harder it will be] to keep it from spreading into [a] general war."

Still, the size of the conflict notwithstanding, Secretary of Defense Neil McElroy said in March 1959 that a response to any aggression from the Soviet Union "really had to be that of massive retaliation." And that was the crux of the matter. The American policy of containment and massive retaliation hinged on the Soviet Union knowing that any act of aggression by them, no matter how small, would result in a nuclear response by the United States. According to Admiral Arthur Radford, "The reason we can intervene in many areas quickly with force is that we can do this with small forces which, armed with atomic weapons, are not in danger of being wiped out." Ike disagreed because he concluded that "we were unfortunately so committed to nuclear weapons that the only practical move would be to start using them from the beginning without any distinction between them and conventional weapons." In other words, the President believed the military would use nuclear weapons as the first line of defense. It frightened him because they needed to contain the Soviets, but no other option was available. [10]

In 1959, as Khrushchev presented his ultimatum regarding Berlin, the U.S. military offered various scenarios to respond with conventional forces should the Russians attack. Ike was adamant that he would not fight "a nice, sweet, World War II type of war" in Europe once again. On the contrary, in March, Eisenhower instructed Congress to reduce the number of U.S. troops on the continent by 55,000 men. "What would these 55,000 men do if we had them?" Ike asked. Ike was sending a message to the Soviets that the U.S. had no intention of engaging in a conventional war. If fighting broke out, the only form of retaliation would be nuclear. The stakes were extremely high, and no wonder Allen Dulles and the President did not want to aggravate the situation by assassinating Castro, as described in the previous chapter.[11]

One person who disagreed with the President was General Maxwell Taylor, Chief of Staff of the Army, who thought retaliating against Soviet aggression with a nuclear response was insanity. "Personally," he said, "I rate this concept of war as only one of the forms, and not necessarily the most likely, which war may take." He thought it "increasingly improbable that an aggressor would intentionally embark on the gamble of atomic war" that the army had the "unique ability to proportion punishment to fit the crime of aggression . . ."[12]

Taylor was a proponent of "flexible response" and that modern warfare demanded the flexibility to use their weapons as required. He proposed the "pentomic division," which consisted of five battle groups designed for flexibility that could quickly adapt to include atomic weapons if needed. As Taylor wrote in his book, *Swords and Plowshares*, "nuclear weapons were the going thing and by including some in the division armament, the Army staked out its claim to a share in the nuclear arsenal."[13]

All Army combat divisions converted to the pentomic concept by early 1958, under Lyman Lemnitzer, the Army's Chief of Staff (By the early 1960s, the Army would revert to a more traditional ground division deployment). The Army did this because troop reductions limited what they could do, and Lemnitzer thought the pentomic concept would enhance the ability of his reduced force to combat aggression more effectively. Taylor agreed but said that one million men were the minimum level the Army could tolerate, more than the 870,000 force the administration proposed.[14]

Eisenhower disagreed, believing that "flexible response" would eventually lead to a more involved war, not prevent one, as did massive retaliation. He turned down Taylor's request to increase the size of the Army's force, as well as the weapons required to fight small wars. He wanted to dispel the idea that the military could control the level of aggression once an engagement began.[15]

Eisenhower ". . . thought General Taylor's position . . . [assumed] that we are opposed by a people that think as we do with regard to the value of human life. But they do not . . . [and] in the event they should decide to go to war, the pressure on them to use atomic weapons in a sudden blow would be extremely great." And he had no intention of giving the Soviets that opportunity, which meant the U.S. had to maintain a nuclear superiority over them, regardless of the cost. For Ike, it was the only way to prevent war from happening.[16]

Eisenhower doubled down and further alienated the military by enacting the Defense Reorganization Act of 1958, which unified commands in the field under the Secretary of Defense, a non-military appointee. The goal was to increase the Secretary's military control by forwarding all defense appropriations through his office rather than individual services.[17]

Eisenhower's refusal to budge on massive retaliation forced General Taylor to resign with disgust in 1959. Shortly after that, he wrote *The Uncertain Trumpet*, which criticized Eisenhower's reliance on nuclear weapons and lamented the reduced role of the Army in planning military strategy. When Taylor testified before

Congress, saying that the allies should "at once" test the Soviets with a military probe, historian Campbell Craig said it "bordered on political insurrection."[18]

Taylor was not the only insubordinate ex-military man Eisenhower faced. General Gavin, like Taylor, disagreed with the administration's massive retaliation approach to national defense. He retired in 1958 and announced he would publicly question Eisenhower's policies, which he vehemently opposed. Later that year, he wrote *War and Peace in the Space Age*, which explained why he chose to retire instead of receiving a fourth star and command of the Seventh Army in Europe. General Lemnitzer had this to say about Gavin: "We in the Army deeply regret the retirement of this able and experienced military commander and staff officer. We [knew] that he was unhappy with the direction our defense policy was taking at the time, particularly . . . the emphasis . . . placed on nuclear weapons . . . This feeling of concern in this regard was not limited to General Gavin, however, but it was shared by the Secretary of the Army, the Chief of Staff, myself, and most other officers in the Department of the Army."

Lemnitzer then added his dig at Eisenhower. "It was obvious to us," he wrote, "that General Gavin was extremely frustrated because his views were [ignored] at higher levels, but so were all of us . . ." The level of insubordination in the Army was unprecedented. It was that way throughout the Cold War. The military thought they knew better than politicians about how the U.S. should fight the war against communism, and it would only worsen after Kennedy became President.[19]

General Ridgway also resented the Army's diminished role and said the President was too "parochial." He was highly critical of Eisenhower's defense policies in his memoirs, which appeared in the *Saturday Evening Post,* followed by the book he eventually wrote.[20]

Then in 1960, the chief of the U.S. Army Ordnance Missile Command, General Medaris, retired in disgust. That same year he wrote *Countdown for Decision,* which also attacked Eisenhower. Medaris dared to write that Ike had a below-average military mind and was making bad military decisions.[21]

The insubordination shown by Medaris, Taylor, Gavin, and Ridgway infuriated the President, who directed the new chairman of the Joint Chiefs, General Nathan Twining, to investigate the legality of retired officers writing books critical of official U.S. defense policy. Eisenhower threatened that they could be "fired" from retirement status if they did not tone down the criticism against the government, recalled to active duty, and court-martialed.[22]

It was an incredibly divisive time in American history. The conduct exhibited by retired generals was nothing short of treason, a behavior military generals had displayed since World War II. The question is, how far was the military capable of going if they thought the nation was in danger and they had to do something to stop it? What would happen when someone without Eisenhower's resume resided in the White House? These were questions Nikita Khrushchev likely asked as well, for he was also concerned. He suspected that Eisenhower was not in control of the government and that powerful militarist forces, including Allen Dulles and Richard Nixon, exercised an unhealthy level of responsibility. He told the Presidium that Ike was "under the influence of various groups and ad hoc situations."[23]

Perhaps what troubled the military was that Eisenhower relied on covert action to counter Communist aggression to maintain plausible deniability in conjunction with massive retaliation. It required virtually no approval but his and allowed him to limit the cost of conventional forces. And a massive retaliation policy in place made the army essentially obsolete. Perhaps it was not a coincidence, considering Khrushchev's concern regarding Allen Dulles' influence. After President Kennedy took office, Dulles brought in General Taylor as CIA's liaison to the White House. Birds of a feather flock together. And Dulles was no stranger to insubordination himself.

* * *

By 1960 the situation in Cuba was in disarray. CIA and Cuban exiles who had supported Batista, disgruntled American businessmen, organized crime figures, and disenchanted ex-supporters of Castro wanted the Cuban leader removed. There were too many groups involved, and each had its plan, which complicated things, for it could potentially jeopardize the plausible deniability the United States needed to maintain. And when Allen Dulles thwarted the attempted coup in Cuba the previous summer to prevent a far-left takeover of Cuba, the right-wing at the CIA took it upon itself to gain control of the Cuban situation and overthrow Castro, even if it meant assassinating him.

In March, the CIA drafted a policy paper titled "A Program of Covert Action Against the Castro Regime." Authorized by the 5412 Committee, it consisted of four points—"the creation of a Cuban government in exile;" "a powerful propaganda offensive;" "a covert intelligence and action organization;" and a "paramilitary force outside of Cuba for future guerrilla action." It was the first indication that the CIA, at the highest levels, was considering the removal of Castro.[24]

J.C. King headed CIA's Western Hemisphere Division at the time. He was an ex-Army attaché stationed in Buenos Aires during World War II and had developed a close relationship with the FBI throughout South America. 1947, when the CIA was born, counterintelligence in Latin America shifted from the FBI to the CIA. King convinced many of his associates at the Bureau to join him in the newly established spy organization. It was from these ranks that the Western Hemisphere Division of the CIA found numerous anti-Communists disciples. Staunch supporters of the radical right who were close to Batista and the American businessmen who had made a fortune in Cuba now characterized King's Western Hemisphere Division. Following Castro's successful revolution, King and his men remained loyal to

Batista, which put them at odds with the State Department, which wanted to give Castro a chance. The Western Hemisphere group wanted to topple Castro at any cost and that Batista, or one of his supporters, should be installed as Castro's successor. As early as December 11, 1959, King had written a memo to Allen Dulles about getting rid of Castro. King said, "that a 'far left' dictatorship now existed in Cuba which, if permitted to stand, will encourage similar action against U.S. holdings in other Latin American countries . . ." He offered two suggestions to prevent this from occurring. First, an anti-Castro group should "establish by force" a beachhead within Cuba and form a new military government. Second, that "thorough consideration be given to the elimination of Fidel Castro."[25]

Dulles crossed out the word "elimination" and replaced it with "removal." The CIA was not yet ready to consider assassinating Fidel Castro. Or at least to put in writing that the Agency was contemplating this.

On January 8, 1960, Dulles instructed his Deputy Director of Plans, Richard Bissell, to set up a task force to overthrow Castro. Then, according to notes written by Gordon Gray, Eisenhower's National Security Advisor, three days later Dulles attended a meeting at the White House that included Eisenhower, Vice President Richard Nixon, and the Secretary of Treasury, Robert Anderson. Dulles brought along "schematic drawings" showing how the CIA intended to sabotage Cuban sugar refineries, and Gray wrote that "the President said that he didn't object to such an undertaking . . ." Ike wanted to go further, believing ". . . that any program should be much more ambitious, and it was probably now [sic] the time to move against Castro in . . . [an] aggressive way which went beyond pure harassment."[26]

Undoubtedly spurred on by the President's enthusiastic suggestion, Dulles went before the 5412 Committee on January 11, and requested that the CIA be allowed to initiate a covert action program against Castro. The Committee agreed, and that same month, Philip Bonsal, the pro-Castro U.S. Ambassador to Cuba, was recalled from Havana. The United States government's war against Castro was officially underway.[27]

Meanwhile, on February 4, Anastas Mikoyan, a First Deputy in the Kremlin and one of the most influential Soviet politicians, arrived in Havana as part of a trade exhibition of Soviet culture and technology. Nine days later, Castro and Mikoyan signed a "trade agreement" that included a Soviet pledge to buy hundreds of thousands of tons of sugar from Cuba and granted them a $100 million low-interest loan, making things much more problematic for the U.S.

Then, on March 4, 1960, the Belgian ship *La Coubre*, which carried arms for Castro's army, exploded in Havana harbor, killing more than one hundred people aboard the vessel and along the adjacent shore. Castro accused the U.S. and Cuban exiles of being responsible, and he was probably right, though nothing was ever proven. In response, Cuba retaliated. They nationalized property owned by U.S. businesses, alienating many Americans. Next, they shut off water to the U.S. base at Guantanamo Bay., mobilized the Cuban military in preparation for an American invasion, and increased their effort to uncover all those involved in the counter-revolutionary movement. The war against Castro was about the enter a new level.[28]

Two days before the *La Coubre* incident, Allen Dulles had briefed Vice President Nixon on the Cuban situation. Entitled "*What We Are Doing in Cuba*," Dulles explained there was a drug "which, if placed in Castro's food, would make him behave in such an irrational manner that a public appearance could have very damaging results for him." By this time, George Hunter White and countless CIA-connected doctors at hospitals throughout the country had been experimenting with LSD on unsuspecting people for around a decade. It was undoubtedly this drug to which Dulles referred. Nothing officially was done, but it is a reminder that mind-altering drugs had become an essential part of the CIA's arsenal, and they were searching for ways to employ them, including assassination.[29]

For a second time, J.C. King wrote that "consideration be given to the elimination of Fidel Castro," in a memo to Allen Dulles. This time Dulles approved the plan. On March 9, 1960, King went one step further during the newly created Cuban Task Force meeting. "Unless Fidel and Raul Castro and Che Guevara [were] eliminated in one package, this operation can be a long, drawn-out affair," he said. "The present government will only be overthrown by the use of force."

Admiral Burke echoed King's words the following day at a meeting of the NSC. He "suggested that any plan for the removal of Cuban leaders should be a package deal since many of the leaders around Castro were even worse than Castro." Everyone was on the same page. However, they ignored King's warning that the operation could be a "long, drawn-out affair." It was not Guatemala, and what King said should have been given more consideration.[30]

The 5412 Committee reconvened on March 14, and Castro's assassination was discussed for the first time. In addition, it was necessary to remove all three—Fidel Castro, Raul Castro, and Che Guevara. The committee met the following day again, with increased urgency, to discuss plans for the overthrow of Castro. The U.S. needed an organized group of anti-Castro Cuban exiles to accomplish this. Also essential was to install a new government in Cuba that was "more devoted to the true interests of the Cuban people and more acceptable to the US in such a manner as to avoid any appearance of US intervention." The CIA confidently reported that the Agency would create a unified political opposition to Castro within two months. They would establish an underground resistance within Cuba. Within six to eight months, an amphibious invasion of Cuba by a CIA-trained exile paramilitary group would happen. There was no mention of assassination, at least not in the official record. However, considering that they raised the topic when they had met the day before, undoubtedly, killing the three Cuban leaders was still part of the plan.[31]

On March 17, the 5412 Committee presented the plan to overthrow Castro to Eisenhower. It was titled "A Program of Covert Action Against the Castro Regime."

Present were Richard Nixon, Christian Herter of State, Admiral Arleigh Burke, who represented the Joint Chiefs, Allen Dulles, Richard Bissell, and J.C. King from the CIA. Once again, the official record does not mention assassination or, for that matter, the use of illicit drugs.

According to the briefing, they told the President that the Cuban operation would include the following:

1. The establishment of a government in exile made up of Cubans in the U.S. who had fled the island.

2. Broadcast into Cuba anti-Castro propaganda from a remote location, similar to Radio Free Europe.

3. An underground within Cuba to gather intelligence and carry out para-military operations (Similar to the Donovan/Dulles stay-behind armies in Europe).

4. "An adequate paramilitary force" to be trained outside Cuba by the CIA and employed in an amphibious island invasion.[32]

It is essential to recognize that the original plan to invade Cuba was dramatical-ly different from the massive assault that became the Bay of Pigs invasion. Richard Bissell described it as a "classic World War II underground activity. Our operation was to train eventually up to seventy-five or more individuals . . . Their primary function was to enter the country, join guerrilla groups already there, and put them in direct communications with an external headquarters, partly to exercise com-mand control and partly to enable them to receive logistic supplies by boat and aircraft."[33] It was a Jedburgh-type, underground army operation, Cuban style.

In March 1960 Howard Hunt, who was CIA's station chief in Uruguay, was re-called to Washington and named Chief of Political Action in charge of assisting the Cuban exiles living in the U.S. to overthrow Fidel Castro. Hunt later recalled in his book, *Give Us This Day*: "The nucleus of the project was already in being—a cadre of officers I had worked with against Arbenz [in Guatemala]. This time, however, all traces of U.S. official involvement must be avoided. . . ."[34]

The most notable people from the Guatemalan operation to whom Hunt re-ferred were David Phillips, David Morales, Tracy Barnes, and Henry Hecksher. In September 1960, Bernard Barker returned from Cuba and was assigned to be Hunt's assistant. Barker was associated with the plot connected to the U.S. Embassy in Havana, including Phillips, Morales, Herksher. Also included were June Cobb and Frank Sturgis. Barker had close ties to organized crime figures, such as Santo Trafficante and John Martino. It appears that the core CIA group from Havana, which was involved in the attempted coup in Cuba, was added to those who had removed Arbenz in Guatemala to create a joint task force mandated to get rid of

Castro. It made sense because the Havana group was already close to the existing underground within Cuba and those within the Cuban military who opposed Castro. Both would be needed for the operation to be a success.

The liberal-minded Richard Bissell, the number two man at CIA, was put in charge of the project. The importance of Guatemala was evident by the chain of command, which descended from Bissell to Tracy Barnes and then to Jake Esterline, who had just taken over Branch 4 in the Western Hemisphere Division. Noticeably absent from the operation were the pro-Batista J.C King, Esterline's boss, and the non-Ivy League Richard Helms, who was opposed to covert action and not part of the OPC fraternity.

King was left out because his conservatism and support of Batista would interfere with Bissell's management of the project. As Tracy Barnes explained to Howard Hunt, there was a belief by some within the Agency that the Cuban people would not embrace the invasion if its leadership consisted of ex-Batista supporters. It was a critical point because the essence of the operation was the Cuban underground which, to a large extent, was made up of ex-followers of Castro who had become disenchanted with the Communist direction he had chosen. It created a rift at CIA because the conservatives within the Agency wanted a pro-American, pro-big business Batista government in power. However, as Bissell said, "They [Ike and CIA conservatives] don't know it, but we're the real revolutionaries."[35]

In April, Hunt reported to the Cuban task force and provided a list of recommendations, including: "Assassinate Castro before or coincident with the invasion." It was clear that the CIA leadership had passed down the word to Hunt to liquidate the Cuban leaders.[36]

The CIA in Cuba was made aware that assassination was part of the operation on July 21, 1960, when Tracy Barnes cabled the Havana station stating, "Possible removal of top three [Cuban] leaders is receiving serious considerations at [headquarters]." In response to Havana's information, a Cuban operative, who had previously gathered intelligence for CIA, indicated he would be close to Raul Castro shortly. It was never explicitly stated that this operative was willing to assassinate Raul, but the implication was obvious.

How the CIA managed to maintain plausible deniability is shown in these back-and-forth cables between Barnes and Havana. First, Havana advised Barnes that a Cuban operative would be near Raul Castro, but there was no mention of assassination. In response, Barnes does not tell Havana to assassinate Raul, just that headquarters is considering the removal of the top three Cuban leaders. There is no mention of killing, but the implication was clear. Discretely, Havana asked if they should try to assassinate Raul Castro. Barnes told them indirectly that this was what headquarters wanted. By reading between the lines, one could easily discern what they were discussing, but both sides could deny that Barnes ordered Havana to kill Castro if pressed. The ability to pass along proper instructions and maintain "plausible deniability" was an essential art that men like Barnes learned to master.

Richard Bissell described plausible deniability as it applied to assassinations: "What is very difficult for anybody to understand is that if you say in however veiled or murky terms that you are going to do something, and if the terms aren't so murky that the listener doesn't know what you're going to do, and if you don't receive a negative and you think it will advance the cause, you go ahead and do it."[37]

The morality of assassination was rationalized by many within the Agency as the ends justifying the means. Would not the world have been better off an assassin had killed Hitler before World War II began? Of course, this was true, and these were men whose roots were born in the 1950s, who shared the belief that democracy had God on its side in battling communism, as well as being deemed acceptable by the Vatican if the circumstances matched the Church's criteria for assassination. In short, everyone was expendable in the war of good vs. evil. It included Presidents of the United States who, if misguided, could lead the country in an irrevocably wrong direction, with disastrous consequences for the nation. Should such a President be allowed to essentially destroy the American way of life, or should that President be removed from office by whatever means possible before it was too late? As Bissell stated to author John Ranelagh in a 1983 interview, as reported in *The Agency, The Rise and Decline of the CIA*: "Killing people is wrong, but it happens, and if someone had polished off Idi Amin, it would have saved a lot of people a lot of grief. But at the same time, it must be a decision in the hands of people you can trust and who will not take such a decision lightly."[38]

Although the CIA most likely never received specific approval from the 5412 Committee or the President to proceed with plans to assassinate the three Cuban leaders, the Agency was probably under the impression that they were authorized to do so. And therein lies the problem with plausible deniability, for the CIA could interpret any response to fit the narrative they wanted to adhere to. The danger was it allowed them to pursue an agenda without approval, and the government would be unaware of what they were doing. As McGeorge Bundy, the National Security Advisor to both Presidents Kennedy and Johnson, later described: "There is a terrible danger that if you don't listen extremely hard and have a relationship of mutual trust that is very close, you can get a situation where what you think you are authorizing is rather different from what the agency will, in fact, believe it is free to do under that authorization."[39]

There is evidence that Vice President Nixon endorsed assassination as part of the plan to remove Castro. After Eisenhower, Nixon, who was supposed to be the next president, was the project action officer for the Cuban operation within the White House and was directly involved in all facets of the Cuban operation. The original plan was for the Bay of Pigs invasion and the assassination of the Cuban leaders to occur just before the 1960 election, which would have served to catapult Nixon into the presidency.

Highly conservative, Nixon worked alongside Allen Dulles to thwart the State Department's attempt to recognize the Castro regime after Castro came to power. At a December 16, 1959 meeting of the NSC, just five days after King's memo to Dulles which recommended the murder of Castro, Nixon stated that "we need to find a few dramatic things to do with respect to the Cuban situation . . . to indicate that we would not allow ourselves to be kicked around completely. . . ." The reference to "dramatic things" was undoubted proof that Nixon was aware of the plan to assassinate Castro.[40]

Nixon's conservatism led the right-wingers at CIA to introduce him to an ultra-right Cuban exile named Mario Garcia Kohly, who had strong international radical right-wing connections, which included the Vatican. Kohly was interested in replacing Fidel Castro and becoming the president of Cuba himself. He was a stark contrast to who the State Department and CIA liberals intended Castro's successor to be, for he was considered an unguided missile. CIA agent Robert Morrow took part in the Bay of Pigs invasion with David Ferrie. He would later claim the CIA was involved in JFK's assassination. In his book *First Hand Knowledge*, he wrote that Kohly was "a distinguished statesman and diplomat . . . one of the most illustrious members of Cuba's investment banking elite . . . Cuba's premier trade and financial representative to the international community at large and major American energy-related industries in particular . . . [He] represented, in Cuba, an extraordinary number of prominent American corporations in industries . . . [such] as banking and energy, foodstuffs and finance, corporate finance and real estate development."[41]

According to Morrow, Kohly's CIA case officer was Tracy Barnes, who disagreed with Bissell's desire to keep Batistaites out of the operation. Barnes wanted to involve Kohly. As the Cuban exile leader told Nixon during their meeting, not only had he formed a group in the United States composed of former Cuban military personnel, but he also had an established underground within Cuba that numbered 42,000 strong. A strong underground was considered essential, and Morrow claimed that Nixon approved of Kohly's involvement in the operation.[42]

Unfortunately for Kohly and his right-wing CIA collaborators, William Wieland at the State Department, who had previously undermined William Pawley's attempt to replace Batista with a military junta, got wind of Kohly's meeting with Nixon. Fearing the invasion force would be labeled Batistaite, Wieland convinced the liberals at the CIA to limit the Cuban exile involvement to ex-Castro supporters only. Kohly was out, which doomed the operation from the beginning.

In addition to different factions operating within the Agency, the CIA managed a Cuban exile community rife with division. All exiles were united in their desire to overthrow Castro; however, infighting and struggles for power characterized them, as there were bitter enemies within the various groups. There were right-wingers like Mario Garcia Kohly, who had prospered under Batista. They had little tolerance for the exiles who had supported Castro and had chased them out. Conversely, the one-time Castro supporters, who vividly recalled how BRAC had terrorized them while Batista was in power, hated the Batistaites. Many had lost family members at the hands of this notorious group. Others among the exiles, like Carlos Prio, had reason to distrust both the Batistaites and the ex-Castro supporters. Mixed in were drug traffickers and gangsters who had lost a small fortune when the casinos were closed in Cuba. They were now offering financial assistance to various exile groups in the hope of returning to Cuba once again. Also filtered in were American paramilitary types and agents of Castro who had infiltrated the exiles.

When Howard Hunt entered the picture the exiles were mismanaged, in total disarray, and going in various directions. One of his initial responsibilities was to establish a Cuban government in exile. The right-winger Hunt steadfastly maintained a desire to form a new government made up of Batistaites alone. His choice to take over for Castro was a Batista follower named Dr. Antonio Rubio Padilla, who also happened to be a close friend of William Pawley. However, William Wieland intervened once more, and the new exile government became more liberal than Howard Hunt and the conservatives would have liked. The new Cuban government in exile was called The Cuban Revolutionary Front (FRD). It consisted of ex-Castro supporters such as Jose Miro Cardona, Castro's first Prime Minister, and Manuel Artime. They had fought against Batista and joined forces with Castro three days before the overthrow of Batista. Artime eventually fled Cuba and formed the Movement of Revolutionary Recovery (MRR) to fight against Castro from the U.S. Another member was Jose Ignacio, the leader of the Christian Democratic Movement.[43]

Also represented in the Frente were one-time members of the Prio government. Justo Carrillo had been president of the Bank for Industrial Development. Aureliano Sanchez Arango had been the Foreign Minister and present leader of the exile group known as Triple A, and Tony Varona had been Prio's Prime Minister. Noticeably absent from this collection was Mario Garcia Kohly or any other supporter of Batista.[44]

In May 1960, Castro's Minister of Public Works, Manuel Ray, broke away from the Cuban government and went underground. He escaped to the United States in November, clinging to the original goals of the revolution. His leftist leanings posed a more significant threat to conservatives than any other leader in the exile community.

While the CIA task force was getting its ducks in a row establishing an anti-Batista Cuban government in exile and invasion force, it propelled ardent right-wingers like William Pawley and Richard Nixon to pursue a different agenda. "Find me one man, just one man who can go it alone and get Castro," Pawley told a Miami newsman shortly after Castro's takeover. "I'll pay anything—almost anything."[45]

Pawley's circle of associates included business people who had lost a fortune in Cuba, like his friend, Dr. Antonio Rubio Padilla, mentioned above. Another was Frank Bartes, a wealthy Cuban exile whose company, Consolidated Railways of Cuba, had employed thousands of pre-Castro Cubans, with assets of $100 million, until Castro nationalized it in 1960. Frank Sturgis associate Gerry Patrick Hemming knew Bartes and described him as ". . . a very distinguished guy, a close friend of Bill Pawley. He was of Spanish descent, very patrician . . . a goddamn aristocrat. The guy is honorable."[46]

What made Bartes a person of interest was his association with Oswald during the summer of 1963 in New Orleans. On August 12 of that year, he was at the courthouse during Oswald's trial for his involvement in a street altercation, which occurred after Oswald handed out Fair Play for Cuba fliers in front of Clay Shaw's International Trade Mart building. After the trial, Bartes stood on the courthouse steps as the media surrounded Oswald looking for a statement. Bartes was visibly upset and chastised the media, telling them they ignored the anti-Castro Cuban perspective. Bartes also talked to an FBI agent that day and told him Oswald was a dangerous man, but he did not disclose that he was an FBI informant himself, which was strange. Then, a month later, on September 9, the FBI interviewed Bartes again regarding potential Communist activity in New Orleans. When Oswald's name came up, Bartes told the FBI agents that Oswald was unknown to him, which was a blatant lie.

Bartes was also a CIA contact asset. CIA files show that on January 4, 1961, the Operational and Support Division asked the Office of Security for a check on Bartes for use in a "contact and assessment" role in the area "WH [Western Hemisphere] Cuba."[47]

One wonders why it was necessary for the well-connected Bartes to deny any knowledge of Oswald over two months before the assassination. The accused killer of the president was still relatively unknown and admitting that he knew Oswald would not have placed Bartes in jeopardy. That is unless the right-wing Cuban exile, FBI informant, and CIA asset already knew more about Oswald than he let on.[48]

Perhaps an answer was provided by author Alan Jules Weberman, who points out in his book, *The Oswald Code*, that the name "Bardes" appeared in Oswald's notebook. Considering that Oswald was a notoriously bad speller, he must have meant Bartes when he wrote Bardes. It possibly proves that Bartes and Oswald were well-acquainted long before JFK's assassination, for why else would Oswald have written Bartes' name in his notebook?[49]

Joan Mellen wrote that Frank Bartes, whose real name was Francisco Bartes Clarens, was a CIA mercenary who flew murderous missions for the Agency in the Congo. Amazingly, Bartes' cousin was Dr. Frank Silva. As described in Chapter

One, he studied at Tulane and was involved in drug experimentation on unsuspecting patients at East Louisiana State Hospital. He had a conversation with Oswald in the hospital lobby in the late summer of 1963. He had also attended a party at the home of Dr. Robert Heath, with whom he had co-authored a paper on LSD and mind control experimentation. Sergio Arcacha Smith was also at the party and would know Frank Bartes from their shared interest in anti-Castro activity in New Orleans. Was this additional proof that there was a connection between Oswald and drug experimentation that somehow involved the New Orleans anti-Castro community? And can it be written off as another strange coincidence that Oswald would meet two cousins, in places roughly a two-hour drive apart, where one of the cousins, Silva, was a psychiatrist involved in mind-altering drug testing? And the other cousin, Bartes, was an FBI informant and CIA asset connected to anti-Castro Cubans in New Orleans, whose name appeared in Oswald's notebook. It could not have been. It was a right-wing connection that brought Oswald into their presence. It is an allegation also supported by the fact that Bartes associated with William Pawley. And what Pawley was involved in with Cuban exiles warrants further examination as well.[50]

* * *

By September 1959, the month after the American embassy in Havana's coup failed to overthrow Castro, William Pawley was contacted at his Miami office by Cuban exiles interested in organizing an invasion of Cuba to regain their country. Pawley had lost a fortune when Castro came to power, and the Cuban exile community was well aware of Pawley's desire to remove Castro. Pawley notified J.C. King, and the CIA subsequently installed a listening device in Pawley's office to monitor what the Cubans had to say when they returned. It is not surprising that Pawley and King already knew each other, considering how far-right and anti-Castro each man was. Pawley was then issued a covert security approval by the CIA to "assist WH [Western Hemisphere] Division by making available . . . reports of conversations held by Mr. Pawley at Miami, Florida, with his contacts among Caribbean revolutionary groups, especially anti-Castro Cuban exile leaders."

Pawley had been involved in the war against Castro even before Batista was overthrown, to the extent that Eisenhower wanted to appoint him Undersecretary in Latin American Affairs. "I told Secretary [of State] Herter that if I was to be put off on this matter again, I wanted to have some very convincing reason," Ike wrote in his diary. Pawley was not given the appointment because of pushback from the State Department. However, it still demonstrated how Pawley was part of Eisenhower's inner circle trying to remove Castro from power. What concerned the State Department was the type of Cubans to which Pawley was aligned. According to the notes taken by White House staff secretary Andrew Goodpaster, during a June 10 meeting with the President, Herter told Ike that ". . . William Pawley had been working with a right-wing group of Cubans, including former Batista police. The CIA is working with former Castro people who have left . . . [Castro because] he has 'betrayed the revolution.' Their work will be spoiled . . . if this right-wing group can show US support . . ." Ike then told Herter to tell Pawley "to get out of this operation."[51]

Undeterred, Pawley secretly contacted Nixon, who shared his view that ex-Batista followers should head the new Cuban government. And even though the CIA was placating the State Department by restricting the operation to ex-Castro Cuban exiles, Pawley did not give up. "I'm in touch with Allen Dulles' people almost daily," Pawley wrote Nixon after Ike dismissed him. "And things are shaping up reasonably well . . . [Killing Castro] is a very delicate problem, and . . . so as not to affect our . . . political [presidential] campaign," they should be careful to ensure this was not made known.

Pawley remained determined. The night before an Organization of American States (OAS) meeting in Costa Rica, he complained that the group was ready to condemn Trujillo while letting the Communist Castro go forward without repercussions. "It seems that the American government is sympathetic to dictators to the left and is only too ready to condemn dictators to the right," Pawley said, "even though in many cases dictators to the right practice greater human rights." He would reiterate his support for Trujillo while testifying before a Senate subcommittee the following month. Still, not everyone agreed that right-wing dictators had a place in the war against Castro.[52]

Much to Nixon's chagrin, the Cuban invasion did not occur before the presidential election, so he did not receive the much-needed bump he needed. CIA had dragged its feet, saying there was a problem with airdropping equipment to the rebel underground inside Cuba and something else had to be changed to get the underground what they needed. It is possible that CIA liberals purposely delayed the invasion to ensure that the right-wing Nixon would lose, knowing that Eisenhower and Nixon would both introduce the U.S. military, if required, to guarantee the operation's success. And at the same time, the CIA kept presidential candidate Kennedy informed, which hurt Nixon during their debates. Why was this done? Recall Allen Dulles' sabotage of the 1959 coup orchestrated by the Embassy cabal to prevent a left-wing Cuban exile government from taking over in Cuba, which was not to the CIA's liking. Or the fear that an invasion of Cuba might spark a Soviet retaliation against West Berlin. Perhaps the same thing happened here. Dulles once again sabotaged the operation. It is just conjecture, but it would explain why the CIA seemed to favor Kennedy over Nixon, a decision which has always been hard to understand. The Agency considered the risks of a Nixon Presidency far outweighed the rewards, especially as it applied to Cuba.

Despite these setbacks, Pawley intended to do something, so he asked J.C. King, who remained out of the Cuban operation, to provide him with an army technical manual on demolition that he could give to one of his Cubans exile groups. Jose A. Benitez, the former Chairman of the Democratic State Committee of Puerto Rico, recommended that Pawley contact Capt. Eladio Del Valle, an ex-Congressman and former Cuban police officer under Batista, was active in the Free Cuba Committee, created by Sergio Arcacha Smith. As we know, Arcacha's associates included Guy Banister, David Ferrie, and Lee Oswald. And as previously discussed, D.A. Henry Wade may have been right when he said Oswald belonged to "Free Cuba," which may have been a reference to Arcacha's Free Cuba Committee, which included del Valle. And this would not be surprising, considering the relationship between del Valle and David Ferrie.

On February 22, 1967, the police found Del Valle's body with a shot in the heart, and his head split open with an ax, violently murdered. David Ferrie died in his apartment on the same day. Jim Garrison was trying to locate del Valle to be a witness in the Clay Shaw trial. Del Valle was also close to Trafficante, and reportedly the two smuggled drugs into the United States from Cuba together. "Captain Del Valle has 150 men . . . ," Benitez's letter to Pawley said. "They are well equipped with arms. . . . His theory is that different battlefronts should be opened . . . directed by people who know about military movements. . . . With your help, Captain Del Valle can make bigger movement than the one he is ready to launch."[53]

Pawley likely took Benitez's advice, for someone like del Valle would have appealed to him. During a November 29 meeting at the White House, he told Eisenhower that "the effort in training..the people [Cuban exiles] in Guatemala was too slow and . . . going backward[ ]." Increasing the size of the Cuban invasion was necessary, but what concerned Pawley was the make-up of the Cuban exile provisional government. They were too far to the left. Pawley made a list of prominent Cubans he felt "could . . . function as one in the interest of the overthrow of Castro." However, Howard Hunt cautioned him not to push too hard to include right-wing Cubans, fearing this would alienate the State Department and the liberal element within the CIA. The feeling was that Pawley was unaware the Cubans he supported were already "dead but did not know it."

Kennedy's victory over Nixon guaranteed that Kohly's underground would not be part of Cuba's operation. It was no longer as important as it once was; the CIA drastically changed the invasion plan four days before the election. The Agency ordered a reduction in the guerrilla force, and from that point on, it was to be a World War II-type amphibious landing. Richard Bissell was responsible for the change, and no longer was an internal underground an essential part of the plan. It is hard to understand because they all knew, including Bissell, that the operation would not succeed without an active underground inside Cuba unless they could rely upon American airpower. And this was unlikely to be approved. Once again, it seemed as if the CIA was looking to sabotage the operation.[54]

With the election of John Kennedy, the American support of the Cuban invasion remained loyal to the leftist ex-Castro supporters. Nowhere was this more evident than with the arrest of Rolando Masferrer just before the Bay of Pigs invasion.
Recall that Masferer was the head of the notorious Los Tigres under Batista. U.S.
authorities apprehended him after Robert Kennedy received a letter from Secretary
of State Dean Rusk. Rusk stated that "The continued presence at large of Rolando
Masferrer . . . is prejudicial to our national interest from the point of view of our
foreign relations." Two days later, the United States charged Masferrer with conspiring to send a military expedition against Cuba. It was a violation of neutrality laws
and an incredibly arrogant charge, considering the Bay of Pigs invasion, which also
violated neutrality laws, was only a few days away. Authorities sent Masferrer to a
detention camp in Texas, where he stayed until ten days after the invasion was over.
He was then quietly released, and they dropped all charges against him. It was a
graphic example for the right-wing and former Batistaites of how isolated they had
become from plans to remove Castro from power.[55]

As the Bay of Pigs invasion approached, Howard Hunt did all he could to create discord among the liberal leaders of the Frente, the Cuban government in exile.
In response to Hunt, in March 1961, with the invasion a month away, the left-
leaning Bissell inexplicably ordered the removal of Hunt and replaced the Frente
with the CRC (Cuban Revolutionary Council), which was even further to the left
than the Frente had been. Others in the exile community accused the CRC of being
Communists. Unlike his right-wing CIA colleagues, Bissell supported a left-wing
anti-Castro invasion force.

Miro Cardona, Castro's first Premier, was named to head the CRC. Manuel
Ray, Castro's former Minister of Public Works, was named Chief of Sabotage and
Internal Affairs. Tony Varona was Secretary of War; Antonio Maceo was named
Secretary of Health, and Justo Carillo was named Economic Administrator. Manuel Artime, Howard Hunt's close friend, who was far too conservative for the CRC,
managed to survive the transition. His responsibility was to lead the invasion, but
the CRC restricted Artime's usefulness to the battlefield alone. The CRC would not
grant Artime a position in the new Cuban government.[56]

Not one to give up easily, Mario Garcia Kohly and his conservative supporters
at the CIA had a plan to prevent ex-Castroites from taking over the new government. Before the 1960 election, there was a meeting between Kohly, his case officer
Tracy Barnes, CIA Deputy General Charles Cabell, and Vice President Nixon. And
according to Robert Morrow, the outcome of this gathering was a plan that became
known as Operation 40, and the significant points were chilling. The idea was for
Kohly to take over Cuba once the Cuban exile invaders had successfully established
a beachhead on the island. Meanwhile, the leftist Cuban government in exile was
held prisoner in the United States by the CIA until it was safe to bring them to
Cuba. Once on the island, Operation 40, Kohly's men, would murder the entire

group. Morrow was told of the plan by Tracy Barnes and received corroboration with a deathbed statement from Kohly in 1975 and a notarized affidavit by Kohly's son, Mario Jr.[57]

One cannot fathom that the murder of the Cuban government in exile could have been a viable option, even in a world where anything was acceptable in the war against communism. However, as incredible as it may seem, there is corroboration. Shortly after the invasion began, the CRC leaders were flown to Miami and kept in a deserted house at an old, abandoned airfield against their will. The CIA held them there under armed guard. Howard Hunt said that ". . . for both personal and operational security, those who wanted to learn the assault plans—and be flown to the beachhead—would have to agree to isolation from the outside world." The CRC did not see it that way and was furious over the detention. Antonio Varona accused his captors of "treason."[58]

There is additional corroboration. Arthur Schlesinger Jr. wrote a memo to Richard Goodwin, a JFK's Task Force member on Latin American Affairs, about Operation 40, which stated that "liberal Cuban exiles believe that the real purpose of Operation 40 [after the Bay of Pigs invasion was to] kill Communists—and, after eliminating hard-core Fedalistas . . . to eliminate first the followers of [Manuel] Ray, then the followers of [Tony] Varona and finally to set up a right-wing dictatorship, presumably under [Manuel] Artime." Not surprisingly, there is also documentation reporting that David Morales was involved with Operation 40 as well.[59]

There was also the recollection of Gerry Patrick Hemming regarding Orlando Piedra, a Cuban exile close to Sergio Arcacha Smith and whose name was also in Oswald's notebook after the assassination. "Piedra was a Godfather kind of guy who had a private detective agency," said Hemming. "Very personable. He belonged to the Junta of National Liberation. William K. Harvey's people supported it . . . ," and Harvey "was setting up this team of people . . . call[ed] OPERATION FORTY . . . They were setting up this team of people to eliminate Fidelista without Fidel, like Manuel Ray. They were to eliminate everybody if accidentally the former Castro people got into power militarily, or civilly, during the anarchy that would follow a victory over Castro. Frank Sturgis was kept on tap to blow a few fucking people away. It was an extension of ZR RIFLE. Ethnic cleansing of the new government after the Bay of Pigs . . . These people were fucking war criminals . . ."[60]

The failure at the Bay of Pigs meant the CIA did not transport the CRC to Cuba. And although the circumstantial evidence is strong, there is no definitive proof that the murder of the government in exile by Operation 40 was part of the plan. Still, with so much corroboration, including a respected person like Arthur Schlesinger, if the operation were successful, it likely would have occurred. There was no limit to what these people were capable of.

Robert Morrow continued to work closely with Kohly. On October 2, 1963, the two men attempted to flood the Cuban economy with counterfeit pesos, but their arrest ended to the plan. Morrow's information has generally proven to be credible, and he has demonstrated he was privy to sensitive information that only a CIA insider would know. It does not prove that Operation 40 was going to kill the CRC. However, the only way for Batistaites to take control of the new Cuban government was to eliminate the CRC.

Operation 40 was fully capable of carrying out the mass murder of the CRC as Morrow suggested they intended to do. *The Fish is Red*, written by Warren Hinckle and William Turner, called Operation 40 "the secret police of the Cuban invasion force . . . [with] nonpolitical conservative exile businessmen . . . its hardcore was made up of dice players at the foot of the cross-informers, assassins-for-hire, and mob henchmen whose sworn goal was to make the counterrevolution safe for the comfortable ways of the old Cuba. They were the elite troops of the old guard within the exile movement, who made an effective alliance with CIA right-wingers against CIA liberals . . . to exclude from power any Cubans who wanted, albeit without Castro, Castro-type reforms . . . Their hero was Manuel Artime, who became the CIA's Golden Boy . . ."[61]

Hinckle and Turner said Operation 40 was "a phalanx of right-wing cutthroats who were to follow in the path of the invading brigade . . ." They would then "murder any middle-of-the-road leaders in towns and villages who might object to a restoration of the Batista status quo . . . [and] to purge the Cuban exile ranks of the anti-Castro left, the exponents of Fidelismo sin Fidel. Operation 40 agents spied on their comrades for the CIA. They were the thought police of the Cuban invasion. After the Bay of Pigs, the CIA kept Operation 40 intact in Miami. . . ."[62]

Frank Sturgis later admitted to being a member of Operation 40 and called it a ". . . top-secret government operation who worked for the Central Intelligence Agency . . ." They "train[ed] people to infiltrate a foreign country, to make contact with members of the underground, to make contact with people in the political sector of the government . . . make contact with people in the military sector . . ." There was also "the assassination section, which I was a part of . . . this assassination group would upon orders, naturally, assassinate either members of the military . . . members of the political parties of the foreign country . . . This is what the Operation of 40 was trained for by the Agency . . ."[63]

Operation 40 was no different from the OAS assassins in Europe trying to kill de Gaulle or the Dulles/Donovan stay-behind armies in Europe. The inclusion of Sturgis means the group involved with the U.S. embassy in Havana that tried to orchestrate a coup in the summer of 1959 must have been part of Operation 40 as well. David Morales would undoubtedly have been a logical choice, and perhaps, June Cobb.

* * *

An organization like Operation 40 involved in the war against Castro, as part of the right-wing Fascist effort operating independently of the U.S. government in the failed Bay of Pigs invasion, is well within the realm of possibility. For the operation to have succeeded, U.S. military intervention was required, including bombers, followed by Operation 40 murdering the Cuban government in exile on the beaches of Cuba, then murdering anyone on the island who opposed the return of Batistaites to power. But Kennedy would cancel the air support, which doomed the operation. The radical right would not forget.

After the Bay of Pigs, right-wingers in the private sector became involved in the effort to oust Castro, with assassination an acceptable option to bring this about. And if they could not accomplish that, perhaps the answer was to have a Castro sympathizer murder an American of sufficient importance, such as JFK, whose death would be the impetus for a full military invasion of Cuba.

As mentioned in the previous chapter, the Omega Plan was the second invasion of Cuba involving the U.S. military that was to occur in December 1963. Consider that in May 1963, roughly seven months after the Cuban Missile Crisis brought the world to the brink of destruction, the Joint Chiefs of Staff recommended that, "The US should . . . at a propitious time, launch appropriate military action to remove the Castro . . . government.."

Opponents thought the Omega Plan was too risky. The military would require a catalyst to justify an invasion of Cuba once again. Eloy Gutierrez Menoyo led the Cuban exile paramilitary group SNFE, involved in the 1959 coup to oust Castro. He was close to the U.S. Embassy group in Havana. According to a chilling CIA memo, Gutierrez said on the day before JFK's assassination that "something very big would happen soon that would advance the Cuban cause."[64] Was the catalyst needed the murder of JFK, done so that the Omega Plan, an invasion of Cuba, and the removal of Castro, could be justified? It is mentioned here as a reminder that as right-wing radicals continued to get ignored and shut out of operations, they would resort to whatever was necessary to ensure their plan came to fruition.

On the other hand, was JFK's assassination and the set up of an alleged Castro supporter named Lee Harvey Oswald designed to take the blame for the murder, to stop the Omega Plan? CIA sabotaged every attempt to kill Castro and takeover Cuba, so it is possible. Could it have been the left-wing at the CIA who killed JFK to stop the right-wing from starting World War III? More about this later.

William Pawley was close to the Cuban Student Directorate (DRE), which was now operating in the United States, and he got Clare Boothe Luce involved with the group in the war against Castro. In the spring of 1963, Clare and her husband Henry actively supported the cause of the Cuban exiles so intensely that they were summoned to the White House by President Kennedy, who wanted them to curtail their fanatical activity. The meeting did not have any effect, for they completely ignored the President. According to reports, an Italian Fascist friend convinced Henry that the best way to topple Castro was to keep the fires burning in the press incessantly.[65]

The reference to Italian Fascists is also interesting considering that the Italian Fascist groups Permindex and Centro Mondiale Commerciale were funding the French OAS generals to assassinate Charles de Gaulle. Recall that Americans like Clay Shaw and Maurice Gatlin were both connected to Permindex and Centro. It meant the entire New Orleans group, which included Guy Banister and David Ferrie. It involved Carlos Marcello, probably Dallas oilmen, their paramilitary associates, and right-wing Fascist groups in Dallas and New Orleans involved with Permindex and the Centro.

In addition to Pawley and the Luces, Frank Sturgis and John Martino were also involved with the Cuban Student Directorate in the months leading up to JFK's assassination and the immediate aftermath to label Oswald a Communist sympathizer. The DRE consisted of right-wing radicals ostracized by the CIA and left out of the Agency's official war against Castro. It was understandable that they would align themselves with American Fascists who operated outside of government control. An FBI report after the assassination stated that the DRE's Miami Chief, Jose Lanusa, "described OSWALD . . . a communist and a supporter of FIDEL CASTRO." Lanusa also claimed that FIDEL CASTRO, in early September at a function at the Brazilian Embassy in Havana, remarked that if the United States causes him difficulty, he has facilities to "knock off" United States leaders.[66]

On January 13, 1967, more than three years after the assassination, one of Jim Garrison's investigators, Frank Klein, interviewed Carlos Quiroga of the DRE. When Klein asked Quiroga what he thought they were looking into, he "answered that he believed that we were investigating the assassination of President Kennedy with relation to David Ferrie. I asked him why he believed this, and he said that Ferrie had called [Carlos] Bringuier, [who was involved in the public altercation with Oswald that led to Oswald's trial where Frank Bartes was present] and told him this after Ferrie was subpoenaed by [the] DA's office . . . He also said that Ferrie is 'plenty scared.'" So, the DRE knew Ferrie and Bringuier, which meant they must have known Bartes as well, while the DRE was close to Pawley, the Luces, Sturgis, and Martino. Another example of how closely intertwined all these right-wing groups were. Be they Americans with money, Cuban exiles, or U.S. paramilitary types.[67]

In January 1977, the HSCA wanted to interview William Pawley because of his close relationship to the Cuban exile community and that he may have been privy to information pertinent to the assassination of JFK. Unfortunately, they never got the chance. That same month, Pawley was found in bed in his Miami Beach mansion with a gunshot wound to his chest. An official inquiry ruled it a suicide.

Carlos Prio was also close to the DRE, having funded the group while Batista was still in power. He was connected to them in the U.S. in the months leading up to the assassination. He was close to Sturgis and a host of others. Two months after the death of Pawley, the HSCA was interested in talking to Prio, but once again, they never had the opportunity. He was also found dead in Miami from a pistol shot. Once again, an investigation ruled it a suicide.

The deaths of Pawley and Prio have fueled speculation that assassins murdered them so they could reveal information that was better kept hidden. It does not prove they were involved in the assassination. However, by the spring of 1963, John Kennedy was perceived to be worse than Castro, for he had abandoned the exiles after leading them to believe he would support them. Both Prio and Pawley were integral parts of that effort, operating outside the CIA's official attempt to remove Castro, and undoubtedly could have known if the hatred of any group was turned from Castro and redirected at JFK. We should not ignore that both were close to the group that Marita Lorenz contended was an active participant in the assassination. Nor should we disregard the fact that members of the Lorenz caravan were part of Operation 40 and that Robert Morrow claimed this group participated in the murder of JFK.

On March 29, 1977, George de Mohrenschildt was also found dead in his home from a gunshot wound to his head, thirteen days after returning to the United States from a trip abroad. An inquiry once again ruled it a suicide. Earlier that day, researcher Edward Jay Epstein interviewed de Mohrenschildt. He told Epstein that he had initially approached Oswald on behalf of J. Walton Moore of CIA's Domestic Contacts Division, which Tracy Barnes ran. Also, that day, Gaeton Fonzi of the HSCA left de Mohrenschildt a message that they wanted to speak with him.

Pawley, Prio, and De Mohrenschildt were all killed mysteriously within two months of each other. We should consider these deaths along with the assassinations of others the CIA wanted to keep quiet. There were suspected Communists within the U.S. government. CIA agents were blackmailed by the Soviets into revealing classified information. Mobsters scheduled to testify in court, who could have admitted their involvement in CIA operations. People like Frank Olson, who was aware of drug experimentation programs, could not be revealed to the general public. And others who knew something about the JFK assassination. It is hard to accept that it was a coincidence. It is undeniable that something sinister was going on throughout the 1950s and 60s. People were dying mysteriously at an alarming rate for no reason other than the CIA could be hurt if they disclosed what they knew. The common thread that joined many together was direct, or at the very least, indirect, connection to JFK's assassination.

Regarding the war against Castro, the facts as the Eisenhower administration came to an end were as follows. Both Eisenhower and Kennedy would keep the military out of the Cuban operation, which infuriated them. The armed forces believed they could get rid of Castro in short order, without much effort, if they were permitted to do so. They would soon set their sights on Vietnam as the place where they intended to fight communism head-on. The right-wing element within the CIA and their pro-Batista Cuban associates also felt betrayed. Ike and JFK kept them out of the Cuban operation, but they had no intention of going down without a fight. It was dangerous business. The military, CIA, right-wing Cuban exiles, Dallas oilmen, Fascist American businessmen, American mercenaries, and paramilitary organizations all believed there was an influx of communism at high levels within the U.S. government, which put the American way of life in jeopardy. These groups repeatedly crossed paths as they worked together on various projects, and all had reasons to rebel against the left-wing establishment. And, perhaps in retaliation, the Omega Plan, which likely would have installed a liberal government in Cuba to placate whoever was President. As a result, the military scrapped the second invasion of Cuba, years after the CIA sabotaged the Bay of Pigs invasion for the same reason.

The assassination of JFK was a right-wing Fascist undertaking that involved Lee Harvey Oswald. Richard Nagell called him the indispensable part of the plan. But it was a complex plan, including characters outside official U.S. government operations, which was the only way the right-wing could achieve what they wanted. It included organized crime elements, which were already associated with the groups listed above in various unsavory operations.

In the late 1950s and early 1960s, the Mafia was involved in the war against Castro and attempted to kill the Cuban leader on the CIA's behalf. Meanwhile, Robert Kennedy was simultaneously investigating them on behalf of the U.S. government. The Mafia felt disrespected, which was something they would not tolerate. Nor would the other groups who thought those in power threatened the American way of life. Recall how often right-wing government overthrows and the assassination of national leaders occurred around the time of Kennedy's assassination. Eventually, something had to give, and considering how commonplace assassination had become, it would not have been hard to redirect one's hatred away from a Cuban dictator toward another perceived dictator, even if that was the President of the United States. All evidence points to this being a radical right-wing murder. However, as we have discussed, JFK's assassination may have been a left-wing conspiracy to prevent the right-wing at the CIA and the military from aggressively carrying out their plan to rid the world of communism. As we move forward and we reveal more facts, who was responsible shall become more apparent. There are many threads to investigate if we want to learn who the likely conspirators were. Some are guilty by association only and had nothing to do with the assassination. Others were aware that JFK was going to be hit but did nothing to stop it. Then there were others who the actual perpetrators set up to blame for JFK's murder because their hatred for JFK made them an easy target. It is a complex investigation. And how organized crime became so disenchanted with the Kennedy brothers is part of that story.

- 5 -

Deadly Liaisons

"I have now learned that one out of every four Presidents dies in office, and I am a gambling man!"

—Senate Majority Leader Lyndon Baines Johnson

During the 1950s, organized crime was still working with the CIA, importing and distributing drugs to finance covert intelligence operations. Crooked Southern politicians, most notably Lyndon Johnson and Texas oilmen, were involved with the mob. Then, Jack Ruby was a busy man, repeatedly traveling to Cuba to get mob boss Santo Trafficante freed from a Cuban prison. Meanwhile, as McClellan Commission Chief Counsel Robert Kennedy grilled the leading Mafia bosses in the country in the late 1950s, his father Joe turned to the Mafia for help to get his other son John elected President. The Mafia obliged. Joe then approached Lyndon Johnson, and he guaranteed LBJ that he could be his son's running mate if he wanted it. Johnson did covet it because he was aware that only one Texan had risen as high as the vice presidency since the Civil War. His best chance of becoming President was to accept the second spot and hope the President died in office. And with Kennedy's victory in 1960, the Mafia, CIA, the military, Texas oilmen, and big business all knew there was someone they could control waiting in the wings, should something happen to JFK.

* * *

There was something peculiar about the relationship between Senator Joseph McCarthy and the Kennedy family. How was it that the anti-Communist bulldog from Wisconsin got along so well with the dynasty of Democrats from Massachusetts? It starts with the Kennedy family patriarch, Joe Sr., and his involvement with McCarthy in numerous unsavory endeavors, including an alleged attempt to undermine Eisenhower and elect McCarthy as President. Perhaps Catholicism brought them together, but there was a more profound connection than simply sharing the same religion. McCarthy socialized with the Kennedys and was a frequent guest at their compound in Hyannis Port. He dated two Kennedy sisters, Eunice and Pat, and would attend Eunice's wedding. There was a relationship between McCarthy and the Kennedy brothers, and both John and Bobby would attend McCarthy's wedding in return.[1]

And the relationship was strong. In 1954 Edward R. Morrow, who had made his famous anti-McCarthy broadcast the previous year, rose to speak at a banquet honoring the Ten Outstanding Men of 1954, including Bobby Kennedy. The future attorney general got up and walked out. Bobby and his wife asked McCarthy to be the godfather of their first child, Kathleen, and he accepted. After McCarthy died, Bobby accompanied his body back to Wisconsin for burial. Brother John was equally supportive. When a vote was taken in the Senate to censure McCarthy, he made sure he was unavailable and did not vote.

Was it possible that the progressive-minded Kennedy brothers leaned more to the radical right than they wanted anyone to believe? Consider some of the speeches John Kennedy made while he was still a Senator. JFK spoke on the Senate floor on June 14, 1960. He said the United States must have ". . . a nuclear retaliatory power second to none." To do this meant "stepping up development and production of the ultimate missiles that can close the gap and will not be wiped out in a surprise attack . . . increasing our production of Atlas missiles, hardening our bases and improving our continental defense and warning systems . . . We must regain the ability to intervene effectively and swiftly in any limited war anywhere in the world . . ."[2]

The previous year, in October 1959, he discussed the importance of conventional forces in a world of nuclear tension, words which were dramatically different from the actions he would later take while President. "No problem is of greater importance to every American than our national security and defense," he said. "And no aspect of our defense capabilities under this [Eisenhower] Administration should be cause for greater concern than our lag in conventional weapons and ground forces . . . our nuclear retaliatory power is not enough. It cannot deter Communist aggression, which is too limited to justify atomic war. It cannot protect uncommitted nations against a Communist takeover using local or guerrilla forces . . . and history demonstrates that this is the greater threat—not an all-out nuclear attack . . . We need tactical atomic weapons . . . to serve as a shield for our conventional forces on the battlefront . . . We need not match the Russians and Chinese man for man . . . but we can build . . . atomic might, conventional forces, and weapons that will prevent any quick Communist takeovers on the ground— enough to let them know that they will be in for a long, costly struggle if they pursue this means of attaining their objectives . . ."[3]

The best nuclear weapons supported by the largest conventional army—that was the defense program Kennedy proposed. It was almost as if Generals Maxwell

Taylor and Lyman Lemnitzer had written the speeches for him. Knowing the relationship between JFK and Senator McCarthy, the military, CIA, and the Fascist
right-wing may have been willing to support a Kennedy presidency, thinking he was
more conservative than he was. And if that were the case, it is safe to assume they
would have felt betrayed if he demonstrated, after being elected, that everything he
claimed to stand for regarding national defense in the 1950s was a bald-faced lie.

* * *

   In December 1952, the Senate Committee on Government Operations named
Robert Kennedy their assistant counsel, which McCarthy headed when he terrorized a large part of the population. When the Democrats regained a Senate majority
in January 1955, Kennedy became the committee's chief counsel, and they began
holding hearings to investigate labor racketeering. Much of what they uncovered
involved the Teamster head, Jimmy Hoffa. On January 30, 1957, the United States
Senate Select Committee on Improper Activities in Labor and Management, commonly known as the McClellan Committee, came into being. Joe McCarthy and
John Kennedy served on this committee, with Robert Kennedy its chief counsel
and investigator. The committee's mandate was to investigate the extent that organized crime had infiltrated labor-management relations. Once again, they focused
on the Teamsters.
   On February 22, working with the FBI, the McClellan Committee broadcast
wiretaps conversations between mobsters Johnny Dio and Hoffa to a nationally
televised audience. Their discussion involved what were known as paper locals, fake
unions that existed on paper only, designed to increase Hoffa's delegate totals. Before that, the hearings had opened with an investigation of corruption in Portland,
Oregon, which included a live television broadcast of tape-recorded conversations
between Portland crime boss Jim Elkins and two Seattle mobsters about a joint
venture to take over Portland's vice operations. A stunned nation learned of a mob-
sponsored plot by Oregon Teamsters to bribe, extort, and blackmail the state's legislature, police, and attorney general's offices.
   The Elkins testimony was critical to the Committee's success, and to a large
extent, their interest in Elkins was due to Joe Kennedy. The eastern Mafia had not
wholly accepted Joe because he was Irish, so he advised his sons to ingratiate themselves with the Elkins family as the McClellan hearings got underway. And Robert
Kennedy heeded his father's advice. In *Enemy Within*, Bobby described Elkins in
favorable terms. He was "a slim, rugged-looking man with a rather kindly face and
a very attractive and devoted wife," and "once he [Elkins] made up his mind that
he was going to co-operate, he went the whole way." However, Bobby left out of
his book the meetings held near Phoenix, Arizona, between the Kennedy brothers,
Elkins, and one other trusted member of the Elkins family. It was there that Elkins
warned the Kennedys to proceed with caution because they could wind up dead if

they went after the Teamsters too hard. The Kennedys said they understood. Once Elkins was confident of their commitment, he gave the brothers the wiretap recordings where mobsters had approached him posing as Teamsters.

Elkins was not a choirboy, which did not seem to matter to RFK. "I learned that [Elkins] had manufactured illicit whiskey during prohibition," Robert Kennedy wrote. He had "been given a twenty-to-thirty-year sentence for assault with intent to kill, a one-year sentence for possession of narcotics, and had been arrested several times on gambling charges." To get out of prison, the Elkins family paid a substantial fifty-thousand-dollar bribe to Arizona's first governor, George W.P. Hunt.[4]

A *Newsweek* article was impressed with Elkins' cooperation and reported that what he provided ". . . made it possible for committee counsel Robert Kennedy to crack the teamster case wide open. Without Elkins, there might have been no indictment of Teamster vice president Jimmy Hoffa. Without Elkins, the Teamsters' powerful president Dave Beck would not be defending himself on the witness stand . . ."[5]

Robert Kennedy's relationship with Elkins would develop into a personal one that was even more strange than what he had with Joe McCarthy. How close were they? Elkins and his family would stay at Kennedy's home in McLean, Virginia, whenever they traveled to Washington, confirmed by a note found in 1986 at the JFK Library in Boston. On December 17, 1957, Elkins sent a Christmas card to Bobby and his family. His wife sent a personal handwritten note addressed to Robert and Ethel Kennedy and family, saying, "We watched Edward R. Murrow's program the night he was at your home," and "we certainly enjoyed it. Jim said it reminded him of 'Old Home week.' The children were just as cute as could be, and the baby had grown, so we hardly knew her."[6]

How does one explain Robert Kennedy's friendship with both McCarthy and Elkins? Was it the previous relationship that each man had with Joe Kennedy that made it possible? Maybe, but it was ill-advised. Bobby was supposed to be a liberal champion of the people, and neither Elkins nor McCarthy cared about what was best for the American people. Even after the hearings, Elkins advised Attorney General Robert Kennedy in his war against organized crime. They shared a mutual hatred for Jimmy Hoffa, which might have been the impetus behind their strange alliance. Elkins allegedly alerted Bobby in 1963 that the word on the street was that the mob intended to assassinate his brother with a high-powered scoped rifle from a tall building while he traveled in a motorcade. Then in 1968, Bobby was supposedly warned by Elkins that there was a hit out on him and that it would occur while he was in Los Angeles during the California presidential primary, which was when RFK's assassination happened. Elkins would also die under suspicious circumstances, on October 17, 1968, when the car he was driving was pushed off the road by another driver. The police never identified the driver.[7]

It was a dangerous game Bobby Kennedy was playing. And it was his father, for his selfish reasons, who was directing him. And Joe should have known better because you did not take on the Mafia and come out unscathed.

* * *

On November 14, 1957, ten months after the McClellan Committee came into being, a secret gathering of over one hundred Mafia bosses took place at a private home in Apalachin, New York. It was inadvertently uncovered by authorities, resulting in the police detaining sixty underworld kingpins. It would result in the indictment of twenty mobsters. The reason for the meeting begins with Vito Genovese. In 1937, he had relinquished his role as acting crime boss of the Luciano crime family to Frank Costello (described in Volume One). Genovese was making waves because he wanted Luciano to reinstate him. Things came to a head on May 2, when Genovese henchman Vincent Gigante shot and wounded Frank Costello outside his New York apartment, which prompted Costello to step down and cede control back to Genovese.

Meanwhile, Albert Anastasia, who had started Murder, Inc., wanted to be the new boss. At the same time, Anastasia tried to muscle in on Meyer Lansky by opening casinos in Havana. On October 25, 1957, most likely at the behest of Santo Trafficante and Vito Genovese, Anastasia was shot and killed in New York City. So, the Apalachin meeting also had to do with the Anastasia murder and the recent Mafia struggle for power.

Santo Trafficante, who was one of those arrested at Apalachin, immediately left the United States after he was released and went to Cuba, fearing he might be charged with Anastasia's murder if he remained behind. Convenient for Trafficante was that the police arrested Genovese and fourteen accomplices that day as well. Genovese would be convicted two years later for conspiring to smuggle heroin into the United States from Cuba, Mexico, and Puerto Rico, leaving Trafficante as the only man standing and the new mob boss.[8]

Jimmy Hoffa also had prison on his mind when he testified before the Mc-Clellan Committee in August 1957, three months before Apalachin. He had been arrested the previous March for trying to bribe the committee. At that time, Robert Kennedy knew that the Teamster boss had paid an attorney named John Cye Cheasty to get a job with the committee to spy on Hoffa's behalf. And when Cheasty handed Hoffa authentic committee documents that March and was given $2,000 by Hoffa in return, the Teamster's head was unaware that Robert Kennedy and the FBI had set him up. The Justice Department would try Hoffa for bribery and conspiracy, but a suspicious not guilty verdict kept him out of jail.

When asked a question during his testimony before the committee in August, Hoffa said he could not remember one hundred and eleven times. Senator McClellan eventually took over the questioning, listing evidence the committee had uncovered regarding Hoffa's wrongdoing, including questionable loans, misuse of union funds, and hiring mobsters and ex-murderers as Teamster employees. In return, Hoffa accused the committee of trying to bust the union.[9]

Based to a large extent on the Apalachin raid, Hoffa's testimony, and the information provided by Elkins, the pressing issue of the McClellan Committee became the relationship between organized crime and the Teamsters union. In January 1958, FBN agent John Cusack told the committee that Joseph Civello, also arrested at Apalachin, ran the Dallas heroin business for Carlos Marcello. Investigators would link Civello to Santo Trafficante and Jimmy Hoffa (The court would eventually sentence Civello to five years for a conspiracy charge stemming from the Apalachin meeting, but in 1961 the conviction was reversed on appeal). And with the introduction of Cusack's testimony, there was no doubt that organized crime existed in the United States. As a result, in February 1959, the committee began to focus more on organized crime, which resulted in public hearings involving some of the country's leading Mafioso.

Price Daniel, the junior senator from Texas, was controlled by the senior senator, Lyndon Johnson, to the extent that Daniel's staff worked out of Johnson's office. In 1956, Senator Daniel investigated drug trafficking in Texas. Critics severely criticized him for recommending stiff jail sentences for convicted drug users, while those at the top making millions remained untouchable. Robert Kennedy watched as Daniel, who had authored a report about drug trafficking along the Mexican border and the Gulf Coast, protected Joe Civello and failed to expose his involvement in the narcotics trade. Bobby realized that local politicians such as LBJ and Daniel protected the Mafia in Texas and Louisiana, and he intended to do something about it.

But other witnesses who testified revealed Marcello's involvement in the French Connection drug operation and other criminal activity, including illegal gambling, prostitution, bribery of government officials, terrorizing honest business people, and a host of other offenses. Senators on the committee questioned why Marcello, who was subject to deportation from the United States since 1953 because of a felony conviction, was still in the country. Senator Sam Ervin of South Carolina accused Marcello of preying "upon law-abiding people [and he] ought to be removed."[10] It was the beginning of a concerted effort to have Marcello deported.

The committee called Sam Giancana to testify on June 9, 1959. "Would you tell us, if you have opposition from anybody, that you dispose of them by having them stuffed in a trunk? Is that what you do, Mr. Giancana?" Robert Kennedy asked. He questioned the mobster about a deputy county prosecutor and four unsolved murders in Chicago that Giancana may have been responsible for, including a man who held Giancana's $100,000 mortgage on a hotel. The mobster just smiled and took the Fifth. "Is there something funny about it, Mr. Giancana?" Kennedy asked again. "Would you tell us anything about any of your operations, or will you just giggle every time I ask you a question? I thought only little girls giggled, Mr. Giancana."[11]

In July 1959, FBN Agent Ike Wurms told the committee that Teamster official Abe Gordon had laundered drug profits through a union welfare fund. Carlo Gambino was involved with the Teamsters through his labor-consulting firm in Manhattan. And Jimmy Hoffa had protected Detroit's major drug traffickers John Priziola and Raffaele Quasarano, by assigning them to Teamsters Local 985. In addition, Marcello was involved with the Teamsters and the Longshoremen's unions in Louisiana, and Trafficante had an office at a Teamsters Local in Miami. Without question, there was a connection between the Mafia and the Teamster.[12]

As Robert Kennedy listened to the testimony of witnesses, he began to understand how far the tentacles of organized crime had spread throughout the world. Like the Teamsters, the Mafia was an international brotherhood, which became apparent as the McClellan Committee learned of the Corsican and Sicilian involvement in cities like Havana, Montreal, and Mexico City, in the French Connection operation.[13]

A person of interest for Robert Kennedy and the committee was the Corsican drug trafficker Antoine D'Agostino. D'Agostino smuggled drugs with Paul Mondoloni as part of the French Connection operation until both men were arrested in Mexico by federal authorities in the early 1950s. Mondoloni, whose name was used as an alias by Jean Lafitte, like so many others, managed to quickly get released from incarceration and, shortly after that, left Mexico and settled in Cuba. D'Agostino was not as fortunate. He was held in San Antonio, then transferred to an Austin jail located within blocks of Senator Daniel's committee, before which D'Agostino was supposed to testify. The FBN had advised Daniel during the initial Washington hearings that the prisoner was a person of importance. However, Daniel elected not to have D'Agostino interviewed during the televised hearings, which would have provided invaluable details regarding Civello's heroin operation. Instead, Daniel waited until the hearings were over and interviewed D'Agostino privately in his Austin jail cell, and what they discussed would be left out of Daniel's report. Whether or not the McClellan Committee knew about this is unknown. Still, it was another example that Texas politicians were in bed with organized crime, and the two groups would do anything to protect each other.[14]

Meanwhile, Robert Kennedy learned that Civello's Texas mob was part of the Marcello crime family. It led to Marcello's subpoena to testify before the Committee. "Are you an associate of Joseph Civello of Dallas?" Kennedy asked Marcello. To which the Louisiana mobster responded by taking the Fifth.

The Committee would learn that Civello had numerous ties to the drug cartel that operated in the northeast part of the United States and Canada, including John Ormento and the Magaddino family in Buffalo, with connections in Marseilles, New York City, Tampa, Havana, and Mexico City. That D'Agostino and

Mondoloni were crucial members of the French Canadian "Controni mob of Montreal." That "French traffickers . . . found it necessary to establish an operating point in Mexico City because of seizures in . . . Montreal . . . ," and that the Marcello and Civello mob families were Mondoloni's connection in southern Texas. The pieces of the puzzle began to come together for Kennedy and the committee. However, they were still unaware that the CIA was involved with organized crime and that the importation of heroin into the U.S. was a vital part of curtailing the spread of communism throughout the Western World. It is understandable for no sane person would have believed that such an alliance could have existed.[15]

The committee also did not know of a relationship between Civello and Jack Ruby, who was relatively unknown in 1959. It was unfortunate, for as they listened to Civello's testimony, the committee searched for the mysterious Jack LaRue, an alias used by a Jimmy Hoffa associate. It all occurred at the same time that Hoffa's mob connections were trying to sell surplus planes to Castro, financed with Teamster money, which would involve Ruby, while Jack Ruby was also trying to sell guns to the new Cuban leader. Jack Ruby was the Jack LaRue the committee was trying to track down.[16]

As author Douglas Valentine asked in *The Strength of the Wolf,* "How could the FBN not know that Ruby was part of Civello's organization, or that the FBI, in 1956, had identified Ruby as a central figure in John Ormento's operation between Texas, Mexico, and New York?" They had to have known the answer, and the only explanation is they did not want to reveal the identity of a valuable informant to the McClellan Committee.[17]

The committee was also unaware that New York mobster Frank Costello was involved in illegal race wires with Bugsy Siegel in Los Angeles in the 1940s. In 1947 Siegel was murdered, so Costello partnered with mobster Mickey Cohen, whose attorney was Melvin Belli, who represented Jack Ruby for killing Oswald. Reporter Dorothy Kilgallen, who curiously was a friend of Costello's in New York, had private conversations with Ruby, arranged by Belli, during Ruby's trial for killing Oswald. Exactly what Ruby told Kilgallen is unknown. In November 1965, someone murdered her, in her apartment, under suspicious circumstances. Her notebook, which contained information about her discussions with Ruby, mysteriously vanished before she could disclose what she knew. But it was well known to her friends that she was investigating the JFK assassination, and she claimed that she was going to break the case wide open after making a trip to New Orleans. A city, as we have shown, with a solid connection to JFK's murder. But that would all be in the future. In 1959, while the committee was still in session, Costello's partner Mickey Cohen was also running guns to Cuba, and "Ruby told one of his business partners . . . he was a close friend of Mickey Cohen." In addition, the FBI would document numerous ties between Ruby and Cohen's girlfriend, stripper Candy Barr.[18]

How significant were Cohen and Barr? In the 1970s, the House Select Committee on Assassinations said there were "a mobster and a stripper" who could add critical information regarding the assassinations of JFK and RFK. It was Cohen and Barr to whom they referred.

Barr was a well-known stripper who performed in Dallas at two establishments near Jack Ruby's Carousel Club. Ads in the *Dallas Morning News* said she danced at Ruby's Colony Club in 1956 until authorities charged her with attempted murder for shooting her estranged husband in the abdomen. Mob-friend and future Ruby prosecutor Henry Wade dismissed the charges. Then in 1957, Barr was arrested for drug possession. During the trial, Judge Joe Brown, who would preside at Ruby's trial, denied the defense's request to prove the police entrapped her. During final arguments, prosecutor Bill Alexander, who would be the chief prosecutor during the Ruby trial, told the jury, "[Candy] may be cute, but under the evidence, she's soiled and dirty." She was convicted and sentenced to fifteen years in prison, despite having no prior convictions. In 1959, while Candy was free on a $15,000 bond and performing in Las Vegas, Mickey Cohen came to her aid, saying he had retained attorney Melvin Belli to appeal to the United States Supreme Court to have her sentence reversed. Cohen even agreed to marry her, but all appeals failed, and Barr entered Goree State Farm for Women in Huntsville, Texas. She would serve three years and ninety-one days until Governor John Connally approved her bid for parole, the same John Connally who sat in front of John Kennedy in the limousine motorcade during JFK's assassination.

Connally was close to Lyndon Johnson and was a typical Texas politician who somehow thought it was necessary to parole a stripper with mob connections. Perhaps it was an indication that the mob owned Connally, just like they did LBJ.

Amazingly, while Ruby was in jail awaiting his trial for killing Oswald, he wanted to hire Barr as a stripper at his club, going so far as to contact authorities to try and get the terms of Barr's parole changed so she could strip again. It went nowhere, for she turned Ruby down, but why all this attention from the imprisoned Jack Ruby? Didn't he have more important things on his mind? Barr said Ruby began acting like her big brother, buying her presents and giving her money. Was there something related to Barr that Jack Ruby felt guilty about, or did Barr know something that Ruby wanted to keep hidden?

On November 25, 1963, in an article in the *Dallas Morning News*, Barr compared Ruby and Oswald. She called Ruby a "good-natured heavyweight," while Oswald "dripped with political venom with a narrow group of acquaintances." How did she know this about Oswald, that he had a narrow group of acquaintances, three days after the assassination, at a time when newspapers were calling him a loner? Was it possible that she had met Oswald through Ruby before the assassination? Was this why Ruby tried to get her reinstated as a stripper so she would keep quiet about what she knew? We know numerous eyewitnesses saw Oswald at Ruby's

Carousel Club. If Barr also saw Oswald and Ruby together, it would destroy Ruby's claim that his desire to murder Oswald was spontaneous and not deliberate. If this were true, Ruby's only chance of getting out of jail hinged on Barr remaining quiet.

The article also referenced a call Ruby made to Barr shortly before JFK's assassination, where Ruby "was trying to get in touch with Mickey Cohen . . ." According to author John H. Davis, "Ruby often boasted of his friendship with . . . Cohen and took pride in the fact that he had had an affair with a woman [Barr] who had been engaged to the Los Angeles mobster." Davis also wrote that "It was no more than ten hours after Ruby's shooting of Oswald that the FBI came to interrogate Juanita [Candy Barr] concerning her part in an alleged plot to kill the president. The interrogation went on hour after hour." The FBI was aware of the Ruby/Cohen/ Barr connection immediately after the Dallas police arrested Ruby. They believed Barr knew something, while J. Edgard Hoover was saying the Bureau had to convince the public that Oswald was the lone assassin. The FBI had no choice but to let it go.

As described in *The Poison Patriarch, How The Betrayals of Joseph P. Kennedy Caused the Assassination of JFK*, Bill Alexander told author Mark Shaw he "understood that Belli had told Cohen that he, Belli, could fix the Barr case through Judge Brown." In his book, *Dallas and the Jack Ruby Trial*, Brown would write that "my first contact with Melvin Belli . . . had occurred five years [before the Ruby trial]. Then, "When a Dallas bondsman went off [Candy's] bond, and a warrant went out for Candy's arrest, her gangster boyfriend, Mickey Cohen, telephoned me. I refused to talk to him."[19]

When Joseph Civello was found guilty of conspiracy and obstruction following the raid at Apalachin, the presiding judge at the time said that Civello needed to be "segregated from society . . . he is a high-ranking criminal who cloaked himself with the facade of legitimate business." For his appeal, Civello hired Percy Foreman, who had already gained notoriety for representing none other than Candy Barr. Foreman somehow obtained a reversal of Civello's conviction.[20]

By the time of JFK's assassination, there was, to put it nicely, an understanding between mobsters, drug traffickers, gun smugglers, and Dallas legal professionals, and in the middle of it all was Jack Ruby. Local authorities knew much of what Ruby was engaged in, yet they hid this information from the McClellan investigation. It was hard to differentiate between the good guys and the bad guys in the city of Dallas.

The committee would also learn that the drug smuggling operation involving D'Agostino, Mondoloni, Civello, and Marcello included Santo Trafficante. They wanted to question the Tampa mobster about this and the murder of Albert Anastasia. But he remained in Cuba. The committee had to settle for the testimony of the Miami Crime Commission chief, who described Trafficante's heroin network in detail, including his mob's unsolved "twenty-one gang killings" over twenty years.

Then, in a demonstration of total defiance, on the day before the chief's testimony, Trafficante ordered another mob hit, and Robert Kennedy had to reveal that "there was another one [murdered] yesterday." If they did not know it before, it became clear to the committee that they were dangerous and played for keeps.[21]

* * *

By 1960, Arizona mobster and CIA asset Joe Bonanno had a connection to Trafficante and Marcello. He was offered protection from prosecution by the Agency if he was willing to perform some delicate tasks. According to author Seymour Hersh, Bonanno had access to Richard Bissell during the period leading up to the Bay of Pigs invasion, always secretly calling him on an outside line. He would eventually write a letter to Bissell saying he was willing to do what Bissell "wanted him to do," which was having people killed. The Mafia "soldiers" who worked for Mafia Capo Joseph Zicarelli were the ones who were to carry out assassinations for Bonanno on Bissell's behalf. Zicarelli was a busy man, for, with the help of CIA asset Robert Maheu, he was involved in the Dominican Republic, selling Trujillo guns and reportedly murdering one of Trujillo's political opponents in New York.

As might be expected, Zicarelli had political protection in the execution of his unsavory operations. Initially, it was through his Congressman, Cornelius E. Galagher. However, the CIA would eventually come to his rescue when the Agency granted him temporary immunity from prosecution on the federal narcotics charges he faced. It was unfortunate for the FBN, for Zicarelli had recently replaced Carmine Galante as the Bonanno family's narcotics manager, and they had their eye on him. The FBN knew what Zicarelli was involved in—murder, drug trafficking, and selling guns to anti-Castro Cuban exiles and their supporters—but they were powerless to do anything about it. They knew of the relationship with the CIA, which meant Bonanno, Zicarelli, and their minions were untouchable, whether the FBN liked it or not. FBN head Harry Anslinger would complain about "higher authorities" (i.e., CIA) within the U.S. government subverting a grand jury in a case involving top mobsters because "delicate investigations conducted by another government agency were underway." It was "a dodge to call us off, and it succeeded," Anslinger complained. [22]

As the relationship between the CIA and the Mafia became even more prolific, Miami became inundated with CIA front companies, questionable assets and informers, and paramilitary types looking for a moment of glory in support of their country for a price. Wealthy right-wing supporters like William Pawley and Henry Luce continued to provide financing. Still, it was not enough, which was why Paul Helliwell, who had set up the drug-financed stay behind army operation for Dulles and Donovan in Europe, entered the picture again.

At the time, Helliwell was general counsel for the Thai Consulate in Miami and active in Florida's Republican Party, which undoubtedly was how he knew to contact William Pawley. He was also a friend of Bebe Rebozo, who was a close confidant of Richard Nixon. Helliwell recreated what he had done previously for the CIA, setting up banks in Miami to launder drug money and finance the Agency's war against communism in Latin America. Meanwhile, the World Commerce Corporation, which staunch Republican William Donovan had founded, was doing the same thing in Panama, even though Donovan was no longer officially involved with U.S. intelligence. The same applied to Richard Greenlee in Honduras, who was part of Donovan's law firm and a former OSS officer in Bangkok under him.[23]

Then, Meyer Lansky tried to reestablish his gambling business with Louis A. Chesler and Wallace Groves. Chesler was a Canadian millionaire and former rumrunner who made a fortune in Florida land deals, then moved to Freeport in the Bahamas and formed the Grand Bahama Development Company in 1961 with Groves. They employed the expertise of Helliwell and Donovan, using Asian drug money allegedly invested in Florida real estate deals through Chesler's General Development Company. With Lansky financier John Pullman, they incorporated the bank of World Commerce in the Bahamas to handle the skim from several Las Vegas casinos. It led to Pullman merging his Atlas bank with Itrabank in Beirut. Palestinian Youseff Beidas established Intrabank. Several Arab nations under the direction of a Saudi Arabian arms trader financed the bank, including a Lansky drug smuggling Corsican contact named Marcel Francisci. Intrabank's Bahamian branch and those mentioned above in Latin America laundered Mafia gambling and drug money with the full knowledge of the CIA.[24]

The bottom line is that in 1959, Robert Kennedy and the McClellan Committee only scratched the surface of Teamster and Mafia operations involving drug deals, arms trafficking, and other illegal activity. Unaware of the CIA's involvement in all this, the committee had no way of knowing how complex the actual operations were. And while the committee was investigating organized crime, U.S. intelligence was employing their services in an international, multi-nation network that included politicians worldwide who were in the pocket of organized crime and did all they could to protect the mobsters. The mob did not take kindly to betrayal, primarily when they worked with the CIA on behalf of the U.S. government, so pursuing them was a dangerous proposition. The time would come when John Kennedy was President, and they would no longer tolerate the intrusion into their business by a young, upstart attorney general. Something had to give.

* * *

Michael Sindona was an attorney in Italy who gave up his practice during World War II to become a black-market racketeer. By the end of the war, he was a Lucky Luciano/Don Calo crime family member and a leading financial adviser to the Sicilian Mafia. Between 1952 and 1955, he was in New York City, acting as Luciano's emissary to Vito Genovese. He became a CIA operative in 1955, passing money obtained illegally to leading Catholic dignitaries in Italy, including Giovanni Montini, the future Pope Paul VI. At this juncture, Sindona had become an essential cog in the CIA, Mafia, and Vatican machine, and his importance with this group would grow in the coming years.[25]

In October 1957, Sindona attended a mob gathering in Palermo. Luciano, Joe Bonanno, Carmine Galante, and Frank Costello were there, along with the head of the Sicilian families, Don Giuseppe Genco Russo. They created a Sicilian Commission that was to oversee all aspects of the multibillion-dollar international heroin trade. It proved to be a jackpot for Sindona, who completely controlled the cash distribution from American inner cities to the Vatican Bank. Genovese's imprisonment in 1959 in the wake of Apalachin served to propel the rise of Sindona, who, with the blessing of Don Carlo's successor, Giuseppe Genco, and Luciano, became involved with the Gambino crime family.

Sindona began his dirty work almost immediately, using mob and CIA money to create Fasco AG, a Liechtenstein holding company that became the cornerstone of his financial empire. Under the Fasco umbrella, he purchased his first bank, the Banca Privata Finanziaria (BPF) in Milan. It became the primary means of transferring drug money to the stay-behind armies in Europe. CIA's William Harvey arranged for Sir Jocelyn Hambro, the owner of Hambros Bank, and David M. Kennedy, the chairman of Continental Illinois Bank in Chicago, to become minority shareholders in Sindona's operation. Around the same time, Paul Helliwell was busy in Miami establishing banks to service the mob's and CIA's drug laundering needs. Harvey connected Hambro and Kennedy with Sindona to perform the same service.

Hambro was part of England's most prestigious merchant banking families and strongly tied to the intelligence community. He was one of the founders of the OSS during World War II, and he maintained a presence on the board of the World Commerce Company, the organization founded by Bill Donovan.

Meanwhile, Kennedy's Continental Illinois Bank held shares in an Opus Dei bank in Barcelona, and in 1955 he became a "conspicuous friend" of the religious order. As a result, Continental Illinois Bank became the main conduit for the Vatican's real estate and corporate investments, which connected him to Prince Massimo Spada, another Knight of Malta and the lay delegate of the Vatican Bank, as well as Sindona, Spada's assistant. Through Kennedy, Sindona developed a close relationship with Monsignor Paul Marcinkus, aka "the Gorilla." A street brawler, lover of good bourbon, fine cigars, and young woman, he would become Pope Paul VI's assigned protector. Thanks to Sindona, Marcinkus became head of the Vatican Bank. He was now responsible for more than ten thousand accounts belonging to religious orders and private Catholic dignitaries, including the Pope.

Sindona then acquired the Banca of Messina, which gave the Gambino, Inzerillo, and Spatola crime clan unlimited access to a financial firm in Sicily. He then bought a third bank, the Banquet de Financement (Finabank), in Geneva. He used it to move money out of Italy. After Sindona purchased the majority interest, the Vatican retained a twenty-nine percent share, and Hambro and Kennedy kept the remaining portion on behalf of their financial firms.

The "Family Jewels," a set of CIA reports under the Freedom of Information Act, shows that Sam Giancana was one of the pivotal figures in this money-laundering operation. Members of the Giancana family made deposits in Continental Illinois, which Continental transferred to Sindona's banks. Giancana's men transported more money to Washington, D.C., to be converted into bonds and forwarded to Finibank in Geneva. Even more money was transported from Chicago to Mexico in suitcases carried by thugs dressed as Catholic priests. A string of shell companies in Panama received the money and sent it to the Vatican Bank. Throughout this process, the CIA worked closely with Archbishop Marcinkus.

While Sindona was purchasing banks with funding from the Mafia, Vatican, and CIA, Paul Helliwell and Meyer Lansky were setting up Castle Bank & Trust in Miami and the Bahamas. Castle Bank became "the conduit for millions of dollars earmarked by CIA for the funding of clandestine operations directed at countries in Latin America and the Far East."[26]

Understanding the Sindona connection is critical. It demonstrates that the relationship between organized crime, the Vatican, and U.S. intelligence, which began in World War II, and in the early 1950s developed into the Helliwell/Luciano/WCC operation, was still active in the early 1960s. Through the auspices of Michael Sindona, it had expanded considerably. It further proves an international network fighting communism around the world existed, and its role remained the same as it always was. It provided funding for projects the CIA needed done without the U.S. Congress knowing about them. The fact that Robert Maheu and Sam Giancana were both involved in this international network is not surprising, considering the operation they were about to embark on together.

* * *

The CIA needed to eliminate Castro in conjunction with their proposed invasion of Cuba if their plan to take over the Cuban government would be successful. As described in Chapter Two, this was something Agency's operatives connected to the U.S. Embassy in Havana attempted to do but were unable to without jeopardizing plausible deniability. Eventually, the CIA turned in a different direction, and once again, it was the American Mafia whom they approached looking for help. "I hoped the Mafia would achieve success," admitted Richard Bissell. "My philosophy during my last two or three years in the Agency was very definitely that the ends justified the means, and I was not going to be held back." It would turn out to be a significant mistake.[27]

The end justifying the means was the CIA's disclaimer that made any operation acceptable, no matter how unsavory. But we should not forget that while Bissell was planning the assassination of Castro, he was very much aware of the nationally televised McClellan hearings and what they were uncovering regarding organized crime. With that in mind, how could he have decided to use the Mafia to kill Castro in total defiance of the U.S. Congress? The only explanation is that men like Bissell believed what they were doing was so important that they were above the law. During the Cold War, right-wing anti-Communist zealots thought they knew better than politicians what was best for the country, and they inundated U.S. intelligence and the military. It was treasonous.

Jim O'Connell was the CIA case officer responsible for coordinating the Castro assassination operation. He would testify to the U.S. Select Committee on Intelligence in 1975 that it began when Bissell approached Colonel Sheffield Edwards, CIA's Chief of Security, asking "whether we [CIA] had any assets" that could handle such an operation. Edwards did have someone specific in mind who already had Agency clearance, whom they had used before for sensitive work and could be trusted to keep silent. "The thing was to get rid of Castro—there was no question of what the assignment was," O'Connell recalled. "Colonel Edwards doesn't mince words; he will [sic] just tell you."[28]

Robert Maheu was the man Sheffield Edwards recommended to O'Connell. A former leading figure at the FBI, Maheu left the Bureau to start his own private investigation company in 1954, Robert A. Maheu Associates. The CIA put him on a retainer of $500/month almost immediately, a sum that exceeded the salary of many full-time agents. His specialty was to handle unsavory cases that the CIA wanted to distance itself from in the event of failure. Prostitution, illegal wiretaps, pornography—nothing was out of the question for Robert Maheu.[29]

An example of his handiwork was producing a pornographic film where a Maheu employee and his wife posed as Tito of Yugoslavia and a female KGB agent in a compromising situation. Similarly, there was a pornographic film that depicted an imposter posing as Sukarno at the time when the Indonesian military was trying to take over the government. In 1959, Maheu arranged for a B-actress to spend time with Jordan's twenty-three-year-old King Hussein at a Long Island beach house, which remained secret until 2017. And, as described above, Maheu was involved with Joseph Zicarelli in selling guns to Trujillo in the Dominican Republic, so he was no stranger to Latin America. In short, if the CIA had an operation that they had no business getting involved in, they would call Robert Maheu.[30]

CIA files confirm that Maheu also helped the Agency in the "procurement of feminine companionship" for certain foreign dignitaries during their official state visits to the U.S. In addition, former CIA officials have since revealed that Maheu also recruited "women of less than upstanding character" for employment in the Washington D.C. safe house used by Technical Services Staff (TSS) and other

Agency branches. As previously discussed, in the 1950s, the TSS experimented with drugs and hypnosis on military personnel and civilians, which led to the creation of Project Bluebird. And it was Sheffield Edwards, the same man that directed Jim O'Connell to contact Robert Maheu, who started Bluebird in 1950. And the person who helped Maheu's firm with its "procurement of feminine companionship" for TSS was mobster John Roselli. It was Roselli who Maheu would use as a liaison to the Mafia when he accepted the CIA's assignment to find mobsters capable of assassinating Castro.[31] Roselli was a logical person for Maheu to approach. In addition to supplying the super sleuth with unsuspecting women used in mind-altering drug experiments, Roselli provided the "grease" for Howard Hughes's entry into Las Vegas, who was Maheu's primary employer. The two men had a history of working together.[32]

Jim O'Connell and Sheffield Edwards first met Roselli at a barbecue at Robert Maheu's home sometime in 1959. "They independently learned that Johnny had access to the highest levels of the Mafia," Maheu would recall, and they were both impressed. Roselli and Maheu saw each other again around Labor Day. Maheu claimed that he represented international business people who had lost a great deal of money in Cuba after Castro came to power. These titans of industry wanted Castro killed, and they were willing to pay $150,000 to have it done, but Maheu could not fool Roselli. He knew it was a CIA operation, for he had been involved with the Agency before and could sense the involvement of U.S. intelligence, and he told this to Maheu. He decided not to accept payment for the assignment, saying it was his patriotic duty to get involved. It was probably a lie, for this was post-Apalachin, and the McClellan Committee, FBI, and FBN were applying pressure to the Mafia. Maheu presented the mob with potential leverage to force the feds to back off. But first things first. Roselli needed to get approval from his main boss, Sam Giancana from Chicago.

It turned out that Giancana was equally interested and for the same reasons as Roselli. He also had someone in mind who he wanted to bring into the operation. Giancana's Chicago outfit had run the Sans Souci in Havana. Roselli was sent there during the 1950s to ensure the people in Havana were managing the club properly. They eventually asked Santo Trafficante to take over that operation. And in 1960, it was the well-connected Trafficante whom Giancana approached to assemble a group in Cuba to carry out the Castro assassination.

In September, at the Brown Derby in California, Roselli told Maheu he wanted to meet someone from the CIA. In New York, posing as a businessman named Jim Olds, O'Connell joined Roselli and Maheu. He also told Roselli they were part of a group that had lost money in Cuba, but Roselli was on to O'Connell from the start. He recognized O'Connell from the barbecue at Maheu's house during the previous summer and knew he was CIA. On the other hand, O'Connell was sufficiently convinced that Roselli had the mob connections to carry out the operation, but he wanted to meet "Sam Gold," whom Roselli said "knew the Cuban crowd." Sam Gold, of course, was Sam Giancana.

Giancana and Roselli met with Maheu and O'Connell at the Fountainbleau Hotel in Miami, calling themselves "John Rawlston" and "Sam Gold," respectively. Santo Trafficante was also present, using the name "Joe" as someone who "could serve as a courier to Cuba and make arrangements there." CIA wanted a classic mob hit, with Castro killed in the street by a spray of bullets, but Giancana objected, saying it was too messy and made it impossible for the murderers to escape. He preferred slipping Castro a poison pill. CIA went along with what Giancana wanted. As Trafficante would later tell the HSCA: "The thing that I got is that anything that could have been done to assassinate Castro or eliminate his associates or overthrow the Government of Cuba short of an atomic bomb, everything was permissible."[33]

We should consider Trafficante's involvement in the Castro assassination plot in its proper context. It occurred soon after he was released in Cuba and was allowed to return to the United States. Roselli knew Jack Ruby, whom he described as "one of our boys," and there is a strong possibility that Roselli and Ruby knew each other as far back as 1933 when they became involved in the newly opened Santa Anita Racetrack in Los Angeles. When Ruby first contacted Robert McKeown about a letter of introduction to Castro to get three people out of prison, he mentioned that a man from Las Vegas would provide the financing. It may have been John Roselli. Therefore, although there is nothing to connect Jack Ruby to the assassination plots against Castro, it was clear he was acquainted with those involved.[34]

Several days later, a concerned Robert Maheu called Jim O'Connell. He had seen photos of Giancana and Trafficante in *Parade Magazine*, and he now knew they were not dealing with some low-level mobsters who had connections inside Cuba. These were mob bosses, ones that the McClellan Committee was trying to put in jail. Men you did not mess with if you wanted to stay alive. O'Connell alerted Sheffield Edwards about who they were, then Edwards told Bissell, but Bissell went forward with the plan anyway. "I knew it was serious," Bissell later recalled. "I knew these were Mafia leaders. And I knew they were in a position to make very damning revelations about the Agency. But we thought it was all under control."[35] Bissell had no idea how wrong he was.

In October 1960, the FBI kept a watchful eye on the Fountainbleau in Miami, which was why Roselli and Maheu decided to stay at a different hotel. The two men were aware that ever since Apalachin, Hoover had a newfound interest in the surveillance of top mobsters, for the FBI Director could no longer say that organized crime did not exist. But the Miami G-men knew nothing about the mob and CIA working together or that Giancana had returned to Chicago. They did not realize that Roselli and Maheu were in town staying at a different location. Hence, their stakeout at the Fountainbleau was fruitless. It was too bad, for the CIA/Mafia assassination plots were proceeding nicely, and it would have been good for the nation had the FBI stumbled on what this band of cutthroats was up to and put a stop to it.

During that October trip, Trafficante picked up Roselli and Maheu at their hotel, and the three men drove to the home of Tony Varona. With Varona were several other prominent Cuban exiles. One was Rafael "Macho" Gener, a red-haired Cuban who had first met Trafficante while working at the mob-run casinos in Havana. Another was Jose Aleman, who had lost a fortune in Cuban investments when Castro came to power. The group discussed the plan's details, which essentially was that Juan Orta Cordova would be given pills to poison Castro.

As already described, Tony Varona was a former Prime Minister of Cuba under Carlos Prio, part of the Cuban government in exile in the United States. The relationship between these two men was excellent and extended long after the two had fled Cuba together on the day Batista came to power in 1952. The Ansan Group connected Prio to Meyer Lansky, which bought Florida real estate with money smuggled out of Cuba. Through Prio, Varona contacted Meyer Lansky, who offered to back his efforts against Castro. Lansky turned Varona over to Trafficante, which is how Varona entered the CIA/Mafia operation.[36]

Those at the meeting at Varona's home did not know that Jose Aleman was an FBI informant. "Informant [Aleman], who is a Cuban exile, has furnished extremely valuable information regarding criminal activities of the Cubans in exile here in Miami," reported an FBI memo. Not knowing the CIA was in bed with the Mafia trying to kill Castro, the FBI warned the Agency about Trafficante. They thought the meeting had to do with Trafficante and Cuban exiles. The FBI had learned "U.S. racketeers were making efforts to finance anti-Castro activities in hopes of securing gambling, prostitution, and dope monopolies in Cuba in the event Castro was overthrown." Another FBI memo was more specific and said that Trafficante told Aleman there were "clients who wanted to do away with Castro and that they would pay big money for the job." It must have alarmed the CIA, for Trafficante should have remained quiet, but he told people that a group wanted Castro killed. And if he were earnest about assassinating the Cuban leader, Trafficante would not have whispered a word to anyone. Based on this alone, the CIA should have walked away and aborted the operation, but they did not.[37]

* * *

Around the same time that the meeting at Tony Varona's house was taking place, Judith Campbell spent the weekend at the Fountainbleau Hotel as a guest of Frank Sinatra. He had initially been introduced to Campbell by Johnny Roselli. As mentioned above, the FBI had men stationed at the Fountainbleau, and Campbell caught their attention because her description matched previous FBI reports of an attractive woman in the company of Roselli. Muddying the waters further was that last February, Senator John Kennedy had been introduced to Campbell while in Las

Vegas watching Sinatra perform with the Rat Pack. By the following month, Kennedy and Campbell would be spending a night together at the Plaza Hotel in New York City. It kickstarted an affair that would still be active after JFK became President and J. Edgar Hoover let Kennedy know the FBI was aware of the relationship.

Then, the same month that Kennedy and Campbell got together at the Plaza Hotel, Sinatra introduced her to "Sam Gold" at the Fountainbleau. The timing was suspicious and would compromise the young senator if he were to become President. She had an affair with Giancana and later claimed she was used by him as a courier, delivering suitcases filled with money to JFK.[38] So the future President of the United States was having an affair with a woman seeing Sam Giancana at the same time. She was delivering money from the mobster to the candidate in support of his campaign. At the same time, Giancana was involved with the CIA trying to kill Castro. Meanwhile, Kennedy's brother Bobby was grilling Giancana as part of the McClellan Committee and trying to put him in jail. One does not have to be a detective to know that this was going to end badly.

Giancana, who did not attend the meeting at Varona's house, may have tried to kill Castro independent of the CIA plot. It involved an ex-Chicago policeman named Richard Cain, who had resigned from the force in 1960 to start a security firm. Cain also worked for the CIA. In October 1960, he visited the CIA office in Chicago, followed by a trip to Miami, where he used electronic eavesdropping equipment to spy on Cuban exiles. From this, he learned there were Castro agents who had infiltrated anti-Castro groups within the U.S. Years later, a House of Representatives panel concluded that "Several of Cain's activities during the fall of 1960, together with his past experience, support the proposition that if Giancana were involved in any Cuban affairs, specifically an assassination of Castro independent of the CIA plot, he would have recruited Cain to assist him." Giancana may have believed that Castro agents had infiltrated the CIA plot, and it was compromised. He asked Cain to investigate to determine if that were true.

There was also a report that "Trafficante had infiltrated Operation Forty with Syndicate henchman" and Richard Cain was responsible, recruiting killers and other nefarious figures on Trafficante's behalf. The June 16, 1975 edition of *Time* magazine reported: "With the consent of the CIA, intelligence sources say, Detective Cain began recruiting Spanish-speaking toughs on the Windy City's East Side. Some of the hoodlums were sent to Miami and Central America for training in commando tactics . . . U.S. sources say that the CIA spent more than $100,000 on the operation, while Giancana laid out $90,000 of the Mob's funds for Cain's expenses. When some Mafia officials objected to the payments, Giancana contented that the funds should be considered 'ice' [protection money]."[39]

That fall, Cain met with Tony Varona in Miami, and after that, he secretly visited Cuba on more than one occasion. He allegedly once traveled with an unidentified woman who intended to poison Castro, but the effort failed. Cain claimed she was captured and executed. Congressional investigators believed she had been "a mistress of Castro."[40]

Could this have been Marita Lorenz, the Castro mistress close to Frank Sturgis, Alexander Rorke, and Gerry Patrick Hemming? According to FBI records, Lorenz did know Roselli, first meeting the mobster at the Riviera Hotel in Havana in 1959. She would also claim that Roselli introduced her to Giancana at the Fountainbleau. It is impossible to confirm if Lorenz was the woman who traveled with Cain to Cuba. However, exactly how many ex-mistresses of Castro were being sent from the U.S. to Cuba by CIA-connected Mafia and paramilitary types with the intent of killing the Cuban dictator with poison pills? This author knows of only one.

Meanwhile, Giancana also had other things on his mind. He had been dating Phyllis McGuire of the McGuire Sisters, a famous singing trio at the time. Trouble began in July 1960, when John W. Teeter, married to Phyllis' sister Christine, approached the FBI with information that Phyllis was dating Sam Giancana. Two months later, Teeter contacted the FBI again regarding a plot to kill Castro, which Giancana had disclosed to Teeter and the two McGuire sisters over dinner. There was no mention of the CIA, so the FBI likely thought the plot involved only mobsters who wanted to kill Castro independently.

By October 1960, Roselli and Trafficante were meeting at Tony Varona's house. Richard Cain was visiting the CIA office in Chicago. And Sam Giancana was preoccupied with rumors that his girlfriend Phyllis was spending time with comedian Dan Rowan. If true, it was a virtual death sentence for the comedian and would have certainly put an end to the CIA/Mafia plot to kill Castro. To deal with it, Rosselli contacted Maheu, who knew Las Vegas well because of his relationship with Howard Hughes. Maheu then solicited another ex-FBI man turned private detective, Edward Dubois, to find out what was going on between Rowan and McGuire. Dubois then farmed the work out to a third private detective named Arthur J. Balletti. It turned out to be a mistake, for when Balletti wiretapped Rowan's phone, he carelessly left his tools lying around. A maid discovered them, which resulted in the arrest of Balletti on October 31. After the Las Vegas sheriff learned what Balletti was up to, he contacted the FBI. Shortly after that, Sam Giancana had a wiretap placed inside his office in Chicago.

The FBI would eventually contact Edward Dubois, who told them Robert Maheu hired him. A trace of Maheu led them to the Kenilworth Hotel in Miami, where Maheu paid for himself and another man named J.A. Rollins, who hotels workers said looked like Roselli when shown photos of the mobster. Hotel phone records revealed that Rollins had called Chicago and the Desert Inn in Las Vegas. When confronted, Maheu disclosed to the FBI that the CIA had hired him in the summer of 1960. He was involved in an operation with Giancana and Roselli, and that Sheffield Edwards had asked him to approach Giancana because of his Cuban connections.

From the wiretap they had placed in Giancana's office, the FBI recorded the mobster discussing the plot to kill Castro, along with the mention of Roselli and the CIA. It was not hard for the FBI to put the pieces together that CIA had involved mobsters Giancana and Rosselli, through Robert Maheu, to murder Fidel Castro. Meanwhile, Giancana was having an affair with Judith Campbell, as was presidential candidate John Kennedy, which the FBI must have known. Within weeks, Hoover approached Richard Bissell. "During recent conversations with several friends, Giancana stated that Fidel Castro was to be done away with very shortly," Hoover said. "He allegedly indicated that he had already met with the assassins-to-be on three occasions. . . . [and] Giancana claimed that everything had been perfected for the killing of Castro . . . The 'assassin' had arranged with a girl . . . to drop a 'pill' in some drink of Castro's."[41] The FBI Director wanted the CIA to know he was aware of what they were doing, but it did not stop Bissell from continuing.

* * *

J. Edgar Hoover loved to let people know he was privy to something they were doing that they wanted to be kept hidden. It made them indebted to him. In August 1962, he would send Attorney General Robert Kennedy a memo detailing his father's ties to organized crime. "Before the last presidential election, Joseph P. Kennedy . . . had been visited by many gangsters with gambling interests," Hoover wrote. "A deal was made which resulted in Peter Lawford, Frank Sinatra, Dean Martin, and others obtaining a lucrative gambling establishment, the Cal-Neva Hotel, at Lake Tahoe. These gangsters reportedly met with Joseph Kennedy at the Cal-Neva, where Kennedy was staying at the time."[42]

There was more to tell if the FBI Director wanted to do so, for Hoover also knew that during 1960, to ensure his son would be elected President, Joe Kennedy met with some of the top mobsters in the country at Felix Young's restaurant in New York. "I took the reservation, and it was as though every gangster chief in the United States was there," recalled Edna Donovan, who worked at the time as a hostess at the restaurant. "I don't remember all the names now, but there was John Roselli, Carlos Marcello from New Orleans, the two brothers from Dallas, the top men from Buffalo, California, and Colorado. They were all the top people, not soldiers. I was amazed Joe Kennedy would take the risk."[43]

In *Mob Lawyer*, Mafia attorney Frank Ragano recalled that months after JFK's assassination, Giancana "blustered in no uncertain terms that his organization won—or, rather, stole—the 1960 election for Kennedy by fixing votes for him in Cook County [Illinois]."[44] "The presidency was really stolen in Chicago," proclaimed gangster Mickey Cohen years later. It also applied to Texas, where authorities disqualified 100,000 opposition votes without explanation. [45]

Furthermore, on February 29, 1960, Joseph Kennedy met with Giancana at a restaurant in New York, along with Roselli, and Mario Brod (James Angleton's liaison to the Mafia), to negotiate the terms by which the Mafia's constituents in Illinois would vote for JFK in the upcoming presidential election. Joe also wanted the mobsters to contribute $500,000 to JFK's campaign. Reportedly, Angleton would later deeply resent Bobby's interference in CIA counterintelligence operations after his brother became President and would only tell Bobby about Mario Brod in 1963. However, in 1960 Angleton supported JFK on behalf of the CIA.[46]

According to mobster Bill Bonanno, the mob was concerned and wanted assurances that if JFK were elected, Bobby would no longer be able to pursue the Mafia, as he was doing with the McClellan Committee. "The old man [Joe Kennedy] specifically told us that if Jack was elected, he was gonna make Bobby ambassador to Ireland or something like that." When Bobby did become Attorney General and went after big-time Mafioso and Jimmy Hoffa, it goes without saying that the mob was furious.[47]

So, while John Kennedy was President, the Mafia joined the CIA, the military, and the radical right groups who felt the Kennedys had betrayed them. After being confronted by Hoover with information regarding the assassination plots against Castro, the CIA also must have realized that they had made a mistake involving organized crime, for Giancana talked too much. And it is puzzling that despite this, the Agency continued to try and kill Castro with the mob's help, even though it brought with it the threat of blackmail if something went wrong. Probably, the CIA was also aware of John Kennedy's interaction with Giancana while both men were having an affair with Judith Campbell. Even if they didn't, by this time, they knew that Santo Trafficante might have secretly been working for Fidel Castro while he was working with the CIA to kill him, and this alone should have caused the termination of the operation.

In *The Secret History of the CIA*, Joseph J. Trento explains that when the CIA first considered using mobsters to assassinate Castro, the Agency was unaware that Trafficante and Castro had made a deal before his revolution toppled Batista. The arrangement was that Trafficante would supply Castro with weapons, and in return, Castro promised Trafficante control of gambling in Cuba once the rebellion succeeded. Trafficante also allowed Castro's supporters to import heroin into Miami and sell it on his turf to help finance the war against Batista.[48]

A 1961 report referenced "unconfirmed rumors in the Cuban refugee population in Miami." Apparently, "when Fidel Castro ran the American racketeers out of Cuba and seized the casinos, he kept Santo Trafficante Jr. in jail to make it appear that he had a personal dislike for Trafficante, when in fact Trafficante is an agent of Castro. Trafficante is allegedly Castro's outlet for illegal contraband in the country."[49]

It is also possible that Castro incarcerated Trafficante to protect him from the McClellan Committee and prosecution for the Anastasia murder. After he was released and returned to the United States, Trafficante provided the winning numbers in the Bolita Lottery in Tampa in advance to Castro's men, guaranteeing that they would win. Cuban American Ricardo Canete, who worked for William Harvey's anti-Castro operation, eventually learned what Trafficante was doing. "Fidel needed money, and he needed information," Canete said. "A man out of the Cuban Mission to the UN named Fernandez ran the Cuban DGI [Cuban Intelligence in the United States]. He took orders from Trafficante. It was clear by the late 1960s that drugs and protection [ ] run through Little Havana were far more profitable than anything the mob had done in Cuba." Informant Jose Aleman told the FBI of conversations with Trafficante where the mobster sounded "like Karl Marx."[50]

The FBN's Charles Siragusa would later recall, "The implication was that he [Trafficante] had sabotaged the CIA's first assassination attempt on Castro and had probably betrayed the CIA in other ways as well." Recall that Siragusa knew Angleton had worked with Brod in Italy during the war, and reportedly Angleton was so dependent on Siragusa for his Mafia contacts that he would have "kissed Siragusa's ass in Macy's window at noon" if he had to.[51]

The FBI also knew what was happening in Cuba. An informant told them that on August 20, 1959, he saw "Santo Trafficante and Henry Saavedra with Jack [sic] Lansky and numerous other gamblers drinking a toast." They were "celebrating the release of Trafficante and Henry Saavedra from jail." The next day, they talked "about opening the Casino del Rio . . . there was some discussion regarding the possibility of Trafficante's opening the Oriental Park Race Track in Marianao . . ." Trafficante was still in Havana on October 5 and said, "the gambling business is very poor . . . and almost no American tourists are observed in the various gambling casinos in Havana."[52]

One would have expected Trafficante to have fled Cuba the moment the Cubans released him from prison. Instead, he drank a toast to his freedom with his mob friends, considered opening a casino and a racetrack, and almost two months later was still in Havana. It was not the behavior of a man who felt threatened by Castro. On the contrary, it appears Trafficante only decided to leave Cuba because the casino business there was essentially dead. One can deduce that he and the Cuban leader were working together, supporting the idea that Trafficante kept Castro apprised of the assassination attempts against him.

There is also the possibility that Giancana staged the Dan Rowan episode to sabotage the Castro assassination plots. When Giancana found out what had happened, Roselli recalled that he was "Smoking a cigar—he almost swallowed it, laughing about it."[53] So, before long, the CIA must have concluded that Giancana and Trafficante were trying to sabotage the operation. It is probably why when the CIA did terminate the assassination plot, the only mobster they would retain in the war against Castro was Roselli. Meanwhile, Joseph Kennedy was in contact with the same mobsters trying to get his son elected President, and his son John was sleeping with the same woman as Giancana. There must have been those at the CIA who felt the mob and the Kennedy family were conning them. It had the potential to derail the drug-money laundering operation organized crime had established on behalf of the CIA. And it was Attorney General Robert Kennedy's pursuit of the mob that placed the CIA in a blackmailable position.

Then there was the far-left Richard Bissell, who wanted mobsters involved in the attempt to kill Castro. Bissell had rejected the far-right Havana group who had tried to overthrow Castro and instead chose the mob over them. If true, the right-wing arm of CIA, including James Angleton, Howard Hunt, Tracy Barnes, David Phillips, Henry Hecksher, June Cobb, and David Morales, would not have taken kindly to this. And if they were aware that Giancana and Trafficante were sabotaging the Castro assassination plots, they would have allowed it to happen to embarrass Bissell. The same thing happened at the Bay of Pigs, where Bissell was duped into failing again, costing Allen Dulles his job, the man who sabotaged Morgan's attempted coup in Cuba.

Still, if true, it does not explain why the Mafia fixed the 1960 election so that John Kennedy would be elected, for the shadow of Bobby Kennedy loomed large over the mob if a Kennedy presidency put the Mafia in harm's way. There had to be a rational explanation for this as well. Enter Joe Kennedy once again.

* * *

In the latter part of 1956, Joe Kennedy approached Senate Majority leader Lyndon Johnson. It was unexpected, for Johnson knew Joe was positioning JFK to run for president in 1960. It was something Johnson was interested in as well. "Joe Kennedy bombarded me with phone calls," LBJ recalled. "One day, he came right out and pleaded with me to put Jack on the Foreign Relations Committee, telling me that if I did, he'd never forget the favor for the rest of his life. Now, I knew Kefauver wanted the seat bad . . . But I kept picturing old Joe Kennedy sitting there with all the power and wealth, feeling indebted to me for the rest of his life, and I sure liked that picture."[54]

On January 8, 1957, Senator Kennedy would be appointed to the Senate Foreign Relations Committee, cementing Joe Kennedy's indebtedness to Johnson. Three years later, Johnson wanted to be the Democratic nominee for president. However, many around Johnson thought it was not the top slot he was after, but the vice presidency instead. Kennedy's selection of Johnson as his running mate was equally curious. It did not transpire without a bitter debate among members of the Kennedy camp; Robert Kennedy included, for most did not want anything to do with Johnson, a man with a history of corruption. The turn of events bewildered political insiders. Still, Joe Kennedy may have made a deal with LBJ to be Kennedy's choice as vice president.

Consider that Johnson was keenly aware of one simple fact—since the Civil War, the Democratic Party had never nominated a man from the Old Confederacy to be President. As the Democratic convention of 1960 approached, Johnson's chance of being selected was slim, and he knew it. Johnson hoped for a deadlock after the first ballot so that someone could submit his name for nomination on the second. It was there he believed he could capture the moment and win the Democratic nomination, but it did not happen.

In their book, *Lyndon B. Johnson: The Exercise of Power*, written during the Johnson Presidency, respected authors Rowland Evans and Robert Novak offered a different explanation for what had motivated Johnson. "Was it just barely possible," they wrote, "that that master-planner, Lyndon Johnson, whose sense of timing was legendary, whose ego did not court defeat and who always knew the odds, knew from the beginning that he could not beat Kennedy? Could he have been angling not for the presidency but for something else? Can a case be made that not the presidential nomination but the nomination for Vice President was his secret goal?"[55]

Evans and Novak offered numerous examples to support their position. In the spring of 1960, Johnson had discussed the virtues of Kennedy with various political associates. He talked about his class, education, and political instincts, which Johnson thought were good. When he finished complimenting Kennedy, he despondently said, "A fellow from my part of the country probably couldn't be anything more than another John Nance Garner." Garner was the only Texan since the Civil War who had risen as high as the vice presidency. Johnson clearly understood that the odds were against him above the Mason-Dixon line.

On another occasion, three weeks before the Democratic Convention, Representative Hale Boggs of Louisiana, a well-schooled political insider and future Warren Commission member, bet a friend that the winning ticket would be Kennedy-Johnson, in that order. At the time, it was foolish to suggest such a thing, especially for a Southerner to do so.

In June 1960, less than a month before the convention, Johnson's right-hand man Bobby Baker told Kennedy's chief policy aide Theodore Sorensen that he foresaw a Kennedy-Johnson ticket. It was a complete reversal from what Baker had been saying the previous year. "I think that would be wonderful," Sorensen replied. "But I doubt very much that the second man on that ticket [Johnson] would agree to it." "Don't be too sure," Baker fired back.

In 1960, Johnson confided to a friend, lobbyist Tim McInerney, that John Kennedy was the Democrat best suited to run for the presidency. McInerney believed that Johnson considered himself the number two man.

Representative Joe Kilgore, a staunch, conservative Texas Democrat, was one of Johnson's closest allies. He spoke to Johnson's man Walter Jenkins shortly after Johnson accepted the second position on the ticket behind Kennedy. Kilgore was furious with Johnson for taking a back seat to Kennedy, and Jenkins told him to calm down. "This is what we've been waiting for all this time," he said.[56]

John Curington was a chief aide to H.L. Hunt during the early 1960s. In an interview with author Dick Russell, Curington described his knowledge of the events surrounding the Democratic convention of 1960:

> "Mr. Hunt and I went to the Convention in L.A. Up to within ten days of the nomination, nobody on earth could have convinced LBJ he wasn't gonna get it. But I had enough information and knowledge that I concluded, if he ever wanted to be president, he had to take the second spot. So, Mr. Hunt and I . . . went to Lyndon and outlined this . . . he had to take a calculated risk that Kennedy would not be nominated in '64, and that would give him the opportunity to be president.
> "Jack and Bobby Kennedy hated LBJ. We went to Bobby first, who said he wouldn't have that Blankety-blank on the second spot under any consideration. Jack didn't want him either. Finally, we went to Joe [Kennedy Sr.], and he had enough gumption to know they needed LBJ on the ticket because he was from the right geographical area, the South.
> "Then in '64, they were not gonna keep Johnson on . . . the only way Lyndon gets to be president is if something happened to John F. Kennedy."[57]

To everyone's surprise, Johnson accepted Kennedy's offer to be the number two man on the ticket, and he provided the reason behind his decision. "I have now learned that one out of every four Presidents dies in office . . . ," he said, "and I am a gambling man!"[58]

Was it possible that the Mafia complied with Joe Kennedy's request to help get his son elected, knowing that Lyndon Johnson would get the second spot on the ticket? Was it done so that if the Kennedys double-crossed the mob, or if they had to blackmail Kennedy out of the White House, that by 1964 Johnson could replace Kennedy, a man the Mafia controlled, who was also a favorite of the right-wing? If true, and it became apparent that there was no guarantee of JFK losing the election in 1964, there was no choice but to remove him from office forcibly. Which they did, but it was not just the Mafia who felt that Kennedy had to go.

* * *

Returning to the CIA/Mafia assassination plots, one question is, when Giancana requested poison pills to kill Castro, how did he even know that CIA had this capability? Who told him? Consider what we know. Robert Maheu and John Roselli were involved with a TSS safe house and "women of less than upstanding character," which sounds similar to the LSD testing George Hunter White performed on unsuspecting women in New York City and San Francisco. Was there a connection between Maheu, Roselli, and White? Was Sheffield Edwards already aware of Maheu and Roselli because of their involvement in Operation Bluebird, the program where drug testing began?

George White and Jean Lafitte were involved in operations in Las Vegas, and it was there that White gave LSD to unsuspecting women working at a local brothel. The two also became involved in the city's less-desirable activities, including those involving Howard Hughes, Robert Maheu's number-one client. That Hughes worked with the CIA on special projects, such as leasing his private islands to train anti-Castro Cubans, is common knowledge. So, it stands to reason that Robert Maheu was aware of White and Lafitte before Giancana requested poison pills to kill Castro. Lafitte admitted he helped broker international drug deals for Meyer Lansky and occasionally worked for Robert Maheu in New York City and Las Vegas. George White's private papers reveal that on at least three occasions in 1954 and 1955, while he was still working for the CIA, Lafitte was assisted by a man named Allan Hughes in undercover assignments for CIA. Hughes was also present at the gathering where Frank Olson was given LSD without his knowledge.

Allen Hughes was an Army Counterintelligence Officer who reportedly was an expert in electronic surveillance and interrogation techniques. He was assigned to work at the CIA, the Technical Services Staff, and the Special Operations Division. FBI files confirm that in 1955 he went to work for Robert Maheu. Maheu's office was located just blocks from the Washington D.C. safe house. Intelligence sources have stated that Hughes outfitted the safe place with video, sound, and surveillance equipment. His importance is that he had a connection to White, Lafitte, and Maheu all around the same time.

Hughes also worked with a former shady Washington D.C. police detective and expert wireman named Joe Shimon. The police department would dismiss Shimon for conducting illegal wiretaps. He was also mob-connected. According to a source who had once worked for Washington Post columnist Jack Anderson: "Hughes worked at least a couple of times with Shimon . . . [mostly] doing secret film jobs on visiting dignitaries staying in either the Madison or Mayflower hotels. For a while, one could find Shimon and Hughes at Duke Zeibert's or late nights at the Old Ebbitt Grill. One night, drunk, the two threatened to toss an FBI agent off the garden roof of the Hotel Washington."[59]

For his book *Mary's Mosaic*, author Peter Janney interviewed Shimon's daughter Toni, who provided valuable information about her father. "Shimon confided that he was the CIA's principal liaison to the Mafia," Janney wrote. "When they started working on Castro's assassination, the meetings were held in Shimon's house. People like Roselli, Giancana, Trafficante, Bill Harvey, and sometimes Angleton. 'My father loved Bill Harvey,' said Toni. 'He was also close friends with Jim Angleton, and of course Sam and Johnny.'"

Officially, Shimon served in the White House as a "Washington Police Inspector." According to what he told his daughter, "Angleton ran everything, controlled everything in the CIA." Angleton, of course, was part of the right-wing group, which suggests the meetings at Shimon's house may have had to do with the sabotage of Bissell's effort to murder Castro and embarrass the left-wing within CIA. Shimon also said he was the principal liaison to Johnny Roselli, and with his connections, Shimon's involvement in the Castro assassination plots is plausible. "Our government has murdered a lot of people when they get in the way . . . Among my many jobs, I used to kill people," he told her. "Our government hired me and others to do this sort of work."[60]

In March 1961, after Kennedy was already in office and a month before the Bay of Pigs invasion, Giancana, Trafficante, and Roselli met with Maheu at the Fountainbleau. Joe Shimon was also present, brought along by Maheu. The men knew the FBI had the hotel under surveillance, but they did not seem to care. There was no longer a reason to maintain secrecy. They met in a suite with Tony Varona and Rafael Gener, who accepted cash and poison pills from the group. Still, the attempted assassination of Castro never happened because Orta got cold feet. When it looked like G-2, Cuba's counterpart to the CIA, was on to him, he asked for and received asylum from the Venezuelan embassy in Havana, where he stayed for three years. Maybe that was all part of the setup to sabotage the operation, and Varona was in on it as well. The key was to ensure the plot to overthrow Castro would be directed by the right-wing and that a Batista follower would replace Castro. And the involvement of James Angleton in the sabotage operation pointed in that direction.

* * *

David Morales, who we know was connected to the U.S. Embassy in Havana after Castro came to power, initially met William Harvey, Ted Shackley, and Henry Hecksher when they worked together in Germany early in the 1950s. Hecksher and Morales wound up in Guatemala in 1954, where Morales reported to CIA officer Enno Hobbing. Hobbing had been involved in Germany after World War II as part of Operation Paperclip. And along with Boris Pash, who served as Chief of Program Branch 7, the group responsible for assassinations when the CIA came into existence, brought Nazi Werner von Braun to the United States. In addition, the file of June Cobb inexplicably contains CIA cables related to Hobbing. Cobb, as we know, was connected to the U.S. Embassy in Havana and worked for the CIA in Mexico City in 1962 and 1963. It further connects Cobb to the assassination group.

The cables show that in Mexico City, Hobbing worked on Project ZR/AWARD. It was part of the CIA's ongoing hypnosis and behavior-modification operations, such as Project ZR/ALERT, which the CIA handled in Mexico, and possibly New Orleans. It may also have been part of the CIA's assassination program ZR/RIFLE, which made sense if it involved hypnosis and behavior modification. At least two assassins had a connection to ZR/ALERT, Harold Meltzer and Hanna Yazbeck. Both were recruited into the CIA by William Harvey and David Morales.[61]

The significance of this assassination squad is that Meltzer worked with Morales from 1960 until around 1963, primarily through Johnny Roselli, who was his CIA "control" mobster. Roselli was also closely associated with Morales. According to former FBI special agent Ted Meacham, the FBI was aware that Meltzer and Roselli had an extensive criminal history together, "going back to the early 1950s in Los Angeles and Las Vegas, with some minor dealings in New York."

In 1959, Roselli told Sheffield Edwards about Meltzer. It is how the CIA first became aware of the assassin. Earlier that same year, George Hunter White wrote a letter to Garland Williams at the FBN. It stated that White and Siragusa had recommended Meltzer to Roselli in a meeting in Miami that included two attendees identified only as "D.M." and "J.E." Most likely, the initials referred to David Morales and Jake Esterline. It was the year Castro came to power and when the plots being run out of Havana to kill him took place.[62]

Meltzer was also involved in drug trafficking, primarily through Mexico City, which extended to the mid-1940s. By the 1950s, he became involved with one of the two Colombian brothers involved with June Cobb.

There appears to be something wrong here. Recall that at the beginning, Richard Bissell asked Sheffield Edwards if the CIA had any assets to assassinate Castro. As described above, Edwards knew the Agency had such people, namely Harold Meltzer. Meltzer already had a connection to Johnny Roselli, David Morales, and the group trying to overthrow Castro from within Cuba. But Edwards elected not to recommend this group and opted instead for Robert Maheu. Maheu then asked Johnny Roselli to find mobsters willing to get involved, which got the Castro assassination operation underway. It cannot be a coincidence that Roselli had a history with Meltzer, yet Roselli bypassed Meltzer, bringing in Giancana and eventually Trafficante. Why wouldn't he have contacted Meltzer, which was logical, unless someone at the CIA told Maheu that Roselli should stay away from Meltzer, which would have connected the operation to the CIA group working out of the U.S. Embassy in Havana? Perhaps the fear was that plausible deniability could be more easily maintained if Roselli brought mobsters into the operation with connections inside Cuba. Had Roselli contacted Meltzer, the potential for disclosure of U.S. involvement in Castro's assassination plot would have been too great. It raises the possibility that the right-wing U.S. Havana Embassy group was ignored and passed over in favor of the Mafia, which complied with the desire to keep this a left-wing operation. And this would have made the right-wing group in Havana angry over having been left out of an operation they were most qualified to undertake. And making people like that angry was not a smart thing to do. It was why the intent was to sabotage Richard Bissell whenever they could. In the war against communism, the radical right had to prevail.

- 6 -

No Ordinary Marine

"By coercion, they meant a number of things. One was blackmail. Another was exploiting links with illegal activities or criminal conduct . . . Potential agents were confronted with proof of their past misdeeds and promised immunity from prosecution in exchange for their espionage services."

— Joseph B. Smith, ex-CIA agent

Only two American enlisted men defected to the Soviet bloc between 1945 and 1959, but in the eighteen months before 1960, a rash of service members fled the U.S. One of those who defected was Lee Harvey Oswald, and he was part of a program to obtain information from behind the Iron Curtain. The CIA likely blackmailed Oswald into becoming part of this operation and subjected him to mind control experimentation at Atsugi Air Base in Japan in preparation for his mission. The evidence confirms that this was so. Oswald spends only fourteen months in Japan. In that short period, a Japanese "hostess" who likely had KGB connections approached him, and he encounters a Soviet military intelligence officer. He purposely shoots himself. He is repeatedly removed from his unit and placed in either a hospital or the brig. It was then that U.S. intelligence subjected him to drug testing. He is removed from guard duty in Formosa and flown back to Atsugi by military plane, showing signs of emotional instability. There was something different about this Marine.

* * *

On October 24, 1956, just six days after his seventeenth birthday, Lee Oswald joined the Marine Corps. After roughly five months at boot camp, with temporary stops for training at Camp Pendleton, California, and Jacksonville, Florida, Oswald was sent to Keesler Air Force Base in Mississippi, where he completed training to become a radar operator. Following a standard check, the Marines granted him a security clearance at Keesler at the "confidential" level. He did well in his training and finished seventh in a class of thirty; he qualified as an Aviation Electronics Operator, an assignment only given to those credited with above-average intelligence. At Jacksonville, he had previously received ratings of 4.7 in conduct and 4.5 in proficiency, the highest rating being a 5.0. He appeared to be doing well.

Oswald kept to himself and was considered a loner, and while at Keesler, he used his weekend passes to travel to New Orleans, about 100 miles away. His mother was still in Fort Worth, so he wasn't visiting her. But David Ferrie and the Civil Air Patrol were still in New Orleans, as was Guy Banister, so maybe it was one of them Oswald was interested in traveling so far to see. However, precisely what he was doing cannot be proven and remains a mystery.[1]

After completing his training requirements, the Marines assigned Oswald to Marine Air Control Squadron One (MACS-1), stationed at Atsugi Air Base in Japan. Inherited from the Japanese after World War II and located a few miles southwest of Tokyo, when Oswald arrived, Atsugi was a jump-off point for Marine jet fighters equipped to detect enemy radar. What was known as "the bubble" was a radar control room responsible for monitoring aircraft, communicating with pilots by radio, and looking for incoming Russian or Chinese aircraft which had strayed off course, a monotonously laborious task.[2]

A group of buildings in one section housed the "Joint Technical Advisory Group," which was the CIA's main operational base in the Far East. From here the super-secretive U-2 flights originated, and the CIA conducted experimental drug testing with LSD on military personnel.[3]

Atsugi was also where the U.S. stockpiled nuclear weapons, violating the treaty between the United States and Japan. According to Lieutenant Charles Rhodes, at least three stories underground, he observed bombs stored in vast numbers. Colonel Fletcher Prouty also remembered that a "monstrous stairway went down into caverns, you could drive a truck into it. A huge underground base. The agency used it for a lot of things."[4]

Lee Oswald arrived at Atsugi on September 12, 1957, and immediately began his duties as a radar operator. His supervisor would recall he did an adequate job, saying, "I would desire to have him work for me at any time . . . he minds his business and does his job well." In general, he made a good impression on his colleagues and superiors. One of the Marines in his group said, "He had the sort of intelligence where you could show him how to do something once, and he'd know how to do it, even if it was pretty complicated." A fellow Marine, Zack Stout, recalled Oswald reading some serious books, including *Mein Kampf* and *The Rise and Fall of the Roman Empire*. Stout said that Oswald "was absolutely truthful, the kind of guy I'd trust completely."[5]

Mein Kampf, of course, was Hitler's manifesto about his plan to rebuild Germany, the struggle against what he believed were the two greatest evils in the world,

Judaism and communism, and the new world order he intended to establish. The reasons for the fall of the Roman Empire are subject to debate. Still, it was mainly due to over-taxing its people to finance the military, an increase in the disparity between the wealthy and the poor, welfare programs for the less fortunate to compensate for that disparity (which drained the economy), political corruption, and instability. The Praetorian Guard, the emperor's bodyguards, assassinated emperors at will and once even gave the position to the highest bidder. The Roman Senate was equally corrupt. So, considering that just a year before Atsugi Oswald had written to the Socialist Party of America asking for information, it appears that the young Marine was beginning to formulate in his mind a political philosophy he could embrace. And that philosophy seemed to be a willingness to overthrow political corruption forcibly, assassinate oppressors if necessary, eliminate over-taxation of the people, and rejecting a system that promoted welfare programs. In many ways, it mirrored what the right-wing proponents of self-determination were looking to accomplish.

The center of attention for Oswald and his Marine buddies were the U-2 flights that mysteriously departed in the morning and would not return until the late afternoon or evening. The planes were shrouded in secrecy, making the official story that they were weather reconnaissance aircraft unbelievable. After landing, a crew rushed out and covered the plane's head to conceal it from the view of unauthorized personnel. Oswald and the other radar operators did not monitor the U-2 flights on their radar screens—the CIA radar operators handled that. However, they could still track the planes, following them as high as 100,000 feet. They listened to U-2 pilots talking to the control tower, and, on occasion, they spoke to the pilots themselves. An unconfirmed rumor among the men was that the planes were flying secret missions over the Soviet Union.[6]

Being assigned to Atsugi placed Oswald at the center of one of America's intelligence hubs in Southeast Asia. Like all personnel stationed there, he was subject to the scrutiny of CIA and Military Intelligence, who considered the armed services a particularly fertile area to draw recruits for various covert operations. At first glance, it is difficult to imagine why a person like Oswald would be considered for intelligence work, for he was not the prototypical Marine, as demonstrated by his interest in Marxism. One would naturally believe that this should have precluded any interest in him, especially a covert assignment that would send him into the Soviet Union as a disenchanted American defector. However, the fact is that with Oswald, they found the perfect candidate.

There is no official confirmation that Oswald's superiors knew of his interest in Marxism when he first arrived in Japan. However, considering his security clearance and the sensitive nature of the work at Atsugi, we can assume he was subject to periodic security checks, including lie detector tests, which may have uncovered something about Oswald that made him a person of interest. And there is evidence to support this, for in his book *Portrait of a Cold Warrior*, ex-CIA agent Joseph B. Smith explained that the Agency was looking for people like Oswald to conduct specialized missions against the Soviets. According to Smith:

"Assessing a potential agent was a matter of looking for one . . . A person who was willing to work because . . . he hated Communists so much or admired the United States so [much] that he gladly joined the team was . . . a mixed blessing. For one thing, his cover for really sensitive missions, where his true feelings had to be . . . unsuspected, was bad. A violently anti-Communist individual could not possibly penetrate a Communist front or party; a person who was known to be sympathetic to the United States was unsuitable for a large number of political intelligence collection or action missions. There, too, the manipulation of a person's ideological convictions posed a problem of understanding the mind that our instructors preferred to stay away from. They liked coercion as the . . . method of motivating an agent.

"By coercion, they meant a number of things. One was blackmail. Another was exploiting links with illegal activities or criminal conduct . . . Potential agents were confronted with proof of their past misdeeds and promised immunity from prosecution in exchange for their espionage services."[7]

Smith's description of the criteria CIA looked for in a potential covert operative applied to Oswald. He was not overly patriotic, nor was his interest in Marxism a passionate one. As for blackmail, there is evidence this may have applied to him as well.

James Wilcott and his wife Elsie worked for the CIA at the Tokyo Station from 1960 to 1964—Jim with the finance group and Elsie as the station's secretary. According to James, the station went on alert after the assassination, and the CIA assigned him to twenty-four-hour security duty. As time passed, people at the station began to talk freely, some of it induced by alcohol, and he learned that Oswald had been "recruited from the military [by CIA] for the express purpose of becoming a double agent assignment to the USSR . . . More than once, I was told something like 'so-and-so was working on the Oswald project back in the late '50s.'"

"At first, I thought 'These guys are nuts,'" Wilcott said, "but then a man I knew and had worked with before showed up to take a disbursement and told me Lee Harvey Oswald was a CIA employee. I didn't believe him until he told me the cryptonym under which Oswald had drawn funds when he returned from Russia to the US." According to Wilcott, this man was a CIA case officer who supervised agents who had handled the Oswald project's funds to the Soviet Union. "It was a cryptonym that I was familiar with," Wilcott told the House Select Committee on Assassinations. "It must have been at least two or three times that I had remembered it, and it did ring a bell."

"It was common knowledge in the Tokyo CIA station that Oswald worked for the agency," Wilcott told the *San Francisco Chronicle* in 1978. "That's true," Elsie

Wilcott said. Immediately after JFK's assassination, "people in the Tokyo station [talked] openly about Oswald having gone to Russia for the CIA. Everyone was wondering how the agency was going to be able to keep the lid on Oswald. But I guess they did."[8]

The Wilcotts then learned that the CIA had obtained incriminating information on Oswald and was blackmailing him. James Wilcott believed the CIA had learned that Oswald had "murdered someone or committed some other serious crime, during a routine lie-detector test."[9]

There was a suspicious murder while Oswald served overseas. On January 5, 1958, fellow Marine Martin Schrand was shot to death while he and Oswald were temporarily stationed with their unit at Cubi Point in the Philippines. According to the Warren Commission testimony of another Marine, part of their responsibility while they were at Cubi Point was "closely guarding a hangar for a U-2 aircraft." Schrand, whom Oswald had known since they trained together in Biloxi, Mississippi, was shot and killed at his post, guarding the hangar. The bullet was fired from Schrand's weapon and had entered below his left arm and exited his left shoulder. On March 31, 1958, an official inquiry concluded that Schrand "died in the line of duty and not due to misconduct." It was considered accidental. However, no one could explain why Schrand violated regulations that stated live ammunition was not to be loaded in a gun while on guard duty. Schrand had loaded a single round into his rifle. In addition, four unused bullets were in his pocket. Interestingly, fellow Marine Donald Camarata told the Warren Commission of a "rumor that Oswald had been in some way responsible for the death."[10]

There is no concrete evidence that Oswald was responsible for killing Schrand. Still, even if that were the case, it does not mean that Wilcott's allegation was wrong that a lie-detector test revealed something about Oswald that U.S. intelligence used against him. And this had to have been significant enough to coerce Oswald into becoming part of a covert operation to send him behind the Iron Curtain.

Oswald's interest in Marxism, no matter how fleeting, would certainly have triggered a lie detector and would have probably warranted dismissal from the Marines, considering the country's mindset in the 1950s. As would his sexuality. That is, if he were gay, which remains an unknown. However, he and David Ferrie were close, and as we previously discussed, Ferrie had a penchant for young boys. Then in 1963, in New Orleans, he was frequently seen in the company of young gay men, even visiting attorney Dean Andrews with a group of gay Cubans looking for legal advice. There is also a possible connection to Clay Shaw, who was gay.

Several witnesses also recall a bar in Yamato, Japan pronounced "Negashaya," where men wore dresses and lipstick. One individual called it a "queer bar" and reported that he once went with Oswald after Oswald had suggested the place. "Oswald seemed to know his way around in the place," recalled the witness, who preferred that his identity remained hidden. "I don't remember that he knew anyone by name, but he was comfortable there."[11]

None of this proves that Oswald was gay or blackmailed because of it, but it suggests the possibility existed. The military considered such behavior immoral during World War II. One could argue that the hatred against gays in the late 1950s was even more significant than during the war. Recall that the CIA may have murdered their people who were gay to protect the Agency from Senator McCarthy's anti-Communist wrath. In *Nightmare in Red*, author Richard M. Fried describes how during World War II, "many men received . . . disciplinary proceedings based on their lives before induction. Some whose loyalty was impeached were kept in uniform but assigned meaningless duties [such as mess duty]; many received unfavorable discharges. The activities that flagged a GI's file typically occurred in his teens . . . In other cases, three soldiers encountered trouble because their stepmothers assertedly belonged to the CP [Communist Party]. Another was said to have a Communist mother-in-law who was 'lying low' but was soon to become active again. In fact, she had died in 1940, when the draftee was ten—a decade before he would meet his wife."[12]

So, the idea that the U.S. intelligence blackmailed Oswald into defecting to the Soviet Union is undoubtedly possible, and there is evidence that he may have alluded to this himself on more than one occasion.

By May 1961, Oswald had enough living behind the Iron Curtain and wanted to return home. "I wish to make it clear," his letter to the American Embassy stated, "that I am asking not only for the right to return to the United States but also for full guarantees that I shall not, under any circumstances, be persecuted [*sic*] for any act pertaining to this case. . . ." He added that unless the embassy agreed, he would ask his relatives "to see about getting something done in Washington."[13]

What exactly did Oswald mean when he referred to not being prosecuted regarding "any act pertaining to this case"? Was he asking for confirmation that he would not be held responsible for something he did before going to the Soviet Union that had to do with him going there in the first place? And why did Oswald, who allegedly had defected and said he would provide the Soviets with classified information, think he could intimidate the embassy by threatening to have his family pursue the matter in Washington? It was a veiled threat that Oswald and his family would disclose the truth about his defection if he were not guaranteed an unconditional return to the United States. But where was his leverage? What possibly could he have revealed? Unless something had occurred during Oswald's tour of duty in the Marines connected to his defection to the Soviet Union, he knew the government preferred to keep secret.

On January 30, 1962, Oswald wrote another letter from the Soviet Union, to John Connally, who he incorrectly assumed was still Secretary of the Navy. Oswald wrote that he intended to "employ all means to right this gross mistake or injustice. . . ." and that he had "always [*sic*] had the full sanction of the U.S. Embassy . . . and hence the U.S. government."[14]

Was Oswald again suggesting that he defected with the cooperation and backing of the U.S. government? To what "gross mistake or injustice" did he refer? If he had defected on his own without assistance, he had no one to blame but himself. So, it is reasonable to assume that the U.S. government did something to Oswald that was unjustified. Perhaps it was the dishonorable discharge he received after he defected, which would be a gross mistake or injustice if his defection were part of a covert intelligence operation, but this seemed more important than that.

Oswald may have revealed his true intention for going to Russia after returning home. He disclosed that "after a certain time after the Russians had assured themselves that I was the naïve American and believed in Communism, they arranged for me to receive a certain amount of money each month."

Oswald's most blatant admission that he had gone to the Soviet Union with the blessing of the United States came during a radio debate in New Orleans during the summer of 1963. Just days before, he was involved in the previously discussed street altercation with an anti-Castro Cuban exile named Carlos Bringuier. The radio debate was a follow-up to that. But Oswald did not know the FBI had briefed the host of the radio program regarding his background. As a result, the debate did not begin with issues about Cuba, but instead with Oswald's defection, and when asked why he went to the Soviet Union, Oswald stated: "I worked in Russia. I was under uh, the protection of the uh . . . of the uh . . . that is to say, I was not under the protection of the uh . . . American government. But that is I was at all times considered an American citizen."[15]

The debaters had caught Oswald by surprise. Flustered, he inadvertently admitted that he was under the protection of the U.S. government while in the Soviet Union. He quickly corrected himself, but it was too late. Oswald's admission can be heard clearly on a recording of the debate, despite that the Warren Commission indefensibly added the word "not" to their transcript of the broadcast, altering the meaning of what Oswald had said to hide his clear admission.

So, on numerous occasions, there is evidence that Oswald alluded to the fact that he was sent to the Soviet Union by U.S. intelligence. And if Wilcott is correct, the CIA blackmailed him into doing so. And according to Agent Smith's description of the type of person CIA was looking for, Oswald, who was not a rabid Marxist, Socialist, or Communist, was the perfect candidate for an intelligence mission involving a feigned defection to the Soviet Union. And blackmail, without question, was a means employed by recruiting agents looking for vulnerable service members. And that there is similar information regarding others who defected behind the Iron Curtain around the same time as Oswald further supports the allegation that he was not a legitimate defector and was on a covert intelligence mission.

* * *

As explained by CIA's Victor Marchetti to author Anthony Summer: "At the time, in 1959, the United States was having real difficulty in acquiring information out of the Soviet Union; the technical systems had, of course, not developed to the point that they are at today, and we were resorting to all sorts of activities. One of these activities was an ONI [Office of Naval Intelligence] program which involved three dozen, maybe forty, young men . . . made to appear disenchanted, poor, American youths who had been turned off and wanted to see what communism [entailed]. Some of these people lasted only a few weeks. They were sent into the Soviet Union, or into eastern Europe, with the specific intention the Soviets would pick them up and 'double' them if they suspected them of being U.S. agents or recruit them as KGB agents. They were trained at various naval installations both here and abroad. . . ."[16]

The program described by Marchetti may explain why only two American enlisted men defected to the Soviet bloc during the period between 1945 and 1959. However, in the eighteen months before 1960, there was a sudden rash of servicemen who did, including Oswald. Five Army men stationed in Germany and two former Navy men working for the National Security Agency defected. Among the civilians who defected were a former member of the OSS and a former member of the Navy employed by the CIA think tank, the Rand Corporation.[17]

Determining which defectors were genuine and intelligence plants was a matter of concern to those who could not access this information. One group that desperately wanted to know more was the State Department. On October 25, 1960, Hugh Cumming, the State Department's Intelligence and Research Bureau (INR) director, wrote to the CIA's Richard Bissell. "Though the CIA and FBI have detailed [American] defectors . . . recruited as intelligence agents by [Soviet] Bloc countries," Cumming stated, "there . . . [is not] a complete listing of those Americans now living in Bloc countries who might be called 'defectors.'" And they could provide "useful intelligence [and have been] significantly exploited for communist propaganda purposes."[18]

Cumming enclosed a list of eighteen American defectors, including Lee Harvey Oswald, who Cumming curiously listed as a tourist. At the time, Oswald was still living in the Soviet Union. Bissell turned it over to James Angleton's Counterintelligence (CI) and Sheffield Edwards' Office of Security (OS). Edwards was the CIA's security officer for Artichoke, which, as previously described, was part of CIA's mind control program MK-ULTRA. The CIA could not penetrate agents behind the Iron Curtain, which led to the creation of the MK-ULTRA mind control program in the first place. It may have included Oswald as one of its victims.

Robert L. Bannerman, the OS Deputy Chief under Sheffield Edwards, had a close relationship with Otto Otepka of the State Department Security Office. He also instructed his group to work closely with Angleton's people at CI. A memo written during this period says Bannerman ordered OS's Chief of Security Research Staff (SRS), Paul Gaynor, to assemble information on American defectors. Gaynor assigned the task to Marguerite Stevens (who would later investigate Clay Shaw as described in Chapter One). However, Stevens would recollect that Gaynor worded his request to persuade her not to investigate seven people, including Lee Harvey Oswald. We can only assume that Oswald would not have been on the list of seven was he the innocent defector he claimed to be.

While this was going on, Counterintelligence was formulating data on the seven defectors who were off-limits to Stevens, intending to provide this information to the State Department themselves. In addition to Oswald, the list included Army Sergeant Joseph Dutkanicz, Libero Ricciardelli, another "tourist," Army private Vladimir Sloboda, Robert E. Webster of the Rand Corporation, and Bruce Davis of the Army. On November 18, Angleton's Deputy Chief presented Richard Bissell with the letter they intended to send to the State Department. Bissell signed it three days later with an attached list of defectors. The tenth on the list was Lee Oswald. The entry next to his name stated "SECRET," a suspicious notation for a legitimate defector. Precisely what was it about Oswald that the CIA wanted to keep hidden?[19]

In 1963, Otto Otepka attempted to determine which defectors were genuine and those who weren't because the intelligence community was unwilling to reveal the truth. One of the cases he studied was Oswald's. According to Otepka, only five months before the assassination, the State Department was still undecided if he had been "one of ours or one of theirs."

Otepka was treading on dangerous ground, and in June 1963, the State Department dismissed him from his job. In addition, he was locked out of his office, and his safe was drilled open. The State Department removed everything from the safe. It would be years before they disclosed that the only information of importance in the safe was his study of American defectors, which included Oswald. Otepka complained, "We had not made up our minds [regarding Oswald] when my safe was drilled, and we were thrown out of the office."[20]

To borrow the words of Lyndon Johnson, stated in a 1969 interview with CBS television, Oswald "was quite a mysterious fellow, and he did have connections that bore examination."[21]

It is clear there was a high degree of interest at both CIA and the State Department regarding Oswald, and the Agency's need to maintain secrecy confirmed there was more to this man than the official story made him out to be. Could all this be attributed to what Oswald may have disclosed to the Soviets after his defection? The answer to this question is a definitive no. If that were the case, the U.S. government would have prosecuted Oswald after he returned home. The fact is they could not disclose the details of Oswald's defection because it would incriminate the CIA and anyone else who had a hand in sending him to Russia.

Army Private Vladimir Sloboda defected to the Soviet Union on August 3, 1960, less than one year after Oswald. He was one of the seven defectors, including Oswald, whom Marguerite Stevens was told not to investigate in October of that year. Despite this, Stevens did obtain some information. Sloboda was in Army Military Intelligence (MI) when he defected. He had worked as a translator-interrogator and documentary clerk with the Army's 513th MI Group in Frankfurt, Germany. "Sloboda is currently of interest to Security." Stevens wrote. Due to "his assignment prior to his defection to the Soviet Union, via East Germany, on 3 August."

Sloboda's intelligence background worried the CIA. As Stevens wrote, he "was in a position to [have] learned the identities of CIA personnel. . . ." However, the Agency was concerned that Sloboda had initially been a Polish or Soviet agent before defecting to the West. According to a CIA report: "Sloboda's prior KGB involvement was confirmed by [redacted] . . . Further indications are the facts that Sloboda was a KGB resettlement case and that he later told an American Embassy Moscow official that he had been blackmailed and framed into going to the USSR. . . ."[22]

The reference to blackmail is significant in that it may apply to Oswald as well. Also noteworthy was that Sloboda was possibly working for the KGB while he was in the U.S. Army, which was also applicable to the defection of John Joseph Dutkanicz, which occurred around the same time as Sloboda's.

On July 28, 1960, the Soviet news agency Tass reported that Dutkanicz had requested asylum in the Soviet Union. A CIA memo written in 1964 stated that although the Army officially assigned him to the 32nd Signal Battalion in Darmstadt, Germany, "his wife indicated that he had CIC [Counterintelligence Corp] connections." His CIA 201 file confirmed this, with the handwritten notation that "his Army assignment may have included intelligence functions of some kind."

Dutkanicz "told American Embassy officials in Moscow that he had been approached by KGB representatives in a bar near Darmstadt in 1958 and had accepted recruitment as a result of their threats and inducements [as we will see, this may have also happened to Oswald]. He claimed to have given them minimum cooperation from then until his defection, although the Army considered it probable that he had done more than he admitted. . . ."

Like Sloboda and Oswald, Dutkanicz had Communist tendencies. In November 1960, a Counterintelligence Staff summary for the State Department stated: "Dutkanicz has had difficulties with his wife and that she reported that he had relatives in the USSR and that he admitted that he was a Communist and that he had associated with German Nationals and Communists."[23]

Shortly after arriving in the Soviet Union, Dutkanicz spoke with a clergyman at the Intourist Hotel in Lvov, who subsequently reported the conversation to the CIA. The clergyman said Dutkanicz had recognized him and the two men went up to his room, where they talked for a short while. It is unknown if this was an innocent encounter or if the clergyman was a CIA contact for Dutkanicz, whose defection was an intelligence mission for the United States.

U.S. intelligence recruited Sloboda and Dutkanicz in Germany and Oswald in Japan. Still, there is a reference in *The Man Who Knew Too Much* by Dick Russell, suggesting there may have been a joint program that placed disenchanted service members from both areas behind the Iron Curtain. Russell referred to a passage from *The Secret War* by Sanche De Gramont, which references a link between the CIA and the military's Counterintelligence Corps (CIC) in West Germany. Recall it was CIC for whom Dutkanicz reportedly worked. According to Gramont:

"The CIC's main task is finding Communist agents in US military installations, such as clerical or kitchen help, and helping to sift agents who come to West Berlin as refugees. Agents thus found are turned over to the CIA for possible use as double agents. Army Intelligence in West Germany also had an operational espionage group, the mysterious Field Operations Intelligence (FOI). But CIA crowns all other agencies and takes over any case it chooses to handle . . ."[24]

FOI might be just a footnote in the Oswald saga were it not that Richard Case Nagell claimed to have belonged to this underground intelligence network. During the 1950s, FOI was a most specialized and revered branch of Military Intelligence (MI). It was highly secretive, and upon his entry into and departure from the organization, Nagell said: "I was required to sign papers subjecting myself to ten years' imprisonment or a ten-thousand-dollar fine, or both, if I disclosed to unauthorized persons the nature of my duties or other classified information, including the fact that an organization like FOI existed . . ."

On paper, FOI was part of the Army, believed to have been created by General MacArthur's "Little Fascist," General Charles Willoughby, during the occupation of Japan and the Korean War. It was part of CIA special (military) operations, "in effect a covert extension of CIA policy and activity designed to conceal the true nature of CIA objectives."

Nagell was with FOI in the Far East until he became disenchanted with their illegal activities, including assassinations. In 1957, while Oswald was at Atsugi, Nagell was transferred out of FOI and into Army Counterintelligence in Tokyo, where he worked for the CIA. It was here that Nagell claimed he first encountered Oswald, seen loitering outside the Soviet Embassy in Tokyo. Nagell subsequently learned that Oswald had entered the embassy and spoke with Soviet Colonel Nikolai G. Eroshkin, believed to be a military intelligence officer. According to Nagell, the CIA was trying to entice Eroshkin to defect and work for the United States, which was why he was at the embassy.[25]

If Nagell's account is accurate, the question becomes, what was Oswald doing at the Soviet Embassy speaking with a Soviet intelligence officer? Was Oswald working with U.S. intelligence, trying to get the Soviet Colonel to defect, or planting the seeds for his defection to the Soviet Union? We will revisit this in short order, but whatever the reason for Oswald's appearance at the Soviet Embassy, it would have been logical for the Soviets to turn a Marine from Atsugi, especially a radar operator. And it is just as likely that U.S. intelligence may have turned the tables on the KGB the following year by having Oswald show up in Moscow unannounced.

One item of interest is that Oswald was the first U.S. Marine to ever defect to the Soviet Union. More importantly, he was a radar operator who tracked U-2 flights, and having worked at the super-secret Atsugi airbase, he had access to a great deal of information, much of which was classified. Yet even though the Soviets usually paraded American military defectors before the press for propaganda purposes, ranting about American imperialism and the shortcomings of capitalism, they did not do that with Oswald. He remained hidden. It was the case even after the Soviets shot down the U-2 flown by Francis Gary Powers, which should have been a significant propaganda coup. Yet, the Russians decided not to exploit Oswald. There was something about him that the Russians were aware of, and they thought it best to keep him hidden from public view. It did not happen by accident. Precisely what was it about this relatively unknown Marine that made the Russians so nervous?

* * *

The first sign that Lee Oswald was involved in something clandestine occurred soon after he arrived in Japan. The Queen Bee was one of the most expensive nightclubs in Tokyo, catering to an exclusive clientele. Officers and pilots, including U-2 pilots, frequented the club, for only they could afford the costly price tag that the Queen Bee could request. A typical date cost anywhere from $60 to $100 for the evening, well beyond what Oswald could afford on his $85 a month take-home pay. Despite this, he developed a relationship with one of the Queen Bee hostesses, dating her on several occasions and taking her to the base numerous times. The other Marines were astonished that someone of her "class" would be interested in a lowly private like Oswald. According to one source, Naval Intelligence had speculated that hostesses from the Queen Bee were being used to gather intelligence and that Oswald was receiving money from someone who worked there.[26]

Oswald's fellow Marines were stunned when the Queen Bee hostess he had been dating visited him at the base. It undoubtedly came to the attention of military security (maybe FOI) and the CIA, Queen Bee hostesses were reportedly on the KGB payroll. According to James Angleton, the Queen Bee was one of the KGB's most intensive recruiting operations because of its proximity to the Atsugi base. "Unfortunately," said Angleton, "we found out later that [several] CIA officers and U-2 pilots began relationships with hostesses in that bar."[27]

According to Marine Corps friend David Bucknell, who was with Oswald in California after returning from Japan, Oswald told him he was alone in a bar when an attractive Japanese woman approached him. She was curious about what he did at Atsugi and asked him questions related to his work. Oswald reported the conversation to one of his superiors, who then arranged for Oswald to meet with an intelligence officer dressed in civilian clothes. Base authorities told Oswald the woman was a KGB contact, and he could do his country a service by providing her with false information. He was given money to spend at the Queen Bee and instructed to pursue the relationship.[28]

Since other Marines knew Oswald was spending time with a Queen Been hostess, there was something to the story. And according to Oswald's account, he met the woman sitting at a bar (like Dutkanicz). Based on what he could afford, it was probably not the Queen Bee where they met, and she was likely a prostitute. Still, it is not in doubt that she was a Queen Bee hostess who developed a relationship with Oswald. But how did this happen? One possibility is that Oswald was already involved with U.S. intelligence and was a "dangle," instructed to go to a bar where someone interested in obtaining information about the Atsugi base would likely approach him. Another possibility is what Oswald described to Bucknell. He then notified his superiors that he was innocently sitting at a bar, and a woman came to him asking questions about Atsugi. U.S. intelligence then gave him money to continue the relationship. Either way, after the encounter, Oswald was involved with U.S. intelligence. His fellow Marines saw Oswald walking around the base with a camera, photographing various sites.[29] It is hard to believe he would have done this so brazenly unless it was part of an intelligence operation that U.S. intelligence was directing.

We should also consider Richard Nagell's story involving Soviet military intelligence officer Colonel Nikolai Eroshkin and the alleged encounter with Oswald at the Soviet Embassy in Tokyo. For if Oswald were in contact with Eroshkin, there had to have been a connection to the Queen Bee hostess incident. We can safely rule out that Oswald was involved with Nagell to get Eroshkin to defect, for that would grossly inflate Oswald's importance to U.S. intelligence at that time. He was a lowly private who had an encounter with a likely Communist woman spy—nothing more. But Nagell learned that Oswald had met with Eroshkin, so if that was true, how did it come to be that Oswald and Eroshkin knew each other?

It is possible that Oswald, who was interested in Marxism, decided to visit the Soviet Embassy, perhaps with interest in traveling to the Soviet Union. In such a scenario, it is not surprising that the Soviets had an intelligence officer meet with the young Marine from Atsugi, so an Oswald encounter with Eroshkin was plausible. The Soviets would be suspicious, which would explain why the Queen Bee hostess later approached a lowly private like Oswald. The KGB had instructed her to do so, to find out what she could about this man. Based on what else we know, Oswald then reported the incident to his superiors. They told him to continue the relationship, which probably led to additional meetings with Eroshkin and a chance meeting with Nagell outside the Soviet Embassy. But was it a chance meeting? We can assume that U.S> intelligence photographed Oswald going in and out of the embassy every time he visited. With that in mind, was it possible that Nagell was following Oswald on behalf of U.S. intelligence, trying to find out what he was doing at the Soviet Embassy? For after they had photographed Oswald, wouldn't U.S. intelligence have wanted to verify that the story Oswald told them was true? If so, it follows that Nagell's story about trying to get Eroshkin to defect was a lie to provide him with a reason for being at the Embassy himself. It does make sense, for why would the U.S. want to encourage Eroshkin to defect? They would have preferred to keep him in place to obtain as much valuable information as they could from him. And if Nagell were lying, it would explain why he reencountered Oswald in the spring of 1963 back in the U.S. For it seems unlikely that Nagell would have investigated Oswald in Texas, and he turned out to be the same man that Nagell had accidentally encountered in front of the Soviet Embassy in Japan years before. What is more believable is that U.S. intelligence told Nagell to investigate Oswald in Japan, which he did. His renewed interest in Oswald in 1963 was just a continuation of that initial assignment.

Another possibility is that the Queen Bee hostess notified the Soviet Embassy after she met Oswald. She subsequently sent Oswald to the embassy to see Eroshkin, but this scenario is less believable. The Soviets would have assumed that the U.S. was photographing all people entering and leaving the embassy, so they would not have wanted to meet Oswald there. Doing so would have ended any chance they had of obtaining intelligence information from the Atsugi radar operator. For this reason alone, we should rule this out. So, the only plausible explanation is the first scenario. Oswald approached the Soviet embassy on his own, which prompted the encounter with the Queen Bee hostess, who the KGB told to investigate Oswald. Oswald then subsequently notified his superiors about the meeting. It led to the surveillance of Oswald by Richard Case Nagell.

We should also consider this scenario in conjunction with Oswald's warning not to prosecute him upon returning from the Soviet Union. He called it a "gross mistake or injustice." Was Oswald blackmailed into traveling to the Soviet Union on an intelligence mission because he had visited the Soviet Embassy, possibly looking to obtain more information about life in Russia because he wanted to travel there someday? Was he falsely accused of providing classified information to a Soviet spy, information he was given by U.S. intelligence, to generate interest from the hostess or Eroshkin, to see where this would lead? And what if he were later given a lie detector test by people who were not involved in the Queen Bee/Eroshkin incident. Wouldn't that have disclosed classified information and placed Oswald in a compromising position? Or was Oswald set up to develop a relationship with the woman and Eroshkin, then given a lie detector test that U.S. intelligence knew he would fail? No one knows for sure what happened, but it appears that Oswald became a pawn of U.S. intelligence, which was why he was so enraged about the "injustice" he faced.

In *On the Trail of the JFK Assassins*, author Dick Russell describes his discussion with Frank Camper, a twenty-year intelligence veteran with numerous CIA and FBI contacts. He served in Vietnam with the elite Special Operations Group and later worked under deep cover, penetrating terrorist organizations worldwide. According to Camper, "Oswald reported a Japanese Communist approach to him to Naval Intelligence and then the CIA picked him up. He fit the profile for [an] MKULTRA [mind control program]." Camper thought it was evident because Oswald "was frequently in the brig or base hospital, was recalled from a unit movement to Formosa to return to the Atsugi hospital, and ended up being assigned to the hospital on a layover or casual basis."[30]

Camper's explanation has merit, for Oswald did frequent hospitals under suspicious circumstances, and his conduct throughout his tour at Atsugi further supports what Camper claims to have occurred.

* * *

A month after Oswald arrived in Japan, officers told his unit they were going to the Philippines. On October 27, a .22-caliber derringer, which Oswald had ordered from a mail-order house in the United States and illegally had in his possession, fell as he gathered gear from his locker and accidentally discharged, grazing his left elbow. The wound was superficial and caused minor damage. Two Marines who came rushing into his room claimed the bullet never touched Oswald. Marine Paul Murphy told the Warren Commission that Oswald sat on his bunk and said calmly: "I believe I shot myself."[31]

Many believed Oswald staged the incident to create an excuse for staying at Atsugi while his unit traveled to the Philippines. Undoubtedly this was true, but questions abound. First, could Oswald have ordered a gun by mail from the U.S. and shipped it to Japan in less than a month? And why did he need the gun? By this time, the Queen Bee hostess Oswald was seeing was already spending time with someone else, so the faked shooting was unrelated to her. Maybe it was the meeting with Eroshkin and Oswald's visits to the Soviet Embassy, but this does not make sense. What is significant is that even though the shooting left Oswald virtually uninjured, the record shows he spent nineteen days in a hospital, an unjustifiable amount of time for such a minor wound. It is hard to understand unless the entire affair was a convenient cover for pulling Oswald out of his unit.

The shooting incident occurred only six weeks after Oswald arrived in Japan. Allowing for the Queen Bee affair to develop, it probably was a maximum of two to three weeks before the shooting accident that intelligence officers would have questioned Oswald about his encounter with the hostess and Eroshkin. The timing is such that the staged event that kept him at Atsugi was not because of the Queen Bee and Eroshkin encounters, at least not directly. For if Oswald was blackmail by U.S. intelligence after failing a lie detector test, it is a good possibility that Frank

Camper's assertion was true, and he was pulled out of his unit and placed in a program involving mind-altering drugs.

Oswald was released from the hospital on November 15 and rejoined his unit to accompany them to the Philippines five days later. Other than the shooting death of Private Schrand on January 15, the trip was essentially uneventful. Interestingly, Oswald was kept on mess duty for almost the entire trip, despite making such an initial favorable impression on his superiors at Atsugi.

On March 18, 1958, Oswald and his unit returned to Atsugi, and he immediately applied for reinstatement as a radar operator. His superiors denied his request, and he remained on mess duty. Thinking the Marines had singled him out for harsh treatment, he applied for a hardship discharge, a rather drastic action. His request once again was turned down. His fellow Marines would later remember him as becoming increasingly bitter over the treatment he was receiving.[32]

In April, authorities at Atsugi court-martialed Oswald for illegal possession of the firearm he shot himself with the previous fall. He applied for and received an extension to his overseas duty three days later, contradicting the hardship discharge he had requested roughly a month before. His sentence for the gun possession charge was 20 days in the brig, suspended for six months. Assuming Oswald behaved himself for that period, the base would suspend the sentence.

The next couple of months were relatively uneventful for Oswald, and the official record does not mention anything occurring that was out of the ordinary. However, by the end of June, he was in trouble again when he had an altercation with a sergeant whom he felt had singled him out for mess duty. One evening Oswald tried to instigate a fight with a sergeant at the Enlisted Men's Club, telling him, "You've got guts to come in here." Not having the desired effect, Oswald spilled a drink on the sergeant at a local Marine hangout three days later, and the military police had to intervene.

Provoking a fight and violent behavior was entirely out of character for Oswald. His fellow Marines remembered him as being "almost frail, shy and quiet" when he arrived in Japan. People do change as they mature, so Oswald's aggressiveness can be attributed to this. On the other hand, mind-altering drugs can have the same effect, which could explain why Oswald acted in such a violent manner.

For his altercation with the sergeant, the sentence Lee Oswald received was 28 days in the brig. His original sentence of 20 days for possession of the illegal firearm, which was on hold, pending his good behavior, should now have gone into effect as well. As a result, the base should have imprisoned Oswald for a total of 48 days. However, according to the official record, he was released after serving only 17 days. It seems impossible. Oswald spilled a drink on a sergeant, and he didn't even have to serve the complete sentence applicable to that charge alone? Maybe the amount of time served is less significant than the fact that for the second time in nine months, Oswald was away from his unit for an extended period. A time where his whereabouts are unknown. And we should not assume it was the brig where Oswald spent his time. Authorities can doctor military records when necessary, including the actual time he was incarcerated, especially if what Oswald was involved in could not be revealed to anyone.

Years later, and unrelated to Oswald, *Time* magazine ran an article that could shed light on Oswald's alleged time in the brig. "If a soldier is assigned highly clandestine work," *Time* reported, "his records are changed to make it appear as if he resigned from the military or was given civilian status." It was "called sheep dipping, after the practice of bathing sheep before they are sheered."[33]

Oswald was released from the brig on August 13 and was, according to the recollection of fellow Marine Joseph D. Macedo, "a completely changed person . . ." "I've seen enough of a democratic society here in MACS-1," Oswald said. "When I get out, I'm going to try something else." He began to associate less with fellow Marines and more with his Japanese friends (Communists, perhaps). Then, in September, as the Communist Chinese appeared on the brink of moving militarily against the islands of Quemoy and Matsu, Oswald and his unit were sent to Formosa. It was here that the official record regarding him becomes even more confusing. The Department of Defense told the HSCA in 1978 that Oswald stayed with a "rear echelon" at Atsugi while his unit traveled to Formosa without him. It is contradictory to Oswald's recollection that he was in Formosa, and one of his officers, Lieutenant Charles Rhodes, confirmed he was there. Why then did Defense Department records show otherwise?[34]

The Defense Department's error may have had something to do with an incident while Oswald was in Formosa. Shortly after his unit arrived, Oswald was assigned to guard duty. Around midnight, Lieutenant Rhodes heard four or five shots ring out from the position that Oswald was protecting. Arriving at the scene, Rhodes found Oswald slumped against a tree. According to Rhodes, "When I got to him, he was shaking and crying. He said he had seen men in the woods and that he challenged them and then started shooting . . . He kept saying he couldn't bear guard duty."[35]

Once again, something is wrong here, for the facts do not add up, not the least of which was an apparent change in Oswald's emotional state, which mind-altering drugs could have also caused. In approximately one year, we have a young Marine who starts spending time with a beautiful Japanese "hostess," a woman who likely had KGB connections. He encounters a Soviet military intelligence officer as well. Shortly after that, officials charged Oswald with shooting himself with an illegal firearm. He does not serve time but spends eighteen days in the hospital for a flesh wound. Upon release, he travels with his unit to the Philippines, where Private Schrand dies while on guard duty, and some thought Oswald was a suspect. He remains on mess duty, which continued after his release from the hospital. Then, Oswald instigates a confrontation with a sergeant, throwing a drink at him. He is supposed to spend forty-eight days in the brig, but he serves only seventeen days.

After all this, Oswald fires multiple shots from his rifle while on guard duty in Formosa, which we know from the Schrand incident violated regulations.

Oswald's conduct that night on guard duty was unacceptable and out of character for him. And a thorough investigation was warranted. But after everything he had done, in only one year, his punishment for firing his gun and breaking down in tears was to be flown back to Atsugi by military plane, and he arrived there on October 5. How could that be? And how could a lowly private, who kept breaking the rules, who showed signs of emotional instability, be provided such preferential treatment? And what happened next is even more bizarre. The official record states that Oswald was returned from Formosa to Atsugi for medical treatment because he suffered from urethritis, a mild case of gonorrhea. It further defies logic. First, why wasn't Oswald treated with medication in Formosa and allowed to go about his regular duties like so many other soldiers were forced to do when inflicted with venereal disease? Second, why wasn't he disciplined for contracting venereal disease, which would have been typical for the military at the time, or for firing live ammo while on guard duty? Third, how could the official medical record state that he contracted the disease ". . . in line of duty, not due to own misconduct." If this last item is genuine, it could have something to do with the Queen Bee hostess. However, taken in its entirety, the official explanation does not add up.

There is also something to consider about the urethritis diagnosis. Oswald reportedly was also treated repeatedly while in Japan for bleeding from the rectum."[36] Was this confirmation of Oswald's homosexuality? Perhaps, but it seems the real reason for Oswald's hasty departure from Formosa was his emotional state of mind when they found him slumped against a tree crying and shaking. He was removed from his unit again and placed in a hospital for the second known time in roughly a year, an excessive reaction to his "line of duty" misadventure. We should also not forget his stint in the brig for seventeen days. There was something out of the ordinary going on here. Oswald displayed emotional problems and bouts of aggressive anger. Yet, they treated him with kid gloves and repeatedly kept him in isolation. Why?

The entire Formosa episode is highly suspect. In addition, there is ambiguity regarding Oswald's pay records for this period. The Warren Commission requested the pay records early in their investigation, but they did not receive them until right before submitting their report. At one point, the records placed Oswald in a different unit than he was assigned to and showed that his pay scale changed when he returned to Japan from Formosa. How they changed is unknown, for that part of his pay records was blanked out. Precisely what could have been in the pay records of a lowly private, albeit Oswald, that had to remain hidden is hard to imagine. Still, as we have seen, secrecy regarding Oswald was not an unusual occurrence. And in this instance, with the other questions surrounding Oswald's first year in the Marines, his pay records changed for a reason, and how this related to his work could not be revealed. So, what could there have been that caused this?[37]

There is ample evidence to believe that Oswald was involved in a drug experimentation program at Atsugi, which would have been part of his defection to the Soviet Union. As has been previously discussed, the CIA, George White, and military intelligence all conducted drug experimentation on innocent victims at hospitals across the United States in the decade leading up to Oswald's service in the Marines. Oswald likely had already been subject to drug experimentation. At the same time, he was a teenager assigned to the Bordentown Reformatory, where both the CIA and the U.S. Army had experimented on young boys there. There was also something strange about Oswald's brief relationship with David Ferrie in New Orleans, a well-versed man in hypnotism who brought CAP cadets to the East Louisiana State Hospital, with which Oswald also seemed to have been familiar. There were the overseas trips Ferrie took the cadets on, which could have involved mind-altering drug experimentation. What happened in Haiti was just one example. Ferrie may also have been instrumental in getting Oswald to join the Marines in the first place. It is possible that while Oswald was at Atsugi, authorities learned about his experience at Bordentown. It could have happened during a lie-detector test, which is how Wilcott claimed officials became aware of incriminating evidence against Oswald, and they knew they could force Oswald to become involved in a covert operation against his will.

Or maybe his past had nothing to do with it, and Oswald entered a drug experimentation program at Atsugi because he had approached the Soviet Embassy, or because a lie detector showed he was gay, or it revealed he was a Marxist. It may have started at Bordentown, New Jersey. There was also Norman, Oklahoma. Mexico City, East Louisiana State Hospital in Jackson, Louisiana, and Tulane University. Then there was the testimony of New Orleans assistant district attorney Edward G. Gillin and his strange encounter with Oswald. Finally, there was Atsugi. The fact is, the specter of drug experimentation hovered over Oswald his entire adult life. Ignoring this would be irresponsible, for where there is smoke, there is fire. And a person would not have so many close encounters with potential drug experimentation unless there were some truth involved.

Furthermore, we know the military experimented on soldiers, so there is no reason to believe that this could not have happened to Oswald while at Atsugi. At the time, he was just another ordinary Marine, like countless others, who may have willingly, or unwillingly, become involved in a dangerous experiment. It would be wrong to reject this possibility due to what fate had in store for him down the road.

As previously mentioned, we know that the Joint Technical Advisory Group building at Atsugi did experiments using LSD on military personnel. These men were being targeted and used as guinea pigs. It was a practice that was being performed throughout the United States and overseas. "[T]here are some four thousand (4,000) American military men who are serving court-martial sentences in the federal prisons . . . ," read a Project Artichoke memo. We should keep in mind Oswald's intense desire to have the "gross mistake or injustice" removed from his military record. The Artichoke memo continued that military personnel could have their sentences reduced if they were willing to get involved in covert operations that included drug experimentation.[38]

Like the infamous Dr. Sidney Gottlieb, CIA officials traveled to Japan during the mid-to-late 1950s to conduct drug tests using LSD. And several American physicians frequently traveled to Atsugi to perform testing for the CIA as part of Project Artichoke. One prominent physician made over 15 trips to Atsugi, involving experimentation with LSD on unidentified subjects, including American service members. One CIA document related to this was dated 1957, which was while Oswald was at Atsugi. So, the possibility for Oswald to be part of mind-altering drug testing did exist.[39]

We also know what they were trying to accomplish. The MKULTRA program was interested in uncovering "substances which will promote illogical thinking and impulsiveness to the point where the recipient would be discredited in public; substances which increase the efficiency of mentation and perception; materials which will prevent or counteract the intoxicating effect of alcohol; materials which will promote the intoxicating effect of alcohol; materials which will render the induction of hypnosis easier; substances which will enhance the ability of individuals to withstand privation, torture and coercion; materials and physical methods which will produce amnesia for events preceding and during their use; physical methods of producing shock and confusion over extended periods of time and capable of surreptitious use; . . . substances which alter personality structure in such a way that the tendency of the recipient to become dependent upon another person is enhanced; a material which will cause mental confusion of such a type that the individual under its influence will find it difficult to maintain a fabrication under questioning; a material . . . which in very small amounts will make it impossible for a man to perform any physical activity whatever."[40]

Another CIA memo about Artichoke suggested it should "be used as a last resort when all or nearly all the attempts at obtaining information have failed or when a subject is completely recalcitrant or particularly stubborn." The same memo said Artichoke was best "operated in a hospital or a hospital-type area."[41]

The dissection of the two CIA memos is quite revealing as they pertain to Oswald. The reference in the second memo that a hospital was the best setting to conduct drug experimentation certainly applies to him, for he was in the hospital on at least two separate occasions, both of which should not have required hospitalization. It also applies to the time he served in the brig, which Oswald knew would happen when he spilled a drink on the sergeant.

Consider what William K. Trail told the FBI in an interview two weeks after the assassination. "He first became aware of the fact that Lee Harvey Oswald was part of their [1st Marine Air Wing unit] during late August or early September 1958," Trail said. When their group went to Formosa, "Oswald and another Marine were being held prisoners at Atsugi." They "had to be picked up by a 'chaser' with a gun." He saw Oswald "marched from the Marine jail without shoes."[42]

William Trail first saw Oswald when he was removed from the brig, shipped out with him to Formosa on September 14th, then later served with him stateside at the Marine base in Santa Ana. The problem is, the official record says Oswald served only seventeen days in the brig until August 13. It was a month before Trail says he saw him leaving. Either Trail was mistaken, or Oswald was kept in the brig longer than the official states. Or maybe Oswald was placed in a hospital once again for another month. Based on the other evidence we are aware of, it is likely that Trail was telling the truth, for he had no reason to lie.

From the first memo, we learn that the CIA experimented with drugs that would "promote illogical thinking and impulsiveness to the point where the recipient would be discredited in public." Doctors gave recipients w"substances which alter personality structure," which would explain Oswald's uncharacteristic anger and signs of depression. Then there is the reference to a drug that could "promote the intoxicating effect of alcohol . . . ," which is of interest because some of his fellow Marines uncharacteristically recalled Oswald having a severe drinking problem. Peter Cassisi said Oswald came back from leave several times "in a completely drunken condition." In an affidavit, John Heindel said that Oswald "drank a great deal, often becoming intoxicated." Jerry E. Pitts recalled that Oswald "passed out drunk in the parking lot next to the barracks" one evening.[43] Was Oswald's reaction to alcohol not because he drank so excessively that he would pass out but a side effect from the mind-altering drugs he had to take? We will never know.

Curiously, his fellow Marines also reported that when he did return drunk, he would shout, "Save your Confederate money, boys. The South will rise again!" It was strange for an alleged Marxist to say, but not so unusual for a racist who grew up in the South, which he was, as supported by additional examples discussed in previous chapters.[44] The man was complex, and his alleged adherence to Marxism was minimum at best, a diversion to support a narrative he was trying to promote. But apparently, he was betrayed by the liquor, which seemingly put the real Oswald on display.

A drug that would "make it impossible for a man to perform any physical activity whatever" could explain Oswald's prolonged work orders that kept him on mess duty.

Drugs that would "render the induction of hypnosis easier" were also of interest, considering Marine Daniel Powers' testimony before the Warren Commission. Oswald was "an individual you could brainwash, and quite easily," Powers said. "A lot of his mannerisms were closely related to other homosexuals I had seen . . ."

Powers thought Oswald was gay, which is supported by the information previously cited.

Was Powers correct? Could Oswald be easily brainwashed? If true, it suggests doctors subjected Oswald to hypnosis, which the CIA used in conjunction with mind-altering drugs. Under Project Bluebird, the CIA was specific about what they wanted to obtain from hypnosis. "Can we 'condition' by post-hypnotic suggestion, Agency employees (or persons of interest to this agency) to prevent them from giving information to any unauthorized source or for committing any act on behalf of a foreign or domestic enemy?"Can we, in a matter of an hour, two hours, one day, etc., induce a hypnotized condition in an unwilling subject to such an extent that he will perform an act for our benefit?; "Could we seize a subject and in the space of an hour or two by post-hypnotic control have him crash an airplane, wreck a train, etc.?; Can we through post-hypnotic control induce a subject to commit violence against another individual, or induce a subject to murder another individual or group of individuals?; "Can we, through post-hypnotic control, create a condition whereby a subject would forget any such induced act after the subject is brought out of his 'conditional' state?"[45]

In 1958, the Bureau of Social Science Research, a subcontractor to the Rand Corporation, issued a report to the Air Force entitled, "The Use of Hypnosis in Intelligence and Related Military Situations." The chief investigator, Albert Biderman, looked into brainwashing techniques for the Army and Air Force since the early 1950s. The author, Seymour Fisher of the National Institute for Mental Health, wrote in his introduction that "hypnosis has long been a potentially powerful instrument for controlling human behavior. Undoubtedly, the intelligence divisions of many countries have given serious thought to this potential and have done classified research in various areas of hypnosis . . . these techniques could have been used and covered up so successfully that they might be impossible to recognize."

The researchers determined that hypnotic techniques were limited as an "offensive measure" due to "the relatively small percentage of individuals susceptible to deep hypnosis." However, for agents subject to capture and interrogation, which would apply to someone on a covert mission behind the Iron Curtain, the report said hypnosis had merit, as described below:

> "In defensive applications, subjects can be . . . selected by a criterion of hypnotizability [sic], and subsequently trained in accord[ance] with their anticipated military function . . . Personnel . . . could be prepared against possible capture in many different ways: (a) by simple hypnotic suggestion, they could be "immunized" against hypnotic interrogation and suggestion by the enemy; (b) with posthypnotic and autosuggestive [sic] training, appropriately timed amnesias . . . ; (c) posthypnotic depersonalization and related dissociative states could be built into the subjects

so that if they fall into enemy hands, they would no longer function as rational, integrated individuals . . ."[46]

Indeed, sufficient supporting evidence convincingly suggests that Oswald's Soviet adventure included preparation with mind-altering drugs. As previously discussed, the CIA had already concluded that drugs could be helpful to control agents placed behind the Iron Curtain by the time Oswald arrived at Atsugi. Therefore, if Oswald was working for American intelligence when he defected, which the evidence supports, he was likely administered drugs at Atsugi in preparation for this and was probably subject to hypnosis as well, which is further supported by a CIA report which contained the following passage:

"As a result of several years' effort devoted primarily to attempts at [the] penetration of denied areas through various black techniques, the Agency has concluded that the vehicle of legal travel offers greater opportunities to place controlled agents within denied areas.

"In the case of long-range operations, [a] lapse of time alone will erode motivation. There is, therefore, the immediate requirement for the development of every technique . . . devised to precondition the agent mind and to create within him viable and long-lasting [sic] motivation impervious to [the] lapse of time and direct psychological attacks by the enemy."[47]

* * *

With his unit still in Taiwan, Oswald was temporarily assigned to an airbase 430 miles southwest of Tokyo, essentially removing him from Atsugi's activities and those who knew him in Japan up to this point. Owen Dejanovich, who had attended radar school at Keesler Air Base with Oswald, approached his old acquaintance but found he had grown bitter. According to Dejanovich, "He kept referring to the Marines at the center as 'You Americans,' as if he was some sort of foreigner simply observing what we were doing." He spoke about "American imperialism" and "exploitation." Dejanovich also saw Oswald in the company of a Eurasian woman, and he wondered why such an attractive "roundeye" would waste her time with a guy like Oswald. It was reminiscent of Atsugi and the hostess from the Queen Bee, for once again, Oswald was keeping company with a woman who should not have been interested in him. She taught him to speak Russian, so we should not reject the possibility that she worked for the KGB.

On November 2, 1958, Lee Harvey Oswald returned to the United States, having spent less than fourteen months in Japan, and a lot had happened in such a short period. Unknown to the nineteen-year-old Marine, he had a little over five years left to live. Many questions remain unanswered regarding this period, but it is hard to accept that this was an ordinary Marine. Viewed in light of his defection to the Soviet Union, the record of his tour of duty in Japan indicates he was trained for an operation behind the Iron Curtain and was subject to drug experimentation and hypnosis as part of this operation. One thing is sure. If U.S. intelligence had trained Oswald for a covert assignment, it didn't end with his departure from Japan. For the mystery surrounding this man had only just begun.

Young Lee Harvey Oswald was looking for a political ideology when he moved to New Orleans with his mother in 1954. He left New York City behind and the reformatory where he likely was involved in mind-altering drug experimentation, something that would hover over him the remainder of his life.

David Ferrie was a right-wing, anti-Communist fanatic, close to Mafia boss Carlos Marcello and Guy Banister. A pedophile, Ferrie first met Oswald in 1955 in New Orleans and was likely the one who introduced him to Guy Banister and the neo-Nazi types with whom Ferrie associated.

Stephen Fritchman was the Communist pastor at the First Unitarian Church of Los Angeles that Oswald attended. The Unitarian Church worked closely with the Albert Schweitzer College in Switzerland, where Oswald was enrolled but never showed up. He defected to the Soviet Union instead.

Lincoln Rockwell headed the American Nazi Party. Oswald's notebook contained Rockwell's name, along with Daniel Burros, another Nazi. Rockwell wrote to J. Edgar Hoover five days after the assassination, listing twenty-seven Nazi storm troopers Rockwell thought were potential assassins. It may have been an admission that Oswald belonged to his group.

Clay Shaw had military intelligence and CIA connections and was close to the radical right-wing group operating in New Orleans. Lee Harvey Oswald was close to the group as well, and Shaw may have known him.

General Charles Willoughby (facing forward) was known as MacArthur's "Little Fascist." He was close to Bill Donovan, Allen Dulles, Reinhard Gehlen, and ex-Nazis operating out of Madrid. He belonged to right-wing paramilitary groups in the United States in the 1950s and 60s looking to overthrow the U.S. government.

General Walker was a right-wing fire-brand who preached military insurrection. After leaving the army in 1961, he resided in Dallas and became close to the radical right-wing Fascist groups. He was a member of the Minutemen, a paramilitary group that wanted to remove the "Communists" who ran the U.S. government from power.

General Pedro del Valle wrote a letter to President Truman calling him a traitor for the way he handled the Korean War. A disciple of MacArthur, in the late 1950s he aligned himself with violent right-wing paramilitary groups that wanted to take over the U.S. government. A racist and an anti-Semite, del Valle was an avid supporter of the Fascist movement that by 1960 thought the American way of life was in jeopardy.

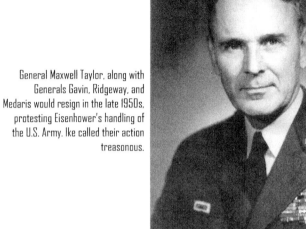

General Maxwell Taylor, along with Generals Gavin, Ridgeway, and Medaris would resign in the late 1950s, protesting Eisenhower's handling of the U.S. Army. Ike called their action treasonous.

John Foster Dulles was Eisenhower's Secretary of State. He repeatedly sabotaged any effort by Ike to normalize relations with the Soviets.

The CIA-connected George de Mohren-schildt controlled Oswald during the year leading up to the JFK assassination, had CIA connections, and was involved in the CIA attempt to assassinate President Duvalier in Haiti. In the 1950s, he had U.S. intelligence connections as an émigré working with the CIA's stay-behind armies in Europe.

Lousiana Senator James Eastland worked with Guy Banister and leading Southern racists to maintain racial segregation in the 1950s and 60s. They all believed the Soviet Union and Cuba financed the civil rights movement to create unrest in the United States.

CIA agent Howard Hunt, who was close to the Cuban exile community and CIA assassins like David Morales and Frank Sturgis, was part of the right-wing group that wanted to remove Castro from power.

Dallas District Attorney Henry Wade immediately called the JFK assassination an international conspiracy until Lyndon Johnson's people in Washington put a stop to it.

Vice President Richard Nixon was the White House's connection to the Cuban operation to take over Cuba and assassinate Castro. Extremely far-right, he only supported Cubans who wanted Batista to remain in power. He received pushback from the leftists at the CIA, who did not wish to see a Nixon Presidency.

Francis Gary Powers piloted the U-2 plane that was shot down over the Soviet Union, ending Eisenhower's hopes to sign a nuclear test ban treaty with the Russians. The CIA likely sabotaged the plane, which occurred while Oswald was living in the Soviet Union.

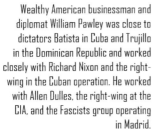

Wealthy American businessman and diplomat William Pawley was close to dictators Batista in Cuba and Trujillo in the Dominican Republic and worked closely with Richard Nixon and the right-wing in the Cuban operation. He worked with Allen Dulles, the right-wing at the CIA, and the Fascists group operating in Madrid.

American mercenary William Morgan supported Castro but became part of June Cobb's plot to overthrow the Cuban leader. The operation was sabotaged by Allen Dulles because many involved, like Morgan, had previously supported Castro and leaned too far to the left. It resulted in Morgan's arrest and death by firing squad.

Rolando Cubela, called "Castro's gun-toting bully boy" by Henry Luce's Time magazine, in 1956 was part of the Cuban Student Directorate, who tried to assassinate Batista. On the day of JFK's assassination, he met with the CIA's Desmond FitzGerald in Paris to discuss the possibility of killing Castro. He may have been a Cuban double agent.

CIA agent June Cobb had penetrated the Castro government and was involved in a 1959 attempt run out of the U.S. Embassy in Havana to overthrow Castro. She was connected to the CIA's assassination section and appeared to have shadowed Oswald the year before JFK's assassination.

Cardinal Spellman was a far-right, anti-Communist Roman Catholic cleric who worked with Joseph Kennedy on numerous occasions. Spellman sent priests throughout Latin America for the CIA and worked closely with the Vatican in fighting communism in Italy.

Joseph Kennedy, shown here in an early photo with his wife and eight children, desperately wanted one of his sons to be elected president. He made secret deals with the Mafia to get John elected in 1960. His mob dealings placed both his sons in danger after JFK became president.

Santo Trafficante, Jr. worked for Fidel Castro when he allegedly tried to assassinate the Cuban leader for the CIA. He was part of the Luciano/Dulles/Donovan drug operation in Cuba that funded the stay-behind armies in Europe.

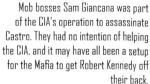

Mob bosses Sam Giancana was part of the CIA's operation to assassinate Castro. They had no intention of helping the CIA, and it may have all been a setup for the Mafia to get Robert Kennedy off their back.

Jimmy Hoffa (shown seated) with mob-connected electronic surveillance expert Bernard Spindel. Hoffa worked with Santo Trafficante and Carlos Marcello in drug trafficking and arms smuggling to Cuba. He was associated with the mob-connected Irv Davidson in Haiti while George de Mohrenschildt was there looking to assassinate Duvalier. A number of his illegal endeavors involved Jack Ruby.

L.A. mobster Mickey Cohen ran guns to Cuba with Hoffa and Jack Ruby in the 1950s. He was romantically involved with stripper Candy Barr. Three days after the JFK assassination, Barr called Ruby a "good-natured heavyweight" and said Oswald "dripped with political venom with a narrow group of acquaintances." How did she know this?

Ruth Paine (shown sitting on the left with Marina Oswald and Lee's mother Marguerite after the assassination) was one in a string of Unitarians who "babysat" Lee and Marina from the time they returned from the Soviet Union until the assassination. Paine's father and sister had CIA connections.

Cord Meyer was responsible for tracking student movements around the world for the CIA. The evidence suggests that, along with Priscilla Johnson, the MIT Center for International Studies, and Harvard's Russian Research Center, he was involved in Oswald's defection to the Soviet Union on behalf of the CIA.

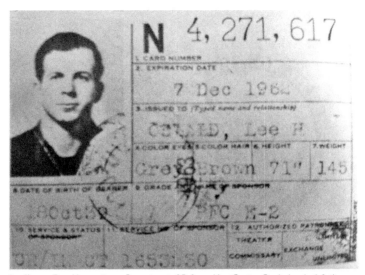

Lee Harvey Oswald was given a Department of Defense Identification Card when he left the Marines. The ID card's image was not of Oswald, proving the card was a forgery. Notice the photo on his passport below, taken around the same time, which was different from the ID card photo. The passport photo was likely the real Oswald.

Lee Harvey Oswald's passport photo when he left the Marines included the image of the real Oswald. Note it was not the same photo as the ID card above. By design, Oswald left his passport at the U.S. Embassy in Moscow when he defected.

Notice of Classification card of Alex James Hidell with the same forged photo as Oswald's Department of Defense Identification Card. The card was found in Oswald's wallet after the Dallas police arrested him. The reason for Oswald's defection in 1959 may have been to make it appear that the Russians forged his documents while he lived there.

The so-called "Minsk Photo" showing the same false image of Oswald. Notice the cutout at the bottom right, which matched the postmark location on the DOD ID Card. The illusion created by U.S. intelligence was that the Soviets had killed Oswald in Russia, and a phony "sleeper agent" had taken his place, who they could set up to take the fall for any crime.

Dean Rusk, Secretary of State under Kennedy, worried that an impostor had taken Oswald's place. He wrote the U.S. Embassy in Moscow, "It is assumed that the person who has been in communication with the Embassy is the person who was issued a passport in the name of Lee Harvey Oswald."

FBI Director J. Edgar Hoover was also concerned about an Oswald impostor returning to the U.S. He wrote the State Department's Office of Security stating, "Since there is a possibility that an impostor is using Oswald's birth certificate, any current information the Department of State may have concerning subject will be appreciated."

- 7 -

Give Peace a Chance and
Other Fairy Tales

"There is a growing realization that the enemies of freedom are not
foreign powers . . . there are forces at work within the nation which
are just as dangerous . . . Our only protection . . . is a real revival of
the spiritual life from which freedom flowed through our founding
fathers."

—R.L. Decker, National Association of
Evangelicals executive director

*A radical right-wing Christian religious revival occurred in the 1950s, spawned by elites
and driven by anti-communism, resistance to civil rights, and preserving the American
way of life. It would result in federal edicts that made prayer in school mandatory.
They added "In God We Trust" to currency and changed the Pledge of Allegiance to
include "One Nation Under God." It served to unite all racist hate groups that fought
segregation because God was on their side. It was especially true in Dallas and New
Orleans, where right-wing Christian ministers used their pulpit to spew messages of hate
to congregations who hung on their every word. It was why when Kennedy's running
mate, Texas Senator Lyndon B. Johnson, and his wife arrived at a Dallas hotel just four
days before the election, a group of Republican women known as the "Mink Coat Mob"
attacked them. The senior Senator from Texas was called a Socialist and a traitor for
supporting JFK, and roughly three years later, Kennedy's assassination would occur in
the same bible-toting city.*

* * *

In September 1959, less than six months after his Berlin ultimatum deadline passed without incident, Nikita Khrushchev, his wife, two daughters, and

son-in-law made a thirteen-day visit to the United States, the first Soviet leader ever to do so. They arrived in Washington on September 15. If they expected a warm reception, they were soon disappointed, for the limousine route from the airport was lined with stone-faced people who remained silent along the entire fifteen-mile ride. Khrushchev accused Eisenhower's people of instructing onlookers to react that way, but he knew better. At a National Press Club gathering, the first question asked of Khrushchev was to describe his role during Stalin's reign of terror, which prompted derisive laughter from the audience. The Soviet leader was not pleased.

Two days later, the entourage took a train to New York, where speeches by Mayor Robert Wagner and U.N. Ambassador Henry Cabot Lodge were interpreted as "provocations" by their guests. Out on the street, Khrushchev got into a confrontation with hecklers protesting his visit. At an affair at the Economic Club, attended by two thousand guests, Khrushchev spoke of free trade and peaceful coexistence, but his audience was not buying what he had to say. *Look* magazine's publisher, Gardner Cowles, asked the Soviet leader to explain how peaceful coexistence aligned with Russia's insistence that communism would inevitably triumph over capitalism. When Khrushchev tried to describe the finer points of a Marxist system, someone from the balcony shouted, "That doesn't answer the question." When he later tried to work around another question about why Soviet citizens were not allowed to read American newspapers or listen to the Voice of America, shouts of "Answer the Question" rang out from the crowd. It was clear that average Americans did not respect the Soviet leader or the Communist system he represented.

In California, Khrushchev faced more animosity, a response to the Premier's constant refrain during his trip that the Soviet system was superior to what the United States had to offer. Los Angeles Mayor Norris Poulson, referring to Khrushchev's "We will bury you" threat to the U.S. made three years prior, boldly challenged the Russian leader: "You will not bury us . . . We are happy with our way of life . . . we shall fight to the death to preserve it." Walt Disney even refused the visitor's request to visit Disneyland. Denied access to the theme park, Khrushchev was driven around Los Angeles instead, and at one point passed a woman dressed in black with a black flag in one hand and a sign that read, "Death To Khrushchev, The Butcher Of Hungary." No one showed up at the train station to see them off when they left for San Francisco.[1]

The anger and disdain that Khrushchev experienced during his trip were indicative of how most of the country felt. Throughout the decade, the anti-Communist mood conditioned the American people into believing in the moral superiority of the American way of life over the "Godless enemy" that opposed them. Khrushchev was the country leader that forced Americans to live in constant fear of instant destruction, and the angry nation directed all their pent-up frustration at him. Never mind that the U.S. policy of containment and increased military spending tried to break the Soviet economy and destroy Khrushchev's own country. It was a "holy war" of good vs. evil. And it led to a religious revival in the 1950s that united right-wing Christianity with an anti-Communist Fascist political ideology based on racism and a let the fittest survive mentality. And appeasement and turning the other cheek had no place in this national philosophy, for promoting what America stood for, or at least what the nation was supposed to stand for, was all that mattered.

Spiritual Mobilization was an organization whose mission was "to arouse the ministers of all denominations in America to check the trends toward pagan statism [Communists in government], which would destroy our basic freedom and spiritual ideals." Their message reflected the political idealism of the nation's wealthy right-wing. "Inalienable rights and responsibilities" were endowed to everyone, and it specifically applied "where the liberty and dignity of the individual, in which freedom of choice, of enterprise and of property is inherent." They preached self-determination and rejected social programs that took money from the rich without their consent. Churches, it asserted, had a solemn duty to defend those rights.[2]

In June 1951, *Spiritual Mobilization's* leaders formed the Committee to Proclaim Liberty, which chose the 175th anniversary of the Declaration of Independence to plan "Freedom Under God" celebrations on the Fourth of July. Their goal was the advancement of conservatism. Its membership included military leaders and conservative politicians, such as Douglas MacArthur, Admiral Ben Moreell, Herbert Hoover, heads of patriotic groups, and right-wing public figures like Henry Luce, Conrad Hilton Walt Disney, Bing Crosby, and Ronald Reagan.[3]

The Committee to Proclaim Liberty designated July 1, 1951, as Independence Sunday and asked ministers across the country to promote a conservative agenda in their weekly sermons. The preachers did not disappoint. "The effort to establish socialism in our country has probably progressed farther than most of us fully realize," asserted a Lutheran minister in Kansas. "It would be well to remember that every act or law passed by which the government promises to 'give' us something is a step in the direction of socialism."[4]

"The growing acceptance of the philosophy of the Welfare State is a graver peril to freedom in America today than the threat of military aggression," cautioned a Missouri Baptist. A Baptist minister from Mendota, Illinois, echoed the sentiment. "For 175 years," he proclaimed, "we have focused our attention so much on 'the enjoyment of our liberty' that we have been perfectly willing to pass all kinds of legislation limiting the other fellow's liberty for our benefit," he argued. "'Government of the people, by the people, for the people' has become government of the people by pressure groups for the benefit of minorities. 'Give me liberty or give me death' has been shortened to just plain 'Give me.'" ". . . Communism, socialism, the Welfare State—they are all cut from the same pattern. The other road leads to the only freedom there is"—free enterprise.[5]

The message was clear. Social programs would lead to the United States becoming a Socialist country, which was unacceptable. It was the same right-wing mantra that began in the 1930s with the attempted forced removal of FDR from office, as well as a belief that eugenics could cleanse the nation of those who did not carry their weight. The difference by the 1950s was that there now existed a Communist adversary, so for right-wing Fascists in America, preserving the status quo had become a matter of life and death.

It was not just the Committee to Proclaim Liberty that felt this way, for the well-known preacher Billy Graham was also touting an anti-organized labor message based on the same right-wing ideology. He told a rally in 1952 that the Garden of Eden was a paradise with "no union dues, no labor leader, no snakes, no disease." Graham said a genuinely Christian worker "would not stoop to take unfair advantage" of his employer by unionizing. He warned that a looming steel stoppage would hurt American troops fighting in Korea during the Korean War.

Oilman Sid Richardson, who financed the careers of Sam Rayburn and Lyndon Johnson, and hired John Connally as his executive secretary, was one of Graham's most ardent supporters. At his funeral, Graham eulogized Richardson, saying "he was willing to go to any end to see that our American way of life was maintained." And that was what was behind this Christian revival movement. Maintaining the American way of life included segregation, anti-Semitism, anti-communism, and anti-everything that did not fit into the neat right-wing picture, representing what the radical right believed America stood for.[6]

In July 1953, the National Association of Evangelicals arranged for President Eisenhower, Vice President Nixon, and other high-ranking officials to sign a statement declaring biblical principles formed the foundation for the American system of government. On June 14, 1954, the phrase "under God" was added to the Pledge of Allegiance, and "In God We Trust" was placed on postage stamps. Two years later, "In God We Trust" became the official motto of the United States, and President Eisenhower mandated that all paper currency have the phrase printed on it. Another Congressional bill was to "acknowledge the dependence of our people and our Government upon . . . the Creator . . . [and] deny the atheistic and materialistic concept of communism." On June 14, 1954 (Flag Day), the enactment of a bill made public school prayer mandatory. "From this day forward," Ike declared, "the millions of our school children will proclaim daily in every city and town, every village and rural schoolhouse, the dedication of our nation and our people to the Almighty."[7]

The Supreme Court would rule against the law in 1962, saying it was unconstitutional, but this only served to confirm what the radical right already knew. President John Kennedy and Chief Justice Earl Warren were Communists trying to destroy what the United States stood for.

Fred Schwarz was an Australian political activist and founder of the Christian Anti-Communist Crusade (CACC), who made numerous speaking tours throughout the United States during the 1950s. "I stressed the role that atheism played in the formation of Communist doctrines and the logical consequences," he later recalled, and he "challenged Christians to be as dedicated to Christian regeneration as the Communists were to creating a godless utopia." His book, *You Can Trust Communists (. . . To Do Exactly as They Say)*, became a national best-seller. In 1958 he opened his first School for Anti-Communism, where for $5 a day or $20 a week, teachers exposed students to various anti-Communist films, lectures, and discussions. Guest speakers included Herbert Philbrick, Lee Harvey Oswald's hero.[8]

Schwarz's remarkable success was a product of the times and the fear that Communists had already taken over the country. "There is a growing realization that the enemies of freedom are not foreign powers," said R.L. Decker, the National Association of Evangelicals executive director. "There are forces at work within the nation which are just as dangerous and more sinister than any foreign foe," Decker said. "Our only protection . . . is a real revival of the spiritual life from which freedom flowed through our founding fathers into the very essence of American life." They needed "to change the pattern of thinking . . . from the present prevailing socialistic, collectivist, secularist, agnostic pattern to the original God-centered freedom idea as expressed in the Declaration of Independence and the Preamble to the United States Constitution."[9]

Once again, the radical right thought the left was violating the U.S. Constitution. Recall General MacArthur's lament that ". . . a new and . . . unknown and dangerous concept that the members of our armed forces owe primary allegiance or loyalty to those who temporarily exercise the authority of the Executive Branch of the Government rather than to the country and to the Constitution which they are sworn to defend. No proposition could be more dangerous."

For American Fascists, there was no higher authority than the Constitution, for adherence to it was considered the cornerstone of preserving the American way of life. But in reality, the use of the word "Constitution" was just a code for self-determination. Communist politicians could not change the American way of life without the people's consent. And the Constitution's promise to "promote the general Welfare," many believed, applied only to radical right-wing, Christian, Anglo-Saxon, anti-Communist, racist, anti-Semitic eugenicists, and that the way of life they promoted had to remain in place. As the election of 1960 approached, the radical right was still clinging to the same convoluted, Fascist principles they had adopted in the immediate aftermath of World War II. But things were getting much more heated and dangerous as the proponents of this Fascist agenda became less tolerant and more violent than they had previously been. And a lot of it had to do with race.

* * *

As the decade was coming to a close in Louisiana, Southern racists continued their quest to keep a segregated America in place. Radical right Fascist leaders like

Leander Perez, Senator James Eastland, Hubert Badeaux, State Senator Willie Rainach, and Guy Banister were at the forefront. Despite the 1957 Brown vs. Board of Education decision, they would not relent. They were determined to prove that all civil rights groups were Communist front organizations funded by the Soviet Union. The possibility that a northern liberal from Massachusetts might be the Democratic Party's nominee for President in 1960 only made matters worse.

The stakes were high for Southern racists in the summer of 1960 as the election loomed on the horizon, for school desegregation was inevitable throughout the South, and it was becoming abundantly clear that short of a revolution, there was nothing they could do to stop it. In 1958, Guy Banister, Leander Perez, and Hubert Badeaux testified before the Joint Legislative Committee on Segregation to report the Communist influence in the integration movement. In 1960, the Sovereignty Commission replaced the Joint Legislative Committee on Segregation, a much less antagonistic name whose title suggested they were interested in preserving state's rights instead of segregation. It didn't matter, for they couldn't hide that what they stood for was self-determination, and in the South, that meant the right to segregate schools without northern interference. Both Guy Banister and his secretary Delphine Roberts were part of the Sovereignty Commission.

Leander Perez had created the Louisiana Sovereignty Commission in response to the court-mandated integration of New Orleans Public Schools. Louisiana federal district court judge Skelly Wright had ordered desegregation to take effect in 1960. It prompted Mississippi Supreme Court Justice Tom Brady to telegraph Governor Ross Barnett the following: "If the battle of New Orleans [were] lost, they would be fighting it in Mississippi." In the Deep South, segregation was a non-negotiable issue even at the highest levels of state government.

Perez and Rainich attended the Democratic convention that July in Los Angeles. Perez said that he was "1,001 percent" opposed to Kennedy and called him a "stooge of [labor leader] Walter Reuther, a student of Moscow." He also despised the Democratic platform, calling it "the Congolese Constitution."[10]

Despite objections from Southerners, the 1960 Democratic platform contained the most extensive civil rights endorsement in party history. "The time has come to assure equal access for all Americans to all areas of community life, including voting booths, schoolrooms, jobs, housing, and public facilities," it stated. It made clear that Democrats supported the sit-ins at segregated lunch counters. "The peaceful demonstrations for first-class citizenship which have recently taken place in many parts of this country are a signal to all of us to make good at long last the guarantees of our Constitution." There was no confusion regarding what the new Democratic Party wanted to achieve and that their idea of what the Constitution stood for was different from what the radical right thought it did.[11]

The lunch counter sit-ins were a contentious issue. In New Orleans in the summer of 1960, black and white Congress of Racial Equality (CORE) members, mostly college students, held sit-ins at Woolworth's and McCrory's lunch counters reserved for white patrons only. In response, New Orleans mayor Delesseps Morrison advised CORE that they would no longer tolerate their activities.[12]

Dallas was no different than New Orleans, as movie theaters, public schools, and lunch counters remained segregated. It was probably the largest city in the United States which continued to reject the progressive efforts of the courts to eliminate separation by race.[13]

Leander Perez intended to maintain the Southern way of life and ensure that self-determination did not become a thing of the past. In this regard, he was one of the most vocal proponents of the "Free Electors" movement, which originated to prevent John Kennedy from getting the Democratic party nomination. In 1960 there were 537 Electoral College votes up for grabs, with 269 required to obtain a majority in the House of Representatives. The Free Electors movement wanted to unite the southern voting bloc and withhold the electoral votes from southern states so that Kennedy could not obtain the required majority. They would cast their votes only for a candidate who pledged to support segregation. On August 4, 1960, less than a month after the convention, Perez convened a Free Electors meeting in New Orleans, still trying to undermine Kennedy's nomination. But the movement was defeated when the State Democratic Central Committee voted 51-48 to back Kennedy, only a three-vote differential. Undeterred, Perez threw his support behind the Louisiana States' Rights Party, whose steering committee included Perez, Kent Courtney, Delphine Roberts, Louis P. Davis, and Emmett Irwin. These were all dangerous people, prone to embrace violence to get what they wanted, and their propensity for armed resistance would only worsen after JFK became President.

Kent Courtney and his wife Phoebe were active in the White Citizens Council, which came into being to fight desegregation in public schools after the Supreme Court Brown ruling. The Council published a journal called *The Citizen: A Journal of Fact and Opinion,* whose managing editor was Medford Evans of Jackson, Mississippi. Courtney and Evans vehemently opposed the integration of blacks and whites. Evans tried to justify his position by stating that African Americans were far better off economically living under segregation in the United States than in Africa. It was a belief held by many Southern racists to justify the conditions under which black Americans had to live. Desegregation, they believed, was a Communist plot to create unrest in the United States.

In 1954, Courtney's rabid racism entered the public domain when he was named chairman of the New Orleans branch of *Ten Million Americans Mobilizing For Justice.* Courtney and his wife were both described as being "so far right the only thing beyond is Outer Space." In October 1959, they sponsored a two-day "New Party" meeting in Chicago, which included a banquet to honor Robert Welch of Massachusetts, the founder of the John Birch Society. Welch and fellow segregationist Dan Smoot spoke at the meeting, which was Courtney's attempt to establish a new political party, with retired Lieutenant General Pedro del Valle acting as "Temporary Chairman." As we have seen, military generals, especially those who served under MacArthur, which applied to del Valle, avidly supported right-wing Fascist movements.

Courtney was also a member of the ultra-right Constitution Party. On April 19, 1960, he was the Louisiana States Rights Party nominee for governor, but he was unsuccessful in his bid. In the general presidential election held on November 8, 1960, Kent and Leander Perez were presidential electors of the States Rights Party.[14]

Louis P. Davis was a leading National Citizen's Council member, who on October 10, 1956, was a featured speaker at their national convention in Jackson, Mississippi. Like Banister, with whom he was close, he had people infiltrate pro-integration groups and labeled the NAACP and the Congress of Racial Equality as "Zionist" organizations. Davis was also close to General Walker and Mississippi governor Ross Barnett, who headed the Mississippi Citizens' Council. He was known for rejecting the court order mandating the integration of public schools in New Orleans, which he tried to prevent from occurring. On December 12, 1960, immediately after the presidential election, the FBI opened a file on Davis, sensing he was a dangerous man.[15]

Emmett Irwin was the president of the New Orleans Citizens' Council. At a Citizens' Council meeting in 1956, he spoke about the NAACP being part of the "Communist conspiracy." Later that year, he presided over a mass segregation rally in New Orleans attended by over 8,000 people, including Leander Perez and Willie Rainach. He knew Senator Eastland, Roy V. Harris, Guy Banister, and numerous Banister associates, including Joseph Milteer. On May 7, 1960, at a New Orleans Citizens' Council meeting, Harris said this about the NAACP: "We can stop them if we united [sic] . . . When mothers start teaching their kids to ostracize the niggers, they'll catch on, and the kids will find a thousand ways to make them miserable."[16]

Joseph Milteer was perhaps a racist second to none, belonging to For America, the Constitution Party, the Federation for Constitutional Government, which operated out of New Orleans, and the Dixie Klan of Georgia. Principal members of the Federation were Leander Perez and J. Evetts Haley from Dallas, a close associate of General Walker and H.L. Hunt. Years later, Milteer would write, "Back in 1958 I went around to many parts of the country trying to get the Right Wing Groups to get together and form one big front and select men for public office, and we all work together to that end." He knew Kent Courtney and another prominent racist, Dan Smoot, who was close to H.L. Hunt.[17]

Milteer is best known for being secretly tape-recorded on November 9, 1963, thirteen days before the assassination, saying that JFK would be killed from a tall building by an assassin with a high-powered rifle. The man who taped Milteer without his knowledge was an FBI informant named Willie Somersett, who had supplied the FBI with information since 1949 when he infiltrated the leadership of the Ku Klux Klan. He was considered highly reliable by the Bureau. They considered him ". . . one of the few Klan informants who possessed the ability, incentive, and appropriate cover to go anywhere in the southeast section of the United States concerning Bureau matters. He is also personally acquainted with . . . various political figures throughout the southeast . . . as well as a large number of Klansmen and hoodlums."

In November 1960, the FBI sent Somersett to New Orleans to investigate the Catholic school integration crisis, which involved Leander Perez. How determined was Perez about preventing school integration? A Roman Catholic himself, Perez encouraged parents to remove their children from integrated public schools and enroll them in private schools instead. He was so unrelenting in his support of segregation that the Catholic Church excommunicated him.

Leander Perez was the leader of this resistance movement in New Orleans, and he was instrumental in Somersett's introduction to the city's racist underground. Somersett joined the New Orleans Citizens' Council, which connected him to Courtney, Banister, and Delphine Roberts. It was how Somersett became involved with segregationists, which would eventually lead him to Joseph Milteer.[18]

The Constitution Party, to which Milteer belonged, was founded in 1950, and Robert Welch of the John Birch Society was a contributing writer to its newspaper. In 1952, the party supported MacArthur for President, which was not surprising considering MacArthur's firm adherence to the Constitution. Two MacArthur proteges, General Pedro del Valle and Colonel William Potter Gale, both extreme racists and anti-Semites, also belonged to the party, and by 1956 they were organized in fifteen states, with Milteer a delegate from Georgia. In 1957, William Gale was elected the party's California chairman.

Del Valle had a connection to the John Birch Society, the Citizens' Council, the National States' Rights Party, the Congress of Freedom, and the American Nazi Party. And as previously mentioned, he was the general who wrote a letter to President Truman calling him a traitor for the way he handled the Korean War. He would become even more aggressive during Kennedy's presidency, for his tolerance for traitors by that time had grown increasingly thin.

Gale was closely associated with Wesley Swift, considered by the FBI to have been the most significant figure in the early years of the *Christian Identity* movement. *Christian Identity* was a white supremacist, racist, and anti-Semitic "religion" that preached only Anglo-Saxon and Aryan people were the true children of God. Like Gale, Swift lived in California during the 1950s and was the west coast representative of the *Christian Nationalist Crusade*. It was part of *Christian Identity*. In 1957, the name of the church was changed to The Church of Jesus Christ—Christian, which is still used by Aryan Nation churches today.

Both Willie Somersett and Joseph Milteer knew that in 1960, Swift predicted that JFK would not survive his first term in office. The FBI was also aware of this, for numerous people from Swift's church contacted the Bureau, alarmed at the vitriol Swift was spouting.

Perhaps because he was aware that Swift and Milteer had each predicted Kennedy's fate, Somersett contacted authorities after the assassination regarding Gale and Swift. The FBI investigated them and concluded that both were at their homes at the time of the assassination.

It is interesting that Gale, on November 16, 1963, had already been interviewed by the FBI. It was just six days before Kennedy's assassination. What prompted them to visit Gale? The timing of this is quite suspicious. It suggests the FBI wanted to let Gale know he was on their radar as Kennedy was only days away from visiting Texas.[19]

The FBI had also interviewed Swift in 1958 regarding bombings in the South and learned he had organized a "Black Shirt fully armed Fascist-like organization" which he intended to merge with Gerald L.K. Smith's America First Party. Not surprisingly, Swift was also associated with like-minded neo-Nazi organizations and individuals, such as the American Nazi Party and the National States Rights Party.[20]

Recall that authorities found Oswald's notebook after the assassination, and it contained the names and addresses of American Nazi Party members. And that Oswald traveled almost exclusively in the company of Fascists in the last year of his life. And as we will see in the following chapter, in New Orleans in the summer of 1963, Oswald and a friend named Kerry Thornley were seen dressed identically, all in black, just like the black shirt members of Wesley Swift's Nazi group. These connections may provide clues to who Oswald's accomplices were in the JFK assassination, for these people were willing to resort to the most extreme levels of violence to preserve the American way of life, which they believed was slipping away. And Oswald would not have had Nazi names in his notebook unless he was involved with them because these were not people with whom he could have had a passing relationship. You either supported them totally, or you were against them, and the evidence suggests that Oswald approved of the message they promoted, for these were his companions that final, fateful year. He knew what he was doing.

Joseph Milteer claimed that as early as 1958, he was trying to unite the various right-wing racist groups into a single paramilitary organization. And by 1963, this was happening. The question then becomes, was this united racist, anti-Communist group, which was in bed with so many ex-MacArthur military generals and protégés, and connected to Oswald, responsible for the assassination? If so, did they commit the crime alone, were they part of a larger group, or were they the perfect group to set up to take the fall? Suffice it to say that this group had the required propensity for violence to pull off such a crime.

* * *

There were many similarities between Dallas and New Orleans around 1960. The anger each city felt over the possibility that the next President of the United States might be a Catholic was one example. Roman Catholicism "is not only a religion, [but] a political tyranny" that "threatens those basic freedoms [and] those constitutional rights for which our forefathers died," sermonized Reverend W.A. Criswell in his Dallas First Baptist Church. If Criswell only knew that the Vatican was directly involved in the war against communism with CIA and organized crime, he would have been livid. But, of course, very few were aware of this.

Then there was Criswell's opinion regarding the Soviet Union. "Communism is a denial of God," said the preacher, and ". . . communism is like a kingdom of darkness presided over by a prince of evil . . . the greatest challenge the Christian faith had ever faced in 2,000 years of history." And then there was what he had to say regarding politicians from the north who wanted to change the Southern way of life: "They are not our folks. They are not our kind. They don't belong to the same world in which we live [and] there are people who are trying to force upon us a situation and a thing that is a denial of all that we believe in."[21]

Reading Criswell's words, one can almost feel the hatred, as if the Civil War had never ended, that northerners were "not our kind" in the South. Such thinking left no room for debate and insisted, by its implied message, that those from the north should remain in the north or suffer the consequences. As hard as it is for people in the Twenty-First century to understand, Criswell managed to capsulize the mood of many in the South who felt the same way.

Another Dallas preacher, the governor's cousin, wrote a book entitled *God the Original Segregationist*, which claimed that African Americans were purposely made black by God to keep them segregated by color. "There is absolutely nothing the Communists would love more than a mongrelized America that they could easily enslave . . . ," the preacher said. "When those meddlesome white politicians and troublemakers leave them alone, the Negro are quite happy and satisfied in their segregated condition . . . God knows my heart, and He knows I am anything but a 'nigger-hater' . . . the land of Dixie has always been a veritable Paradise for the Negro."[22]

It would be nice to write that these two preachers were the exception and not the norm, but of course, this was not the case. And these were supposedly men of God! If they thought this way, there was no telling how far others might go to prevent interference from northern politicians and judges who wanted to change the Southern way of life. These people didn't realize it, but the Civil War was over, even if they still wanted to continue the fight.

Leander Perez and Willie Rainich were not the only prominent racist, anti-Semitic white supremacists present at the Democratic National convention. As we know, oilman H.L. Hunt of Dallas was there as well, for he had already sent tens of thousands of Criswell's anti-Kennedy sermon to Protestant ministers across the country to try and derail Kennedy.[23]

As we have discussed, Hunt connected to Guy Banister and other members of the segregationist movement. The Joseph Milteer associate, Texas rancher J. Evetts Haley, was one example. A member of the Congress of Freedom, the Constitution Party, We the People, and the Citizens' Council, Haley was the founder of Texans for America. An insight into his intellect is his belief that all vegetarians were Socialists and his work to ban "communist-influenced" textbooks from Texas public schools. Haley was connected with Dan Smoot, General Walker, and Robert Surrey, Joseph Milteer and Leander Perez associates. Since 1956 he had worked with General del Valle in support of various right-wing causes. Without question, the racists in Dallas and New Orleans were interchangeable and well connected.

Dan Smoot was a racist who said desegregation was "an American tragedy" caused by Communists. He believed that Brown vs. the Board of Education "poisoned our Constitution" and that "the government of the United States . . . is plotting the surrender of our country to world Communist-Socialist control." On October 26, 1960, there was a "Free Electors" meeting in New Orleans. Smoot was there and called Kennedy the "personification of the evil which American constitutionalists want to get out of Washington." Another Haley associate named Robert Surrey was the head of the Dallas American Nazi Party, a member of the Minutemen, and an aide to General Walker. Walker, Surrey, and H.L Hunt all belonged to the John Birch Society.

Haley supported the use of violence as a deterrent against the civil rights movement. He served with Leander Perez on the board of the Federation for Constitutional Government in 1956. Senator Eastland was also involved with the organization, stating the Federation's objective was to fight the Supreme Court, the union labor group C.I.O. (which was considered Communist), the NAACP, and all groups "who are attempting our destruction." Haley was also a member of Kent Courtney's Committee to Form The Independent American Federation of State Parties. He attended a meeting with Courtney on November 4, 1959, which included Medford Evans. He was an early supporter of General Walker, and when Walker moved to Dallas, Haley guaranteed the lease on Walker's home. These people were drawn together by self-determination. Their mentality was that it was up to each state to decide if segregation was what it wanted. They adhered to a sincere anti-Communist philosophy that thought the Red Menace had infiltrated the United States government at the highest levels. And what brought them together was a deep-seated desire to use violence to achieve their objectives.[24]

* * *

By 1960 Lyndon Johnson, who had become the youngest Senate Majority Leader in the nation's history, was one of the most powerful politicians in the country. So complete was his control of Texas politics that he was permitted to remain a U.S. Senator while he ran for vice president. It ensured he would keep his Senate seat if he and Kennedy lost the election. The man had connections and knew how to take advantage of them. Still, he was considered a traitor by Southern radical right-wing Fascists for agreeing to be Kennedy's running mate. There was hatred for LBJ, which was evident in a research report Kennedy received after becoming the Democratic nominee, which stated that, "He [Johnson], of course, should campaign for the ticket outside of Texas. It is extremely doubtful if he can be effective in Texas . . . [He cannot jusify] his adoption of the [party's civil rights] platform . . . the more he defends it in Texas, the more it will hurt." The South could not accept the fact that one of their own could support desegregation. In Texas, they would never forget.[25]

Almost immediately after the Kennedy/Johnson ticket was announced officially, there was talk that oilmen, who were almost exclusively Democrats from the South, would not support the Democratic candidate for President because of their hatred for the liberal Kennedy. As a result, Johnson and Sid Richardson's old Texas friend Sam Rayburn, the Speaker of the House, gave an ultimatum to the oil industry giants. They could not be Democrats 364 days a year and then vote Republican in the presidential election. If they did, the oil depletion allowance, which they so dearly coveted because of the fortune in tax payments it saved them, might be repealed in Washington. Politics aside, the oilmen heeded Rayburn's warning and supported JFK. However, it was an ominous sign of how intense the opposition to Massachusetts's liberal, Catholic candidate was.[26]

Race, of course, was a significant issue with Southern voters in 1960. On October 12, Kennedy gave a speech in Harlem in front of the Hotel Theresa. "I am delighted to come to Harlem," he said, "and I think the whole world should come here . . . [and] recognize that we all live right next to each other . . . We should not fear the Twentieth Century, for the worldwide revolution which we see all around us is part of the original American revolution."

Based on what else Kennedy had to say that day, the reference to revolution highlighted that a portion of the country failed to understand that the "all men are created equal" inalienable right, which the Declaration of Independence promised, applied to African Americans as well. "If a Negro baby is born here and a white baby is born next door," Kennedy continued, "the Negro baby's chance of finishing high school is about 60 percent of the white baby . . . His chance of being unemployed is four times that baby's . . . White people are a minority in the world . . . [and] I believe it is important that the president of the United States . . . speak[s] out on this, [and] associate ourselves with the great fight for equality."[27]

One week after Kennedy's Harlem speech, on October 19, Dr. Martin Luther King was arrested in Atlanta for sitting in a department store. Six months previously, he had been given a suspended sentence for a minor traffic violation. However, the traffic violation charge went into effect because of the department store incident, and King received four months of hard labor. It was incredibly severe, and the fear was that it was a death sentence for Dr. King. The campaign reached out to King's wife Coretta, and JFK spoke to her on the phone, which angered Bobby when he found out. "You bomb-throwers [*sic*] probably lost the election," he said. "You've probably lost three states, and . . . the civil rights section isn't going to do another damn thing in this campaign." However, the future Attorney General soon had second thoughts, so he called the judge who passed the sentence. "The more I thought about the injustice of it, the more I thought what a son of a bitch that judge was," Bobby would recall. "I made it clear to him that it was not a political call; that I am a lawyer . . . one who has seen the rights of defendants misused in various ways . . . and I wanted to make it clear that I opposed this. I felt it was disgraceful."[28]

The next day King was released from prison, but the judge issued a public statement that he had done so because Bobby complained that King was not allowed to post bail. The campaign put out a denial, but undoubtedly those in the South believed the judge's explanation.

There was no ambiguity regarding the Democratic candidate's position on race relations, which created alarm among voters in the South. It would not take long for Johnson to experience the hatred that Kennedy faced himself. For many in Texas, Johnson was worse than Kennedy, for he should have known better.

On November 4, just four days before the election, a limousine containing Johnson and his wife pulled up to the Baker Hotel in Dallas, where they were staying. As they exited the car, a group of angry Republican women known as the "Mink Coat Mob" assaulted them. Republican right-wing Congressman and H.L. Hunt supporter Bruce Alger had riled up the group. LBJ and his wife had to force their way through the angry crowd. "We're gonna show Johnson he's not wanted in Dallas," Alger yelled. The women carried picket signs which called Johnson a "Traitor" and a "Judas." They manage to force their way into the hotel.

Then, the Johnsons had to rerun the gauntlet because they had a scheduled appearance at the Adolphus Hotel across the street. Meanwhile, the crowd had grown and was more boisterous than it was before. The Johnsons made it to the Adolphus, but not before Lady Bird was spat on and hit on the head with a picket sign. "LBJ SOLD OUT TO YANKEE SOCIALISTS," read the sign held by Congressman Alger. The group was out for blood, and if there was any doubt how vehemently the majority in the South wanted to maintain the status quo, it ended that day. Three years before Kennedy's assassination, the signs were there that Dixie would not tolerate Northern liberalism.[29]

In the election, Nixon would defeat Kennedy in Dallas by a two-to-one margin, but the rest of Texas went for Kennedy, who won the state by forty-six thousand votes. The black vote was pivotal and was credited with the Kennedy victory, organized crime interference notwithstanding.

There was a great deal of anger circulating against Kennedy around the time of the election. And there was a concern for his safety, especially after the Chicago police arrested a man at a Kennedy rally carrying a .38 revolver in a brown paper bag. Police arrested a second man in Chicago after he began running towards Kennedy's motorcade. The arresting officers who wrestled him to the ground found he was carrying a .25-caliber automatic pistol. On December 11, 1960, in Palm Beach, Florida, Richard Paul Pavlick loaded his car with dynamite to assassinate Kennedy by blowing him up in his car. He got close enough to Kennedy to have pulled it off, but JFK had his wife and children with him, and Pavlick changed his mind. He told the arresting police four days later that he did not want to harm the children.[30]

There was visible hatred on the streets of the United States in 1960. Whether it was Nikita Khrushchev or John Kennedy, there was no denying that passions ran high. One man represented the Soviet Union, the Godless enemy that most Americans blamed because they lived in constant fear of a nuclear attack. The other man dared to be an Irish Catholic and support civil rights. The radical right called him a Communist. It was a divided country, and it would stay that way for years.

Interestingly, both men were hated for essentially the same reason, albeit each from a different perspective. That is, each threatened to change the American way of life and put self-determination in jeopardy. The United States had to stop Khrushchev from bringing his dream of worldwide Communist domination to fruition, so no expense was spared, and no life was too great to sacrifice. As far as Kennedy, it was much easier to kill him and have him replaced with the Southern racist, mob-connected, oilman-friendly, pro-military, highly blackmailable Lyndon Johnson. He had accepted the second slot on the ticket because it put him a heartbeat away from the presidency, and he was a man who the powers at be could direct and control.

One final word about the election of 1960. On November 12th, the press reported that "the Republican National Committee [was investigating] purported presidential election fraud in 11 states . . ." The next day, "GOP leaders in Illinois, where Mr. Kennedy held a lead of less than 8,000 [votes], were demanding recounts in Cook County (Chicago)."

Organized crime had stolen the election, and press reports tracked developments that this was the case.

November 16th: "Riding a wave of absentee ballots, Vice President Richard M. Nixon grabbed California's 32 electoral votes . . . The switchover . . . boosted . . . Nixon's . . . total to 223. It dropped . . . Kennedy's from 332 to 300 . . ."

November 19th: "The Justice Dept. said . . . it has asked the FBI to investigate several alleged voting frauds in the presidential election . . ."

November 20th: Press reports regarding an FBI investigation of voter fraud: "It would be several weeks before the FBI completes all the investigations and determines whether further federal action is warranted." (December 19th was the day the Electoral College officially counted the electoral votes. If J. Edgar Hoover could stall the investigation into voter fraud until then, the election would be Kennedy's.)

December 4th: The Texas GOP charged voter fraud in Texas and claimed the state's twenty-four electoral votes belonged to Nixon. The FBI actively investigated "reports of such things as voters being 'coerced and intimidated' by pistol-packing election officials; many cases of alleged 'fixed' voting machines; widespread disregard of the secret ballot; numerous instances of clearly illegal voting; disqualified ballots." It would take some time to gather the necessary information they require to determine what happened.

December 19th: The electoral college tallied the official vote. The final count stood at JFK 300, Nixon 219.[31]

The election was nothing short of robbery. And as previously mentioned, the Mafia and CIA had their reasons for wanting Kennedy to win. But for the Southern right-wing Christian racists, the outcome was a disaster, even though LBJ was on the ticket. From their perspective, what Kennedy wanted to do violated their religious beliefs. History has shown that whenever religious fervor is the foundation for political unrest, people have nowhere left to turn, and they take matters into their own hands. By 1963 things had changed. For segregation to remain, for the pressure to be taken off the mob, for self-determination to continue, for the American way of life to be preserved, and for the war to be taken straight to the Communists, a Son of the South from Texas had to be catapulted into the White House. Of course, the odds on the happening were slim, unless that was the plan right from the beginning. These various groups would increasingly come together during the last year of Kennedy's life. There was talk of removing the traitors from government, including the President, by whatever means possible. And it was more than talk, for they formulated plans to bring this about. And when their well-known dissatisfaction became known to others who shared their disgust for the direction the country was heading, JFK's assassination changed things. Were Fascist religious zealots part of the conspiracy? Probably not directly. However, consider the right-wing Christian group *Spiritual Mobilization*, which combined religion, capitalism, and big business to maintain the status quo in America. There is no doubt that this would have united Texas oilmen, the Suite 8F group, and radical Christian racist groups, for they shared a common cause. The religious revival brought people together who hated Kennedy, so, to a certain extent, they had blood on their hands.

William Pawley wrote Richard Nixon in a long letter after the Bay of Pigs disaster, "All of the Cubans and most Americans in this part of the country [Miami] believe that to remove Castro, you must first remove Kennedy, and that is not going to be easy."[32]

Pawley was wrong. It was not that difficult, for the hatred against the young President was so widespread. Consider that in the spring of 1963, a flyer was distributed among Cuban exiles in Miami, signed by "a Texan who resents the Oriental influence that has come to control, to degrade, to pollute and enslave his own people . . . Only through one development will you Cuban patriots ever live again in your homeland as freemen . . ." The flyer called for "an inspired Act of God [to] place in the White House within weeks a Texan known to be a friend of all Latin Americans . . . though he must under present conditions bow to the Zionists who since 1905 came into control of the United States, and for whom Jack Kennedy and Nelson Rockefeller and other members of the Council of Foreign Relations and allied agencies are only stooges and pawns. Though Johnson must now bow to these crafty and cunning Communist-hatching Jews, yet, did an Act of God suddenly elevate him into the top position [he] would revert to what his beloved father and grandfather were, and to their values and principles and loyalties."[33]

The references to the enslavement of God's people, inspired Act of God, Zionists, and Communist-hatching Jews left no doubt that a member of the radical Christian right wrote this letter. Someone was reaching out to the Cuban community, whom the writer believed wanted Kennedy killed as badly as Southern Fascists did. What is also interesting is the hate targeted at Nelson Rockefeller and the Council on Foreign Relations. Rockefeller was considered a liberal Republican who supported civil rights, taxation, and other programs that the radical right proponents of self-determination abhorred. It proves that a new world order based upon open borders and a globalist economic structure was never the objective. By the time of Kennedy's assassination, "America First" had become the mantra of the White Christian Racist Fascist community. It was why religious zealots ruled the day in the decade leading up to the murder of JFK. And the repercussions from this are still being felt today.

- 8 -

The Defector Who Wasn't

"... there was good reason for the unenlightened SS [*sic*] and F.B.I.
to suspect I might've had a hand in it [the JFK assassination]. We
had some political conversations, and finally, I guess, I was cleared.
No word from them lately . . . When it is all over, though, I may yet
go piss on JFK's grave, RIP."

—Kerry Thornley, Oswald's Marine buddy and
friend in New Orleans

*Physical evidence proves Lee Harvey Oswald's defection to the Soviet Union was part of
a U.S. intelligence operation. Separate identification documents issued upon his release
from the military show the photos of two different people. In addition, the "Oswald"
who returned from the Soviet Union was 5'9" tall while the man who initially left the
U.S. was two inches taller. The Warren Commission was lied to by the FBI. They covered
up evidence of a "replacement" Oswald after the assassination for a good reason. It was
all part of an illusion created by U.S. intelligence to make it appear that the real Oswald
died in Russia. A Soviet "sleeper agent" returned to the United States in June 1962,
who could take the blame for any crime. Seventeen months later, JFK's assassination
happened. Coincidence or conspiracy?*

* * *

On October 2, 1958, Lee Harvey Oswald boarded the USS Barrett in Yoko-
suka, Japan, to return to the United States. After a thirty-day leave where he visited
his mother in Fort Worth, Texas, he boarded a bus on December 21 and reported
for duty at the Marine Corps Air Station at El Toro, California. He became part of
a small radar crew (seven enlisted men and three officers) who conducted aircraft
surveillance. As at Atsugi, according to his superiors, he was "competent in all functions." John F. Donovan, Oswald's training officer, told the Warren Commission

that El Toro's primary function was "basically to train both enlisted [men] and officers for later assignment overseas." A "Secret" clearance was the minimum requirement at the base. It was an odd arrangement for a Marine who had been court-martialed twice, spent time in the brig, had requested an early discharge, had demonstrated emotional instability, and was rejected when he asked for a foreign duty extension.[1]

As was the case during the latter part of his stay in Japan, Oswald remained outwardly bitter towards the United States. According to the Warren Commission Report, he related "increasingly with Russia and the Russian way of life," and he was "anxious to publicize his liking for things Russian." He was called "Oswaldskovitch" and "had his name written in Russian on one of his jackets" He played Russian songs on his record player, used expressions like "da" or "nyet," and addressed others as Comrade. What was happening? It was the Marines.[2]

The Marines who were close to Oswald knew of his antics, and they kidded him about being a Russian spy. Oswald always chose the red players when they played chess because he said, "The Red Army is always victorious." Mailroom clerks became alarmed when Oswald received "leftist" literature, but complaints to a superior officer did not lead to any disciplinary action.[3]

Why Oswald conducted himself in this manner is difficult to comprehend. If he were a legitimate Russian sympathizer who honestly planned to defect to the Soviet Union, one would think such public pro-Soviet displays would have been counterproductive. Someone who truly wanted to defect would have gone to considerable lengths to keep his feelings hidden, as other defectors had done in the past. And that those around him were aware of what he was doing and did nothing to reprimand him meant they did not take his behavior seriously. Otherwise, they would not have tolerated Oswald's conduct. Precisely what he was trying to prove remains a mystery, but one thing is sure. When U.S. intelligence investigated Oswald after he defected, his fellow Marines would recall the outward affection for the Soviet Union he had displayed, which served to validate the narrative that Oswald voluntarily fled the United States for a better life behind the Iron Curtain.

Another oddity was that despite his desire to give the impression he was pro-Soviet, the Marines who knew him could not later recall that Oswald ever professed a belief in the virtues of communism. Lt. John E. Donovan told the Warren Commission that he never heard Oswald "in any way, shape or form confess that he was a Communist . . ." When asked if Oswald ever professed an interest in Communist principles, Marine Dan Powers said, "None that I recall." Donald Peter Camarata testified, "I have no recollection . . . of any remarks on his part concerning Communism, Russia or Cuba." Mack Osborne recalled the same. Richard Dennis Call stated, "I do not recall Oswald's making serious remarks [regarding] the Soviet Union or Cuba."[4]

Recall from Chapter One that Oswald's roommate at El Toro was future California judge James Botelho, who stated, "Oswald was not a Communist . . . If he [were], I would have taken violent action against him, and so would many of the other Marines in the unit."[5] "My impression is that although he believed in pure Marxist theory, he did not believe in the way Communism was practiced by the Russians . . ."[6]

It was consistent with how Oswald described himself. Oswald never said he was a Communist and called himself a Marxist-Leninist, so the recollections of his fellow Marines were consistent with this. When asked by the Warren Commission if Oswald "read philosophy" and which philosophers interested him, Lt. Donovan replied philosophers interested in "social revolutions."[7] It was who Oswald was. He was interested in helping people remove the yoke of oppression from tyrannical despots who abused their power. His writings would later show he was not interested in the Soviet system, which subjugated its people. As Botelho wrote, "I was quite surprised when I learned Oswald had gone to Russia."

* * *

The only Marine at El Toro who recalled Oswald promoting the virtues of communism was Pvt. Kerry Thornley, but there is reason to view Thornley with skepticism. In the summer of 1963, Thornley and Oswald lived in New Orleans when Oswald handed out pro-Castro Fair Play for Cuba Committee leaflets in public. Thornley would later deny that he knew Oswald at that time. He was lying, for there is credible evidence that the two men spent considerable time together during this period and may have worked together.

Both Thornley and Oswald resided at the Hotel McBeath in New Orleans and frequented the Ryder Coffee House, and Oswald's signature was in their guest book. Douglas Jones, the owner of Jones Printing Company (who printed Oswald's FPCC leaflets), was shown photos of Thornley with a beard added, and Jones identified all four pictures as the man who picked up the FPCC leaflets. "He called himself 'Lee Osborne,'" Jones said, which was the name on the printing order, which indicates Thornley was involved with Oswald in the handing out of the pro-Castro leaflets. Barbara Reid provided a sworn statement that she had seen Thornley and Oswald together at the Bourbon House. "I am positive that the person sitting at the table with Kerry Thornley was Lee Harvey Oswald," Reid said, and she called them "the gold dust twins." Peter Deageano was at Reid's table and saw Oswald walk in and join Thornley. He had also seen the two together on another occasion, "in either August or September." He saw Oswald distributing his leaflets on Canal Street. He identified him as "being identical" to the person he saw at the Bourbon House. L.P. Davis also saw Oswald and Thornley at the Bourbon House, wearing the same black pants and white shirts. Newsman Cliff Hall reported that Thornley admitted to him shortly after the assassination that he had seen Oswald during the summer of 1963. Another witness, Jeanne Hack, said Thornley knew about Oswald's FPCC activity. On the day of the assassination, he told her, "Oswald did not do it alone but had help."[8]

Four days after the assassination, the Los Angeles Sheriff's Department conducted a "confidential" interview with a friend of Thornley's father. They discovered that Thornley and Oswald had corresponded regularly and that Thornley's father claimed his son had received "numerous letters from Oswald, some of which are of recent date." It is interesting how quickly authorities interviewed people who were close to Thornley. They must have been aware of a connection between the two in New Orleans, for what else would have drawn them to Thornley so quickly?[9]

Doris Dowell, the assistant manager of an apartment complex in Arlington, Virginia, where Thornley worked from December 1963 until mid-1964, claimed he said he had known Oswald in New Orleans the previous summer. The official report of her interview with Garrison's office stated that Thornley and Oswald "were buddies in New Orleans. He [Thornley] said that he had met Oswald again in New Orleans and that they had met at a place in the French Quarter that she would probably not like."[10] If true, this was very revealing because Thornley said that he and Oswald were friends in New Orleans before 1963, and they then met again in the summer of 1963. It means their initial encounter had to have occurred when Oswald briefly lived in New Orleans with his mother in 1955/56, as described in Chapter One. Oswald was involved with David Ferrie's CAP group, which involved drug experimentation on CAP cadets and a connection to East Louisiana State Hospital. Does this imply that Thornley, born the year before Oswald, was also part of the CAP group? In Garrison's book, *On the Trail of the Assassins*," he wrote that Thornley admitted he had met Ferrie and Guy Banister, who worked out of the same office building. Add to that that Thornley and Oswald looked alike and had the same build (they were the gold dust twins), one starts to think there was something suspicious about their relationship.

What exactly did Thornley know? Was he involved in the assassination? He hinted in a letter he wrote to a friend just months after JFK's murder that he may have been privy to something. "The whole thing was very interesting for a while," Thornley wrote, "the assassination, because—on the surface—there was good reason for the unenlightened SS [*sic*] and F.B.I. to suspect I might've had a hand in it. We had some political conversations, and finally, I guess, I was cleared. No word from them lately . . . When it is all over, though, I may yet go piss on JFK's grave, RIP."

These were strong words, but why did Thornley think there was good reason for the Secret Service and FBI to believe he might have been part of the assassination plot? A relationship with Oswald was not sufficient for authorities to draw such a conclusion without supporting evidence. It must have had something to do with Ferrie and Banister, who Thornley admitted he had known.[11] And in this regard, a Fascist, neo-Nazi connection is a possibility, considering L.P. Davis' recollection that he saw Thornley and Oswald together "wearing the same black pants and white shirts." Why would two men be dressed the same way? For one reason only. They were involved in something that required everyone to dress accordingly. And a neo-Nazi group, with their penchant for having their rank-and-file dress identically in black and white so that they could emulate Nazi storm troopers, would certainly have fit the bill.

Consider a document in Department of Defense files that said Thornley was a CIA employee who attended Chemical and Biological Warfare School. He received "technical instruction" in Washington, and his security rating went from "confidential" to "secret." Amazingly, his course was in "Atomic, Biological and Chemical Warfare," and ran from June to August 1960 and began at Atsugi, Japan.[12]

Chapter Six discussed how Oswald might have been administered mind-altering drugs at Atsugi in preparation for defection to the Soviet Union. Before Oswald's service at Atsugi, Thornley indicated that he and Oswald knew each other in New Orleans, which may have involved David Ferrie's CAP, which we know included drug experimentation on CAP cadets. We also know that Ferrie had CIA connections and that Thornley knew Ferrie and Guy Banister. Then, after returning from Atsugi, Oswald was assigned to El Toro, and so was Thornley. Thornley then became the only Marine at El Toro who claimed Oswald said he was a Communist. It was a necessary disclosure at the time, for without Thornley's statement, we have a Marine acting like a Communist sympathizer, without anyone at the base being able to recall him ever professing an interest in communism, which would have been difficult to explain. Then, while Oswald was in the Soviet Union, Thornley was sent to Atsugi by the CIA to study chemical and biological warfare, which would have involved mind-altering drugs. After Oswald returns from Russia, he travels to New Orleans once again and coincidently spends a great deal of time with Thornley while he was there, if the witnesses who claimed to have seen them together were telling the truth. But Thornley lied about ever seeing Oswald in New Orleans. Why did he do this if he had nothing to hide?

Meanwhile, while he and Thornley spent time together, Oswald mysteriously approached New Orleans assistant district attorney Edward G. Gillin. Less than two months before the assassination, he asked about a specific drug that he had read in a book entitled *Brave New World*. He visited East Louisiana State Hospital, where doctors experimented on CAP cadets and other unsuspecting individuals with mind-altering drugs. That all this happened by coincidence does not make sense. It appears that Thornley, like Richard Case Nagell, was tracking Oswald, conveniently appearing wherever Oswald turned up, from New Orleans to El Toro and back to New Orleans. And if Oswald's exposure to mind-altering drugs began during his first stint in New Orleans, one would expect that he would have been monitored closely, wherever he went, by someone with whom he was familiar. In this case, that someone was Kerry Thornley.

An interesting sidebar to Kerry Thornley's story is that in 1961, while Oswald was still in the Soviet Union, Thornley wrote a book about a character based on Oswald entitled *Idle Warriors*. He claimed he was inspired to write the book after learning about Oswald's defection. Maybe that is true, but this was years before Oswald became a household name for murdering JFK. Perhaps this is proof that Thorney already knew more about Oswald than the official record suggests.

On the night of the assassination, Thornley was with Allen Campbell, who worked out of Guy Banister's office and knew Oswald as well. Thornley admitted to Campbell that he had known Oswald that summer in New Orleans, and regarding Oswald's arrest for assassinating JFK, Thornley said, "It could not have happened to a nicer guy."[13] Thornley's curious choice of words implied that Oswald was the fall guy in the assassination plot. And, of course, it also meant that Thornley was likely aware of the assassination before it occurred.

* * *

Returning to El Toro, in addition to outwardly professing to be a supporter of the Soviet Union, Oswald developed a high level of proficiency in the Russian language while stationed there. As Lieutenant Donovan testified, "Yes, he said he was interested in learning Russian. And he took great pride in the fact that he could speak it . . ." "According to Botelho," . . . It was common knowledge that Oswald had taught himself to speak Russian."[14] As mentioned in Chapter Six, Marine Dan Powers, who served briefly with Oswald at the end of his time in Japan, believed Oswald had been tutored there in Russian by a Eurasian woman.

At El Toro, the Marines tested Oswald in his Russian language ability. If Oswald was just an ordinary private, it is hard to understand why they would do this. Shouldn't a red flag have been raised when a Marine, a radar operator who walked around the base acting like a Communist and had Russian newspapers delivered to El Toro, was permitted to take such a test? The fact is he did remarkably well, scoring +4 in Russian reading (four more right than wrong), +3 in written Russian, and -5 in understanding spoken Russian. The Warren Commission tried to downplay his success, saying the results were "poor," but getting more right than wrong, considering his limited experience, was quite an achievement. The Warren Commission should have addressed the real issue—not how well he did, but why he was allowed to take such a test at all.[15]

By the summer of 1959, Oswald had improved so dramatically in speaking Russian that a fellow Marine arranged a meeting between Oswald and his aunt. She had been studying Russian with a Berlitz instructor for over a year. By her admission, Oswald was more at ease with the language than was the aunt. She recalled that he was capable of stringing complete sentences together. It was a remarkable display for a man who allegedly was not receiving any formal training.[16]

Oswald told the woman he learned Russian by listening to Radio Moscow, which was unlikely. The truth may lie in a top-secret record of a Warren Commission session only released in 1974. Chief Council Lee Rankin told the Commission: "We are trying to track that down, to find out what he studied at the Monterey School of the Army in the way of languages. . . ."[17]

The military, the CIA, and the U.S. government used the Monterey School to provide crash courses for personnel destined for overseas work. Ike Feldman of the FBN, who studied Russian and Mandarin Chinese at the Monterey School in the late 1940s when CIA recruited him, called it an intensive program—eight hours per day, seven days per week.[18]

Years later, Oswald's wife, Marina, was interviewed by the *San Jose Mercury News.* She said Lee "seemed professionally schooled in secretiveness . . . I believe he worked for the American government. He was taught the Russian language when he was in the military." She wondered, Is it normal "that an ordinary soldier is taught [to speak] Russian? Also, he got in and out of Russia quite easily, and he got me out quite easily."[19]

Lee Rankin was not questioning if Oswald had studied at Monterey—his words indicate it was a foregone conclusion that he did. Rankin just wanted to know which language he studied, which was understandable since another fellow Marine, Nelson Delgado, testified before the Warren Commission that Oswald also spoke some Spanish. Lt. Donovan testified that ". . . He [Oswald] may have known a few words. But he did not—I don't believe he had a command of Spanish."[20] So, there is little doubt that Russian was the language Oswald was studying at Monterey.

Despite how poorly he spoke Spanish, Cuba was very much on Oswald's mind during the summer of 1959 at El Toro. Soon after Castro came to power, the world did not yet know that he would turn Cuba into a Communist satellite of the Soviet Union. "I know that Cuba interested him [Oswald] more than most other situations," Donovan told the Warren Commission. Oswald knew "about Mr. Batista. He referred to atrocities in general . . . I think that we all know that there were injustices committed under the Batista administration. And he was against that. And he was against this sort of dictatorship." When asked, "Did you hear him [Oswald] express sympathy for Castro specifically," Donovan responded, "Yes—but . . . so did *Time* magazine at that time. Harvard accepted him de facto . . . At any rate, what he said about Castro was not an unpopular belief at that time."[21]

According to Nelson Delgado, he and Oswald discussed getting honorable discharges and becoming officers in Castro's army. Oswald wanted to go to Cuba and be like William Morgan, the Marine turned soldier of fortune who Allen Dulles would eventually betray. At the time, many politically minded paramilitary types in search of adventure wanted to emulate Morgan. Right-wing Minutemen leader Robert DePugh said he became interested in Castro after reading an article by the Cuban revolutionary in the February 1958 issue of *Coronet* magazine entitled "Why We Fight." Two of his associates even went to Havana, intent on joining Castro's army. "But they found that if you wanted to contact Castro," DePugh said, "you went through the Left Wing instead of through the general people. So, they came back quite disillusioned." [22]

To Delgado, it was all talk, but not to Oswald. Delgado testified that "he [Oswald] started [ ] making plans, he wanted to know . . . how to get to Cuba and things like that. I was shying away from him. He kept asking me questions like 'how can . . . an English [speaking] person, get with a Cuban, you know, people, be part of that revolution[ary] movement?'"[23]

Delgado told Oswald to get in touch with the Cuban Embassy. Shortly after that, Delgado noticed an "envelope in his [Oswald's] footlocker, and as far as I could recollect that was mail from Los Angeles, and he was telling me there was a Cuban Consul." Delgado noticed the Cuban seal on some of the letters Oswald received. On one occasion, a civilian came to the front gate to see Oswald, and "they spent about an hour and a half, two hours talking. . . ." The man had on an overcoat and, to Delgado, looked like a Cuban.[24]

Castro was a Communist supported by the Soviet Union. He had abandoned his people and subjected them to atrocities similar to what Batista had done. Based on Oswald's Marxist philosophy, we can assume Oswald lost interest in Cuban affairs once it became known Castro had done this. And by the spring of 1959, Oswald's mind had already shifted to another part of the world.

* * *

Oswald's first sign he intended to defect to the Soviet Union was on March 19, 1959, when he applied for admission for the 1960 spring term at Albert Schweitzer College in Churwalden, Switzerland. Oswald said he was fluent in Russian and spoke some German (which was why the Warren Commission asked Donovan if Oswald was well-versed in the German language). Oswald also mentioned an interest in "ideology" in his application, another word for philosophy and psychology. He listed Norman Vincent Peale, Charles Darwin, and Jack London as his favorite authors. He also intended to take a summer course at the University of Turku in Finland.[25]

The three authors Oswald listed provide insight into what was on his mind at that time. Jack London was an advocate of socialism and eugenics. He joined the Socialist Party of America and published two essays entitled *The War of the Classes* and *Revolution and other Essays,* both topics that Oswald embraced. Regarding eugenics, London was for forced sterilization of criminals and "feeble-minded" people. "I believe the future belongs to eugenics," London wrote. In 1910, he wrote *"The Unparalleled Invasion,"* set in the future between 1976 and 1987, in which China planned to colonize its neighbors with the intent of taking over the Earth. In response, western nations used biological weapons with the most infectious diseases to thwart them. London was not far off, just a bit early in when he expected this to occur.[26]

Darwinism took on a special meaning during the 1950s. As *Spiritual Mobilization*, the right-wing Christian movement that combined religion, capitalism, and big business, as described in the previous chapter, became popular throughout the U.S. One of the group's founders, James Fifield, said that capitalism should follow social Darwinism. "Much of the energy of our so-called 'most civilized' people," Fifield wrote, "has been quite unconsciously spent in trying to thwart the laws of nature." Let the fittest survive was the philosophy that Capitalists should pursue. In supporting the weak who, "if not allowed to pass off the scene as nature has decreed, rapidly multiply and numerically overpower those very people and nations who have sacrificed for their very existence."

Fifield was against the state working to end racial discrimination. The "efforts of minorities to push in where they are not wanted . . ." was "an abomination unto the Lord." [27] Was Oswald's interest in Charles Darwin a sign that he supported this form of extreme eugenics and racism?

An interesting detail about *Spiritual Mobilization* is that it began in pre-war Japan. It was known as the *National Spiritual Mobilization Movement* and was part of a Japanese "New Order." It relied on celebrities to promote its plan, just like the American version. And the purpose of the movement was to rally Japan for a war against China. It was a macabre connection to Jack London's novel about a Chinese attempt to colonize neighboring countries.[28]

Norman Vincent Peale was a religious leader in the 1950s. He combined psychotherapy with religion, and his detractors accused him of advising people to accept social conditions as they were rather than trying to make things better. It was a subtle allusion to eugenics and race relations. Peale was also chairman of the far-right Committee for Constitutional Government, which was against social programs.[29]

The similarities of the three writers Oswald referenced were striking. A consistent theme favored eugenics, natural selection, racial discrimination, the support of Socialist principles, and the elimination of social welfare-type programs. It alluded to class warfare and revolution. These were the principles Oswald believed in as he was about to leave the Marines, and mind-altering drugs may have played a role in developing these principles.

Consider also that Oswald wrote on his application that he had participated in a "student body movement in school" to control juvenile delinquency, which could only refer to his detention in Youth Center in New York as a teenager.[30] Why mention this unless Oswald found humor in admitting that New York City's correctional system had sent him to the New Jersey Reformatory at Bordentown, who experimented on him with mind-altering drugs?

The stated aim of Albert Schweitzer College was "opening communication with those in all lands who are striving to unite Pure Religion and Perfect Liberty, and to increase fellowship and cooperation among them." Schweitzer started the school in 1955. It was a highly liberal institution of approximately 25–30 students, owned and operated by the International Association for Religious Freedom (IARF), with a solid association with Unitarian-Universalists. The college was unknown to most people in the United States, and it had no intention of increasing its exposure, for they advertised on a limited basis at best. Even Swiss authorities had trouble locating the school in 1960 after the FBI contacted them about Oswald's defection. Which raises the question, how did a Marine stationed in California, who had recently returned from overseas duty in Japan, find out about a college that very few Americans knew existed? And where did Oswald get an application form for the college?

The answer is it was likely Kerry Thornley who told Oswald about the school. During his Warren Commission testimony, Thornley said that while at El Toro, he "had been going to the First Unitarian Church in Los Angeles," where the congregation was "a group of quite far-left people politically." And more importantly, they were closely associated with Albert Schweitzer College.[31]

Pastor Stephen Fritchman, who admitted being a Communist and testified before the House Un-American Activities Committee on two separate occasions, ran the Los Angeles church. The National Archives and Records Administration contains a sixty-page FBI report on him. His congregation favored one "world government" run by the United Nations, which had become a left-wing utopian idea.

One of Albert Schweitzer College's directors was Percival Flack Brundage, a principal Unitarian Church officer. At the time, the Unitarian Church provided significant funding for the college, which they would do over several years. Dr. Robert Schacht, the pastor of the First Unitarian Church in Providence, Rhode Island, would review Oswald's application. And on May 13, 1959, Schacht submitted the names of the American applicants, including Oswald, to the college in Switzerland. The connection between the Unitarian Church and Albert Schweitzer College was strong.[32]

Regarding the Los Angeles church's political affiliation, a congregation member said: "A church member invited me to attend a Communist Party social gathering . . . many good things were said about the Soviet Union, as were often said from the pulpit . . ."[33]

The Warren Commission investigated Fritchman to see if he, or someone connected to his parish, might have provided Oswald information about the college. U.S. investigators were also interested, and after the assassination, they visited Unitarian churches throughout the country to see if there was a connection to Oswald. The correspondence of Albert Schweitzer College was being monitored by the CIA and the FBI at least since April 1956, and the commission was now searching for anything nefarious connected to Oswald's 1959 application.

The FBI was also suspicious of the parish and asked Thornley about Oswald's connection to the First Unitarian Church. He responded, "there was none." It was not reassuring. Maybe they were aware of Thornley's right-wing belief system that may have included neo-Nazism and wondered why he was attracted to such a left-wing parish. Did they believe he had an ulterior motive for attending such a leftist church? Perhaps Thornley was infiltrating left-wing groups, like he and Oswald may have already done together in New Orleans.

Was there a connection between the Los Angeles church and Oswald? In the summer of 1963, after his arrest for distributing FPCC literature in New Orleans, Oswald told officer Francis L. Martello that "he became interested in that committee in Los Angeles . . . in 1958 while in the U.S. Marine Corps." The problem is the FPCC did not start until April 6, 1960. But the pro-Castro Communists, who would later establish the FPCC's Los Angeles chapter, did attend the Unitarian Church run by Fritchman in 1958. It was when Oswald would have been there.[34] So, maybe this is what confused Oswald. We know he would have initially been sympathetic to the idea of fair play for the Cuban people, which meant allowing them to determine what type of government they wanted for themselves.

It brings us to a potentially relevant exchange during Thornley's Warren Commission questioning, involving Sylvia Bortin, who attended the same Unitarian Church in Los Angeles. When asked where Bortin lived at the time in question, Thornley responded, "In Whittier, California . . . ," so he must have known her well. Regarding a possible connection to Oswald, Thornley testified that "Miss Bortin never knew Oswald and vice versa . . . There was this civilian compartment and the military compartment [in his life], and I never intermingled them." It is telling because if Thornley never brought Oswald to the parish, why not just say that and be done with it. The way he answered suggests Thornley did get Oswald there but kept him separate from his relationship with Bortin.

Not satisfied, the interviewer continued to pursue this line of questioning:

Mr. JENNER (WC): This young lady [got] married, and her husband is now in Havana, Cuba?

Mr. THORNLEY: That is what she told me last summer; yes. He was going to school in Cuba.

Mr. JENNER: I take it this had nothing to do with yourself and Oswald's views [concerning] Castro . . .

Mr. THORNLEY: No, this happened, I think, later; In fact, I am sure it happened later. At that time, Miss Bortin, she was then unmarried, did not know Robert [redacted], I believe. I met him [in] September a year later.[35]

Bortin must have felt very strongly about Fidel Castro and a Communist Cuba if she married a man in school in Havana in 1962. Thornley tried to downplay Bortin's significance, saying her marriage to this man happened after Oswald would have attended the Church, but it does not diminish her potential importance. We can assume her pro-Castro leanings were in place long before her marriage; at the time, she would have met Oswald when he was interested in going to Cuba and fighting with Castro. Perhaps there was a connection between Oswald and Bortin, and Thornley was willing to commit perjury so that it remained hidden.

Consider another portion of Thornley's testimony that dealt with George Orwell's book 1984. It was Oswald who suggested Thornley should read it (Orwell was the same author of *Brave New World*, which Oswald would ask New Orleans district attorney Gillin about in September 1963). Thornley explained that *1984* was about "a projection into the future . . . in 1984 in England under a complete police state. It is, I would say, an anti-utopian novel . . . a criticism of English socialism and what it might lead to in which a mythical leader called Big Brother dominates everybody's life . . ."[36]

The book was a political statement that Oswald would have rejected. We know he adhered to a Marxist philosophy based upon what radical right proponents of self-determination believed. But how did Thornley feel about this? He testified that "I would say I am an extreme rightist. I call myself a libertarian, which is that I believe in the complete sovereignty of the individual, or at least as much individual liberty as is practical under any given system. To which Mr. Jenner of the WC replied, "You don't have to be an extreme rightist to believe in the sovereignty of the individual." "Well," replied Thornley, "it is getting that way in this country today. At least most people who listen to me [ ] call me a rightist . . ."

Thornley said he believed in the "complete sovereignty of the individual," which was self-determination, that no one could force you to do something against your will. In addition, he was an "extreme rightist," and most people who knew him agreed with this assessment. And at the same time, he was a libertarian. In short, his philosophy was identical to Oswald's. And maybe it was Fidel Castro that attracted them to the Unitarian Church, for in a convoluted way, they equated their right-wing self-determination beliefs with those of the Cuban revolutionary fight for justice.

Even though much of this is speculation, there is sufficient circumstantial evidence that Oswald was told about Albert Schweitzer College by someone associated with the Unitarian Church in Los Angeles. It was likely Kerry Thornley who did so. And, when considered alongside the other information described in this chapter, it reinforces the possibility that Thornley may have played a role in Oswald's defection, and possibly it all somehow related to Cuba. And it is for these reasons that the Unitarian Church bears further examination.

* * *

During World War II, the Unitarian Church became heavily involved in émigrés' relief and rescue efforts throughout Europe. In this endeavor, they received support from the OSS, who then placed undercover agents within the church so they could, in the course of the charitable work they engaged in, access restricted areas that the OSS could not get to on their own. In addition, the Unitarian Service Committee (USC) worked closely with the OSS in "the rescue of Europe's intellectual, academic and [anti-Nazi] political leaders . . ." By 1945, the War Relief Control Board recognized the USC, and the National Defense Fund endorsed it. On May 17, 1944, in connection to this, Percival Brundage sent a memo to fellow board members of the Refugee Relief Trustees entitled "Statement Regarding Relation of Unitarian Service Committee to War Refugee Board." The message concerned Unitarians and their involvement in government-sponsored refugee activity and intelligence gathering. There was more to this church than attending services on Sunday.

The Unitarians maintained offices in Lisbon and Madrid. In Marseilles, they worked with Corsican "gangster families," who helped resolve some of their pressing refugee problems. It helped establish an early relationship between American religious service organizations, American intelligence, and the Corsican Mafia, which would lead to the Helliwell operation and the trafficking of illicit narcotics to fund the Dulles/Donovan stay-behind armies.

During the war, Allen Dulles utilized humanitarian groups in Switzerland because there were "individuals who happened to have access to different parties . . . [and were] willing to make their access available." Quakers and Unitarians connected Dulles with emigre groups that had intelligence and political connections throughout Europe. The American Friends of German Freedom was a U.S. intelligence operation that worked with the OSS-supported Emergency Rescue Committee. David Seiferheld, an OSS counterintelligence officer who became secretary of the American Friends of German Freedom, was "an early recruit into the OSS and a confidant William Donovan."[37]

Robert Dexter, the Unitarian Service Committee director in Lisbon in 1941, worked undercover for the OSS. He put Allen Dulles in touch with Noel Field, who had successfully created underground routes from France to Switzerland. However, neither Dexter nor Dulles knew that Field was a Communist. Or that Field directed the food and other aid to be sent to Communists only.[38]

After the war, Central Intelligence Group Directive No.155 called for the "Exploitation of American . . . Religious Organizations with Connections Abroad as Sources of Foreign Intelligence Information." This practice continued after the CIA came into being. Since the Unitarian's humanitarian work brought them into third-world countries, U.S. intelligence was again interested in the church. This time it was the CIA. Many church leaders supported CIA programs around the world, including church-related resistance groups. From 1946 until 1948, Allen Dulles ran private intelligence operations inside Eastern Europe, which involved numerous religious and charitable institutions covering covert operations.

Percival Brundage had ties to James R. Killian, Jr., a highly placed Unitarian who in 1949 became president of MIT. Within a year, he allowed Harvard to conduct meetings of their "Project Troy" on the MIT campus as part of what the Center for International Studies was doing. It may have played a role in Oswald's defection to the Soviet Union, for the name Troy may have come from the Trojan Horse, where Greek soldiers entered Troy secretly, under the pretext of friendship, with the intent of destroying that city. It became even more relevant in 1954 when Killian became chairman of the Technological Capabilities Panel, which studied military and intelligence applications of "high-flight reconnaissance," which included the U-2 spy plane.[39]

While James Killian was busy at Harvard putting together a program to infiltrate the Soviet Union, Noel Field continued doing what he had done during the war, arranging for anti-Nazi Communists to return to Germany. By 1946, the Unitarian Service Committee in France was run by Communists exclusively, and as a result, non-Communists groups failed to receive Unitarian assistance out of France.[40] Before Communist Stephen Fritchman became pastor of the Los Angeles parish, he was editor of the *Christian Register*, the publication put out by the Unitarian Church. It led to Unitarian Linscott Tyler, a former FBI agent, alerting the church about Fritchman. The FBI investigated him, and they were filming his meetings and monitoring his telephone conversations. Understandably, Fritchman's pro-Communist background outraged some congregation members.[41]

The January 1947 *Christian Register* reported that some Unitarians thought the publication was not only pro-Russian but anti-American. A group called *Friends of Democracy* complained. They said that ". . . The *Christian Register* consistently defended the policy of the Soviet Union while attacking our own . . . In domestic issues, it was in substantial agreement with the Communist organ, *The Daily Worker* . . ." One congregant said that ". . . If any Unitarian believing in the principle of the free mind and cherishing the methods democracy can be a Communist, he [was] either a schizophrenic or a Communist conspirator." Another said the *Register* ". . . has been encouraging . . . communist ideology . . . and humanistic philosophies detrimental to Unitarian Christianity." Another accused *The Christian Register* ". . . of unadulterated admiration of Soviet Russia. . . ."[42] It was clear what Fritchman and the leftist Unitarians stood for.

Recall that growing up, Oswald's hero was Herbert Philbrick, who infiltrated Communist cells on behalf of the FBI. When Philbrick's book, *I Led Three Lives: Citizen, "Communist," Counterspy* was published, it claimed Philbrick had been a member of a Communist cell led by Martha Fletcher, a onetime associate director of American Unitarian Youth. According to Philbrick, the Unitarian Church never joined the Communist Party USA (CPUSA), "but their sympathies were with the Soviet Union . . . Some of it [dealt with] the dogma that 'capitalist imperialism' was certain to die and socialism was the wave of the future . . ."[43]

Fritchman eventually resigned as *Christian Register* editor and became pastor of the First Unitarian Church of Los Angeles, which compelled members who objected to communism to leave. Those that stayed supported his far-left views and created an overall pro-Socialist, if not pro-Communist, congregation. As reported in *Stephen Fritchman: The American Unitarians and Communism*, Fritchman maintained "a fierce socialist dream and . . . high hopes for the Russian and Chinese (and Cuban) experiments. It attracted political radicals and Communists to the Los Angeles Unitarian congregation."[44]

But not all Unitarians were Communists. As stated above, the church also has a long relationship with U.S. intelligence going back to World War II, which included an association with Allen Dulles, the Corsican Mafia, and Eastern European resistance groups Dulles was establishing. A prime example was Percival Brundage, director of the Unitarian Service Committee from 1949 thru 1954, which means he dealt with the CIA during the early 1950s. In 1954, while Brundage was an active member of the Council on Foreign Relations, Brundage became Deputy Director of the Bureau of the Budget (BOB) in the Eisenhower administration. Brundage was also likely a member of the Century Club. He exhibited his paintings there. Recall from Volume One that this club's membership consisted of elites who opposed FDR and were looking to create a "New World Order." After leaving BOB, he and an associate, former Assistant Secretary of Defense E. Perkins McGuire, were asked to become majority stockholders "in name only" of a new airline, Southern Air Transport. Recall that Paul Helliwell had established Air America to transport drugs in Southeast Asia. Southern Air Transport was the CIA airline that controlled the Caribbean part of the same operation.[45]

Then there was Ruth Paine, the woman who lived with Marina Oswald in Irving, Texas, in the months leading up to the assassination. Ruth and her husband Michael were both Unitarians. Both of Ruth's parents, William Avery and Carol Hyde, were Unitarians as well. William Avery Hyde worked for the Agency for International Development (AID), a CIA offshoot, as did Ruth's brother-in-law, John Hoke. Ruth's sister Silvia, the wife of John Hoke, worked for the CIA.

Meanwhile, Ruth's husband, Michael Paine, the son of George Lyman Paine, was a Marxist who lived in California. His mother, Ruth Forbes Paine Young, was very close friends with Mary Bancroft, who amazingly was Allen Dulles' mistress, while Dulles was with OSS in Europe during World War II. Shortly after the war, Ruth Forbes Paine joined the World Federalist Movement, founded the International Peace Academy. And with her second husband, she created the Institute for the Study of Consciousness at Berkeley, California.[46]

The leftist credentials of Ruth and Michael Paine and their extended families rivaled anyone at that time. Which made it quite odd that when the FBI asked for character references from Ruth and Michael, they provided the names of Nancy and Frederick Osborn, Jr., two elitist right-wingers with whom the two leftists should have had nothing in common. Unless we consider Kerry Thornley and Lee Oswald were right-wing radicals who also supported left-wing causes. And that if Thornley used the name Osborne in ordering Oswald's FPCC handbills, it was just another coincidence and had nothing to do with the Osborns, who were friends with the Paines. Regardless, the Paine/Osborn connection is odd because the Osborn family history was such that it should have made Michael and Ruth Paine run for cover.

Henry Fairfield Osborn, the uncle of Frederick Osborn Jr.'s father, was a eugenicist. So involved was he that in 1921 he was president of the Second International Congress of Eugenics. By 1937, responsibility for the furtherance of eugenics passed to the Pioneer Fund and its secretary, Frederick Henry Osborn, Sr., the father of the character witness for Michael and Ruth Paine. He was also a "leading proponent of racial eugenics." The Roosevelts and the Rockefellers were his friends; he was a trustee of Princeton, the Carnegie Corporation, the Population Association of America, and the American Society of Human Genetics.

The Pioneer Fund was established in 1937 by Frederick Osborn and "a group of wealthy Northeastern conservatives" who were well known for supporting southern segregationists. Osborn was a boyhood friend of Franklin Roosevelt. He had at least two meetings with Harry H. Woodring, FDR's secretary of war, to promote the Pioneer Fund's eugenic program to improve the breeding stock of the US Army Air Corps, which also included a program on behavior modification.

In 1956, Nancy and Frederick Osborn, Jr. kept the family tradition going and were members of the leading American "genetics" group that supported the senior Osborn's eugenics organization. How was it possible for the Osborns, with their family history, to be associated with the Paines? How could the left-wing Paines tolerate the eugenicist Osborns? Is it possible that, like Kerry Thornley, the Paines were libertarians who considered themselves extreme rightists and supported right-wing causes that did not conflict with Marxist principles? In the Oswald saga, his connections were primarily radical right Fascists who supported self-determination. Still, there was also a Unitarian angle that seemingly assisted him to defect to the Soviet Union, kept a watchful eye over him, and guided him to the Texas School Book Depository and the assassination of JFK. Are we to believe that everything in between was unrelated, that the involvement of Unitarians was just bookends, or was this all part of the same operation? When Lee and Marina Oswald moved to Fort Worth, Texas, they were visited during the summer of 1962 by George de Mohrenschildt and Colonel Lawrence Orlov. Orlov knew Dallas CIA agent J. Walton Moore, who had asked George de Mohrenschildt to keep tabs on Oswald. Was there a significance that Orlov visited the Oswalds with de Mohrenschildt, even though there was no other known contact between them, and after that, Orlov seemed to disappear? The Warren Commission never called Orlov to testify, which may have been because he was in the oil business, served in both world wars, and had intelligence connections. There is no record of what this secretive man was doing between 1948 and 1961. But most important, Orlov's obituary stated he was a Unitarian, and the almost constant Unitarian presence throughout the last few years of Oswald's life just seems to be much too odd for it to have been random and coincidental. [47]

* * *

On August 17, 1959, Oswald requested a dependency discharge from the Marines to care for his mother, and a few weeks later, they accepted it. The next day, September 4, he applied for a passport, listing Cuba, the Dominican Republic, England, Turku, Finland, France, Germany, Russia, and Switzerland as countries he intended to visit. His itinerary included stops in places run by Trujillo and Castro, two Latin American dictators, and the Soviet Union, America's sworn enemy. It should have raised a red flag at the passport office, but it did not.

Oswald's passport application also included a document that said he was ". . . to be released from Active Duty and Transferred to the Marine Corps Reserves (Inactive) on September 11, 1959. It was signed by a Sergeant Stout over the typed signature block of Lt. A.G. Ayers. Ayers was the officer who prepared and signed the discharge entry on Oswald's military record, as well as the back of the Department of Defense ID card Oswald was issued when he left the Marines. It should have been a straightforward process, but Ayers could not remember working with a sergeant Stout when asked about it years later.[48]

Stout's signature on Oswald's document was a forgery, for we can assume that Ayers would have remembered him if they had worked together. Especially if they were so familiar that Stout was authorized to sign documents for Ayers in his absence. We could rule out that someone in Ayers' office did the forged signature because even Ayers admitted that he would have gladly signed the document if given to him. It means someone helped Oswald prepare a letter with a forged signature to submit to the Passport Office with his application. Did Oswald do this because of a need to expedite the passport, and he thought submitting additional information would help? Perhaps, but consider that service members generally would not receive an early honorable discharge because they wanted to travel to Europe and attend college there. It was especially true if they were being transferred to the reserves, as Oswald was, because, if called upon, they were required to serve in the future. Oswald's application included numerous overseas destinations, including countries the U.S. did not want its citizens to visit. It also included a forged letter confirming his transfer to the reserves. And he wanted his passport in one week, which should have been an impossible request. The fact is, Oswald may have been trying to get out of going to the Soviet Union. There was enough information furnished with his application for the Passport Office to have denied his request to travel abroad, or at least to have contacted the Marines to see if they knew of what Oswald intended to do after his discharge. It may have been the only way for Oswald to extricate himself from an assignment he did not want to accept.

It is not just the issuance of Oswald's passport that is troubling. Like all service members, the military issued Oswald a Department of Defense ID card upon his discharge, which was in his possession at the time of his arrest after JFK's assassination. The card taken from Oswald included his photo, identification number N 4,271,617, and two Post Office postmarks on the front of Oswald's card, one on top of the other. On the reverse side, the card was identified as a "Uniformed Services Identification and Privilege Card," DD Form 1173, issued on September 11, 1959, at El Toro Station, Santa Ana, California. The card was signed on the back by the issuing officer, 1st Lt. A.G. Ayers, Jr., the same man who prepared and signed the discharge entry on Oswald's military record, which said he was released early for "reasons of hardship." [49]

In their book *Oswald Talked*, Mary and Ray La Fontaine explained how they discovered a problem with Oswald's DOD ID card. First, it is essential to understand that the Marine Corps issued primarily three types of cards in 1959. Active-duty officers and enlisted men received a green 2MC card; retired Marines received a gray 2MC(RET) card, and reservists a red 2MC(RES) card. The red card was the one Oswald should have received, which is what all the other Marines who served with him were issued when they left the service. But Oswald was given a buff-colored DOD ID card, not one of the three cards usually distributed.

Mary La Fontaine contacted the Pentagon and was spoke with DOD employee Steve Gammons, who specialized in Department of Defense history. Gammons told Mary that the card Oswald received was known as a military dependent's card. The card was for family members to use the PX, the commissary, etc. The Marines issuing this card to Oswald should never have occurred, for he was an unmarried Marine without children. But there was one exception. These cards, Gammons said, were "sometimes issued to civilian personnel requiring military identification overseas." Remember that Gammons was answering a general question about DOD ID cards posed by Mary La Fontaine and did not know they were talking about Oswald, so something was wrong here. [50]

Recall from Chapter Six that a *Time* magazine article described "sheep dipping." The process involved making it appear that a soldier had "resigned from the military." [51] Did this apply to Oswald's supposed discharge from the Marines? Was it all a charade? Let's examine the facts as we know them.

In front of his fellow Marines at El Toro, Oswald publicly displays support for the Russian way of life. Simultaneously, he studies the Russian language and does not try to hide the fact. Oswald shows an interest in Castro's Cuba, and according to one Marine, receives mail from the Cuban Embassy in Los Angeles. He associates with a Unitarian Church parish in Los Angeles whose pastor was a Communist and whose congregation leaned far to the left. Oswald applied to a college in Switzerland associated with the Unitarians. At the time, the FBI and the CIA were investigating the Unitarians for possible Communist ties. He requests an early discharge from the Marines to allegedly take care of his sick mother. He applies for a passport with a proposed itinerary to visit numerous countries overseas, including Cuba and the Soviet Union. His application includes a forged document, and he wants the passport issued within a week. Then upon his discharge, the Marines issued him a DOD ID card only given to veterans working overseas as civilians. Is there any doubt that the Marine Corp knew Oswald was going overseas on a covert intelligence assignment?

There were also other problems. Oswald was issued the DOD ID card on September 11, the date of his discharge. Since the Marines were adamant that they never gave ID cards earlier than their effective date, it makes sense. But Oswald already had his card with him when he visited the passport office on September 4th, with the correct ID number listed on his passport application. How was that possible if regulations prohibited him from having the card in his possession that early? Military rules also stated that when the Marines took the ID card photo of Oswald, they should have retained one original and the negative in Oswald's file. However, in October 1963, the month before JFK's assassination, the CIA station in Mexico City cabled the Office of Naval Intelligence (ONI), requesting that they forward the most recent photo they had of Oswald, who had just left Mexico City.

ONI should have provided the CIA with the 1959 DOD ID card photo, but they did not. After the assassination, they produced an envelope addressed to the CIA, which contained Oswald's 1956 photo when he joined the Marines. It was the latest photo they had of him, so what happened to the discharge photo, and why was it necessary to keep that photo hidden? The answer to that question is obvious once all the facts are known. Oswald's passport photo and DOD ID card photo, taken around the same time, should have looked the same. However, they are not. They are so different they look like photos of two separate people. How could that be? The passport photo shows Oswald with a crew-cut, military-style haircut, as would be expected for a man about to be discharged from the service. The DOD ID card shows an Oswald with much longer hair, not a photo of someone in the military. The DOD ID card also was not laminated, which it should have been, per regulations. Did Oswald apply for a passport with a fraudulent ID card, and did he then throw away his actual DOD ID card when he was given it on September 11th? Or did the long-haired Oswald photo mean that the man discharged from the Marines was not the same one who obtained a passport and defected to the Soviet Union? It seems too involved to make any sense, for why have two different photos on the DOD ID card and the passport application if it would have been so easy to have the same photo on each. There must be a rational explanation.

The DOD ID card reveals more information. On the front of the card, the expiration date is typed and seen clearly as December 7, 1962. The date of the most recent Post Office postmark stamped on the front of the card is October 23, 1963, positioned right over another postmark and partially obliterates the date of the original postmark. All that is visible on the original is the word "July." On the back of the card are instructions explaining that the finder of the lost card should "drop in any mailbox." The Postmaster would then return the card to the Department of Defense at the address provided on the card. If the card were authentic, it was twice returned to the DOD and then returned to Oswald each time. It is troubling. It seems unlikely that the card was lost twice, and how would the DOD know where Oswald lived in 1963? Also, the card was a forgery. It would have become immediately apparent had the DOD compared the card mailed to them to the original DOD ID card photo in their files.

Since Oswald returned to the U.S. from the Soviet Union in June 1962, we can assume it was either in July 1962 or 1963 that the first postmark appeared on the ID card. If it were 1962, coming one month after his return from Russia, perhaps Oswald had been instructed to drop the card in a mailbox upon his arrival to let people know he was back in the United States. And if it were July 1963, was this a prearranged signal that Oswald wanted out of something in which he was involved just months before the assassination? Was the card returned to him and sent back to DOD again in October 1963, but it was too late by then? Was Oswald looking for help but was left out in the cold? Admittedly, it seems somewhat farfetched, and additional information is required to reach a definitive conclusion, but it is odd. The card was twice returned to DOD, most likely for a specific reason, and then somehow wound up in Oswald's wallet in Dallas at the time of his arrest. There had to be a reason behind this.[52]

Consider also the story of Louise Sweeney and Alveeta Treon, who worked the phone switchboard at Dallas City Hall. On the night of the assassination, two law enforcement officers came into their room to listen in on a call the incarcerated Oswald was about to make. At 10:45 P.M., Mrs. Sweeney took Oswald's call from the jailhouse, and she wrote down the details of the person Oswald wanted to call. She then did what the officers instructed her to do. Mrs. Sweeney did not put the call through. "I was dumbfounded at what happened next," said Alveeta Treon. Mrs. Sweeney told Oswald, 'I'm sorry, the number doesn't answer.' She then disconnected Oswald without ever really trying to put the call through. A few moments later, Mrs. Sweeney tore the page off her notation pad and threw it into the wastepaper basket."

After Mrs. Sweeney left work, Mrs. Treon removed the slip of paper from the wastebasket. She copied the information about Oswald's intended call onto a message slip as her souvenir of the event. In 1970, Chicago researcher Sherman H. Skolnick obtained a copy of the paper through a Freedom of Information Act suit. According to the phone message, Oswald was trying to call a "John Hurt" in Raleigh, North Carolina, at "834-7430 or 833-1253." In November 1963, two men named John Hurt lived in Raleigh—John David Hurt and John William Hurt. Interestingly, during World War II, John David Hurt was in military intelligence serving as a U.S. Army Counterintelligence Special Agent. HSCA lawyer Surell Brady, who investigated the Raleigh call, put it mildly when he described it as "provocative."[53]

Ex-CIA officer Victor Marchetti thought Oswald was following standard intelligence practice. He was trying to contact his case officer through a "cut-out," an intermediary with no direct involvement in an operation who Oswald was to call if he needed help. And for the law enforcement officers not to allow the call to go through meant they knew Oswald did not act alone, and they were afraid of what they might find out.

Returning to the mystery surrounding Oswald's DOD ID card, there is still more to consider. At Oswald's arrest, his wallet also contained a forged Selective Service System, Notice of Classification card issued to A.J. Hidell, the alias Oswald used in New Orleans. This card also had a photo of the same longer-haired man on Oswald's forged DOD ID card, supposedly taken in 1959 at his discharge from the Marines. The phony Hidell card with the same photo had to have been made four years later.[54]

It is indisputable that the A.J. Hidell card was a forgery, and the Warren Report admitted that it was. We also know that a photo of the same man was on Oswald's DOD ID card, which confirms that this card was a forgery as well. If the DOD ID card was authentic, the photo should have matched Oswald's passport photo, not the longer-haired man whose image appeared on the Hidell card, which showed up four years later. It does not make sense. Was someone trying to make it look like the person discharged from the Marines was not the real Oswald? Or that the man who went to the Soviet Union was not the same man released from the Marines in El Toro? Or was the man who went to the Soviet Union not the same one who returned to the U.S.? The FBI was very much aware that something unexplainable had occurred here, and we know this by the information they did and did not provide to the Warren Commission.

The Warren Commission Report included a photo of the forged Hidell Selected Service System card, showing the longer-haired Oswald photo, with a summary describing the card based on a report by FBI special agent Manning C. Clements, made the day after the assassination. Clements wrote that the card contained a photo; he described the writing on both sides and stated that the card was probably a forgery. It was a very detailed account of what was on the card.

Notably, Oswald's DOD ID card, which was supposedly given to him when he left the Marines, did not have the card's photo visible in the Warren Report as an exhibit. Even though the Hidell Selective Service System card with the same image is included as a Warren Commission exhibit with the photo visible. It was a purposeful omission. The DOD ID card contained the same photo as the Hidell Selective Service System card, which was made four years later but was different from Oswald's passport photo made at the same time. They could not disclose this information, for the Warren Commission and the FBI could never have offered a rational explanation for how this could have happened. It pointed to a conspiracy in JFK's assassination, for it would have destroyed the scenario they were presenting that Oswald was an unstable lone gunman. They had no choice but to hide this potential bombshell, even though they may not have understood what it meant.

FBI Agent Clements provided the Warren Commission with the summary of Oswald's DOD card. This time, he limited his description to the front of the card only. It included the card number, expiration date, Oswald's birth date, etc. The reverse side of the card had the place and date of issue, and the issuing officer, which was critical information but was not part of the Warren Commission report. To understand how crucial this omission was, we must consider that the FBI and the Warren Commission needed to convince the public that Oswald and Hidell were not separate individuals. That Hidell was not an accomplice working with Oswald. And this was their opportunity. They had in their possession a card made out in Oswald's name and a second card made out in Hidell's name, both with the same photo. Including both cards in the Commission's report would have put this matter to rest. However, they did not do this because anyone could easily have recognized that the photo was not Oswald when he left the Marines. It is also why a description of the back of the card was not in the Warren Report, for it would have mentioned El Toro, the name of the releasing officer, and the date of issue. They wanted to keep this information hidden from the public to maintain the narrative that Oswald was a disgruntled ex-Marine who assassinated the president after he defected to the Soviet Union.

The deception they attempted to perpetrate gets even worse. The Warren Report includes a photo of Oswald while he was in Russia entitled "Photo taken in Minsk." The picture is identical to the images shown on the phony Hidell Selective Service card and Oswald's DOD ID card. There is even a circular cutout on the Minsk photo in the lower right-hand corner to remove the evidence of the Post Office postmarks on the DOD card, which the Post Office applied in the United States. It means the FBI purposely lied because they knew the image of Oswald was after he returned to the U.S. from Russia. It was impossible for it to occurred before then. In addition, in December 1966, when the DOD card was released and sent to the National Archives, the Archives' Sue McDonough told the La Fontaines that the card arrived "nearly obliterated by FBI testing. The color, the image, the printing, everything is gone; you couldn't use it to show anything." It was "significantly discolored and stained" and had "no visible date stamp [postmark]."[55]

What was the FBI trying to hide? Consider that they submitted the "Minsk photo" and the phony Hidell Selective Service card with the same photo on it to the Warren Commission. It created the illusion that the "Minsk photo" was taken in Russia, and the Hidell card was forged and made with this photo after Oswald returned to the U.S. from the Soviet Union. It was a logical conclusion to draw with the information provided. However, Oswald's DOD ID card, which was given to him when he left the Marines in 1959, had the same "Minsk photo" on it, which destroyed this narrative. And since getting at the truth was never the FBI's objective, and to prevent the Warren Commission and the general public from learning the truth, the Bureau had to do something about the DOD ID card that had the same "Minsk photo," which they knew could not be authentic. So, the FBI provided a written description of the DOD ID card issued when Oswald left the Marines. However, by not including the photo to the Warren Commission, they could not connect the DOD ID card to the Hidell Selective Service card or the Minsk photo. It left the timeline they wanted to follow intact.

The FBI almost got away with this attempt to hide evidence because an actual copy of Oswald's DOD ID card is hard to find. When JFK's assassination occurred, Jesse Curry was the Dallas Police Chief. In his 1969 book about the assassination, he included a copy of the photo. Author Michael Eddowes also had a photocopy of the card in his 1977 book entitled *The Oswald File*. It further proves that the FBI lied and that the DOD ID card was a forgery. The FBI knew that if they provided a copy of the DOD ID card to the Warren Commission, they could not explain how that photo could be the same as the "Minsk photo" taken in Russia years later. They covered up the truth so they could maintain that Oswald was the lone assassin. There is no other conclusion that one can reach.

It also explains why, when the CIA asked for the latest known photo of Oswald in 1963, they received the image of Oswald when he joined the Marines—the picture of Oswald that was on the forged DOD card when he left the Marines was missing. What a surprise. It suggests that when the DOD received Oswald's fake card in the mail, someone must have discovered that the photo on the card did not match the image of the real Oswald in their files, so they destroyed what they had in their files. That this was not pursued further by the DOD is hard to explain unless someone who was privy to what Oswald was up to elected to keep this a secret. And considering that Oswald's Soviet defection was a covert intelligence operation, unconnected to JFK's assassination, it could explain why the FBI was willing to suppress evidence after the fact. It was not to alter evidence related to who murdered JFK. It was to hide the truth about Oswald's trip to Russia. And maybe that was why Oswald had misleading identification on his at the time of his arrest. It was not hard to connect the dots, and any professional would have immediately concluded that something was wrong. That this man should not be looked into too deeply because he had secrets better left uncovered. And it is what happened.

* * *

Oswald's passport was received on September 10, conveniently the day before his discharge from the Marines. He then boarded a bus and visited his mother in Fort Worth, telling her he planned to go into the export-import business. He soon left for New Orleans, where he suspiciously contacted Clay Shaw's travel agent, Lewis E. Hopkins, at the International Trade Mart. He booked a freighter to Europe, the Marion Lykes, scheduled to depart on September 20 for Le Havre, France.

Oswald had a few days to kill in New Orleans, and Joan Mellen tells a story in *A Farewell to Justice* that claims Oswald met with David Ferrie while he waited for his departure date to arrive. According to Mellen, a recent high school graduate named Van Burns worked at a parakeet stand at the Old Pontchartrain Beach amusement park. Burns was waiting to go to Marine boot camp and had some time to kill himself. On this day, a friend of Van's named Bob Boylston, who had been inducted into the Army six months earlier but was no longer in the service, approached him in the company of two men. One of the two was older with odd-looking hair. His name was David Ferrie. The other said his name was Lee Oswald and that he was in recon in the Marines. "We take pictures," he said. Boylston chimed in, saying that Lee had traveled with him and Ferrie to Cuba on recon missions, which was possible since we know that Ferrie took CAP cadets with him on trips to Latin America.[56]

It is possible that Oswald innocently looked up Ferrie when he arrived in New Orleans because Ferrie was someone to whom he was previously close. But it had been three years since he left New Orleans for Fort Worth with his mother, so this was somewhat odd unless Ferrie and Oswald had continued their relationship while in the Marines. And if that were the case, it potentially leads to the more ominous possibility that Ferrie was involved in Oswald's defection plans himself.

We should consider this in conjunction with Oswald's interaction with Clay Shaw's travel agent and the Bolton car dealership incident the following year. When Guy Banister's group, the Friends of a Democratic Cuba, used Oswald's name while he was in Russia. Kerry Thornley's involvement with Ferrie and Banister. Ferrie's possible connection to mind-altering drug testing at East Louisiana State Hospital, Tulane, and various Latin American countries, all of which may have involved Oswald. Thornley's relationship with Oswald over several years in multiple locations. When looked at collectively, the evidence provides a virtual bombshell of information. This group might have associated with Oswald before his defection, which means they may have played a part in it. Did Oswald's Russian defection have something to do with Cuba and the desire to remove Castro from power, and did this eventually morph into blaming Oswald for the assassination of JFK? Or was the defection connected to the attempt by Guy Banister and his associates to discredit civil rights and pro-Castro groups in the U.S.? Was this why Oswald started a Fair Play for Cuba chapter when he returned from Russia to infiltrate these groups (like June Cobb) and then testify against them, as others had done? It is something we will investigate as our narrative moves forward.

There are also questions regarding how Oswald financed a $1500 voyage when his bank account contained only $203, suggesting someone must have helped him pay for it. In addition, his passport showed that he traveled from Le Havre, France, by ship to England on October 9 and then left England for Helsinki, Finland, the following day. It should have been straightforward, but it poses a problem. The only commercial flight from London to Helsinki did not arrive in Finland in time for Oswald to have checked in at the hour recorded in the registration book of the Torni Hotel, where he stayed that night. It has led to speculation that Oswald may have traveled by private plane or military aircraft to reach his destination. Oddly enough, Oswald spent only one night at this hotel and the following day transferred to the Hotel Klaus Kurki. Both were first-class hotels in downtown Helsinki, so what prompted him to switch from one to the other is unknown, other than he might have been trying to make it difficult for anyone looking to follow him to do so.[57]

Then, although the expected turnaround time in Helsinki for obtaining an entry visa to the Soviet Union was seven to fourteen days, Oswald received his in only two, an indication that he was considered somewhat of a unique case by the Soviet consul who issued the visa. There is also some confusion as to if it was Helsinki from where Oswald entered the Soviet Union. On November 25, 1963, the Swedish newspaper *Dagens Nyheters* reported that Oswald "traveled through Sweden . . . on his way to the Soviet Union. According to the paper, he was unsuccessful in Helsinki, so "he went to Stockholm, where he rented a hotel room. Two days later, he was able to continue his journey to Moscow. That indicated the Russian Embassy gave him a visa."

The young ex-Marine arrived in Moscow on October 16. Rima Shirokova, an Intourist guide, met him and helped him register at the Hotel Berlin. Oswald had a series of meetings with Soviet officials over the next five days, who undoubtedly wanted to determine the validity of Oswald's desire to defect, especially if Oswald had an encounter with Eroshkin at the Russian Embassy in Tokyo and then showed up in the Soviet Union unannounced. It seems Oswald failed to convince them that he was a legitimate defector. The Soviets told the ex-Marine his visa had expired, and he had two hours to leave Moscow. They were suspicious, for it is unlikely the Russians would have rejected a defector whom they believed to be genuine. They were not in the habit of turning away a former American serviceman who came knocking at their door.

But Oswald was not going to give up that easy. Later, Shirokova came to Oswald's hotel room to find he had slashed his wrist in an apparent suicide attempt, a dramatic reaction to the Soviet's demand that he leave the country. Perhaps this was another sign of Oswald's emotional instability, caused by the mind-altering drugs taken while in the Marines. Or maybe the drugs he was administered programmed him to slash his wrists if he needed to do something drastic. Or perhaps the attempted suicide never occurred and was used to explain why Oswald spent time in Botkin Hospital in Moscow, where he supposedly spent the next eleven days recuperating from his wound. Once again, Oswald was in a hospital, this time undoubtedly under the intense scrutiny of the KGB.[58]

Years later, Richard Case Nagell told author Dick Russell: "The Soviets were . . . more interested in Lee Harvey Oswald [after his return to the United States] than the Americans. Because when he was in the Soviet Union, they had considered him emotionally unstable, prone to commit some act that could bring embarrassment to the Soviet Union. . . ."[59] Ex-CIA agent James Wilcott echoed what Nagell said, claiming the Russians were on to Oswald immediately and knew he was involved in a deep cover operation.[60]

Despite this, the Soviets changed their minds and allowed Oswald to remain. He left the hospital on October 22 and checked into the Hotel Metropole.

Game on!

- 9 -

Double Trouble from Moscow

"... it seemed to me that there was a possibility that he [Oswald] had been in contact with others before or during his Marine Corps tour who had guided him and encouraged him in his actions."

—John McVickar, American consul at the U.S. Embassy, Moscow

There was immediate concern among investigative bodies in the United States that the man named Lee Harvey Oswald, who had defected to the Soviet Union, was an impostor. And the case of this lowly Marine private would require the attention of J. Edgar Hoover, the Director of the FBI, and Dean Rusk, the Secretary of State.

Oswald would be met at his Moscow hotel by a reporter named Priscilla Johnson, who was really with the CIA. She was brought into the CIA by Cord Meyer, and the evidence suggests these two were part of a network that planned and supervised Oswald's Soviet defection. Then, after JFK's assassination, Johnson conveniently became close to Oswald's widow, Marina, and would write a book about Marina's life with Lee Oswald, much of which Johnson distorted. Adding to the intrigue is that Priscilla Johnson's husband was good friends with George de Mohrenschildt, the suspicious man who befriended Oswald and Marina after returning to Texas from the Soviet Union.

* * *

The CIA had a complicated history of obtaining information from the Communist bloc, which makes the idea that Oswald's defection to the Soviet Union was an intelligence operation so believable. From the beginning of the Cold War, the United States made a concerted attempt to infiltrate agents behind the Iron Curtain, but without success. And because of freedoms inherent in the United States, the Soviets enjoyed a distinct advantage over their American counterparts, who could not move freely within Communist countries.

Allen Dulles voiced his frustration about this in a 1954 interview with *U.S. News and World Report*. He stated that the Soviets "have far greater facilities for operating in the United States than we have [in Russia]. "I would give a good deal if I could know as much about the Soviet Union as [they] can learn about us by merely reading the press."[1]

Attempts by the CIA to secretly place agents within Communist countries failed disastrously. In *The Agency, The Rise and Decline of the CIA*, author John Ranelagh described how the CIA tried desperately to penetrate the wall that separated eastern Europe from the rest of the world:

> OPC sent agents into the Soviet Union and Eastern Europe by sea, land, and air from Norway, Sweden, Finland, Germany, Greece, Iran, Turkey, and Japan, all with the mission of setting up networks and reporting on military and political affairs in the Soviet Union and the Soviet bloc.[2]

As early as 1950, the OPC regarded Poland as the weak link in the Soviet bloc. Thousands remained in the West rather than return to their country and the tyranny of a Communist regime. It proved to be fertile ground for recruiting agents who were more than ready to put their lives on the line. The OPC primarily aligned itself with the Polish Political Council and the Freedom and Independence Movement. The latter, known as WIN because of its Polish initials, claimed to be connected to a group within Poland. The OPC could not verify this because agents sent into Poland were caught almost immediately by the Communists. Despite having reservations, the OPC began airdropping money, arms, and ammunition to WIN agents behind enemy lines. Two years later, as the fear that the Soviets were preparing to sweep across western Europe grew, WIN was considered a formidable force that would stall the anticipated Soviet onslaught. Their numbers were impressive—20,000 members, and with additional funding, there was the potential for 100,000.

In the end, the WIN operation was a failure, for Polish Communists had penetrated the group. By the end of 1952, the OPC/WIN operation ended a significant propaganda coup for the Soviets. Still, there was no remorse at the CIA for the needless loss of life, for innocent deaths were a necessary evil in the war against communism. As David Atlee Phillips explained, "Many entered CIA so soon after World War II, which was regarded as a 'just' war, that they didn't worry too much if civilians were killed in the process. This feeling remained in CIA for a long time afterwards. We were soldiers in a 'just' war."[3]

The CIA determined that unconventional infiltration methods into the Soviet Union and Soviet bloc countries would not suffice as the decade wore on. They began to realize that legal travel offered a better means of obtaining information. But what remained consistent throughout everything the CIA did was their continued disregard for the loss of innocent life.

One creative program involved using average American tourists who were interested in traveling behind the Iron Curtain. Those foolish enough to succumb to the Agency's request for help did so at tremendous personal risk. It was one of the CIA's most thoughtless programs undertaken because it endangered the lives of innocent men and women. It should not come as a surprise, considering that drug experimentation was being conducted by the CIA on other unsuspecting innocents simultaneously. In comparison, this was relatively tame.

William Makinen, a graduate student from the University of Pennsylvania who then attended the University of West Berlin, was a typical example of how ruthless the CIA was. Interested in traveling to Ukraine, he was given a car and expense money by two CIA agents and instructed to take notes of military sites. It did not take long for Ukrainian police to arrest him. Authorities charged him with espionage activity, for unknown to Makinen, his cab driver phoned authorities when his passenger became unusually interested in driving around military installations. Makinen eventually confessed that the CIA had paid for his trip. It resulted in an espionage conviction and a seven-year prison sentence.[4]

William Makinen was not the only civilian to spy for the CIA, nor was he the only one apprehended and punished. CIA considered these students expendable, and the cost of a car and pocket change was a small price to pay for the potential benefits the Agency could reap.

Taking advantage of American tourists traveling legally behind the Iron Curtain was part of a covert operation called REDWOOD, a program run by CIA's Soviet Russian Division SR10. The Chief of Soviet Realities, "Thomas Casasin," a pseudonym he alternately spelled "Cacasin," believed Lee Oswald's trip to Russian might have been part of this operation. It would explain why on the list of military defectors whom CIA's Marguerite Stevens investigated, she listed Oswald as a "tourist."

* * *

Founded in 1945 and recognized by the United Nations, the World Federation of Democratic Youth (WFDY) was an international, pro-peace, anti-nuclear war youth organization that brought together young people from Capitalist and Socialist nations. They characterized themselves as an anti-imperialist and anti-leftist organization. Still, as the Cold War progressed, the group was accused by the U.S. State Department of being a "Moscow front," which was not far from the truth. Many Western groups left the Federation. As a result, the WFDY's membership primarily came from Socialist nations, national liberation movements, and Communist youth organizations.

Generating resistance against such groups was part of the CIA's mandate, so in 1948 Frank Wisner authorized OPC to secretly fund American labor organizations to develop opposition to the World Federation of Trade Unions overseas. And once they determined that the WFDY was a Communist-backed student organization, the CIA set out to limit the spread of this group. The National Student Association

(NSA) was an American student group founded at the University of Wisconsin in 1947. It did not take long before the CIA infiltrated the group and provided funding. CIA recruited dozens of American students and administered security oaths under the Espionage Act while assigning case officers to ensure students complied with their covert objectives. And as the years progressed and the NSA grew in numbers and importance, their participation in covert CIA operations grew.[5]

In 1950, Tom Braden became head of the International Organizations (IO) Division at CIA. Located within OPC, IO tended to engage in operations that leaned left of center, including projects which included Socialists from the outside. OPC believed that this was more effective than the right-wing operations Frank Wisner and others at the Agency preferred in the struggle for heart and minds behind the Iron Curtain and Third World countries. As a result, IO focused on programs that supported more liberal anti-Soviet groups, believing their main objective was to overthrow hardline Communists. An alliance with more moderate leftists could accomplish this. It was a continuation of William Colby and Clare Boothe Luce's struggle years before in Italy. It served to widen the chasm between the liberal and conservative groups within the CIA.

Cord Meyer, a life-long liberal, joined the CIA in 1951 and was assigned to IO, for which he was perfectly suited. A World War II hero, Meyer was severely wounded in combat. After the war, he embraced an anti-war, anti-atomic bomb stance, and commitment to world peace gained him national notoriety. He attended the United Nations Conference on International Organization in 1945, and two years later, he was elected president of the United World Federalists. This international organization promoted a one-world government. In pursuit of his leftist utopia, Meyer had to engage with Communists on several occasions, and these encounters changed his opinion of communism forever. Things came to a head when Communists tried to control the American Veterans Committee, which Meyer prevented by utilizing around-the-clock stakeouts of left-wing students and other covert techniques. The experience had a lasting effect on him, and he no longer was an advocate for world peace; he became an ardent anti-Communist Cold Warrior, albeit a liberal one. In 1954 he succeeded Tom Braden and was appointed head of the IO division, overseeing worldwide youth movements and student group operations, including the National Student Association. It became the defining work of Meyer's career.[6]

Winning the hearts and minds of disenfranchised people became more complex in 1955 when the previously discussed Bandung conference in Indonesia pushed for Third World independence from the U.S. and the USSR. One problem the United States faced was that Bandung supported the Algerian student union (UGEMA), the Algerian Front de Liberation Nationale (FLN) student arm, and their struggle against French colonialism. The U.S. supported France's effort to maintain the status quo.

France regarded the FLN as a terrorist group. And because of their relationship to the FLN, the UGEMA was considered one as well. As a result, even though they were a student organization, UGEMA followers in France were treated with the same brutality which the FLN faced in Algeria. In 1955, UGEMA's thirty-one-year-old vice president disappeared in Paris, never no one ever saw him again. There were other murders, torture, and Algerian students held in prison without trial. The following year, a hunger strike to protest French atrocities brought support from the East German student union, further alienating the UGEMA in France.

Meanwhile, the American NSA backed the Algerian students, as did CIA liberals, contrary to what the Eisenhower administration wanted. Opposing U.S. policy was nothing new for the CIA, but this was different because the rise of the worldwide student movement threatened the American sphere of influence worldwide. And it was not just Algeria where the problem existed, for Cuba and Egypt were two other hot spots where the U.S. position opposed what student groups worldwide supported. It made promoting democracy internationally that much harder.

The most important event for the World Federation of Democratic Youth was the annual Youth Festival, a Socialist and Communist-inspired political and cultural celebration for peace held in a Socialist nation. In 1957 it took place in Moscow and attracted 34,000 people from 130 countries. In protest over the Soviet intervention in Hungary the previous year, America's NSA boycotted the event. Unwilling to allow the Soviets exclusive access to student groups attending the event, the CIA sent a contingent of politically motivated, older American graduate students, including former NSA officials, to the festival. And once in Moscow, they intended to raise the Hungarian issue so the whole world would understand what had happened there.

Twenty-eight-year-old former NSA officer Richard Medalie, a student at Harvard Law, made the trip. "I met a man in Harvard Square," he later said, "who handed me an airline ticket from Boston to Washington with a false identification card to match the false name (Dr. Carlton) on the ticket." Medalie was briefed in Washington to ensure he understood what the CIA expected of him. He recommended another Harvard law student, George Abrams, who later identified his contact simply as "a former NSA person" who had experience dealing with international matters. Abrams had a similar meeting in Harvard Square, where he also received a ticket under a phony name for a briefing in Washington.

From the beginning, problems beset the two men, including being forbidden from entering the Soviet Union directly from the U.S. without violating the McCarran Act, which banned travel to Communist countries. But Medalie had contacts at the Polish student union, ZSP, and they arranged for the Americans to secure entry visas through the Soviet embassy in Poland, bypassing normal travel channels. It was a good plan, except that the two young Americans would be on their own and left out in the cold if something went wrong. Abrams later said that he never fully grasped the risks they faced until he returned to the U.S.

They arrived in Moscow as members of the Polish delegation with copies of the UN report on the Hungarian uprising buried inside their luggage. The report challenged the Soviet version of events, and Medalie and Abrams looked forward to letting the Russians at the Youth Festival know the truth about what had happened in Hungary. Their opportunity came in Red Square in front of Lenin's Tomb. The two Americans discussed various topics with Moscow citizens while roughly one thousand spectators looked on. The crowd questioned them about racial discrimination in the U.S., the KKK, wages, and various other topics. However, when they started reading excerpts from the UN Hungarian uprising report, the Hungarian delegation appeared and defended the Soviet action, saying it was necessary to suppress "fascist counter-revolutionary elements." For several nights similar exchanges took place, which naturally angered the Soviets. The official Communist Party newspaper *Izvestia* called Abrams an FBI spy. The newspaper *Sovetskaya Rossiya* denounced him as a State Department plant.

They were harassed and delayed as they tried to leave the country when it was over, but the two eventually made it back to the United States unharmed. The CIA debriefed both men, and they testified in closed session before the Senate Foreign Relations Committee.

The CIA also sent Rand Corporation Soviet specialist and future CIA career officer Raymond Garthoff to the festival. Alexander Dallin, a young Russian scholar from Columbia University who traveled to Moscow as part of the Swedish delegation, joined him. Dallin's father had gone into exile after fighting as a Menshevik in the Russian revolution, so there was no question about where his allegiance lay. Both men spoke Russian, and they had the opportunity to talk with hundreds of students in Moscow and nearby cities. They obtained valuable intelligence, including a classified Soviet military report, and brazenly took dozens of photographs that showed how deplorable conditions in the Soviet Union were. It was welcome information for the CIA to digest, and the risk justified the reward, at least in the minds of the CIA handlers who sent these two innocents behind enemy lines, with no means of support if something went wrong.[7]

Over the next few years, the NSA concentrated on the two most prominent countries where revolutions were actively taking place—Cuba and Algeria. The American student group backed the revolutionaries in both countries. However, as long as the U.S. government provided support to Batista in Cuba's struggle against Castro's revolutionary army and backed France over the locals in Algeria fighting for their freedom, student groups worldwide questioned the sincerity of NSA's support. It was a critical period for the NSA and the U.S. government. The CIA hoped the NSA's support for Algerian independence could win them friends in other North African and Middle Eastern countries that struggled to achieve their freedom from European colonial rule. These were countries that could not be allowed to fall into the Soviet sphere of influence.

And similarly, the CIA thought that support of the Cuban revolution would resonate positively for NSA and the United States throughout Latin America and keep Western Hemisphere nations in the democratic camp. However, it was an exercise in futility, as the NSA pro-revolution and anti-colonialist message were not trusted worldwide even though it opposed the official U.S. government position. As a result, international student groups painted the NSA with the same brush as the United States.

In the summer of 1959, as Lee Harvey Oswald prepared for his defection to the Soviet Union, which was only a couple of months away, the World Youth Festival was held in Vienna, Austria. The country was split politically between two major parties—the Socialist Party of Austria and the Austrian People's Party. The Austrian Peoples Party was conservative, pro-Catholic, and anti-Socialist. Since this was the first time the festival would occur in a nation that was not part of the Soviet bloc, the CIA saw it as an opportunity to recruit foreign nationals from Asia and Africa and bring them into the Western camp. They also expected an onslaught of Soviet propaganda, and according to Cord Meyer, the CIA intended "to compete more effectively with this obviously successful Communist apparatus."

Meanwhile, right-winger C.D. Jackson recognized the festival's importance "This is the first time commies have held one of these shindigs on our side of the Iron Curtain," he said, "and what goes on, how it goes on, and what the follow-up will be is, I think, extremely important." "Communist ideology," Jackson wrote, "despite all the evidence of the realities of life in the Soviet system—still has a significant appeal to many peoples outside that system."[8]

Eisenhower agreed. "Nationalism is on the march, and world communism is taking advantage of that spirit of nationalism to cause dissension in the free world," Ike wrote in his diary. "Moscow leads many misguided people to believe . . . they can count on communist help to achieve and sustain nationalistic ambitions," Eisenhower continued. "[C]ommunists are hoping to take advantage of the confusion resulting from the destruction of existing relationships . . . to further the aims of world revolution and the Kremlin's domination of all peoples." [9]

Jackson's first step was to approach the always available John McCloy and ask him to write an article about the U.S. occupation of Germany and what America was doing to reconstruct that country. McCloy was a logical person for Jackson to seek out, for he understood the festival's importance. In 1951, while serving as high commissioner of occupied Germany, McCloy had countered the World Youth Festival in East Berlin by hosting a similar festival in the western half of the city at the same time. He agreed to write the article published in five languages in a newspaper distributed by twenty-five-year-old Smith College graduate Gloria Steinem, the future woman's rights activist.

When Jackson first contacted McCloy in the autumn of 1958, he and Cord Meyer had already agreed that the CIA would provide secret funding to an "informal group of activists" who would go to the festival as an "alternate" American delegation. The Agency also intended to distribute books and publish a newspaper in Vienna as part of their propaganda blitz, so Steinem, who had recently returned from a two-year assignment in India as a Chester Bowles Asian Fellow, was brought into the operation. Steinem very much supported a contingent of liberal, anti-Communist American students going to the festival. Through her contacts at the NSA, she learned there was funding available for American participation in the yearly event. Working through Jackson and Meyer, she set up an organization in Cambridge, Massachusetts called the Independent Service for Information on the Vienna Youth Festival. Jackson helped her obtain contributions from various U.S. corporations, but most of the money came from the CIA, which Jackson managed in a "special account." McCloy was involved because he could get the financing to Vienna unnoticed. As Jackson explained to Cord Meyer, "I have been in touch with Jack McCloy on the handling of funds . . . [which] Chase Bank had done it in the past . . . [McCloy] gave me the name of the man in Chase who knew all about such things." In addition, the "money would have to do quite a lot of traveling—from Chase to Switzerland in one of the numbered accounts, from Switzerland to Bresach & Co. in Liechtenstein . . ." From there, Jackson arranged to have one of Henry Luce's *Time* magazine reporters pick up the funds in cash and drive it to Vienna.

How often McCloy allowed the CIA to use Chase Manhattan Bank in this fashion is not known. However, given the tenor of the times, McCloy's close relationship with Allen Dulles, and how the CIA was also secretly laundering money through the Vatican, it would be surprising if Chase's involvement with the CIA was not a relationship that worked together regularly.

About the same time that McCloy helped the agency at the Vienna Youth Festival, Cord Meyer began fund-raising for the American Institute for Free Labor Development (AIFLD), a new organization designed to train labor union officials from Latin America on how to combat communism. It was a significant undertaking since Fidel Castro had come to power earlier that year and threatened to spread his revolution into other Latin American countries. Chase Manhattan Bank, Standard Oil of New Jersey, and several other large corporations subsidized AIFLD's activities.[10]

Meanwhile Steinem continued her work for the Youth Festival, encouraging undergraduates to apply to the left-wing US Committee for International Student Cooperation. At the same time, she and her staff screened candidates, often young professionals, on behalf of C.D. Jackson. One group she may have recruited, recalled Thomas Garrity, a Vienna festival attendee who had been active in the NSA during the late 1940s, involved U.S. Army recruits based at Fort Leavenworth, Kansas. These servicemen grew their hair long enough to pose as students and went to Vienna with a singular purpose—to disrupt the festival. CIA liberals wanted them there to potentially counter right-wing Austrian hardliners who might try to disrupt the conference physically. It would have hurt the American effort to get their pro-peace, democratic message across to student groups they were trying to impress.[11]

So, as Lee Harvey Oswald prepared to defect, there was a significant push by U.S. intelligence to obtain information regarding what life was like behind the Iron Curtain and to thwart the Soviet plan to spread their revolution throughout the Third World. And it was all run by left-leaning CIA operatives like Cord Meyer, not the hardline, right-wing radicals who had failed miserably in their attempt to place people behind the Iron Curtain.

During this time, a rash of military personnel defected to the Soviet Union, including Oswald, as discussed in Chapter Six. It was probably an operation run by CIA liberals as well. Recall that left-leaning Unitarians likely assisted Oswald in the period leading up to his defection, who, like Cord Meyer, were one-time United World Federalist supporters. In addition, the CIA provided funds to unsuspecting American citizens legally traveling to the Soviet Union.

The CIA also secretly sent students to the World Youth Festival and other events. The Agency used others to infiltrate leftist groups to disrupt Soviet propaganda efforts that targeted international students who did not know any better. And in all cases, the action was led by the left-leaning CIA officer Cord Meyer, who believed a more liberal message would be more effective than a far-right one. And undoubtedly, this was not looked upon with disfavor by the right-wing, who steadfastly maintained that unmitigated force was the only acceptable response.

* * *

It was not until October 31, 1959, two weeks after he arrived in Moscow, that Lee Oswald appeared at the U.S. embassy to announce his defection. Embassy staff directed him to Embassy consul Richard Snyder who was a CIA case officer under diplomatic cover, according to the publication *Who's Who in CIA*. Released CIA documents also reveal that Snyder had been a CIA campus recruiter, or "spotter," at Harvard. At the same time, he was a student there, looking for other students interested in going to the Soviet Union. Cord Meyer certainly would have approved of such work.[12]

There were CIA had agents posted within the American Embassy in Moscow when Oswald showed up there. According to *Vanity Fair* magazine: "The official story has it that when Oswald defected, he went to the American Embassy in Moscow only once, visiting only the consular office on the ground floor. Yet the widow of the assistant naval attaché, Joan Hallet, who worked as a receptionist at the embassy, said Consul Richard Snyder and the security officer 'took him [Oswald] upstairs to the working floors, a secure area where the Ambassador and [the] . . .

military officer were. A visitor would never go up there unless he [were] on official business. I was never up there.'" According to Hallett, Oswald came to the embassy on multiple occasions in 1959.[13]

Oswald handed Snyder a handwritten note asserting his desire to renounce his citizenship and that his "allegiance is to the Union of Soviet Socialist Republics." He said he was a Marxist and had planned his defection for two years while in the Marine Corp. If the timing is correct, this means it began when Oswald arrived in Japan, and the Queen Bee incident took place, when he most likely first came to the attention of U.S. intelligence.

Snyder attempted to talk Oswald out of his desire to defect. Still, if he insisted on going ahead with it, Snyder said, Oswald would have to return to the embassy in a couple of days to sign the official defection papers. Upon hearing this, Oswald abruptly left, leaving his passport in Snyder's possession. He would not return to the embassy, even though he remained in Moscow for several weeks after the encounter and had ample time to do so. It was a critical decision, for it meant he never officially renounced his citizenship, leaving open the possibility that he could return to the United States someday if he so desired. Snyder later concluded that Oswald might have staged the entire incident, assuming the KGB had bugged the embassy and listened to their conversations.[14]

John McVickar was the other American consul at the embassy. He recalled for the Warren Commission that "it seemed to me that there was a possibility that he had been in contact with others before or during his Marine Corps tour who had guided him and encouraged him in his actions." As we have shown, there was ample evidence to support this possibility.[15]

According to Snyder, Oswald said he "was warned you would try to talk me out of defecting." Who would have warned him? The Soviets, who initially wished to send him back to the U.S. or his American handlers, helped him plan his defection to Russia. The answer is obvious.[16]

After the encounter with Snyder and his declaration that he intended to defect, Lee Oswald returned to his room at the Hotel Metropole. Around two in the afternoon, he was greeted by a United Press International (UPI) reporter named Robert J. Korengold, who Snyder told of Oswald's intended defection. The attempted interview was unsuccessful, and Korengold had to leave without the story he had hoped to get. Returning to his office, he notified fellow UPI reporter Aline Mosby about Oswald, and she raced to Oswald's hotel and briefly spoke with the young American. Oswald agreed to talk with Mosby again on November 13, roughly two weeks later. One wonders why Oswald wanted to wait so long to tell his story.

The follow-up meeting turned out to be not much of an interview, for Oswald talked almost nonstop for two hours, with only a few questions asked by Mosby. He spoke about American racial problems, which the Soviets were interested in and used as propaganda. The reason Oswald may have mentioned it was that he assumed the Soviets had bugged his room.

In 1964 Mosby would recall the encounter and write that, "Behind his [Oswald's] brown eyes I felt a certain coldness. He displayed neither the impassioned fever of a devout American Communist who at last had reached the land of his dreams nor the wisecracking informality and friendliness of the average American." And although he told Mosby he had been a radar operator in the Marines, he said nothing about disclosing sensitive information to the Soviets.[17]

On November 16, Oswald granted another interview with Priscilla Johnson of the North American News Agency three days later. Oswald told her he had permission to remain in the Soviet Union, and he agreed to an interview to give his side of the story. It was curious, considering he had just spoken to Mosby three days before. Johnson and Oswald talked for five hours, with the conversation once again dominated by Oswald, but nothing of apparent significance transpired. However, in *Oswald and the CIA*, author John Newman observed that, "Neither Priscilla Johnson's 1959 contemporaneous notes nor her 1963 written recollection mentions that Oswald told her he had threatened to reveal radar secrets. Her [Johnson's] book *Marina and Lee* makes no mention of radar secrets. Her newspaper articles then and since make no mention of radar secrets. Under oath, however, she told a very different story. . . ."[18]

Priscilla Johnson told the Warren Commission that Oswald "hoped his experience as a radar operator would make him more desirable to [the Soviets] . . . he felt he had something [to] give them, something that would hurt his country in a way . . . that was quite negative, that he was holding out some kind of bait."[19]

How was it, Newman wondered, that Priscilla Johnson neglected to mention Oswald's intent to furnish radar secrets to the Soviets except during her Warren Commission testimony? Was it possible that Oswald told her this during their interview, and she neglected to include it in her discussion notes? It seems unlikely, for Johnson was not just an innocent reporter and had to recognize the importance of Oswald's disclosure. She was a seasoned veteran and would have included it in anything she published related to Oswald. Because she did not, we can only assume that Oswald never mentioned it, which means her Warren Commission testimony was a fabrication. She lied so that what she had to say about Oswald fit the narrative the Warren Commission wanted to convey. To understand how this was possible, let's take a closer look at who Priscilla Johnson was.

"Like many idealistic young people right after World War II," Priscilla Johnson McMillan later wrote, "I was a World Federalist [and] hoped that the Soviet Union could be persuaded to join a world government. Because of this interest, I majored in Russian at Bryn Mawr and in 1953 received an M.A. in Russian Studies at Harvard. . . ."[20]

We know from the previous chapter that Michael Paine's mother, Ruth Forbes Paine, was also a World Federalist, as was Cord Meyer. Also interesting is that Johnson failed to mention in her brief biographical sketch that she had applied for a job at CIA after leaving college, but the Agency rejected her. "Security disapproved," CIA security officer Sheffield Edwards wrote on her CIA application review the year of her Harvard graduation. A month later, she was working as an aide for Senator John Kennedy.

Priscilla Johnson's affiliation with the United World Federalists caused her to be rejected by the CIA because the organization maintained a leftist bias. Communists had infiltrated the organization and wanted to take it over. Therefore, she was a potential liability. Still, her connection to the UFW is of interest because she first met Cord Meyer there. And as we know, it was Meyer's World Federalist experience that made him disillusioned with Communists and what they stood for.

Throughout the 1950s, Priscilla Johnson spent a great deal of time in the Soviet Union. As she described it: "I went to Russia whenever I could, and in 1955 got a job as a translator [just like June Cobb did in Cuba] for the *Joint Press Reading Service*, run by the British, American, and Canadian embassies in Moscow to provide English-speaking diplomats with Soviet newspaper translations. Then I worked as a translator for *The New York Times*, but I had to leave [Russia] in 1956, with great regret, when my succession of visas ran out. I was in Moscow again from 1958 to 1960 as a correspondent for the *North American Newspaper Alliance* and *The Progressive* magazine. And it was in 1959 that I interviewed a young American who was defecting to the U.S.S.R. His name was Lee Harvey Oswald."[21]

An innocent enough account, but there was so much more to her story, for the record shows that Priscilla Johnson was with the CIA. And, her liaison with Oswald in Moscow was purposeful and by no means accidental.

Consider that her employer, *North American Newspaper Alliance* (NANA), was established in 1922 as a union of fifty prominent newspapers. In 1951, Ernest Cuneo, a former OSS operative, owned the paper. It came to be known as a front for espionage activity. Under Cuneo, NANA published CIA-connected reporters like Victor Lasky and Virginia Prewett, whose husband worked for the CIA.[22]

In 1956, in the middle of her frequent trips to Moscow, the CIA finally showed an interest in Priscilla Johnson. Despite being previously rejected, a CIA Security Office and FBI records check on her was completed satisfactorily. The CIA Security Office subsequently sent a memo to James Angleton's Counterintelligence, notifying them of their favorable review, and no further investigation was necessary. However, redacted from the message was which department showed an interest in her. Still, we can assume it was the Soviet Russian Division, SR/10, the branch in charge of "legal travelers" to the Soviet Union. A January 25, 1957 document from SR/10 to Counterintelligence requested a cancelation of their previous interest in

Johnson because they no longer wanted anything to do with her. "SR/10 has no further operational interest in subject [Johnson]," was the reason given.

The memo mentioned above is critical because it included some disturbing inconsistencies in her biographical profile. Security Office files showed her middle initial was "L for Livingston and not R," and, "She was [ ] born 23 September 1922 in Stockholm, Sweden, rather than 19 July 1928 at Glen Cove, New York," as was previously reported. In addition, "She was utilized by OSO [Office of Special Operations] in 1943 and 1944 [during World War II]." And her clearance rating was based on a Civil Service Commission rating of eligibility which was dependent upon "a favorable investigation and record checks." And Naval Intelligence [NIS] was interested in Johnson as well, for "an FBI record check completed 21 August 1956" was returned to NIS."[23]

We know that OSS's Special Operations was all "cloak and dagger" whose members were skilled in parachuting, sabotage, self-defense, weapons, and trained in leadership ability to support guerrilla or partisan resistance. It was similar to what George Hunter White was involved in during the war.

Priscilla Johnson had a story to tell, as did the CIA, regarding why her information throughout the years had changed. Consider the original 1953 investigation; her records show she was born in 1928, which meant that to have served with OSO in 1943, she would have done so at fifteen. It would have been impossible. Subsequently, her 1956 investigation did not reference her involvement in left-wing activities. It was a significant omission because that was why the CIA had rejected her in 1953. The 1956 CIA standard questionnaire listed her political affiliations, memberships in professional or social organizations, contacts, and family members (other than her parents) as unknown. But we know she was a liberal World Federalist, so we are left with two Priscilla Johnsons. One investigated in 1953, who was born in Glen Cove, New York in 1928 and was a far-left World Federalist. And one investigated in 1956, who was born in Stockholm, Sweden in 1922, and served with the OSO special ops group in World War II, and whose political orientation was unknown.[24]

Were there two separate Priscilla Johnsons, the real Priscilla and an impostor, running around in 1956? Probably not. A more believable explanation is that in 1956, someone at the CIA was interested in hiring her. However, due to her liberal slant and connection to the World Federalists, her previous rejection made this problematic. Essentially, someone at the CIA created a false narrative for Priscilla, one that not only hid her liberalism but placed her in World War II as an intelligence operative. And to do that, it was necessary to make her six years older than she was. And to ensure that no one could verify the integrity of her story, she had no apparent living relatives other than her parents. It makes one wonder if they had intelligence connections and could be relied on to support her cover story. Before one rejects this possibility outright, recall the story of Michael and Ruth Paine, their parents, her sister, brother-in-law, and the apparent involvement with U.S. intelligence on both sides of the family.

John Newman interviewed Priscilla Johnson, and she told him about her father's neighbor, F. Trubee Davidson, who asked to speak with Johnson after she returned from Russia in 1956. Davidson worked for the CIA, so, understandably, he would have been interested in what she had to say regarding her trip. Johnson told Newman that she believed "Davidson was waiting for me to grow up to recruit me." What exactly did she mean by that? Was she insinuating that as she got older, Johnson began to realize that communism was not the utopian society she once thought it was? After spending time in Russia and dealing with Communists regularly, it opened her eyes to how potentially dangerous Communists indeed were? Interestingly, she added, "The other person who was waiting for me to grow up was Cord Meyer," who had a similar awakening to the inherent danger of Soviet communism. It would explain why there was renewed interest in Priscilla Johnson in 1956 and why someone at the Agency falsified her biography to make her recruitment by the CIA more probable.[25]

By March 1958, Johnson was in Paris working for "someone I knew either for Radio Liberty or the Congress for Cultural Freedom," an anti-Communist advocacy group made up of "non-Communist (or former Communist) left-wingers, such as Arthur Schlesinger.[26] The fact that Priscilla associated with this organization at this time, something she would never have done in her World Federalist days, is in line with the idea that though she remained a liberal, she had "grown" into an anti-Communist warrior from the left.

While still in Paris, Johnson applied for entrance into the Soviet Union once again, and in July, she was back in Moscow. Her pending trip to the Soviet Union likely renewed the CIA's interest in her in April 1958.

A cable sent from CIA headquarters to an unknown location that remains classified had Cord Meyer listed as the releasing official on the bottom left of the wire, and he reported the following:

"Subj [Priscilla Johnson] DOB July 1928 [rejecting the later 1922 birthdate from the false identity resume] MA Radcliffe 1952. From wealthy Long Island [Family]. Excellent scholastic rating. Application KUBARK [CIA] employment 1952 [was] rejected because some associates and memberships would have required more investigation than thought worthwhile. Once [a] member of United World Federalist; thought liberal, international-minded, anti-communist. Translator, current *Digest of Soviet Press*, New York, 1954. Considered by present KUBARK employee [who] knew her [at] Harvard to have been 'screwball' then; considered 'goofy, mixed up' when applied KUBARK employment. No recent data. No headquarters record [of] prior KUBARK use."[27]

Johnson had already applied for a visa to return to the Soviet Union when Meyer wrote the above assessment. She arrived in Moscow for the third time on

July 4, 1958. Possibly pertinent is that Meyer described her in his review as being "anti-Communist," and that he did not outright reject her, as was done before.

Another request to utilize Johnson was made on May 6, 1958, most likely again on behalf of Counterintelligence, SR/10. Why the CIA wanted her remains classified, but her status as a "legal traveler" to the Soviet Union must have been the reason. This time, the Security Office submitted a "summary of derogatory information," as they had done in 1953. But now they realized there were two Priscilla Johnson bios in CIA files, and what they did to correct the discrepancy also remains classified. Interest was supposedly canceled on August 28, on paper anyway. Fourteen and a half months later, Priscilla Johnson was on her way back to the Soviet Union, and the evidence suggests she was traveling as an asset of U.S. intelligence, most likely CIA.

Consider that there was concern about why Johnson's name appeared in Oswald's address book after the assassination. A simple explanation may be that Oswald innocently wrote it down after their interview. However, not so easily explained was a previous CIA investigation which revealed she had "apparently [worked] on a part-time basis within the U.S. embassy during two periods of residence in Russia." Then an FBI report written the day after the assassination stated that ". . . one Priscilla Johnston [sic] and Mrs. G. Stanley Brown also had contact with Oswald in Russia. Both these women were formerly State Department employees at the American Embassy [in Moscow], and their contact with Oswald was official business." If true, it is a critical development. Did Priscilla Johnson also work for the embassy where other CIA personnel like Snyder worked undercover? And was her interview with Oswald "official business?" Wouldn't one reasonably conclude from this that she must have been familiar with Oswald before she arrived at his hotel room, and she was probably involved in his defection? Was the idea for her to contact him at the hotel, perhaps to ensure everything was going according to plan? Was this why she never disclosed that Oswald intended to provide the Soviets with classified information until after he was dead because the intent was for Oswald to return to the United States someday?[28]

The mention of Mrs. G. Stanley Brown as an associate of Priscilla Johnson is curious, considering who this woman likely was. This author can find only one reference to someone with this name. Mary (Mollie) Garfield Stanley-Brown was the daughter of President James A. Garfield, who an assassin's bullet killed in 1881. Mary married Joseph Stanley-Brown in 1888, who had served as her father's private secretary. They eventually moved to Cold Spring Harbor, Long Island, New York, which, as described in Volume One, was where the Carnegie Institute established a eugenics laboratory in 1904. It could be a strange coincidence, were it not that in 1911, the Brooklyn Institute of Arts and Sciences' Biological Laboratory, located at Cold Spring Harbor, listed, under "Training Courses for Field Workers in Eugenics," a J. Stanley-Brown as an instructor.[29] Without question, he was the husband of Mary Garfield, for how many J. Stanley-Browns could there have been in Cold Spring Harbor while they lived there?

Mary and Joseph Stanley-Brown had a daughter Ruth, who attended Vassar College, worked in publishing in New York City, and married Herbert Feis in 1922.[30] Feis was an economics professor at Harvard in 1920-1921 and then an advisor to the International Labor Office (ILO) of the League of Nations in Geneva, Switzerland. He was a member of the Council on Foreign Relations from 1930-1931. The State Department then hired him as the Economic Advisor for International Affairs in the Herbert Hoover and Franklin Roosevelt administrations. In later years he became a writer of the history of American foreign policy between 1933 and 1950, including the origins of the Cold War and the change from isolationism to a policy of global intervention.[31] Ruth was also a writer, and in 1962 published a children's book based on her mother's diaries.[32]

What to make of all this is unclear. However, the name G. Stanley-Brown was in an FBI report with Priscilla Johnson the day after JFK's assassination for a reason. And it stated she had met Oswald in Moscow. It had to have been Ruth, whose husband worked with the International Labor Office and the Council on Foreign Relations, areas that would have interested Cord Meyer. Her husband also worked for the State Department, which the FBI said Mrs. G Stanley-Brown worked for when she encountered Oswald. And was Ruth's father's connection to eugenics relevant to Oswald's defection in any way, or was it just a strange coincidence? Feis' connection to the League of Nations and the Council on Foreign Relations suggests a left-leaning political slant and support for a one-world government which Priscilla Johnson and Cord Meyer shared, at least early on in their careers. But, unfortunately, what the Stanley-Brown family had to do with Priscila Johnson and Lee Harvey Oswald, if anything, remains a mystery.

Priscilla Johnson became involved in the Lee Harvey Oswald story after the assassination as well. In June 1964, when the Warren Commission was still trying to establish if Oswald's widow Marina knew anything about the assassination, Johnson met her for the first time. Marina was desperate for money and legitimately concerned, for she was not a citizen and could have faced deportation. And others were afraid of what Marina might disclose and secrets Lee Harvey Oswald may have told her. Recall that before testifying before the Warren Commission, *Life* magazine's Isaac Don Levine spent a whole week with Marina, coaching her to control what she would say. Her story was translated for *Life* by Ilya Mamantov, and it was Jack Crichton of the 488th Military Intelligence Detachment that asked Mamantov to do this. It is not surprising that it was at this time, when keeping Marina quiet seemed to be a significant concern, that she agreed to let Johnson write a book about her life with Lee. The two women spent the next several months together in virtual isolation as Johnson gathered the information needed to write the book. Inexplicably, it was not published until 1977, thirteen years later, which confirms that her interest in Marina was to keep her quiet, not to publish her story. In *Plausible Denial*, Mark Lane wrote that "Johnson prohibited her [Marina] from speaking to anyone about any of the relevant events. After the book was published, Marina told me that much of it was false and was known by Priscilla Johnson to be false."[33]

Priscilla Johnson's story gets even more intriguing. In 1967 Joseph Stalin's daughter, Svetlana Alliluyeva, defected to the United States. She settled into, of all places, the home of the parents of Priscilla Johnson. And as speculated above, the 1956 CIA investigation into Priscilla suggested that her parents had CIA connections, which Svetlana's temporary living arrangement supports, for how else would Stalin's daughter wind up in their home. Also convenient was that when Svetlana arrived, Priscilla was also living with her parents. Not surprisingly, Johnson eventually translated Svetlana's book into English.[34]

It is hard to believe that Priscilla Johnson did not have intelligence connections or that the CIA did not send her to interview Oswald in his hotel room in Moscow. The question is, was Johnson already part of the operation, and was her meeting with Oswald prearranged before he even walked into the American Embassy announcing his intentions?

Priscilla Johnson was an expert in Soviet affairs and connected to the Russian Research Center at Harvard University, which worked closely with the MIT Center for International Studies. And that Unitarian James R. Killian, Jr. was the president of MIT and allowed Harvard to conduct their Project Troy at MIT as part of the Center for International Studies, which likely involved Oswald's defection. The MIT Center, headed by Harold Isaacs, acted as a conduit between CIA and Harvard. In the 1940s, Isaacs was a Communist supporter of Trotsky and a proponent of worldwide revolution. But just like Cord Meyer and Priscilla Johnson, Isaacs "grew up," as Priscilla put it, telling the FBI he no longer felt that way when he began working at the MIT Center.

There was also the relationship between Isaacs and Oswald's cousin, Dorothy Murret, and that her CIA file referred exclusively to Harold Isaacs. Recall that Murret was a schoolteacher who taught at various places around the world for three-and-one-half years, leaving on a steamer in the summer of 1959, just a few months before Oswald did the same. In the latter part of 1966, Murret would apply for a passport to travel to Haiti and Santo Domingo for a "vacation." Frances Knight, who was the director of the Passport Office in 1959 when Oswald received his passport in only six days, was still in charge, and she was concerned about Murret. She wrote to CIA's Deputy Director of Plans requesting "any information of a security nature . . . concerning the individual [Murret] mentioned in the attached memoranda." What motivated Knight to do this? There was no known connection between Oswald and Murret; they were cousins, which should not have been grounds for suspicion. And the fact that Knight became aware of Murret's application suggests Murret was on a watch list of some sort. Why was she a person of interest three years after the assassination, unless there was concern about something she was involved in before. Perhaps something that pertained to Oswald.[35]

The MIT Center for International Studies specialized studying of worldwide youth movements, which could explain the connection between Isaacs and Murret, and is something that would have involved Cord Meyer. We know that Priscilla Johnson had a link to the MIT Center through the Russian Research Center. We also know there was a relationship between her and Cord Meyer and that Meyer may have been responsible for the CIA's interest in her. It is possible that Isaacs, Murret, Meyer, and Johnson were all involved in, or at least aware of, Oswald's defection, which may have been part of a more extensive CIA operation.

Consider the following. If Oswald's defection was a covert operation, whether it involved mind-altering drugs or not, it began at Atsugi. He returned to El Toro and became involved with fellow Marine Kerry Thornley. Thornley introduced Oswald to the Unitarian Church in Los Angeles, which had a pro-Communist pastor and congregation. Oswald applied to Albert Schweitzer College through the Unitarian Church, which was part of the overall defection plan to explain his reason for traveling overseas. Oswald defects to Moscow, and almost immediately, Priscilla Johnson contacts him. Johnson, Harold Isaacs, Dorothy Murret, and Cord Meyer were all moderate leftists. They may all have been part of Project Troy, an operation run out of Harvard, while a Unitarian named Killian was Harvard's president. Oswald returns to the United States and eventually goes to New Orleans, where he and Kerry Thornley meet again. While he is there, his wife Marina is in Fort Worth, Texas, living with Ruth Paine, a Unitarian leftist. Ruth will stay with Marina through the assassination. Her husband, Michael Paine, another Unitarian leftist, will spend time with Oswald the month before the assassination after Oswald returns to Texas from New Orleans. After the assassination, Priscilla Johnson arrives on the scene again, essentially taking over for Ruth Paine and places Marina under her supervision.

Then there were Alice and Raymond Bauer. Alice wrote the *Guide for Interviewing Soviet Escapees,* which involved the MIT Center. The year Oswald defected, Raymond wrote *Nine Soviet Portraits,* a collection of interviews of Soviet refugees, which also involved the MIT Center and the Russian Research Center. And we know Priscilla Johnson had a connection to the latter. Both Alice and Raymond were considered left-leaning anti-Communists. The FBI was particularly interested in Raymond, for they thought he might be a Communist working undercover. Raymond also obtained a passport to travel to France, Switzerland, and Austria to continue his studies in conjunction with the Russian Research Center. It was like the itinerary Oswald put on his passport application when he was supposed to attend the highly liberal Albert Schweitzer College and Murret's itinerary for traveling overseas around the same time.

It is pretty remarkable. After returning to the United States from Russia, Lee Oswald would spend almost his entire time amongst right-wing Fascists, anti-Castro Cubans, and Americans who supported their cause. His notebook contained references to neo-Nazis in the United States. Yet, during this period, Oswald and his wife will have one apparent babysitter after another who could each be categorized as a moderate leftist and a connection to the Unitarian Church, the MIT Center for International Studies, or the Russian Research Center. The same was true for the people who directed Oswald before his defection, such as Cord Meyer, Priscilla Johnson, and Harold Issacs, which was at a time when the CIA was investigating what life was like behind the Iron Curtain. The only piece of the puzzle missing is when Lee and Marina lived in Texas immediately after returning from Russia. But there may be a connection here as well.

In mid-August 1964, George de Mohrenschildt and his wife entertained a writer named George Edwin McMillan, who just happened to be the husband of Priscilla Johnson at that time. McMillan was also employed "within the US Embassy in Moscow during two periods of residence," and de Mohrenschildt described him as a good friend.[36] How was this possible? George de Mohrenschildt, a moderate leftist who essentially controlled Oswald when he first returned from the Soviet Union, was friends with Priscilla's husband? And de Mohrenschildt had an associate named Colonel Lawrence Orlov, whom he introduced to Lee and Marina. Orlov was also a Unitarian. It completes the puzzle. Was it a coincidence that all these leftist moderates, seemingly associated with the CIA, with many of them being Unitarians, acted like "handlers" that hovered around Lee and Marina Oswald for all those years? And that after Lee was dead, what Marina had to say was controlled by Don Levine, Jack Crichton, Ilya Mamantov, and Priscilla Johnson.

Was Oswald part of a program involving the MIT Center for International Studies and the Russian Research Center? Did it include Harold Isaacs, Dorothy Murret, Priscilla Johnson, Cord Meyer, Kerry Thornley, Ruth Paine, Michael Paine, Raymond Bauer, Alice Bauer, and George de Mohrenschildt? It is possible. If so, none needed to know all the operation's details or each other. Each had a specific role to play. Which was to either prepare Oswald for his defection, which included mind-altering drug experimentation, monitoring Oswald while he was in the Soviet Union, or to essentially be a babysitter for him and his wife, before and after his defection, to ensure they stayed on the right path. And wouldn't it be necessary to monitor both Oswalds closely after their return from the Soviet Union, for either one could have been a Russian spy? Oswald's defection may have had nothing to do with the assassination of JFK. Still, the post-assassination whitewash was necessary to ensure that such an operation remained secret, for U.S. intelligence could never allow the public to know the details of what they had done to Oswald.

We should also consider that Oswald's identification papers had photos of two different people on separate documents taken around the same time when he left

the Marines. It must also have been part of this. Oswald was given an alternate resume, just like what the CIA had done for Priscilla Johnson. We should accept that
it was all done for a specific purpose. It brings us to one of the more bizarre aspects
of the Lee Oswald saga, related to the Oswald documents with different photos.
It is a story that researchers have ignored for decades, but its potential significance
dictates that we must address it here.

* * *

Aline Mosby and Priscilla Johnson interviewed Oswald within three days of
each other. Their accounts were informative but not incredibly revealing. However,
there was an exception. A discrepancy that each reporter mentioned in passing went
unnoticed but became quite relevant after the assassination. It involved a difference
in the reported height of Oswald provided by each reporter. Mosby wrote that
Oswald was 5'9" tall, while Johnson said he was 5'11". Such a seemingly insignifi-
cant detail would usually be considered a mistake due to human error by one of
the reporters, were it not that this same two-inch height discrepancy would follow
Oswald throughout the remaining years of his life. What is more, Oswald knowingly promoted this discrepancy himself to intentionally make it appear that he had
lost 2" in height.

Oswald's height was recorded as 5'8" when he enlisted in the Marines Corps,
and his Marine records show that he had grown to 5'11" tall by the time of his
discharge. There was substantial evidence to support this. On September 3, 1959,
Oswald was given a complete medical examination before his release from the Marines. The medical examiner measured Oswald's height as 5'11". It was also the
height Oswald listed on his Albert Schweitzer College application. One month
before his discharge, Oswald wrote he was 5'11" tall on his passport application.
It included Oswald's photo with a crew cut. On September 11, the Marines issued
Oswald his Department of Defense Identification card, the one with the picture
of a longer-haired Oswald. The DOD card also listed his height as 5'11", even
though it was a forgery, for it had to be consistent with the other documentation.
All indications were that Oswald was 5'11" tall when he left the Marines. There was
nothing to indicate otherwise.

The first sign that something was wrong occurred at Oswald's autopsy. It listed
Oswald's measured height as 5'9". A logical person might assume that the autopsy
doctor made a mistake, for a person cannot shrink two inches in height. However,
the record shows that whenever Oswald listed how tall he was after returning to the
United States from the Soviet Union, he wrote that he was 5'9". It was consistent
with the autopsy measurement. And he did so on numerous occasions, including
various job applications. He only listed 5'11" on paper was when he renewed his
passport in the summer of 1963, because the height on the new document had to
match the original. It was deception done on purpose. But why was it essential to

make it appear that the Oswald shot by Ruby was two inches shorter than the one discharged from the Marines?[37]

We know that Oswald did not lose two inches in height. If it were a matter of one doctor's measurement vs. another, the discrepancy could be considered a human error, but clearly, this was not the case. Oswald was 5'11" when he left the Marines and defected to the Soviet Union, but the man who returned to the United States was 5'9" tall. One option is that the Soviets killed Oswald in Russia, and the man who returned to the United States was an impostor who assumed his identity. Another possibility is that the discharged Marine was not the same person who defected to the Soviet Union. Anything was possible, but there must be a rational explanation.

Researcher Michael Eddowes embraced the theory that the Soviets killed Oswald in Russia. In the 1970s, the premise of his book *The Oswald File* was that the Soviets killed Oswald in Russia, and a Soviet assassin assumed Oswald's identity and returned to the United States. Eddowes even had Oswald's body exhumed, but dental records showed that it was the real Oswald's body in the grave, and that body was 5'9" tall.

From a logical point of view, the idea that the Soviets killed Oswald and had an impostor take his place is unlikely. If for no other reason, the Soviets had easy access to the United States and experienced little trouble placing "sleeper agents" throughout the country. Why would they then expose themselves to the inherent risks involved with an Oswald impostor? Second, since the Russian impostor would have been 5'9", this is the man Mosby would have met at the hotel around three weeks after Oswald arrived in Moscow. Was it possible for the Soviets to find someone who looked like Oswald in such a short period? Likely not, but assuming they did, Johnson would have met the real 5'11" tall Oswald three days after Mosby met the impostor. It does not make sense. It is a certainty that the Russians would have ensured that both reporters spoke to the same man. And wouldn't it have been necessary that the impostor matched Oswald's height exactly? Eventually he would have to fool Oswald's mother and brother, whom he spent time with after being discharged from the Marines. We can assume this would have been difficult if he were 2" shorter and not the same man after returning from Russia. So, we can state with certainty that the same man who defected to Russia later returned to the United States.

Another option is that American intelligence intentionally sent an impostor to Russia, two inches shorter, as part of the covert operation behind his defection. Under this scenario, the real Oswald would have been at Atsugi and El Toro while the impostor prepared for his mission. Then, after being discharged from the Marines, Oswald went into hiding while the impostor assumed his identity. If true, wouldn't it have made more sense to alter Oswald's discharge and medical records to reflect that the Oswald who left the Marines was 5'9" to match the height of the man who traveled to Russia? And it would have been simple to list 5'9" on his passport application and DOD ID card as well. However, this did not happen, which means that planting the idea there were two different Oswalds was a necessary part of the plan. But what was behind this? Why not have the photos match? They went to great pains, so it would appear that the returned defector was 2" shorter than the Oswald who left the Marines. It implies they purposely wanted to ensure that any future investigation would uncover that something out of the ordinary had occurred, for it would be impossible to miss. And there had to be a reason behind this because the height of the man shot by Jack Ruby was 2" shorter than his Marine records and passport indicated, which was impossible.

We should also consider that someone may have impersonated Oswald at El Toro. The real Oswald, removed from his unit, was privately training for his assignment in the Soviet Union. Under this scenario, the real Oswald was 5'9", while the impostor at El Toro was 5'11". After the impostor left the Marines, Oswald reassumed his identity before going to the Soviet Union. It could explain why Marine Oswald's height did not match the man who returned from the Soviet Union. However, there are still problems. Wouldn't it have made sense to put 5'9" on the passport application so that it would match the height of the real Oswald who defected? Oswald's height also would have been listed falsely as 5'9" when he left the Marines. And, if someone were impersonating Oswald at El Toro, he would have had to fool three Marines who served with him there and in Japan. And the passport photo and the DOD ID photo should have been the same person, but they were not. Therefore, this scenario seems improbable as well.

So, what was the motivation behind this deception? Let us consider the possibility that the discrepancy in height had nothing to do with two separate "Oswalds." American intelligence wanted it to appear that the Soviets had killed a "taller Oswald" in the Soviet Union. It created the illusion that had an impostor had taken Oswald's place when he returned to America, even though the real Oswald went to the Soviet Union and the same man returned to the U.S. It was a scam, and U.S. intelligence essentially created their own Soviet "sleeper agent" within the United States. It was the perfect ruse—this "Soviet agent" could be manipulated to take the fall for anything. If something happened that warranted an investigation, the Soviets would be held responsible for whatever he had supposedly done. It would look like the real Oswald had died in Russia, and a Russian impostor had taken his place when he returned and committed the crime.

Let's assume that the real Oswald was 5'9" tall, and U.S. intelligence changed El Toro's medical records to make him appear two inches taller, not a difficult thing for them to achieve. His DOD ID card would show 5'11". The intent was to make it appear that the person discharged from the Marines and traveled to the Soviet Union was 5'11" tall, which was why Oswald put that height on both his passport and Albert Schweitzer College applications. If true, it meant Oswald was privy to what was happening and a willing participant in the ruse.

After arriving in the Soviet Union, Oswald would leave his passport at the U.S. embassy, taking it out of circulation. He does not ask for it back until he is ready to return home. Or maybe there were two passports, one showing his height as 5'9", which he used to enter and leave the Soviet Union, and another 5'11" passport after crossing back into the West. Meanwhile, Aline Mosby interviewed him and recorded his height as 5'9". Priscilla Johnson followed and corrected the record. She writes that the Oswald she met was 5'11" tall.

Recapping the evidence to this point, Marine Oswald leaves the service with a DOD ID card that says he is 5'11" and his passport showing the same. The ID card and the passport have different photos, but the ID card is a forgery, so there is no telling what it looked like when Oswald arrived in Russia, but it would appear that it was forged in Russia to match the impostor. Hence the need for a different photo on this card. His application to Albert Schweitzer college lists his height as 5'11". In Moscow, two reporters interview him and record different heights, 5'9" and 5'11", respectively. Anyone interested would conclude that the reporter who thought Oswald was 5'9" tall simply made a mistake. Oswald then leaves his passport at the American Embassy. He does not have any documents in his possession while in the Soviet Union that would list his height as 2" taller than he was. The Oswald who blends into Soviet society is 5'9" tall.

Things got interesting after Oswald returned to the United States. He drops his charade and begins to accurately list his height as 5'9", contradicting his military records, for this was part of the plan. The following list, taken from *The Oswald File*, shows how Oswald perpetrated the myth.

- June 26, 1962: Oswald is interviewed by FBI agents Carter and Fain and verbally gives his height as 5'11". He must do this because the FBI could check his military and passport record, and the height he provides must match those records. When they ask about Marina, Oswald cleverly adds 2" to her height, saying she is 5'5" so that the height differential between the two of them is correct.

- July 13, 1962: Oswald applies for a job at Leslie Welding Company and lists 5'9" on the application.

- October 9, 1962: Oswald registers with the Texas Employment Commission and gives his height as 5'9".

- October 12, 1962: On a completed employment questionnaire at Jaggars-Childs-Stovall, Oswald lists his height as 5'9".

- April 1963: Oswald registers with the local Department of Labor, New Orleans, and gives his height as 5'9".

- May 9, 1963: Oswald lists his height on a job application for William B. Reily Company as 5'9".

- June 24, 1963: Oswald files for a new passport in New Orleans and lists his height as 5'11". It is the only time he would put this height in writing. He had no choice because it had to match his original passport.

- August 9, 1963: The New Orleans police arrest Oswald for a disturbance that occurred while he handed out FPCC literature. The police measure him as being 5'9".

- August 10, 1963: FBI agent Quigley interviews Oswald at the police station and records his height as 5'9".

- October 4, 1963: Oswald fills out a job application form for Weiner Lumber Company in Dallas and lists his height as 5'9".

- October 15, 1963: Oswald fills out a job application for the Texas School Depository and lists his height as 5'9".

- November 9, 1963: Oswald fills out a driver's license application and lists his height as 5'9".

- November 22, 1963: Dallas police arrest Oswald is arrest. Autopsy doctors measure his height as 5'9½".[38]

The pattern was consistent and showed that Oswald knew what was happening. This operation involving the discrepancy in heights was probably unrelated to JFK's assassination when it began but became part of the plot as the deadline to Dealey Plaza approached. If you wanted an assassin authorities would never investigate thoroughly, Oswald was the perfect man to set up for the crime. Let us assume that Oswald was supposed to have escaped or been killed before his arrest, and authorities did not have a chance to interview him. And Jack Ruby would then not have needed to murder him on live television, planting seeds of doubt in the minds of most Americans. If done correctly, a post-assassination investigation would have concluded that the man who returned from the Soviet Union was 2" shorter than the man discharged from the Marines and traveled to Russia. The only explanation would be that the Soviets had killed Oswald and had sent back an impostor who killed the President.

In conjunction with this, we should also consider a letter allegedly written by Oswald to the Soviet Embassy in Washington D.C. on November 9, 1963, thirteen days before the assassination and approximately one month after returning from Mexico City. The letter includes the following passage: "I was unable to remain in Mexico undefinily [sic] because of my Mexican visa restriction which was for

15 days only. *I could not take a chance on requesting a new visa unless I used my real name*, so I returned to the United States . . ." (Author's italics)[39]

The letter implied an impostor was posing as Oswald in Mexico, who could not use his real name when requesting a visa, which did not make sense. Why didn't he get an extension to the original visa in Oswald's name? The reason is quite apparent, for the person who wrote the letter would have known that mentioning this would alert the FBI, who was reading all mail sent to the Soviet Embassy in Washington, which the Post Office before it reached the embassy. The existence of this letter became known after the assassination, and its impostor reference must have been considered alongside the multiple height discrepancies and Marine documents that pointed toward an Oswald impostor as well. What must the FBI have thought? In addition, the same letter referred to a Kostikov who worked in the Russian Embassy in Mexico City, whom U.S. intelligence knew was a KGB assassin. They must have concluded that an Oswald impostor returned from Russia and had killed JFK. No wonder there was a massive coverup to blame Oswald as the lone killer to prevent World War III.

There is also a possibility that Oswald was not the one who wrote the letter. Someone curiously left a draft on Ruth Paine's desk in her house, a place where she was sure to find it. Mrs. Paine secretly copied the letter to give it to the FBI the next time they visited her home. It was a visit that did not occur, so she gave the FBI the letter the first chance she had, the day after the assassination. It is hard to believe. Would Oswald have left such an incriminating letter in a place where Mrs. Paine was sure to find it unless he wanted her to do so? And would she wait almost two weeks to give it to the FBI, considering that she claimed to have realized how important it was? If the answer to the last question is no, then Ruth Paine wrote the letter herself, which means she was involved in the Oswald impostor scheme from the beginning. As we have shown, this was a possibility and would also implicate all the left-leaning individuals listed above who monitored Lee and Marina.

We know the FBI was concerned about an Oswald impostor and that J. Edgar Hoover warned the Bureau about this possibility while Oswald was in Russia. Recall that after the assassination, as described in Chapter Six, the FBI gave the Warren Commission misleading information to hide the fact that there were two different photos on Oswald's ID cards. Factor in the height discrepancies and the Oswald letter to the Soviet Embassy, and there was good reason for the Bureau to be worried. And the more they investigated, the more evidence they uncovered of a possible Oswald impostor.

On December 3, eight days after Oswald's murder, an FBI agent went to Harris Hospital in Fort Worth to examine Oswald's early medical history. He learned that Oswald required surgery for acute mastoiditis of the left ear at the age of six. As would be expected, the Marine Corps doctor who examined Oswald listed the scars in his health records. But there was no mention of the scars or bone removal in Oswald's post-mortem report on November 24, 1963.

The CIA had concerns about an impostor Oswald, at least those within the Agency who were not privy to what transpired around Oswald's defection. Their anxiety was such that they were willing to work with the FBI to try and learn what transpired, something that did not happen that often. On February 18, 1964, Richard Helms, who headed the CIA's covert operations, sent a memo to the FBI asking if Oswald's body had a scar on his left wrist, which should have been there if his attempted suicide in Moscow did happen. Helms wanted any information the FBI could provide, "including the undertakers [recollections], copies of any reports, such as autopsy or other, which may contain information pertinent to this point. . . . The best evidence of a scar or scars on the left wrist would . . . be [a] direct examination by a competent authority, and we recommend that this be done and that a photograph of the inner and outer surfaces of the left wrist be made if there has been other evidence acceptable to the [Warren] Commission that he did in fact attempt suicide by cutting his wrist." Helms said that they should exhume the body if there were no evidence of a left wrist scar. Helms was aware of all the other contradictory evidence and wanted to verify Oswald was in his grave.

A week after Helms' request, two Dallas FBI agents contacted C.J. Price, the Administrator at Parkland Memorial Hospital, where the doctors performed the autopsy on Oswald. The agent's follow-up report said the following: "He [Price] advised he was unable to recall seeing any report or observation on the part of any person who attended [to Oswald] . . . that commented on a scar on OSWALD'S inner left wrist. He said he observed LEE HARVEY OSWALD . . . in the trauma room . . . and he failed to observe any scar on Oswald's wrist."[40]

Price suggested the FBI agents talk with Dr. Earl Rose, one of the two medical examiners who had performed the autopsy. Manning Clements was responsible for providing the Warren Commission with deceptive ID card evidence. He was one of the two agents who went to see Rose. Clements was also at the police station after Oswald's arrest, where Oswald told Clements he was five foot nine inches tall and had no permanent scars. Clements worked with Agent Tom Carter, one of the two agents who had interrogated Oswald after returning from the Soviet Union. That was when Oswald verbally gave his height as 5'11". They asked Dr. Rose about a one-and-three-quarter inch traverse scar on Oswald's inner left wrist and whether this could have resulted from a suicide attempt. Rose said it was possible. The agents also asked about two scars on Oswald's left upper arm identified in the post-mortem report, but they should have already been aware that an earlier Marine record listed three scars, not two. Regardless, Dr. Rose replied that the color slides he had taken were over-exposed. As a result, the doctors could not identify any visible scars. The FBI never asked about the mastoidectomy scars that should have been visible on Oswald's body.

That's where things stood until 1975 when a previously classified Warren Commission document was made available to the public. It referred to a March 13, 1964 memo by Commission investigator W. David Slawson, written the day after the two FBI agents visited Dr. Rose. "The CIA is interested in the scar on Oswald's left wrist . . . ," the memo stated. "The FBI is reluctant to exhume Oswald's body as requested by the CIA." J. Edgar Hoover wanted to let sleeping dogs lie.

The release of the classified document led to the *Dallas Morning News* interviewing Dr. Rose about the mastoidectomy scar not shown on the autopsy report. "I won't say that we couldn't have overlooked a mastoidectomy [scar]," Rose said. "That is a possibility . . . [But] we went into very careful details to note as many of the abrasions or scars or any type of skin blemish to help in identification in case this question arose."[41]

In the spring of 1964, this led to a visitor coming to Marina's home, who asked her to sign a release to install an electronic alarm system at Oswald's gravesite. Marina consented but didn't know what she was signing. "I just did what I was told [to do]," she told the *Dallas Morning News.* After that, the FBI and the CIA's interest in who was in Oswald's grave curiously came to an end. But author Michael Eddows persisted. He contacted Marina, and in 1981, due to the pressure they applied, the body was exhumed, which proved "beyond any doubt" that it was Lee Harvey Oswald's body buried there.

The bottom line is we have a Marine made to look like he was 5'11" tall when he went to the Soviet Union and was 5'9" when he returned. There are forged document cards, with photos, that make it appear there were two Oswalds, for one of the cards found would be in the name of Alek Hidell, and when considered in conjunction with the letter found in Ruth Paine's home, it would be damaging indeed. But the body in the grave was Oswald. If the autopsy did not record a scar on his wrist, most likely, the suicide attempt never happened, and the story was a fabrication. The most logical explanation is that U.S. intelligence doctored evidence and forged medical records to appear that the Soviets had murdered Oswald in Russia. And that an impostor Oswald returned to the United States. It does not necessarily mean that the deception was orchestrated with the assassination of John Kennedy in mind, for the so-called Soviet "sleeper agent" could have been called upon to provide any service. And after the fact, an investigation would conclude the Soviets were responsible. It was probably part of the assassination plot, for both the Americans and the Russians went to great lengths after the assassination to try and show that the Soviets were not involved. Consider that it was the perfect opportunity to get rid of the Russian-puppet Fidel Castro finally, but after JFK's assassination, he was left alone for some reason. Perhaps Oswald's arrest and was alive and could talk changed things. Regardless, what the conspirators created was the perfect cover story. A post-assassination investigation would uncover unexplainable inconsistencies which had to remain hidden from the public. It virtually guaranteed a whitewash cover-up to ensure the truth never came out.

A final word regarding the Soviet "sleeper agent" deception plan and the setup of Oswald after the assassination. Their superiors instructed FBI Special Agent Bob Barrett and Dallas Police Captain Westbrook to go to the corner of 10th Street and Patton, the scene of the murder of Officer Tippit, about one-half hour after JFK's death. "It hadn't been long [after arriving at the murder scene] when Westbrook . . . called me over [to him]," Barrett recalled. "He had this wallet in his hand . . ." Westbrook asked me, 'Do you know who Lee Harvey Oswald is?' and, 'Do you know who Alex Hidell is?' And I said, 'No, I never heard of them.'"

FBI agent James Hosty, responsible for keeping tabs on Oswald during the month leading up to the assassination, discussed the wallet incident in his 1995 book, *Assignment Oswald*.

"Near the puddle of blood where Tippit's body had lain, Westbrook had found a man's leather wallet." Inside he discovered identification for two separate people— Lee Oswald and Alek J. Hidell. "Westbrook called Barrett over and showed him the wallet and [the] identifications . . . Westbrook took the wallet into his custody [and] Barrett told me [Hosty] that if I had been at the scene with Westbrook, I would have immediately known who Oswald was.

"Although official police reports would later state that Oswald's wallet and identification were found on Oswald's person when . . . arrested in the movie theater, Barrett insists that Westbrook found them near where Tippit [died . . . However,] the FBI decided to go with the official police version, even though Barrett's version was further proof Oswald had . . . gunned Officer Tippit down. As Barrett said, the case against Oswald was a 'slam-dunk'."[42]

However, news footage taken immediately after the Tippit shooting shows Dallas Police Sergeant Calvin "Bud" Owens holding a man's leather wallet, which he showed to Dallas Police Captain George Doughty, standing to his left. Owens has the wallet open, and Doughty is examining an item from the wallet in a plastic sleeve as a plainclothes officer, most likely Westbrook, joins them. Oswald's wallet was at the site of the Tippit murder, but when testifying before the Warren Commission, Westbrook never mentioned the wallet there. And we know that the wallet was not Tippit's because his wallet was removed from his pocket at Methodist Hospital after his death. There was only one explanation to account for Westbrook's silence regarding such a critical point. Oswald did have a wallet in his possession when the police arrested him at the Texas Theater, which was well-known and something the Dallas police could not have denied. But two Oswald wallets, each containing a Hidell ID card, one at the Tippit murder scene and the other on Oswald at his arrest, pointed toward a conspiracy and a setup in the Tippit murder. So, Westbrook had no choice but to keep quiet regarding an Oswald wallet at the Tippet murder scene. But why were there two wallets?[43]

For this author, there is only one explanation that makes sense. Consider what would have happened if Oswald had escaped and not been captured by the police in the Texas Theater. Authorities would have found a wallet at the Tippet murder scene containing Oswald's DOD ID card and a Selective Service card in the name of A.J. Hidell. Both cards would have included a photo of a man who looked different from Oswald's original passport photo. There would eventually find the so-called "Minsk photo," which matched the fake Hidell card and the forged DOD ID card. The only conclusion they could have drawn from this was that the photo was taken in Russia and depicted an Oswald imposter. And the fake Hidell and forged ID cards were made in Russia from this photo. And when considered, along with all the evidence provided above, it would have led authorities to conclude that an Oswald impostor from the Soviet Union had assassinated JFK and killed Tippet. The plan was probably to kill Oswald and make it look like he had fled the country, most likely for Cuba. There was a report that a plane waited on the runway in Mexico City for one passenger, and after he arrived, the aircraft left for Havana. And just as important, there would not have been a Jack Ruby shooting of Oswald, for the need to do so no longer existed, and the doubts raised by Oswald's murder would never have become part of the story. It was the perfect plan. That is if nothing went wrong.

- 10 -

What's Wrong With U-2?

"Aggressive imperialist forces in the United States . . . have been taking the most active measures to undermine the summit . . . Was this aggressive act carried out by Pentagon militarists? If such actions are taken by American military men on their own account, it must be of special concern to world opinion."

—Nikita Khrushchev

President Eisenhower wanted to sign a nuclear test ban treaty with the Soviet Union as a first step in halting the arms race. Most right-wing radicals opposed this. They could not trust the Soviets, but Eisenhower remained determined. For years, the super-secret CIA U-2 spy plane had conducted reconnaissance flights over the Soviet Union, photographing military installations. The last U-2 flight scheduled before the summit between Ike and Khrushchev crashed, ending any chance of signing a test ban treaty. Someone, likely the CIA, sabotaged the plane before takeoff. The evidence confirms this, and the reactions of Eisenhower and Khrushchev after the fact support that they were aware this was the case. Two weeks later, the Soviets walked out of the summit in Paris. The President put the U.S. military on alert, and reporters in Washington D.C. wanted to know if the military had taken over the U.S. government. The fact that they would ask such a question reveals there was a fear this could have happened, and rightfully so. JFK's assassination would occur only three and one-half years later.

* * *

For U.S. intelligence, the military, and many in the private sector, the nuclear arms race was a fight for national survival. Eisenhower was perceived to be soft on communism, and confidence in his ability to govern began to wane as the end of his second term drew near. As a result, General MacArthur's idea that the military was not beholden to any President, that their primary responsibility was to uphold the

Constitution and protect the American people from an ineffective leader, began to gain traction within the armed services. This attitude was just as intense in the intelligence community and the private sector. A primary concern was that the Soviets had an edge in long-range nuclear missiles, which was critical because these could directly hit the United States. There was a general belief that if the Soviets were to increase their "missile gap" advantage, the United States would be helpless to thwart the spread of communism throughout the world. For many Americans, the balance of power in the late 1950s hinged solely on the number of Intercontinental Ballistic Missiles (ICBMs) each country possessed. The U.S. believed it could not trust the Soviets, and they would probably attempt a first-strike nuclear attack if they thought their nuclear superiority was large enough for them to be successful.

It seemed almost everyone feared that the U.S. was behind in ICBM development and deployment. Henry Kissinger wrote: "Fifteen more years of a deterioration of our position would find us reduced to fortress America in a world in which we had become largely irrelevant." These were strong words, but even staunch liberal Adlai Stevenson found it necessary to lecture President-elect Kennedy by decade's end. "This revolutionary age confronts us with a potential shift in the balance of power of a magnitude hitherto unknown," Stevenson warned.[1]

The Soviet ballistic missile program had only begun in 1957, and CIA estimates projected Soviet ICBMs to be in the hundreds by the end of the decade. As the Soviet's proficiency increased, American attempts to do likewise failed.[2]

Eisenhower was skeptical, but he agreed to form a commission to develop ". . . active and passive measures to protect [the] civil population in case of nuclear attack."[3] In 1957, the President asked the National Security Council to put together a team to investigate this. Rowan Gaither, chairman of the Ford Foundation and a RAND Corporation co-founder, was chosen to chair the new committee. The NSC chose John McCloy to be a member of its top advisory panel. Others involved were from NORAD (North American Air Defense Command), the Strategic Air Command, the Secretary of Defense's office, the Federal Civil Defense Administration, the Weapons Systems Engineering Group, CIA, and major defense contractors. The common denominator shared by all was that each would benefit financially from an increase in long-range nuclear missile development and manufacture.[4]

It was called the Gaither Commission, and its mandate was to develop a civil defense program. However, they expanded the scope when Gaither said they needed to study the overall balance of power between the U.S. and the Soviet Union. It led to the conclusion that U.S. strategic defenses were unprepared for the deployment of Soviet ICBMs and that the U.S. had to dramatically improve its nuclear deterrent capabilities.[5]

Then on October 4, 1957, just as the committee was about to write their final report, the Soviets launched a satellite into orbit, which created a virtual panic throughout the United States. Eisenhower's Gallup poll rating dropped twenty-two points. Sputnik's distinctive radio "beep" could be detected as it flew over the U.S., and Clare Booth Luce said it was "an intercontinental outer-space 'raspberry' to a decade of American pretensions . . ." *Newsweek* wrote that Sputnik represented a "defeat in three fields: In pure science, in practical know-how, and [ ] psychological Cold War." *Life* magazine agreed: "Let us not pretend that Sputnik is anything but a defeat for the United States." It was compared to Pearl Harbor and confirmed what many Americans already feared. What the President was doing to protect the people was inadequate. Charges of a "missile gap" were leveled against the administration, which was considered incompetent.[6]

But contrary to what the Soviets intended, Sputnik served a purpose for the hardliners in America. It allowed the Gaither Commission to stress the urgency of the situation they were facing. Their report was presented to the President on November 4 and was alarming in what it projected, which was that over the next few years, the Soviets would build thousands of ICBMs. The fear among the radical right was that the Soviets would try to obliterate the United States as soon as they could.[7]

The Gaither report recommended that the United States do whatever was required to maintain nuclear superiority over the Soviets. "The USSR," the report stated, "will probably achieve a significant ICBM delivery capability with megaton warheads by 1959 . . . The U.S. will probably not have achieved such a capability . . . [It] appears to be a very critical period for the U.S." To end the missile gap, the U.S. had to spend between $19 to $44 billion. It was in addition to the roughly $38 billion already spent on defense.[8]

Eisenhower wanted to keep the findings of the Gaither Commission hidden from the public, but it was not possible. On December 20th, the *Washington Post* ran a story with a headline that read: "*Enormous Arms Outlay Is Held Vital For Survival.*" "The still-top-secret Gaither Report portrays the United States in the gravest danger in its history," the article reported. "It pictures the Nation moving in frightening course to the status of a second-class power. It shows an America exposed to an almost immediate threat by the missile-bristling Soviet Union."[9]

The administration had created the problem by purchasing fewer Atlas and Titan missiles, electing to wait to develop more efficient Minuteman ICBMs, not scheduled until 1962. It left five years where the Soviets would be building many more missiles than the United States. The Air Force's Strategic Air Command (SAC) believed that by 1961 the Soviets would have 150 ICBMs, precisely the number required to destroy all thirty SAC bases in the U.S. and twenty other key military and civilian targets, including the nation's capital. The outlook was dire and called for drastic action.[10]

One of the most vocal believers that the "missile gap" had to be addressed was Missouri Democratic Senator Stuart Symington, who thought of running for President in 1960. He charged Eisenhower with being irresponsible for choosing a balanced budget over national security. "What do you do with a government," he said in September 1959, "which decides that money is more important than security?" Around the same time, on the Senate floor, he predicted that the Soviets would have 3,000 ICBMs by 1962.

All the major presidential candidates agreed. Lyndon Johnson fanned the flames of fear that the missile gap was real and had to be corrected. John Kennedy warned in 1958 that the time was fast approaching where "our [ ] offensive and defensive missile capabilities will lag so far behind those of the Soviets as to place us in a position of great peril."[11]

The military chiefs took advantage of the situation, using congressional hearings to support the Gaither Committee recommendations. In the end, Ike agreed to increase the alert status of strategic bombers, disperse their bases, raise the number of ICBMs under development, and deploy ICBMs to Western Europe. But he firmly rejected the Gaither Committee's overall recommendations because he knew the U.S. was ahead of the Soviets and there was no need to worry. Military expenditures as a percentage of Gross National Product would decline from 9.9 percent when Sputnik first orbited the earth to 9.6 percent for fiscal 1959 and 9.1 percent for 1960. A non-panicked President believed this to be more than adequate, despite the hysteria which surrounded him.[12]

Eisenhower's confidence in curtailing military spending was due to one thing—he had access to information that very few other people did. The fact is that, when Symington warned that the Soviets would have 3,000 ICBMs in 1962, Ike knew the actual number would be less than one hundred. He knew Soviet ICBM strength in 1961 would be a small fraction of what his critics anticipated, and the wisdom of waiting for the Minutemen was because there was nothing to fear from the Soviet arsenal, in the present or the future. And it was the U-2 spy plane flights over Russia, kept secret from the American people and most people in government, that provided Eisenhower with an accurate assessment of where the Soviets stood.

* * *

Understanding the nuclear capabilities of the Soviet Union was the biggest problem the Eisenhower administration faced as early as 1954, as the nation tried to determine if there was enough nuclear firepower to deter a surprise Soviet attack. Efforts by the CIA and the Air Force up to this point had limited success, so in the summer of that year, the President asked James Killian, the Unitarian president of MIT, to form a Technological Capabilities Panel to look into the matter. Killian brought aboard his neighbor from Cambridge, Massachusetts, Edwin H. Land, who founded Polaroid and had a history of developing innovative lens products during World War II. Killian put Land in charge of developing a spy plane that utilized high-powered optics, and Land did not disappoint. He designed a camera that could photograph human figures from 70,000 feet in the air. Kelly Johnson, who ran Lockheed's top-secret "Skunk Works," designed the aircraft, and together they successfully tested a plane that would eventually be called the U-2.[13]

The far right-wing General Curtis LeMay, the head of the Air Force Strategic Air Command (SAC), was not interested in a spy plane that could not carry nuclear weapons. LeMay turned the U-2 down, but Richard Bissell at CIA was enthusiastic about it, and eventually, Allen Dulles was as well. It was code-named Aquatone, and the CIA was responsible for the plane's development, manufacturing, and testing. However, once the aircraft was operational, LeMay wanted control of the project returned to SAC. However, by that time, it was too late. "I want this whole thing to be a civilian operation," Ike instructed. "If uniformed personnel of the armed services of the United States [can] fly over Russia, it is an act of war—legally—and I don't want any part of that." It did not please Air Force General Nathan Twining, who said, "They [CIA] took it over lock, stock, and barrel. We had nothing to say about it. Ike approved it too, which he shouldn't have done . . . CIA just kind of talked him into these things."[14] And the distrust between hardline military right-wingers and CIA leftists continued to grow.

There was a potential thaw in the Cold War in 1955 as a possible chance for a peace agreement with the Soviets arose. "I'll give it one shot," Eisenhower said. "Then if they don't accept it, we'll fly the U-2." When Khrushchev rejected Ike's "Open Skies" proposal, the U-2 story began. The plane was flown and tested over United States airspace throughout 1955. It would not be until June 1956 that the first U-2 flew over Eastern Europe, and on July 4 of that year, the first flight into Soviet airspace occurred.

In the meantime, trying to determine Soviet nuclear strength was an ongoing exercise, and other attempts to penetrate Soviet airspace continued. In 1956, as the CIA was still testing the U-2, Eisenhower authorized flights over the Soviet Union by armed American bombers carrying eavesdropping equipment and cameras instead of nuclear weapons. It was called Project Homerun. Planes took off from an airbase in Greenland and flew over the entire northern section of Russia, from the Bering Strait to Murmansk and the Kola Peninsula in European Russia. A flight over the North Pole was the shortest distance for Russian bombers and missiles to reach the United States and was the likely route of a Soviet attack if one were ever to occur, which was why the CIA chose this path. It was a risky operation, for Soviet radar operators would not know if the bombers they detected were taking pictures or traveling over Russia to drop nuclear bombs. Starting in March, for several weeks, the U.S. launched eight to ten bombers every day. The Kremlin filed a protest with the American Embassy in Moscow, but publicly they remained quiet.[15]

Other missions involved American planes probing Soviet territory, darting back and forth across sensitive borders. The intent was to goad the Soviets into turning on their covert tracking system or fire at the planes with their ant-aircraft missile batteries, enabling American signal catchers to pinpoint their locations. Clearly, by the time the U-2 flights began, there was already a history of U.S. planes violating Soviet airspace.[16]

When Eisenhower originally approved the U-2 project in 1954, Allen Dulles told him the planes would fly unnoticed over Soviet territory. However, once the flights began in 1956, the U.S. was aware that Soviet radar could track the aircraft, but their guns could not reach the 70,000-foot altitude at which they flew. Ike still allowed the flights to continue because, as John Foster Dulles told him, the Soviets would never protest and "admit that for years we had been carrying on flights over their territory while they . . . had been helpless to do anything about the matter." Still, Eisenhower reserved the right to suspend the flights in the future if necessary.[17]

By 1958, as the U-2 flights continued to violate Soviet borders, U.S. balloon photographic reconnaissance flights, which traveled across the Soviet Union at high altitudes collecting intelligence photos, continued as well. That is until Ike ordered the Air Force not to send any more balloon flights over Russia. Arms control negotiations were proceeding nicely with the Soviets, and the President did not want to do anything to damage the discussions. Still, despite Ike's directive, the balloon flights continued because disrupting the discussions was what the Air Force wanted to accomplish. Eisenhower's secretary Ann Whitman remembered the President's angry phone call to the Pentagon, full of "salty language" and that the Secretary of Defense should "fire a few people." Servicemen "ought to obey orders or get the hell out of the service," Eisenhower fumed and sent a formal memorandum to Defense Secretary Neil McElroy, stating "there is disturbing evidence of a deterioration in the processes of discipline and responsibility within the armed forces." He mentioned the balloon flights and U-2 flights that continued to travel over routes "that contravened my standing orders," which, especially regarding the U-2s, brought with them potentially serious consequences. He demanded action "at once" to tighten discipline. "If he had done some of the things that [were] done in the last few days," Mrs. Whitman recorded the president lamenting, he would have "shot himself." The treasonous behavior continued.[18]

It took the Soviets until 1958 to protest the U-2 flights, and once they did, Ike believed he had no choice but to end these missions, for he took the Soviet complaints very seriously. The U.S. would consider it an act of war if the Russians violated American airspace, he said. Undoubtedly, Khrushchev felt the same way. However, sixteen months after he stopped the flights, advisers told Eisenhower it was necessary to restart the program. They had learned that the missile gap did not exist, but concern remained because they could not verify the pace at which Soviet nuclear missile production was increasing without more flights. Secretary of State Herter believed the benefits reaped far outweighed the risks, even if the Soviets shot down a U-2.[19]

The CIA and the Pentagon agreed that mothballing the U-2 flights returned the U.S. to a time when obtaining much-needed intelligence was impossible. Satellite reconnaissance capabilities were not yet available, which left the military and U.S. intelligence in the dark. As a result, a secret meeting of the Joint Chiefs and top intelligence officials occurred at Quantico, Virginia. Even though the President had not authorized additional flights, hardliners at the meeting demanded that the U-2 flights take to the air again over Russia. To do so would have been treasonous, but they did not care by this point in the Cold War. From their perspective, to have followed Eisenhower's instructions and done nothing would have been treasonous and a dereliction of duty.

Public pressure intensified as well. An unnamed official warned in *U.S. News and World Report* that it would only get harder to track Soviet progress. The Russians were camouflaging existing ICBM sites and building new ones. "The next President will probably wake up to discover that his military commanders cannot guarantee that they know the sites of Soviet missiles and can knock them out. If you don't know where to strike, your military power is limited."[20]

During the latter part of 1959 and early into 1960, the pressure on President Eisenhower to restart the U-2 flights intensified. General James Doolittle of the President's Board of Consultants on Foreign Intelligence Activities urged him to send as many U-2s as possible over the Soviet Union. Allen Dulles agreed, believing more data increased the accuracy of CIA's estimating capabilities, which had been essentially guesswork since the U-2s stopped flying.

Eisenhower succumbed, approving additional flights for the early part of 1960. Washington was optimistic when a U-2 flew over Kazakhstan and part of the Ural Mountains on April 9 before returning safely home, and the Soviets did not protest the flight. One more flight was approved, but it had to occur by May 1, for Eisenhower did not want to offend the Soviets by flying into their airspace on May Day. The scheduled summit with the Soviets was May 16 in Paris, and Ike hoped he and Khrushchev could agree on a nuclear test ban treaty. "[I] have one tremendous asset in a summit meeting," the President said. "That is [my] reputation for honesty. If one of these aircraft were lost when we were engaged in apparently sincere deliberations, it could be put on display in Moscow and ruin [my] effectiveness."[21]

* * *

Once Khrushchev returned to Moscow from his trip to the U.S. on September 28, 1959, the Cold War entered a period of optimism. The potential for positive change was in the air, something missing throughout the entire decade leading up to this point. "I can tell you in all frankness, dear comrades," Khrushchev said as he addressed officials at Moscow's Vnukovo Airport. "As a result of my talks and discussions of concrete questions with the U.S. president, I have gained the impression that he [Eisenhower] sincerely wishes to see the end of the Cold War . . . I am confident . . . that we can do a great deal for peace." He departed by shouting, "Long live Soviet-American friendship!"[22]

There was good reason for the Soviet leader's apparent giddiness, for he had been worrying for quite some time that his need to keep up with Washington in the arms race would bankrupt his country. He was aware that the Soviets were far behind the Americans in missile capability, but things improved three months after returning from the U.S. The Russians were ready to install two R-7 ICBMs at launch sites, each with a three-megaton nuclear warhead. It meant the Soviet Union could finally hit the U.S. directly with atomic missiles.

Khrushchev's advisers believed they would reach nuclear parity with the United States sometime in the following decade, but the Soviet leader was not interested. He knew that the Soviet Union would never be able to keep up with the U.S., which was determined to manufacture as many ICBMs as possible. In a secret session before the Presidium, he confessed that he no longer believed in the superiority of the Soviet system after visiting America. And U.S. bombers with nuclear weapons were stationed only hours away at NATO installations throughout Europe. Eisenhower could deliver a massive strike with one order, whereas the Soviets were still years away from that. And despite what U.S. alarmists believed, the missile gap would increase in the future in favor of the Americans.

The Soviets were willing to prohibit all nuclear test explosions. Khrushchev pointed out that the technical experts at Geneva had found no obstacle to including verification as part of a test-ban treaty. He wanted to sign a nonaggression pact with the U.S. and afterward negotiate a "reduction in forces" with "the most thorough control with inspection by both armies." To show he meant what he said, Khrushchev told the Presidium he planned to cut one-third of his active army, around one million men. It was approved. The Soviets were desperate to ease tensions and bring military spending under control, but Khrushchev's internal support would not last forever. Top military men began to have second thoughts over the unilateral troop cuts, and this discontent spread broadly throughout the government. Now it was up to Eisenhower to meet him halfway. The problem was that the American military was just as worried about troop cuts and weapons reductions as were their Soviet counterparts.[23]

Ike had a pretty good idea that, despite all of Khrushchev's bluster that the Soviet Union would destroy the United States, things were not going well in Russia. In early 1959, he had studied Khrushchev's seven-year economic plan and knew it was impossible to achieve. The CIA confirmed that the Kremlin's projected rate of economic growth was unrealistic. The only way for the Soviets to increase food production was by reducing the money allocated for defense. But that was something they could not do, for they were already way behind the United States.

Before Eisenhower temporarily grounded the U-2 flights, data gathered by the planes had shown the Soviets were having problems with their missile testing program, which resulted in an interruption in testing between April 1958 and March 1959. As a result, analysts determined that Soviet ICBM deployments would not occur until late 1959, instead of at the beginning of that year, as was previously thought. In addition, information obtained from the U-2s proved that earlier estimates of ICBM deployments in the hundreds were incorrect. By 1961 they would deploy only four.[24]

Eisenhower knew the missile gap was a myth and that increased military spending by the United States could bankrupt the Soviet economy, as George Kennan's containment policy had foreseen. However, Ike still wanted to sign a nuclear test ban treaty with the Soviets before his term in office ended. He believed the unilateral Soviet troop reduction was a positive development. After meeting with Khrushchev at Camp David during his American visit, Ike thought the Soviet Premier was sincere about pursuing world peace. But not all his advisers agreed. Allen Dulles downplayed the significance of the troop reduction and other concessions the Soviets were making. Then, curiously, within a week, the CIA chief did a complete reversal, saying the Agency detected severe concerns within the Soviet military in speeches they had monitored. At an NSC meeting on January 21, 1960, Allen Dulles now said they might be seeing a change for the better in the Cold War. That Khrushchev's decision "seems to exclude general war as a deliberate Soviet policy," and that Moscow could not hope to occupy Europe with the reduced size of the military they now had. So, all of a sudden, based on speeches from Russia by Khrushchev, the man who Allen Dulles and his brother John said could not be trusted, made the CIA chief do an about-face and believe that the Soviet Union would follow through on what they promised to do. He was now in total agreement with the President, but something else is going on here, based upon what we know about Dulles. It just does not seem plausible that the CIA Director would succumb so quickly, especially when weighed against what others in Washington were feeling at the time. Did Dulles have something else in mind—perhaps resorting to sabotage to get what he wanted once again?[25]

Consider that even though Dulles knew that a missile gap did not exist, others did not. All the American public knew was that in the past, Khrushchev claimed the Soviet Union could make missiles "like sausages," and he threatened to set major U.S. cities on fire, and these threats frightened the general populace. Even more threatening was an R-7 Soviet missile successfully launched with a dummy warhead that traveled more than seven thousand miles from the center of the Soviet Union and landed just south of Hawaii, the first of its kind to do so.

Nathan Twining, the Joint Chiefs chairman, and Thomas Gates, the Defense Secretary-designate, tried to downplay the missile launch's significance. They testified on Capitol Hill that even if the Soviets had more ICBMs than the U.S., the nation still had more nuclear firepower in long-range bombers and submarines than the Soviet Union. Their point was that even though there might be a missile gap, there was no deterrence gap, but Congress quickly rejected that argument. The chairman of the Armed Services Committee, Senator Richard Russell of Georgia, responded that "I can't accept the statement that there is no missile gap. I think there is," which was the prevailing opinion of the lawmakers in attendance.

Meanwhile, Eisenhower was criticized in public by his military, an all too familiar occurrence. On the same day that the R-7 missile, aimed at Hawaii, was launched, General Thomas S. Power, the head of the Strategic Air Command, delivered a speech at the Economic Club in New York. He spoke of a future where the Soviets "might accumulate enough missiles to destroy this nation's retaliatory missiles and bombers before they could be fired or take off . . ." Powers called for strategic bombers to be airborne around the clock, with the ability to retaliate against the first strike from Russia.[26]

The press got involved as well. On January 23, Joe Alsop wrote multiple columns warning that the Soviets were well ahead in missile development. Based on what Powers had to say, Alsop foresaw 150 ICBMs and 150 intermediate-range missiles being fired at European targets, resulting in the Soviets destroying all of NATO's nuclear weapons. He then assumed that if the Soviet missile factories could match the U.S. factory production that had produced the SAC's Atlas rockets, the Russians would have 150 ICBMs in ten months. He charged Eisenhower's administration with playing Russian roulette because they refused to increase production until they could prove the Soviets had as many missiles as the critics believed they did. Not knowing that information provided by the U-2s proved that actual Soviet missile production was virtually nonexistent, Alsop wrote: "[N]o intelligence service on earth can be . . . certain that the closed Soviet society . . . has not produced a number of weapons equal to a mere ten months of capacity production in a single American factory." Alsop wrote that the U.S. should assume the worst and accelerate the arms race. The nation agreed, for they did not have all the facts, and found Alsop's position more prudent than Eisenhower's desire to sign a nuclear test ban treaty.

Aware of what the sentiment was in America, a determined Khrushchev offered to destroy all Soviet intercontinental ballistic missiles, in addition to the military downsizing he had previously promised. "They blame us for advocating cuts in conventional forces," he told the Presidium a few days after the Alsop articles were published. "Now, let's call for cuts in an area where they think we are ahead." He was trying to force the U.S. into accepting disarmament, which he knew would benefit the Soviet Union because of the numerical advantage possessed by the United States.[27]

Disarmament, arms reduction, and a test ban treaty were all favorable to Eisenhower as he entered his last year in office. In 1958, eighty-one nuclear detonations occurred worldwide before a pause in testing occurred on October 31, which had to stop.[28]

As would be expected, Eisenhower faced enormous pressure and opposition in his desire to negotiate with the Soviets. The Democrats, who controlled the Joint Congressional Committee on Atomic Energy, were dead set against a test ban treaty. The Pentagon wanted no part of it. The CIA thought it was a significant mistake and insisted on an increase in U-2 flights instead. The new Chairman of the JCS, Admiral Radford, summed it up best when he said: "We cannot trust the Russians on this or anything . . . The Communists have broken their word with every country with which they ever had an agreement."[29] General Curtis LeMay was just as blunt: "Pacifists with their perennial utopian quests can harm the human race as much as conquerors."[30]

The *New York Times* stated categorically that an unverifiable test-ban treaty would "leave the Soviets free to continue experiments behind the Iron Curtain to develop Premier Khrushchev's fantastic weapons." The head of the Atomic Energy Commission, John McCone, said such an agreement "was a surrender of our basic policy." But Eisenhower's ambition before leaving office was to negotiate a test ban treaty. So, in March 1960, he proposed a compromise proposal for a limited two-or-three-year moratorium on such unverifiable testing, followed by further negotiations. The Soviets indicated their agreement, and an Eisenhower/Khrushchev summit would happen that May, despite opposition the President faced from all quarters.[31] But Ike had reached the point where there was nothing that could derail the summit, except perhaps the downing of a U-2 flight. Which was a remote possibility, for only one more flight was scheduled before the conference. What could go wrong?

* * *

Immediately after Oswald visited the U.S. Embassy in Moscow, Ambassador Snyder sent a confidential telegram to the State Department in Washington D.C. for Oswald was not an ordinary defector and had to be treated with the highest priority. Here was a Marine, Snyder's telegram advised, who "has offered Soviets any information he has acquired as [an] enlisted radar operator. . . ."[32] It was a bombshell disclosure because of Oswald's familiarity with the U-2. Snyder followed this up on November 2 by cabling that Oswald "might know something of special interest." American Consul John McVickar confirmed this, telling the Warren Commission that Oswald "mentioned that he knew certain classified things . . . and that he was going to turn this information over to the Soviet authorities. . . ."[33]

The State Department received Snyder's cable on the morning of Saturday, October 31. Two days later, a U.S. naval attaché in Moscow alerted the Navy Department at the Pentagon that Oswald "OFFERED TO FURNISH SOVIETS INFO HE POSSESSES ON US RADAR." On or around November 4, the State Department sent Snyder's cable to the FBI, and the CIA received the naval attaché's cable around the same time.[34] And it was a couple of days before that, that a CIA memo reported that the FBI's liaison to the Agency, "Mr. [Sam] Papich would like to know what we know about this ex-Marine who recently defected in the USSR." Two days later, the CIA replied to the FBI that they had "no info on [the] subject."[35]

According to the official record, throughout the weekend of November 7th and 8th, as well as the next few days, the FBI and CIA were unaware of Oswald's threat to furnish the Soviets secret information, so his defection was treated rather routinely. However, it was not long before the Snyder cable began to circulate, and both investigative agencies took a closer look at the ex-Marine turned defector. By November 9, someone at the CIA put Oswald on a "Watch List," meaning that the CIA authorized the illegal opening of Oswald's mail from that point on. Someone in James Angleton's Counterintelligence group wrote "SECRET EYES ONLY" on Oswald's notecard. The program was called HT/LINGUAL, and Oswald joined a select group of only 300 people who had their mail targeted.[36]

The FBI was also opening mail from the Soviet Union. In January 1958, they initiated "confidential inquiries with appropriate Post Office officials to determine the feasibility of covering outgoing correspondence from the US to the USSR . . ." However, the New York Post Office told the Special Agent in Charge (SAC) they could not authorize the FBI request to open the mail because the CIA was already doing this.[37]

As early as 1955, the CIA was randomly opening mail delivered to the United States from the Soviet Union in the hope of undermining potential subversive activity. According to Angleton, HT/LINGUAL allowed "discreet interior examination and photograph . . . of approximately two percent of all incoming communications from the USSR, or approximately 400 per month." Eventually, the operation expanded to the point where the CIA photographed 14,000 letters annually. It was initially run jointly by William Harvey's Staff C and Sheffield Edwards' Office of Security until it became the responsibility of James Angleton's CI Staff in 1955. Angleton thought it was "probably the most important overview that counterintelligence had."[38]

In January 1958, Angleton learned that the FBI also wanted to open mail from the Soviet Union. Angleton informed Allen Dulles, and they had no choice but to let Hoover know what the CIA had been doing. The Agency and the FBI eventually reached an agreement, and the Bureau joined their operation. So, by 1959 the FBI and CIA were able to obtain more information about the defector Oswald, for they were both reading his mail that came in from Russia.[39]

* * *

As American intelligence began to take a keener interest in Oswald, the Soviet handling of the case remained odd. The arrival of an American ex-Marine defector was usually an event that warranted exploitation by the Soviets. For a nation that required walls and border patrols to prevent its people from escaping to the West, they would not easily dismiss the propaganda benefits someone like Oswald could provide.

A case in point was a Marine named Bruce Davis, one of the defectors Marguerite Stevens was told not to investigate. In August 1960, Davis crossed the border from West Germany into East Germany. Two months later, the Soviet embassy in Washington released a statement, signed by Davis, which included the following passage:

> "Since the end of World II, the American press has been playing up in all ways the Cold War and the Iron Curtain which the Socialist countries . . . [allegedly caused. And] in the USA that the blame for a third World War could rest only with the Socialist countries. These often-repeated declarations of the American press aroused my doubts. The question invariably suggested [is] how the Soviet Union, the country which had suffered the most in World War II, could prepare a new war. At the very time the American public was being made to believe that we Americans seek peace, I could see for myself, while in the Army, that actually we are seeking to extend the might of our army."[40]

There were other similar stories. In 1956, Professor Alexander Kasem-Beg defected to the Soviet Union. Shortly after that, Pravda announced his arrival, and a collection of anti-American articles followed that. In August 1960, two National Security Agency employees named Mitchell and Martin, who were also on Marguerite Stevens' list, defected to the Soviet Union through Mexico and Cuba. Eisenhower's reaction was that they should shoot both men. In response, the Soviet Union issued the following statement written by the two defectors: "The United States Government secretly manipulates money and military supplies to bring about the overthrow of unfriendly governments. It pays code clerks of friendly embassies to get information to break their codes. The NSA gathers communication intelligence from almost all nations of the world, friendly and unfriendly, for use by the Government."[41]

Lee Oswald was an ex-Marine who had supposedly become disenchanted with the military and foreign policies of the United States. He had expressed his disgust over "helping drag up guns for the [Nationalist] Chinese and watching American technicians show the Chinese how to use them." He was a radar operator at Atsugi Air Base, one of the homes of the U-2 spy plane. At the time of Oswald's arrival in Moscow, the U-2 flights were still active and a significant item of concern for the Soviets. They knew the flights were taking place but were helpless to stop them. Oswald's offer to disclose classified information was an apparent reference to his knowledge of the U-2 and the reason why American intelligence in the United States considered his case so serious. It should have been a propaganda coup for the Soviets that they could have easily exploited. However, even after the Soviets shot down Francis Gary Powers's U-2, Oswald was not asked by the Soviets to issue a public statement, even though Powers was on trial for all the world to see. It was odd that they did not choose to reap the benefits that Oswald's defection had to offer unless they were on to him like ex-agent Wilcott professed to know and considered it best to stay away.

* * *

Author John Newman investigated how authorities in Washington analyzed information related to Oswald immediately after he defected and uncovered something curious. Newman called it a "hungry black hole in CIA [which] seemed to be consuming every scrap of paper on Oswald in the days immediately following his defection . . ."

One would have expected the CIA to have provided the Soviet Russian division with this information, but it was not. The material was too sensitive to share outside the Office of Security and Counterintelligence, which meant it was part of a very secretive Agency program. As a result, information was shared on a need-to-know basis only, for such a program would have involved only a handful of people at the CIA.[42]

Under normal circumstances, as the CIA collected information on an individual, they would open a 201 file, which should have applied to Oswald immediately. But Oswald's 201 file was not opened until a year after his defection, on December 8, 1960. The Warren Commission ignored this, but HSCA wanted the CIA to explain the long delay. They discovered that the person who finally opened the 201 file was Ann Egerter, who worked under James Angleton, inside the most sensitive Counterintelligence section in the Agency: the mole-hunting Special Investigations Group (SIG). Egerter was reluctant to talk, but she finally agreed to an interview when threatened with a subpoena by HSCA.

Ann Egerter handled Oswald's files for the last three years of his life, and nothing could be added or removed from these files without her permission. One item of interest the HSCA obtained from Egerter was that it was Monday, November 9, 1959, when someone at the CIA put Oswald on the mail-opening "Watch List." The delay in opening his 201 file might have been to keep hidden that the CIA was opening Oswald's mail. However, a more likely explanation is that the less paperwork circulated about this man during that first year of his defection, the better it was for the CIA.

Her HSCA interviewer asked Egerter if her job description was essentially "to investigate Agency employees who for some reason were under suspicion." To which she replied, "That is correct." She was then asked: "When a 201 file is opened [by the CIA] does that mean that whoever opens the file has either an intelligence interest in the individual or, if not an intelligence interest, he thinks that the individual may present a counterintelligence risk?" Once again, she responded, "Well, in general, I would say that would be correct." And when asked if there was "any other reason for opening a file," Egerter said, "No, I can't think of one."

Egerter called SIG "the office that spies on spies" and involved "investigations of Agency employees where there was an indication of espionage." It applied to Oswald, for he had offered to provide secrets to the Soviets, which was sufficient cause for SIG to investigate him.

The HSCA interviewer offered his opinion that "the purpose of CI/SIG was . . . primarily to investigate Agency employees who for one reason or another might be under suspicion of getting espionage against the United States . . ." "Well, it is employees and also penetration, which is the same thing, of the Agency," was how Egerter replied.

The critical disclosure made by Egerter was that her job was "to investigate Agency employees." On a second occasion, she said SIG was responsible for "investigations of Agency employees where there was an indication of espionage." It leads one to conclude, especially since Egerter chose her words carefully, that she was stating Oswald was a CIA employee, or at least an Agency asset. He was involved in something Counterintelligence knew nothing about in 1959, hence the delay in opening the 201 file. It means that if Oswald was involved in a covert operation, Counterintelligence was not involved, at least not at that time. But the fact remains that Egerter referred to Oswald, on two separate occasions, as an Agency employee investigated for possible espionage.

* * *

Returning to what was happening to Oswald in Russia, on November 3, 1959, about two weeks after his interview with Priscilla Johnson, Lee wrote to Llewellyn Thompson, the American ambassador in Moscow, again asking that the United States revoke his citizenship. Thompson spoke to Snyder, and Snyder replied to Oswald that all he had to do was return to the embassy to renounce his citizenship, which Oswald never did. On November 8, Lee wrote to his brother Robert, saying, "I will never return to the United States, which is a country I hate." He wrote Robert again that he "would like to see the capitalist government of the U.S. overthrown" and "happiness is taking part in the struggle." He will later try to do precisely that when he returns to the United States. And, "In the event of war, I would kill any American who put a uniform on in defense of the American Government—Any American." He added that Robert and their mother were "not objects of affection." In December, he wrote to Robert saying he would not be writing them again.[43] Curiously, despite Oswald's anti-American rant, the Soviets continue to have no desire to exploit him for propaganda purposes. They did not trust this man.

On January 4, 1960, the Russians told Oswald he could stay in the Soviet Union, and they were relocating him to Minsk, 450 miles from Moscow. For the next year, he would drop out of sight, living in virtual obscurity.

Not able to contact her son, Oswald's mother, Marguerite, contacted the FBI in February 1960. Although the FBI never admitted meeting with her at that time, she later recalled that an agent named "Fannan" did come to her home. Most likely, his name was Fain, who officially paid her a visit in April. Fain told Marguerite that it appeared Lee had made the decision himself to go to Russia and suggested she contact her local senators and members of Congress to see who might be able to help her locate her son. Following Fain's advice, she wrote to Congressman Jim Wright and Secretary of State Christian Herter. Wright responded by writing to the State Department himself, who then sent copies of both letters to the American embassy in Moscow on March 21. On March 30, the State Department wrote Marguerite to inform her they had forwarded her letter to Moscow to try and find her son. Meanwhile, on March 22, Marguerite received a letter from Albert Schweitzer College, which indicated Lee was to attend school there from April 19 thru July 20. She promptly wrote to the college to determine if they had any information regarding Lee.

On April 5, the Embassy in Moscow told the State Department that Oswald had not contacted them since he departed from the embassy the previous November. Shortly after that, on April 28, FBI agent Fain got in touch with Marguerite again. He forwarded his report of their discussion to the New York field office, which sent a telegram to FBI headquarters on May 23 that contained the following passage: "There appears to be a possibility of locating Lee Oswald outside the USSR at the Albert Schweitzer College in Switzerland. Furthermore, since Oswald had his birth certificate in his possession, another individual may have assumed his identity."

On June 3, J. Edgar Hoover followed this with a letter to the State Department's Office of Security. Hoover wrote: "Since there is a possibility that an impostor is using Oswald's birth certificate, any current information the Department of State may have concerning subject will be appreciated."[44] There was something strange happening here, for it is odd that this case would have warranted Hoover's attention and compelled him to place the entire Bureau on alert, based solely on a mother's claim that her son took his birth certificate with him. And consider Hoover's reaction in conjunction with the fact that, starting before Oswald's defection, up until the day he died and beyond, the possibility of an impostor hovered over him in so many ways, a myth Oswald even perpetrated himself, as described in the previous chapter. Are we supposed to believe that the FBI director was unaware of this, and it had no bearing on his warning that an Oswald impostor might have existed? Most likely, Hoover already knew more about Oswald than he ever admitted.

The Oswald impostor concerns continued into 1961. On March 31, Edward J. Hickey, Deputy Chief of the Passport Office, sent a letter to the Consular Section of the State Department. Hickey noted that ". . . there is an impostor using Oswald's ID data and that no doubt the Soviets would love to get hold of his valid passport . . ." By this time, the wheels were already in motion for Oswald's eventual return to the U.S. The embassy heeded Hickey's advice, agreeing not to return

Oswald's passport to him unless he appeared at the embassy in person, despite Oswald's desire to have them mail it to him in Minsk.

What is interesting is the way Hickey phrased his letter. He did not say there was the possibility that someone was posing as Oswald. He definitively wrote that "there is an impostor using Oswald's ID data . . ." And what did he mean by ID data, which is an odd way to refer to a birth certificate. Was Hickey referring to Oswald's Department of Defense ID card, the one with the photo of the long-haired Oswald? Hickey follows this by saying that the Soviets would have loved to get hold of Oswald's passport, which suggests that Hickey, based on what he knew, believed the Soviets were responsible for the Oswald impostor. It means there was concern that the real Oswald, whom they assumed had defected, was dead, killed by the Russians. If true, it is consistent with the false Oswald "sleeper agent" scenario discussed in the previous chapter.

By July, the concern over Oswald had reached a climax. None other than Secretary of State Dean Rusk wrote the embassy in Moscow, stating that "careful attention to the involved case of Mr. Oswald is appreciated. It is assumed that the person who has been in communication with the Embassy is the person who was issued a passport in the name of Lee Harvey Oswald."[45]

It appears that Rusk was also worried that the Russians had killed Oswald and had installed an impostor in his place, which reinforced to the embassy that they should not send Oswald his passport but insist that he come to the embassy in person to pick it up. There was also a hint of doubt in Rusk's words. Why tell the embassy to ensure that the person they were communicating with "is the person who was issued a passport in the name of Lee Harvey Oswald?" Why not instruct the embassy to make sure that the person was Lee Oswald? Was there doubt at the State Department that the man who defected may not have been Oswald?[46]

In January 1961, two months before the Hickey letter and six months before the letter from Rusk, the Bolton Ford incident took place in New Orleans involving Guy Banister's group, the Friends of a Democratic Cuba. It included the name "Oswald" on the pending sale documents. The FBI was concerned and conducted some interviews in the early part of 1961 to "obtain background data for leads concerning Oswald." Considering the timing, did the FBI connect the Bolton incident and the possibility that someone was using Oswald's name in the U.S. to the Oswald impostor scenario?

Could an innocent statement by Oswald's mother generate such attention from the FBI, CIA, and the State Department? Did other defectors receive such attention? Should Oswald have warranted such attention? Under normal circumstances, the answer is no. But this was not your garden variety defector, and those investigating Oswald knew that was the case. We are left to ponder the possibility that Oswald's sojourn to the Soviet Union was nothing but an allusion to making it appear that the Soviets killed the real Oswald and that an impostor had assumed his identity. Incredibly, in addition to his mysterious 2" loss in height and falsified documents with different photographs on them, the Director of the FBI, the Secretary of State, and the U.S. Passport Office were concerned that an impostor had assumed Oswald's identity in the Soviet Union. Future associates of Oswald's were using his name in the struggle against Cuba long before the Marine defector returned to the U.S. It does not add up. The possibility that Oswald was an innocent, disenchanted defector becomes increasingly difficult to accept.

* * *

On May 1, 1960, fifteen days before the summit conference in Paris, a U-2 plane piloted by Francis Gary Powers left its base in Peshawar, Turkey. The mission was to photograph ICBM installations in the Soviet Union and land in Norway, but a Soviet missile near Sverdlovsk allegedly shot the plane down. The Russians captured Powers, and the plane, with minimal damage, crash-landed inside the Soviet Union and was secreted away by Soviet authorities.

Initially, Khrushchev considered the incident a credit to the sophistication of Soviet anti-aircraft technology. However, three weeks earlier, his air defense forces could not shoot down another U-2, even though the Soviets knew exactly where that plane was flying. While pursuing that earlier flight, a MiG-19 Soviet fighter crashed at Semipalatinsk, near a secret nuclear testing site that the U-2 plane was photographing. Two newly developed high-altitude interceptors could not catch up to the aircraft as it collected Tyumatom ballistic missile site images. What had changed so suddenly that the Soviets were now able to shoot down a U-2, something they had not been able to do previously? As we will see, this concerned Khrushchev, for the timing related to the upcoming summit was too suspicious.[47]

The exact circumstances surrounding the U-2 incident remain unknown. The Soviets claimed they shot the plane down while it cruised at 70,000 feet which, at the time, was discounted by experts who believed the altitude was out of the range of Soviet missiles. Years later, James Angleton told author Dick Russell: "To this day, we have no finite knowledge as to the fate of Powers' mission. The mind would be boggled with trying to consider all means by which it was eventually brought down. You can't discount anything . . ."[48] Senator William Fulbright never believed that the Senate inquiry into the U-2 affair uncovered what had happened. Years later, he had this to say: "I have often wondered why, [during] these efforts by President Eisenhower and Khrushchev to come to some understanding, the U-2 incident was allowed to take place. No one will ever know whether it was accidental or intentional."[49]

From the beginning, Washington mishandled the crisis, first calling it a weather plane. The U.S. was confident they could lie and cover up what had occurred, based upon Allen Dulles' "absolutely categorical" guarantee that the pilot couldn't survive a crash. Dulles also told the President that the wreckage would be destroyed beyond recognition if the Russians shot the plane down. As Eisenhower's aide, Andrew Goodpaster, would later report, "We had an understanding . . . that the plane would be destroyed and that it was impossible for the pilot to survive." And if he did not know it already, the President would soon learn he could not trust Allen Dulles.[50]

On Thursday morning, May 5, Khrushchev addressed thirteen hundred deputies of the Supreme Soviet in the Great Kremlin Palace. American Ambassador Llewellyn Thompson was invited to attend and was seated in the front row of the diplomatic gallery. In attendance was a young, attractive American correspondent named Priscilla Johnson. The friendly presummit banter she encountered moved her so profoundly that she crossed the gallery to sit with Eastern European Communist journalists. After speaking for three hours, Khrushchev revealed the fate of the U-2 plane but did not mention that the pilot had survived and was in Soviet custody.[51]

At a Soviet Press Day reception that same evening, some Russian journalists invited Priscilla to dinner. She refused to go, or so she claimed, but they took her by the arm anyway and led her into the private dining hall of the House of Journalists, where hundreds of Soviet editors and reporters were to eat and drink. At some point during the meal, *Investia's* thirty-six-year-old editor, Alexei Adzhubei, who was also Khrushchev's son-in-law, stood up and shouted, "Is there an American in the room?" All eyes turned to Johnson. He mimicked a plunging plane with his index finger, then asked her what she thought of the incident Khrushchev had revealed earlier that day. Amidst shouts from the crowd, Johnson had to walk down the long room to drink a toast with Adzhubei. Johnson looked down and saw a row of Chinese faces grinning back as he touched his glass to hers. As she groped her way back to her chair, a Soviet foreign affairs writer rose and proposed a toast to "our only friends, the Chinese."[52]

Perhaps Priscilla Johnson was singled out that day because, as an American reporter, she was an easy target. On the other hand, maybe the Soviets knew she was not so innocent, that she was a CIA asset, one who had met with Oswald, and they enjoyed rubbing her nose in it. We'll never know.

The timing of the U-2 incident, so close to Eisenhower's summit with Khrushchev, made the sabotage of Powers' plane believable. At the time, nuclear testing was considered essential by many, including the scientists who were working to improve America's nuclear arsenal. They believed that a suspension of testing put the country's security at risk. When Ike held a press conference in 1958 and said the U.S. would halt nuclear testing if the Soviets agreed to do so as well, Edward Teller, the man known as the father of the hydrogen bomb, was furious. Teller, an outspoken supporter of a nuclear weapons arsenal, sent a telegram to Brigadier General Alfred Starbird, the defense official at the Pentagon in charge of nuclear weapons tests. Teller warned that a test ban threatened national security and made

America vulnerable to a surprise nuclear attack. According to Teller, ending testing was the first step towards nuclear disarmament with an adversary the United States could not trust to honor any agreement. Those who agreed believed the nation's very existence was in jeopardy, and one would have to assume they would go to any length to prevent this from occurring. To believe otherwise implies that people who thought the nation was in danger stood idly by and were willing to let it happen. We know this was not the case, which means those opposed to the summit with Khrushchev had to prevent it from taking place. And with Ike's mind dead set on signing a treaty, there was only one way to do that.[53]

Powers believed someone sabotaged his plane. He told a radio audience in 1977, shortly before he was to die in an accidental helicopter crash, he thought the aircraft was tampered with before takeoff on the ground in Turkey. He added that since security was so tight, it "would have to have been an inside job." Allen Dulles made a statement shortly after the incident that may have corroborated the concern Powers had. According to Dulles, data obtained by the National Security Agency indicated an autopilot malfunction that caused the plane to fly at only 30,000 feet.[54]

Colonel Fletcher Prouty also had concerns about what happened. He wrote it was supposed to be a "'civilian' aircraft . . . flown by a 'civilian' pilot . . ." However, Powers was "permitted to carry with him . . . his military identification card, complete with name and picture [the same DOD ID card that Oswald was issued], along with a pocketful of other identifying cards . . ." It all "placed him at military installations in military instrument flight schools and on military facilities just days before the flight. He was hardly a deniable spy."[55]

Prouty continued that "all clandestine operations personnel, and especially the select coterie of U-2 pilots, were required to submit to a complete inspection before takeoff." It "included the removal of all clothes and other personal effects and the issue of sanitized, non-identifiable clothing and equipment sufficient only for the flight. Neither pilot nor plane [was] sanitized on this flight as was required on other flights."

Colonel Prouty also has his explanation for why the plane may have descended to a lower altitude:

> "When the plane went down, its signal faded, and it was lost from tracking radar. The engine had stopped, and Powers was gliding the plane down from its extreme altitude, which was so high that the air's oxygen content was insufficient to support combustion. The normal combustion of the jet engine at that altitude had to be assisted by the infusion of a trace of raw hydrogen from a small liquid hydrogen cryogenic storage bottle. If by some chance the engine either coughed itself out or if something happened to this slight hydrogen supply and the engine flamed

out, it could not be restarted at that altitude. The pilot would have no recourse other than to let down and see if he could restart the engine at some lower altitude. The evidence that the engine would not restart even at thirty thousand feet indicates that the trouble was most likely hydrogen deficiency and not a normal fuel flameout. Had it been a simple flameout and had there been plenty of hydrogen, the engine should have restarted, as others had in similar circumstances.

"When the plane did not restart, Powers [had to] to let it continue to spiral toward earth, and then at a safer altitude either bail out or continue [ ] down to the ground . . . some of the early pictures of the U-2 showed an aircraft that was relatively undamaged, when one considers that the Russian story was that it was hit by a rocket in the air and then crashed into the ground. We may never really know whether Powers parachuted because he was hit by Russian rockets or gunfire or whether he parachuted simply to leave a plane that was doomed to crash anyhow. The elaborate pictures of the plane, which the Soviets released at the trial, show neither bullet damage nor rocket fragment damage, although at that point neither would be important; the plane was going to come down. If it had not been on the way down, neither rockets nor bullets would have been able to bring it down in those days."[56]

When Oswald's commander in the Marines at El Toro, First Lieutenant John E. Donovan, testified before the Warren Commission on May 5, 1964, he provided additional light on what may have happened to Powers' plane. "He [Oswald] had been schooled on a piece of machinery called the TPX-1," Donovan reported, ". . . used to transfer radio-radar and radio signals over a great distance. Radar is very susceptible to homing missiles [and] this piece of equipment [can] put your radar antenna several miles away and relay the information back to your site, which you hope is relatively safe . . ."[57]

According to Donovan, not only was the plane flying at 70,000 feet, it had equipment that would send radar signals to the ground that made it appear the plane was several miles away from where it was. No wonder it was impossible for the Soviets to shoot down this plane. The only logical explanation is that the aircraft was flying at a much lower altitude than it was usually capable of doing, where Soviet missiles could reach it, or it had to land on its own due to a mechanical problem.

Allen Dulles, whose credibility is questionable since the CIA may have been responsible for sabotaging the plane, still provided helpful information. Dulles blamed the crash on an autopilot malfunction that forced the plane to fly at 30,000 feet, but how would he know this? There was no way for the U.S. to obtain this information, for the Soviets never let anyone near the wreckage. Why, then, not just say that the Soviets got lucky and shot the plane down, regardless of altitude? A plausible explanation would be that radar operators were aware of the actual elevation at which the aircraft was flying. And if ever questioned, they would be obligated to reveal this information. So, to dispel the possibility that an inquiry would show that the CIA had sabotaged the plane, Dulles said it was flying too low. And the radar operators could then tell the truth, and no one would question them. It means the scenario that Colonel Prouty offers is a more likely explanation for what happened. The plane was tampered with before takeoff.

Based on the evidence, the idea that the plan was not shot down, but had to glide to earth on its own, makes more sense. Photos from the crash site show a plane remarkably intact that likely landed horizontally or close to it. The U-2 was flimsy and lightweight, critical factors in allowing the aircraft to fly so high. If a missile hit it, it is hard to believe the wreckage would have remained as intact as it did. Almost certainly, the plane would have suffered massive damage, or at least gone into a tail-spin and crashed nose-first into the ground. It did not happen, and whether Powers bailed out or landed the plane himself is irrelevant. What is relevant is that someone, likely the CIA, sabotaged the U-2 to prevent the upcoming summit from occurring.

One person who was concerned that the American right-wing had sabotaged the plane was Nikita Khrushchev. "Aggressive imperialist forces in the United States in recent times," he said, as he spoke before the Politburo shortly after the incident, "have been taking the most active measures to undermine the summit or at least to hinder any agreement that might have been reached." "Was this aggressive act," he wondered, "carried out by Pentagon militarists? If such actions are taken by American military men on their own account, it must be of special concern to world opinion."[58]

Khrushchev believed that hard-liners around Eisenhower wanted to derail the summit. He suspected that Allen Dulles had intentionally ordered a U-2 mission destined for failure to disrupt the meeting with Eisenhower and upset relations between the two countries. He blamed "imperialists and militarists" around Ike and said the U-2 was an act of "aggressive provocation aimed at wrecking the summit conference." And what kind of country was it, Khrushchev asked, "in which the military can do what the government opposes . . . if one of our military [generals] allowed himself to behave like that, we would grab him by the ear, right here in the daylight."[59]

"Certain ruling circles in the United States have at present not [concluded] that a relaxation of tension and the solution of controversial problems through negotiation is necessary," the Soviet Premier continued. "Lately, influential forces—imperialist and militarist circles, whose stronghold is the Pentagon—have become noticeably more active in the United States. These aggressive forces stand for [the] continuation of the Cold War and the arms race. And they have been going in for downright provocation."[60]

"The question then arises: who sent this aircraft across the Soviet frontier? Was it the American Commander-in-Chief who, as everyone knows, is the President? Or was this aggressive act performed by Pentagon militarists without the President's knowledge? If American military men can take such actions on their own, the world should be greatly concerned." Khrushchev charged that "American aggressive circles" were trying to "torpedo the Paris Summit or, at any rate, prevent an agreement for which the whole world is waiting."[61]

"I do not doubt the President's intentions to exert all of his will to reach [an] agreement between our two countries . . . ," Khrushchev said on another occasion. "Nevertheless . . . some people in America do not act in the same way as the President. These forces want to continue the Cold War and the arms race . . . I would not be in a hurry to say whether these forces are large or small, powerful or weak and whether the forces supporting the President can win . . ."[62]

Khrushchev decided to ". . . address the American people: In spite of these aggressive acts against our country, we have not forgotten the friendly encounters we had during our visit to America. Even now, I profoundly believe that the American people—except for certain imperialist and monopolist circles—want peace and friendship with the Soviet Union . . . I do not doubt President Eisenhower's sincere desire for peace."[63]

Interestingly, Khrushchev added "monopolistic circles" to who was responsible for downing the U-2. It shows he was aware that the arms race was very profitable for the defense industry in the U.S., and they also had a vested interest in seeing the summit destroyed.

There is also something fascinating about Khrushchev's reaction. He could have achieved better propaganda by saying the U.S. had been flying over Russian airspace for years. However, now the Soviet Union could shoot down this high-flying aircraft. If true, it would have prevented future U-2 flights from occurring. But by suggesting the U.S. had sabotaged the mission to destroy the summit, he admitted that Soviet missiles could not have reached the altitude necessary to have taken the plane down. He even singled out Secretary of State Christian Herter for the attack: "Far from feeling guilty and ashamed of aggressive actions," Khrushchev complained, "he [Herter] justifies them [U-2 flights] and says they will continue . . ."[64]

Would Herter have said the U-2 flights would continue if the Soviets had developed the ability to shoot down the plane at 70,000 feet? Would the U.S. risk having another plane shot down and be embarrassed once again? They would not have. It was an admission by Herter that the U.S. knew the Soviets did not shoot down the aircraft. They could make excuses, like Allen Dulles, that there was an autopilot malfunction, but the truth is sabotage brought down the plane.

The shooting down of a U-2 over Russia destroyed the summit, which began on May 16. When Khrushchev wanted assurances that the U.S. would discontinue flights in the future, he once again confirmed they did not have the technical capability to shoot down the U-2. When Eisenhower refused to agree to this, the Soviets walked out, and hostilities escalated.

Shortly after midnight, the Joint Chiefs in Washington received word from the summit in Paris to put U.S. forces on alert. Around the world, soldiers, sailors, and airmen manned their battle stations, and a civilian radio announcer near Lowry Air Force Base in Denver broadcasted the following: "All fighter pilots F-101 and fighter pilots F-102: Code Three Alert! Hotcake One and Hotcake Six scramble at Lowry immediately!"

In Washington, reporters demanded to know whether the military had tried to seize power while civilian leaders were in Paris. It was an indication that the press in 1960 believed strongly that a military takeover could happen, for why else suggest such a thing. It is telling, for a little more than three years later, President Kennedy's assassination would occur, and there were reports that before the return of Air Force One to Washington from Dallas, the Pentagon said they were in charge of the government. But no one asked about a possible military takeover at that time, and one wonders why that was so.[65]

As he walked on stage to a packed audience at the Palais de Chaillot during the summit, Khrushchev was met with boos and catcalls, what the New Yorker's Janet Flanner called "the noise and violence of a quasi-riot." An angry Khrushchev responded to those in attendance. He told them: "I have already been informed that [West German] Chancellor Adenauer sent here some of those fascist bastards we didn't finish off at Stalingrad. We hit them so hard that we put them ten feet underground right away. If you boo us and attack us again, look out! We will hit you so hard that there won't be a squeal out of you." International tensions were at a fever pitch, and the potential was there for World War III to begin, should one side provoke the other into starting hostilities.[66]

On May 27, an opposition force overthrew the government in Turkey, the country from where Powers' U-2 flight had taken off. Premier Adnan Menderes, who had secretly approved the U-2 base and many other forms of Turkish-American cooperation, was arrested and later hanged. The Turks wanted to make it clear that the United States had acted on its own.

In Japan, the people wanted the U-2s removed before the Soviets had a chance to do it forcibly, and Premier Nobusuke Kishi found himself fighting for his political life. Rioting broke out before Eisenhower's visit, which had been agreed to before the U-2 incident happened. Having little choice, Kishi decided to cancel Eisenhower's invitation, and he resigned from office, but not before he was stabbed five times in the thigh by a right-wing nationalist. In July, Christian Herter informed the President that "we have withdrawn all the U.S. U-2 aircraft from Japan, and the Japanese government is very much relieved."[67]

Then on July 1, an American RB-47 spy plane that took off from its British base flew along the northern coast of the Soviet Union and vanished over the

Barents Sea. In Moscow, Khrushchev admitted that the Soviets had shot down the plane to halt another "gross violation" of their airspace by the United States. The Soviets rescued the two Americans on board who had survived the encounter. This "new act of American perfidy" showed that Eisenhower's pledge to stop the spy flights was "not worth a busted penny," Khrushchev angrily declared. And he added that the British should know that allowing the Americans to use their bases for "aggressive actions" would only endanger their people.

The United States claimed that the plane had been more than thirty miles beyond Soviet airspace, which might have been correct. Still, after the U-2 incident, the Soviet military was looking to regain some respectability. The White House considered publicly providing evidence to support their claim, followed by breaking relations with Moscow, but that would have compromised American tracking stations, so they did nothing.[68]

The 1960 election was "the biggest defeat of my life," said Eisenhower, a repudiation of everything I've done for eight years." A disgusted Richard Nixon blamed his defeat in part on the CIA because they were responsible for the U-2 disaster, which enhanced the animosity between the two superpowers.

A commission conducted an investigation of the CIA in the wake of the U-2 incident. Eisenhower received their report on December 15, 1960, and it was very critical of the Agency. Three weeks later, another report from the President's Board of Consultants on Foreign Intelligence Activities warned that the CIA's power, which was accountable to no one, had gotten out of control. "The structure of our intelligence organization is faulty," the President said after reading the report. "It makes no sense, it has to be reorganized, and we should have done it long ago." Regarding CIA, he said, "I have suffered an eight-year defeat on this," and added that he had left his successor "a legacy of ashes." It was as if he were admitting the CIA had sabotaged the U-2, and had he reigned them in earlier, his precious test ban treaty would have come to fruition. On January 17, 1961, Eisenhower gave his farewell address to the nation, warning about the military-industrial complex that threatened the country, calling it a "disastrous rise of misplaced power . . ." It was the same group about whom Khrushchev said the world should be concerned.

Regarding Oswald, the fact that the Soviets did not exploit his services speaks volumes. The Soviets shot down a U-2 plane, and the pilot survived. At the same time, living in Minsk was an ex-Marine who was a radar operator that monitored U-2 flights. Whether or not Oswald provided them information regarding the U-2 is irrelevant. They could have paraded him at the trial in front of cameras, but they didn't. It was almost like they did not know what to make of Oswald and thought it best to keep him quiet. And what must they have thought? For years, the Soviets could not do anything to stop the overflights. Then a radar operator shows up at their door, and soon after that, the U-2 incident occurs. They would have known it was sabotage, as Khrushchev stated multiple times. Oswald's presence must have worried them greatly, for the timing of his defection would have led them to believe there was a connection to the downing of the plane. It was as if the U.S. wanted the Soviets to put Oswald on display, which would have given the Americans the opportunity to blame Oswald for what happened to the U-2. However, the Soviets recognized this and kept him secreted away. It was a high-stakes international game of cat and mouse.

And what about the American handling of Oswald. He arrived in Moscow, threatening to reveal secrets to the Soviets, which had to deal with the U-2. While he was there, a U-2 was shot down, which was the official American position regarding what had occurred. Why then was Oswald not prosecuted after he returned to the United States from Russia? He should have been, if for no other reason than to let future potential military defectors know there would be consequences for revealing military secrets to the Soviets. But nothing happened. Oswald was left alone. It does not make sense unless he had done nothing wrong, and U.S. intelligence knew it.

One could argue that sacrificing a U-2 and its valuable intelligence, not to mention the public humiliation the United States had to endure, was a high price to pay for canceling the summit. However, although the U-2 provided invaluable information that the U.S. could not have obtained in any other way, it is essential to realize that it was counterproductive to those who wanted U.S. military spending to increase. The U-2 permitted the President to limit military spending. It provided him with accurate information regarding the development of the Soviet missile program, which was way behind the U.S. The same people who benefited from increased military spending did not trust the Russians and believed war was inevitable. Therefore, on both counts, it was necessary to prevent the summit from happening. Not to mention that the U-2 incident also polarized relations with the Soviet Union, which made the signing of a test ban treaty under a future president that much more improbable.

Without question, the U-2 incident was another treasonous act by the American military and intelligence community, and they were getting more daring and less tolerant as the years went by. Little did they know that the next president would sign a test ban treaty with the Russians in three years and would do so without military or intelligence input before they had a chance to stop him. It may have been the last straw that sealed Kennedy's fate.

When the nuclear test ban treaty summit died before discussions could begin, JFK's date with destiny was still three years away. However, the writing was already on the wall. Some would do anything to prevent a naïve president, who underestimated what they could do, from appeasing their Communist antagonists and jeopardizing the country's welfare. Kennedy would learn this lesson the hard way and pay dearly for daring to try and reach an accommodation with Soviet adversaries whom America's military-industrial complex was hell-bent on destroying.

- 11 -

Epilogue

On January 20, 1961, John Fitzgerald Kennedy took the oath of office and became the 35th President of the United States. As he stood before an enthusiastic Washington D.C. audience on that cold winter day, one wonders if he realized that he had no business being there. The Mafia had stolen the election from Richard Nixon, the Republican candidate, by falsifying returns in numerous states due to an understanding the mob had reached with Joseph Kennedy, the new President's father. However, just in case, organized crime provided financial support to Nixon as well. The Mafia knew that the former vice president was a friend to organized crime. The same could not be said about JFK; however, whose brother Robert was waiting in the wings to go after them with a vengeance. On the surface, supporting Kennedy was a foolish thing to do. But the Mafia rarely made stupid decisions, so there must have been a reason behind this one. And there was—it was their relationship with the CIA. The liberals at the Agency did not want Nixon to win, for how to handle Cuba was still an open question and electing Nixon was a dangerous proposition that they tried to avoid. He was a loose cannon who had the potential of starting World War III.

Consider the facts. During the summer of 1959, a right-wing group of cattlemen from Cuba who had joined William Morgan's attempt to overthrow Castro approached Allen Dulles. The CIA Director rejected what the cattlemen had to say and turned them away. He then exposed Morgan's plans, which thwarted the pending revolution and resulted in Morgan's execution. It was a curious decision by Dulles because Morgan's effort may have worked. He had inside Cuban assistance and the backing of right-wing CIA operatives in Havana. But it was too visible an operation that could have been traced back to the U.S., resulting in an aggressive Russian response, such as the taking of West Berlin. So, Dulles threw Morgan under the bus to maintain control of a potentially volatile situation, for this was not Guatemala. The Soviets were involved in Cuba, and the U.S. had to tread carefully. Maintaining plausible deniability was essential.

The Bay of Pigs came next, which started as a fifty-man paramilitary force to be dropped in Cuba to work with the Cuban underground, considered an essential element of the operation. Fidel Castro's assassination was deemed necessary. However, it soon became apparent that Raul Castro and Che Guevara would also have to die. And the plan morphed into a full amphibious invasion. Without U.S. military intervention, it would fail, which the CIA and the military knew from the beginning. It did not matter. They would force the President's hand, as they had done throughout the Cold War.

Even though the CIA had access to professional hitmen to kill the Cuban leaders, they turned to the Mafia instead. Why would Allen Dulles do that unless he knew the Mafia effort would be half-hearted and had no chance of succeeding? And if all three Cuban leaders needed to be killed for the takeover of Cuba to be successful, why was it only Fidel that the Mafia focused on? The answer is CIA wanted it to fail because of the international fallout the U.S. would face if it succeeded. Cuba was not that important that it warranted potentially escalating hostilities somewhere else in the world.

It was the summer of 1960 that Allen Dulles met with candidate Kennedy at the Democratic Convention, accompanied by liberal Cubans who had opposed Batista. Kennedy was fed more information than was necessary, designed to undermine Nixon's chances of getting elected. CIA probably felt they could manipulate Kennedy. Nixon was a different story.

Meanwhile, Nixon was orchestrating his right-wing plan that was supposed to happen just before the 1960 election. William Pawley and Mario Garcia Kohly, two ultra-right conservatives, worked closely with Nixon putting the operation together. It involved Kohly's massive underground paramilitary force inside Cuba and Operation 40, the right-wing assassination group. Still, it was all to no avail as the 1960 Presidential election passed without incident. The CIA made sure the delay happened, and Nixon did not have an opportunity to introduce U.S. military air and land forces into Cuba, which he most likely would have done if given a chance. When it came time for Kennedy to make that decision during the actual Bay of Pigs invasion, as expected, he rejected the request to use the military to support the Cuban exile invasion force. It created intense hatred for the new President among Cuban exiles and their radical right-wing supporters. It was something they would not forget.

* * *

As Kennedy spoke to the large inauguration audience, he challenged his "fellow Americans" to help him make America a better place for all. "Ask not what your country can do for you," he said. "Ask what you can do for your country."

Most Americans found these words electrifying and inspiring, but not everyone felt that way. Many were furious that Nixon hadn't benefited from a Cuban invasion that was supposed to occur before the election. It included a right-wing Fascist element in society, fueled by an elite class that felt betrayed by a government infiltrated with Socialists and Communists at the highest levels. The country was at a crossroads, for one could sense that the American way of life was on the cusp of monumental change, and the radical right believed the young, Catholic, newly elected President from Massachusetts would not be up to the task. They had already decided that JFK was too inexperienced and too liberal to be President. It was especially true in the South. And if he proved incapable of putting America back on the right-wing, Christian, anti-Communist road they were accustomed to traveling upon, he would not survive his Presidency. There is no doubt that this was so, and Lyndon Johnson became his running mate precisely for that reason. In actuality, Kennedy had the deck stacked against him from the outset. To be reelected to a second term, there were fundamental American principles he had to adhere to because the Fascist right found them non-negotiable. Kennedy's three predecessors failed to comply with this, and they faced the consequences for doing so. And unfortunately for the new President, what he would face from the opposition that tried to control him far exceeded what his predecessors had to endure.

The first principle was to restore self-determination to the American psyche and limit the social programs that took money from the wealthy without their consent to give to those in need. For many right-wing Americans, this was unacceptable on various fronts. It was against the U.S. Constitution and its mandate to preserve domestic tranquility. It violated the Declaration of Independence and the inalienable rights of life, liberty, and the pursuit of property. Finally, it rejected eugenics because it perpetuated an element of society that could not sustain itself, which was unacceptable. They believed this weakened the purity of the nation's ruling class and served to lower the country's standing as a whole.

Second: The appeasement of Communists was unacceptable, for the Soviet and Chinese economies would self-destruct if left to their own devices. It included adhering to George Kennan's containment philosophy and not letting Communist countries increase their sphere of influence worldwide. They believed it was an inferior race of people the United States could not trust.

Third: Build a strong, well-rounded military superior to the Soviets and use nuclear weapons if necessary. The radical right believed war was inevitable, so why not engage Communists when the circumstances suited the American position.

Fourth: Limit the civil rights movement, desegregation, and equal rights for all. Many believed that Communists controlled these groups, which attempted to destroy the American way of life. Leaders would die if they ignored this condition.

As outlined throughout this narrative, there was a history of treason and deceit during the Twentieth Century, by individuals and groups, inside and outside government, who were no longer willing to tolerate a President who wanted to "weaken" America and coexist with Communists. By the time Kennedy was elected, for those who truly believed that America was facing potential destruction, a President who failed to understand the gravity of the times in which they lived had to be removed by any means possible. It was especially true when there was a replacement waiting in the wings whom they could control.

The right-wing distrust of politicians they considered Communists began in the early 1930s with numerous industry titans forcibly trying to remove FDR from office. Then there was the assassination of Huey Long, who was considered even more liberal than Roosevelt, and the attempted assassination of President-elect Roosevelt. As World War II approached, the right-wing embraced Nazi Germany and fascism. The plight of the Jews was ignored by the anti-Semitic proponents of eugenics, for it was in the financial best interest of big business to do so.

President Truman attempted to cut military spending dramatically, and he was willing to abandon South Korea, Formosa, and Japan to the Communists. It was unacceptable to the radical right, especially the military, so General MacArthur and the Joint Chiefs created a ruse that North Korea had invaded South Korea, which started the Korean War. Then, every time there was an opportunity for peace, the U.S. military reacted to prevent this from occurring. They either became needlessly more aggressive to try and goad the Chinese into escalating hostilities, or they hastily retreated from a non-existent phantom enemy. They inflated the number of Chinese troops engaged in the conflict or lied about the number of casualties U.S. troops inflicted on the Communists, giving the false impression that they were winning the war, when in fact, there was no enemy in sight. The point is they lied about conditions on the ground to ensure that peace was never achieved, with the hope that they could convince the President into allowing them to launch nuclear weapons directly at China, but Truman held firm.

Under President Eisenhower, a seemingly continuous call from his generals to use nuclear weapons in an unprovoked, first-strike attack. The military repeatedly tried to embarrass the President in public, to the point where he called their conduct treasonous. The relationship between military contractors and generals became so intertwined that Ike would warn about the danger posed by this group when he spoke about the Military-Industrial Complex in his farewell address. When the U.S. tried to orchestrate a coup in Indonesia in 1958 to have Sukarno removed, the Indonesian military shot down the plane of an American pilot named Allen Lawrence Pope. It appeared that the CIA had purposely created an incident to try and force Ike into using U.S. armed forces there, but it did not work. In 1959, Allen Dulles sabotaged an attempted coup in Cuba, resulting in the execution of William Morgan and others who tried to overthrow Fidel Castro. The following year, Eisenhower agreed to sign a nuclear test ban treaty with the Soviets. Allen Dulles lied to him, guaranteeing that if the Soviets ever shot down a U-2, it would destroy the plane, and the pilot would not survive. The CIA then sabotaged the U-2 flight piloted by Francis Gary Powers. The Soviets shot down the plane, and the treaty was not signed. For men like Allen Dulles, the treaty could not be allowed to happen. It was considered appeasement of the Soviets, which they would not tolerate.

Then there were the assassinations, and unexplainable deaths, mostly while Truman and Eisenhower were presidents. There were the suspected Communists within government under Truman, who the CIA most likely murdered. Men like Harry Dexter White, W. Marvin Smith, Laurence Duggan, Morton Kent, Laird Shields Goldsborough, Francis Otto Mathiessen, and Abraham Feller. The Soviets were also blackmailing CIA employees under Eisenhower because of their behavior. The CIA murdered them as well—men like John Montgomery and James Kronthal. Some like Frederick Crockett survived. There were others probably killed to ensure they kept quiet, like James Forrestal and Frank Olson.

Then there were the witnesses during the Kefauver hearings in the early 1950s who the CIA likely murdered because they might expose the working relationship between the CIA and the Mafia. It was the Cold War against a Godless enemy. The American way of life was at stake, so permanently silencing people to protect CIA operations that were illegal and immoral was acceptable. It was a common occurrence that would continue even after JFK's assassination. In the mid-1970s, when the House Select Committee on Assassinations wanted to speak to mobsters regarding their relationship to CIA, Sam Giancana, Johnny Roselli, and Jimmy Hoffa were all killed. When the committee wanted to interview people connected to Oswald or the war against Castro, William Pawley, Carlos Prio, and George de Mohrenschildt all committed "suicide."

There were other alleged "suicides" that conveniently silenced people. Phillip Graham knew too much and had become a liability. Dorothy Kilgallen was going to break the assassination case wide open after meeting with Jack Ruby. And Charles William Thomas stumbled upon information in Haiti and Mexico City, indicating that the assassination was a conspiracy. Then there was the killing of ex-CIA director William Colby, the man who had revealed CIA's "Family Jewels" and had become a threat because who knew what else he might say.

There were the needless deaths of innocents who got caught up in a Cold War with no rules. The CIA sent tourists and students behind the Iron Curtain who did not know the ramifications involved in what they were doing. They gave mind-altering drugs to unsuspecting Americans, experimented on others, and sold narcotics to urban African Americans to finance CIA operations. It resulted in countless deaths and lives ruined. Eastern Europeans were sent back to their native country on suicide missions to fight communism, only to be slaughtered or sent to slave labor camps. Places like Hungary revolted, expecting American support that was promised but never came. The real intent was to reveal the oppressiveness of the Soviet Union to the world. The U.S. military destroyed countries like South Korea in the name of freedom. The murder of thousands of innocents occurred in regions overthrown, such as Indonesia, the Middle East, northern Africa, and

Central and South America. Then there were countries like Cuba and Vietnam where attempts to gain control failed. There were others, but the list is sufficient to prove a point—the extermination of human life was considered collateral damage by people who believed that only eliminating the "Evil Empire" would save the world from Communist subjugation.

Then there was the domestic war being fought against civil rights in the United States, as Southern racists groups joined with Fascist proponents of eugenics who wanted to preserve the purity of the white Anglo-Saxon race. Many in the right-wing groups listed above agreed with what these hate groups espoused. Hence, there was an overlap of anti-Communists and racists who wanted to maintain America's status quo.

The bottom line is those in control had become desensitized to the needless killing, and human life soon had no value in a cause considered just. Any life was expendable in the war against communism. And any life sacrificed to improve the American way of life, especially "subhumans" whose very existence threatened to dilute the white Anglo-Saxon purity they wanted to preserve, was an acceptable loss. And lives lost, be it white or black, to maintain segregation throughout the South and keep alive the southern way of life was worth sacrificing because African Americans did not fit into their Normal Rockwell portrait that these Fascists believed represented America.

So, consider how easily blood was spilled in the name of democracy to maintain self-determination and the American way of life. With that in mind, how can we not accept the possibility that these same right-wing, anti-Communists would murder an American President for the same reasons, especially when the evidence overwhelmingly points in that direction? In examining what transpired during the previous decades during the Cold War, anyone willing to take the time to read the tea leaves would conclude that by 1960 a President who did not go along with the right-wing Fascist agenda placed himself in mortal danger.

John Kennedy was one person who believed that was possible. Recall what Arthur Schlesinger wrote in *Robert Kennedy and His Times*. That ". . . the military leaders were Cold War zealots . . . [and] the alliance between the military and the right disturbed the Kennedys . . . When the popular thriller *Seven Days in May* depicted a Pentagon attempt to take over the government, the President remarked, 'It's possible. It could happen in this country, but the conditions would have to be just right. . . .'"[1]

The conditions were "just right" under JFK. There was the nuclear test-ban treaty he signed with the Soviets in the summer of 1963, where he bypassed Congress and went to the American people directly; he signed a deal to sell wheat to Russia, which was considered appeasement and violated the containment policy; he publicly spoke of coexistence with the Soviets, an inexcusable offense; he began a pullout of troops from Vietnam and was on record that he would institute a complete withdrawal after he was reelected which, it was believed, would have inevitably led to a Communist Southeast Asia; he passed up the opportunity to invade Cuba during the Cuban Missile Crisis, even though this was what the hardliners around him advised he should do; he trusted the Soviets that they would remove missiles from Cuba after the Missile Crisis without verification; he agreed to remove missiles from Turkey after the same crisis; he was willing to never invade Cuba; he initiated talks that could have led to normalization of relations with Castro's Cuba, even though he knew that appeasement of Communists could not be tolerated; he cracked down on sabotage raids against Cuba; he refused to provide military air support during the Bay of Pigs invasion, dooming many Cuban exiles to a certain death; he fired Allen Dullen after the Bay of Pigs, a legend at CIA; he submitted a civil rights bill for Congressional debate; he called on the National Guard to ensure that African American students were allowed to attend the University of Mississippi and the University of Alabama; and a host of other actions that the Deep State found unacceptable. It was why a Kennedy Presidency could no longer be allowed to continue into a second term. The proponents of a new world order based everything on American superiority and preserving the American way of life. The Deep State had a vision for the future of America. They needed to contain communism, and racial segregation had to be maintained, at any cost, to achieve their goals for America. Therefore, there was no choice but to assassinate John Kennedy, for the changes he wanted to introduce during a second term would have turned the United States upside down and could not be allowed to happen.

* * *

From what conditions were like in 1960, there is no doubt that the radical right killed Kennedy. Even the Marxist Lee Harvey Oswald was a misguided racist who equated Marxism with Nazism with the self-determination promoted by right-wing elites. So, the idea that Kennedy's accused assassin was a Communist sympathizer has no merit, for he had much more in common with the Fascists he associated with in the last year of his life.

Knowing that the assassination of JFK was a right-wing conspiracy is not enough to determine who Oswald conspired with executing the crime of the century. The search for suspects begins with the stay-behind armies established by Allen Dulles and William Donovan shortly after World War II, which led to the formation of the World Commerce Corporation. They were privately funded and were not answerable to the U.S. Congress, which meant nothing was off-limits. At the same time, the Service d'Ordre in France was also privately funded. The two groups worked together, essentially creating a private international intelligence organization aligned with the Vatican Bank, which laundered money for their anti-Communist operations. As the group grew, additional funding was needed. So they instituted the Helliwell Plan, which involved opium shipped from Southeast Asia to fund their operations. It led to the involvement of the Corsican Mafia, while mobsters like Lucky Luciano, Santo Trafficante, Vito Genovese, and Carlos Marcello handled the American end of the operation. It was the beginning of a marriage between organized crime and U.S. intelligence that included leading figures at the CIA.

Because the Fascist dictator Francisco Franco was in control in Spain during the Cold War, Madrid became the center of radical right-wing, anti-Communist activity worldwide. SOFINDUS, a Spanish corporation that acted as a cover for Nazi intelligence during World War II, remained in place after the war and attracted many high-profile ex-Nazis, such as Otto Skorzeny, Hjalmar Schacht, and Reinhard Gehlen. It was also likely that Charles Willoughby, MacArthur's "Little Fascist," associated with this ex-Nazi group. Another key figure was Spanish businessman Victor Oswald, who was also connected to SOFINDUS and was an original member of the World Commerce Corporation.

We know that Thomas Eli Davis had a connection to Victor Oswald and that the Tangiers police arrested Davis sixteen days after the JFK assassination with a letter in his possession that referenced Oswald and Kennedy's murder. The letter was for Thomas Proctor, a New York attorney with CIA connections. A relationship with Proctor and Victor Oswald meant Davis was involved with the WCC international drug operation, including the Corsican and American Mafia, CIA, and the Donovan/Dulles stay-behind armies. More importantly, Davis was released from prison in Tangiers with the help of CIA assassin QJ/WIN, who was part of William Harvey's assassination group, ZR/RIFLE.

Thomas Eli Davis was also a Federal Bureau of Narcotics informant who knew George Hunter White and Charles Siragusa, both associates of Jean-Pierre Lafitte. He had met Jean Souetre of the OAS, a man connected to international drug traffickers, and may have been in Dallas when JFK's assassination occurred. Davis was a gun runner to Cuba with Jack Ruby, who was also well connected within the drug trade.

Lafitte and George Hunter White were involved in the CIA's drug experimentation program involving unsuspecting civilians. James Angleton and William Harvey were also. Harvey and White also had a connection to John Roselli, who was involved in the CIA's attempts to kill Castro with Santo Trafficante, Jr., and Sam Giancana.

Lafitte was close to Santos Trafficante Jr., Paul Mondoloni, and the Corsican Mafia, which connected him to the Mafia/WCC/Corsican drug operation, which funded the stay-behind armies started by Donovan and Allen Dulles. Lafitte visited Trafficante in a Cuban prison, as did Charles Siragusa, who also had organized crime connections. Jack Ruby also visited Trafficante in the Cuban jail. Assassination suspect John Martino was incarcerated in the same Cuban detention facility as Trafficante, and Lafitte used his name as an alias. Lafitte used Michael Mertz as an alias, who may have impersonated Jean Souetre in Dallas on the assassination day.

Mertz was associated with Corsican Paul Mondoloni, who was at the heart of the WCC drug operation, and another Lafitte alias.

In the period leading up to the JFK assassination, Davis tried to put together a mercenary army to invade Haiti. At the same time, George de Mohrenschildt, Clint Murchison, and Bobby Baker were all involved in Haiti's suspicious dealings. It is also possible that mind-altering drug experimentation may have happened there, considering Charles William Thomas's encounter with de Mohrenschildt when the two men accidentally met in Haiti.

The likely reason de Mohrenschildt was in Haiti was that he was part of a CIA operation to assassinate Papa Doc Duvalier and install Clemard Charles as President of that country. If accurate, it makes de Mohrenschildt a much more important figure than just a babysitter for Lee Oswald. A plot to assassinate Papa Doc would have involved William Harvey, for he headed the CIA's assassination program. One would also assume that Thomas Eli Davis' mercenary invasion force was part of this operation. The assassination of Fidel Castro was a critical element in the Bay of Pigs invasion. Therefore, one could assume the exact blueprint would be followed in Haiti by the CIA.

Clint Murchison, of course, was connected to Texas oilmen and the Suite 8F group, who all knew de Mohrenschildt well. Then there was the possible connection of de Mohrenschildt to the Donovan/Dulles/WCC stay-behind armies in Europe through CIA's Nicholas Anikeeff. The importance here is that there was a potential political assassination in the works in Haiti. It likely involved Thomas Eli Davis and George de Mohrenschildt. Both men had a connection to the Donovan/Dulles/WCC stay-behind armies, which included the Fascist group of ex-Nazis operating in Madrid.

Then there was the connection to European Monarchists, the Italian CIA front companies, Permindex, and the Centro Mondiale Comerciale, which supported the Fascist agenda on two continents. It seems to imply an international anti-Communist consortium of assassins and right-wing zealots, which on the surface is hard to accept because it would be much too complicated for it to have been the case. That is until we consider all the right-wing assassinations and overthrow of leftist and Communist governments, which occurred worldwide within months of Kennedy's assassination.

Returning to Clint Murchison, his Suite 8F connections included Sid Richardson, H.L. Hunt, and David Harold Byrd. George de Mohrenschildt was very close to Harold Byrd, the owner of the Texas School Book Depository. Byrd was a director of Dorchester Gas Producing with Jack Crichton, which brings us back to the happenings in Madrid. Clint Murchison was also a director of one of Crichton's companies. Crichton was involved with Clint Murchison and the Du Ponts trying to negotiate oil drilling rights in Spain, while fellow Suite 8F member William Pawley was in Madrid trying to secure U.S. military bases there. As we have documented, Pawley was extremely anti-Communist, and a Fascist who strongly supported dictators Batista in Cuba and Trujillo in the Dominican Republic. He was willing to put up the money to assassinate Castro and may have done so. He was close to the far-right Cuban ex-Batistaites who wanted to take back their country and return it to the oppressiveness that characterized Batista. Pawley was also close to Allen Dulles and connected to the world of intelligence. Both in the U.S. and abroad. He fit in well with the Suite 8F group.

In addition to his Madrid connections, former OSS officer Jack Crichton had a history of working with U.S. intelligence. He had organized the 488th Military Intelligence Detachment, a U.S. Army Intelligence unit operating out of Dallas, and was the Army Intelligence officer who had immediate access to Marina Oswald. After the assassination, Crichton asked Ilya Mamantov to act as Marina's interpreter, effectively silencing her. Isaac Don Levine was also coaching Marina around the same time, on behalf of *Life* magazine, which one must assume connected him to Crichton and Mamantov. It is noteworthy because Frank Wisner hired Levine to develop a secret program to export Russian and Ukrainian émigrés into Germany from other European countries. It means a connection existed with the WCC anti-Communist resistance armies created at that time. Levine was also a board member of the American Friends of Paix et Liberte, was associated with Service d'Ordre du RPF, which worked with the WCC and further connected Levine to the Donovan/Dulles stay-behind armies.[2]

The group operating out of the Havana Embassy in Cuba tried to overthrow Castro in 1959/1960. It included several JFK assassination suspects, such as David Atlee Phillips, David Morales, Henry Hecksher, Paul Bethel, Frank Sturgis, Howard Hunt, Bernard Barker, and June Cobb. These individuals are of interest because some admitted they were involved in the JFK assassination, while eyewitnesses have accused others of taking part in the crime.

Hunt, Morales, and Phillips had worked with Tracy Barnes, Johnny Roselli, and William Pawley in Guatemala during the government takeover in 1954. David Morales and Henry Hecksher worked for William Harvey in Germany while Harvey was CIA station chief there. Bechtel was in the military in Germany at the same time. Morales and Phillips remained close after Guatemala, and Morales would admit involvement in the JFK assassination. He was an assassin who worked with Tony Sforza, another Task Force W assassin connected to the Mafia, Corsican Brotherhood, French killers, drug traffickers, and drug smugglers. June Cobb knew Morales and Sforza well and would follow Phillips to Mexico City and work with him there in 1963.

Morales was involved with John Martino in Havana, which Martino admitted to in his book. Martino was close to Santo Trafficante and admitted involvement in the JFK assassination. We know that Trafficante, Carlos Marcello, and Jimmy Hoffa all knew that Kennedy's assassination would occur before it did. They predicted it, which likely means they were in on the crime, at least at some level. And as mentioned above, Martino was also an alias used by Jean-Pierre Lafitte.

Frank Sturgis was with Operation 40, the Bay of Pigs assassination team that would remain in operation after the failed invasion. They were close to Mario Garcia Kohly, the ultra-right Cuban exile, whose case officer was Tracy Barnes. Sturgis knew Howard Hunt well, and both have been considered assassination suspects for years. Recall that Marita Lorenz accused both of being part of the caravan that traveled to Dallas the day before the assassination. Sturgis also knew John Martino when Sturgis was Minister of Games of Chance under Castro, in charge of the casinos. Because of that, Sturgis also knew Lewis McWillie, who brought Jack Ruby to Cuba to try and get Santo Trafficante out of prison. It creates a possible connection between Ruby and the whole network in Cuba. At the very least, the group in Cuba had to have been aware of Ruby.

Howard Hunt became Bernard Barker's CIA case officer in Miami in the war against Castro while JFK was President. The Washington D.C. police arrested Sturgis, Hunt, and Barker as part of the Watergate burglary, so their relationship lasted many years and was a strong one.

June Cobb connected to Thomas Proctor, Victor Oswald, and Thomas Eli Davis through their association with Proctor. One cannot overstate Cobb's importance in our search for the truth because of her possible association with Oswald in the period leading up to the assassination. She also had a close relationship with David Atlee Phillips, who was alleged by Antonio Veciana, the head of the notorious anti-Castro group Alpha 66, to have been in the company of Oswald in the summer of 1963 when Veciana met with Phillips. At the time, Phillips was using the alias Maurice Bishop. The bottom line is that Cobb and Phillips worked closely together in Cuba, then again in Mexico City. There is evidence that they both associated with Oswald, which is critical because someone had to introduce Oswald into the assassination plot.

Richard Case Nagell called Lee Harvey Oswald the "indispensable tool" in the plot to kill JFK. We know Nagell was aware that Kennedy's assassination would happen, for why else shoot up a bank two months before and have yourself arrested. Nagell also used the Hidell alias, as did Lafitte and Lee Oswald. We know that when the El Paso police arrested him, Nagell had in his wallet a mimeographed newsletter from the Fair Play for Cuba Committee addressed to him, which could indicate a connection to both June Cobb and Oswald.

By his admission, at the beginning of 1963, Nagell was "investigating activities of Anti-Castro organizations and their personnel." He "conducted inquiries relative to 'dissident' members of several Cuban refugee groups based in the United States, including Eladio Del Valle, Sergio Arcacha-Smith, David Ferrie, and Rolando Masferrer." There were others, but Nagell mentioned their names for a reason, perhaps based on what he had learned in the summer of 1963. It was then that he became aware of a plot to kill JFK, the activities of Lee Oswald in New Orleans, and the FPCC. And according to Nagell, it was "a domestic-inspired, domestic-formulated, and domestic-sponsored" plan to assassinate President Kennedy.[3]

The reader should recall the Bolton car dealership incident and their use of Oswald's name while he was still in the Soviet Union. Lafitte, who used the alias' Hidell and Jack Martin, worked with Oswald at the Reily Coffee Company. And that the proprietor at the Jones Printing Company identified Kerry Thornley as the man who picked up Oswald's FPCC handbills, using the alias Osborne. Oswald connected to Guy Banister, David Ferrie, Clay Shaw, and numerous anti-Castro Cuban exiles. For multiple reasons, these people in New Orleans are persons of interest, either as assassination suspects or associates of Oswald. They shed light on his activity during that critical summer in New Orleans in 1963.

This New Orleans group connected with multiple people who wanted Kennedy dead, such as right-wing racist organizations that were flourishing in New Orleans, Dallas, and throughout the South at that time. The Suite 8F Group, Texas oilmen, dirty politicians, disgruntled ex-military generals, paramilitary groups—they were all violently opposed to Kennedy. They supported the segregation plan that the group in New Orleans promoted. They were also closely connected to Carlos Marcello and his drug empire, part of the Havana drug distribution operation, which involved Santo Trafficante and the Dallas drug network, including Jack Ruby. It connected the New Orleans group to the Havana Embassy cabal and the Madrid outfit associated with the Dulles/Donovan/WCC operation. There was a great deal of interconnection between pro-Monarchist Fascists groups in Europe and Fascists in the United States who would have wanted Kennedy killed.

* * *

Oswald's defection almost certainly was an independent operation and had nothing to do with the conspiracy to kill Kennedy, at least at the time of the defection. Still, there are essential questions to be answered. Did the intelligence people who were involved in this operation later become part of the assassination plot? Or did another group know the truth about Oswald's defection and involvement in a mind-altering drug program, and they brought him into the operation because he was the perfect fall guy at whom blame for the assassination the conspirators could direct? Which would explain why he was the indispensable tool, as Nagell described him.

The possibility that U.S. intelligence subjected Oswald to drug experimentation and hypnosis is strong and seemed to follow him throughout his life. There was the Bordentown Reformatory. When Oswald was a boy, the CIA, the military, and George Hunter White all provided mind-altering drugs to children, whom they considered expendable, at that facility. There was Oswald's connection to David Ferrie in New Orleans through the Civil Air Patrol. And the indisputable evidence that Ferrie gave mind-altering drugs to, and conducted hypnosis on, other CAP cadets, including taking them to East Louisiana State Hospital and Latin American with false passports to hide the fact that they were ever there. Oswald's Marine duty was at the Atsugi airbase, where the CIA and military intelligence conducted drug experimentation on military personnel. Oswald's inexplicable hospitalization for a minor wound, incarcerations, strange, abnormal behavior, personality changes, and the special attention he received as if he had a mental health condition. East Louisiana State Hospital in Jackson had a long history of drug experimentation and worked with Tulane University, which also involved in questionable programs. Oswald seemed to be involved with both institutions. Oswald's encounter with New Orleans Assistant D.A. Edward G. Gillin just months before the assassination and his effort to learn more about a specific drug, which was probably LSD. And finally, the Norman, Oklahoma connection may have involved June Cobb, Thomas Davis, and Loren Hall.

The evidence is solid that the Russian Research Center at Harvard University and the Center for International Studies at MIT were involved in Oswald's defection to the Soviet Union. The ex-Socialist Harold Isaacs had a prominent position at the Center for International Studies and, according to eyewitness testimony, was involved with Lee Harvey Oswald and David Ferrie. The CIA file on Oswald's mysterious cousin, Dorothy Murret, focused on Isaacs and had nothing to do with her alleged assassin cousin. Priscilla Johnson was part of the Russian Research Center and was brought into the CIA by Cord Meyer. Meyer's expertise was studying student movements worldwide, so his connection to the Russian Research Center and the Center for International Studies has an extremely high probability level. Johnson and Meyer were one-time proponents of a one-world government (which was how they met) until both became disenchanted with Communists they had dealt with and "grew up," as Johnson put it. Raymond Bauer and Alice Bauer were also with the Russian Research Center and the Center for International Studies, interviewing and evaluating émigrés from behind the Iron Curtain. The FBI was suspicious of Raymond, believing he was a Communist spy acting as a double agent, but maybe he also needed time to "grow up," as did Harold Isaacs. It all concludes that Oswald's defection was an operation established by liberals at the CIA to receive first-hand information about life in the Soviet Union.

As we know, the involvement of CIA liberals with Oswald's defection was not just the Russian Research Center and the Center for International Studies alone. The Unitarians, such as the president of MIT at the time of Oswald's defection, James R. Killian, a Unitarian who allowed Harvard to conduct Project Troy at MIT, probably the defector program that involved Oswald. There was the monitoring of Oswald by Unitarians after he returned to the U.S. from Russia, which included Kerry Thornley, Michael and Ruth Paine, and George de Mohrenschildt's friend Colonel Lawrence Orlov.

* * *

The prime suspects in the assassination of JFK are the CIA and the U.S. military. After World War II, each group tried to create foreign policy, regardless of what the President wanted. By the time of the assassination, a military coup was a real possibility. Congress conducted hearings to look into the matter because there was a real fear that the military might take over the U.S. government. Then there was the CIA and their history of assassinations, all in the name of suppressing Communist expansion. Either group could have murdered the President in the name of defending the U.S. against communism, to which all the assassinations and government overthrows around the world at the time of JFK's murder could attest. The first step in the CIA's blueprint for orchestrating a coup was to bring the military on board, which may have occurred in the plot to kill JFK.

Other groups could have taken part in the assassination as well. The Military-Industrial-Complex would have made the arms industry part of the plot, which they would not have been averse to do if Kennedy intended to kill the golden goose of arms development. There was organized crime, which had a strong working relationship with the CIA and the military since World War II, and the Mafia had a strong motive for wanting Kennedy dead. Texan oilmen and other right-wing aristocrats, like the Suite 8F Group, thought Communists and Communist appeasers ran the U.S. government. These Communists also intended to force racial desegregation upon them and destroy the White Supremacist utopia they wanted to maintain. There were Christian/Fascist paramilitary types. Anti-Semitic and anti-African American racist groups. They had a propensity for violence and felt the same way. That the end of self-determination and the American way of life was near unless they did something dramatic to stop it; these groups had a connection to the CIA/military alliance, for many of MacArthur's retired high-level officers were members of these racist groups.

Any of these groups, or individuals from various groups, could have been involved in the JFK assassination conspiracy, for they were so intertwined that anything was possible. Their motives for wanting Kennedy dead varied, but the desired result was the same for all.

Since a liberal group and a conservative group existed within the CIA, would they have worked together in something as monumental as an American president's assassination? The answer is probably not. So, the question then becomes, which group at CIA would have benefited most from a changing of the guard? What was their motivation, and with whom did they associate? And if the liberals at the CIA ran Oswald's defection, does that imply they were involved in the assassination plot? Or did the left-wing apparatus at CIA set up Oswald as the fall guy to destroy the Omega Plan and sabotage a proposed invasion of Cuba right after the assassination? Or was the right-wing responsible for JFK's assassination? They brought Oswald into the plot, knowing that the post-assassination investigation would be a cover-up to hide everything they had done to Oswald related to his defection? It raises another question. Was the arrest of Oswald not supposed to have happened? Did it force the right-wing conspirators to abort the Omega Plan invasion of Cuba because Oswald was supposed to escape? And his arrest destroyed the narrative that a Soviet assassin had been sent to the U.S. to kill Kennedy.

Recall the Oswald height differential, the fake documents, and other information that point in this direction. Had Oswald escaped from Dallas, there would not have been a Jack Ruby murder of Oswald. And the only wallet found would have been at the Tippit murder scene, with A.J. Hidell and Lee Harvey Oswald identification cards within the wallet. It would confirm that a Soviet assassin was responsible for the assassination. With a missing Oswald, wouldn't there have been ample justification for invading Cuba and removing Castro? Of course, there would have, but Oswald's arrest made this impossible.

It is also interesting that after Kennedy's assassination, Cuba would become less critical to the United States. Within a year, the Gulf of Tonkin incident would take place in Vietnam, and the focus of America's military would shift to containing the spread of communism in Southeast Asia. Why was that? Is it possible that the reason behind JFK's assassination was to prevent an invasion of Cuba from occurring because they were afraid the Soviets would retaliate by moving into West Berlin? Did Oswald become involved because the liberal group at the CIA knew the details of his defection, and they understood that authorities would cover up a post-assassination investigation to keep that hidden? Allen Dulles had already thwarted one Cuban invasion to prevent this from happening when he sold out William Morgan and his compadres. Did he do it again?

One thing is sure. Lee Harvey Oswald knew a great deal about things that U.S. intelligence could never disclose. Why else was he murdered live on national television by a small-time thug like Jack Ruby? Ruby silenced Oswald before he could talk. It says a lot about who Oswald was and what he may have known about the assassination plot, as well as things unrelated to the assassination, such as his defection and potential mind-altering drug experiments. It warranted the need to silence him. And who would have forced Jack Ruby to kill Oswald? The Mafia is a logical choice, but Ruby blamed the right-wing, who worked closely with the Mafia for many years, for placing him in his predicament. Perhaps they collaborated once again in Dallas.

Finally, the assassination of John F. Kennedy demonstrates how distorted the official record of American history has been since the founding of the nation. There have always been two American histories—the truth and the sanitized version. We have been fed the latter throughout the years as being a factual representation of what happened. Much of it is a lie. There was a time when Americans accepted this, but this is no longer the case. Twenty-First Century Americans are too smart to blindly accept questionable historical accounts at face value.

Today, those of us who demand that the truth be told have pushed aside the veil that has hidden America's sins, no matter how painful this might be. Many have suffered through the years. And those without the means to protect themselves were especially vulnerable, people of color most of all. It characterized the Cold War. And it was all done as a disguised attempt to preserve the American way of life and self-determination, for those involved in one unconscionable misdeed after another knew the American people would never accept what a misguided minority was doing—if they only knew.

The purpose of Volumes One and Two was to reveal what was happening in America in the years leading up to Kennedy's Presidency, how it eventually led to JFK's murder, and to answer why Kennedy had to die. Because if I could demonstrate that the assassination did not occur in a vacuum, it would be easier to accept and understand that an assassination conspiracy occurred. That it was just a continuation of a series of heinous acts over decades that defy what we thought America stood for. Hopefully, I have succeeded in that endeavor, but it is only the beginning.

The attempt to force America's anti-Communist agenda on the world worsened under JFK. Those opposed to Kennedy assassinated him to prevent the introduction of changes that would alter the basic fabric of America's domestic and foreign policies. That Kennedy was killed for this reason is indisputable. As is the fact that he and his brother Robert tried to reign in the "Deep State" and "Drain the Swamp," long before it was fashionable to want to do that.

My next book will continue where this book leaves off and will focus on 1961 through 1963. It will cover the Kennedy Presidency and examine the assassination in sufficient detail, clearly and concisely, to prove a conspiracy killed JFK. There is no question that this is a fact, and the idea that Oswald acted alone is so riddled with holes that it is impossible to accept.

Oswald's tragic story will be covered, beginning with his time spent in Russia, his return to the United States, his introduction to the assassination plot, and the events connected to November 22, 1963. There is no doubt Oswald was involved. However, this does not preclude the possibility that he was still a patsy. Unraveling this mystery is one of the keys to understanding what transpired that day in Dallas.

We will also investigate Kennedy's Presidency and why his policies so offended the conspirators that their only option was to assassinate him. The likely suspects who were most likely responsible for the assassination will be exposed. And the many questions posed in this book but remain unanswered will be addressed in detail, for the evidence does not lie.

Notes

Chapter One: Fighting Communism in the Big Easy is Not Easy

1. Osgood, Kenneth, *Total Cold War, Eisenhower's Secret Propaganda Battle at Home and Abroad*, Lawrence, Kansas, University Press of Kansas, 2006.

2. Minutaglio, Bill, and Davis, Steven L., *Dallas 1963*, New York, New York, Hachette Book Group, 2013.

3. Caufield, M.D., Jeffrey H., *General Walker and the Murder of President Kennedy, The Extensive New Evidence of a Radical-Right Conspiracy*, Moreland Press, 2015.

4. Fried, Richard M., *Nightmare in Red*, The McCarthy Era in Perspective, New York, New York, Oxford University Press, 1990.

5. Caufield, *General Walker and the Murder of President Kennedy, The Extensive New Evidence of a Radical-Right Conspiracy*.

6. Johnson, Robert David, *Congress and the Cold War*, Cambridge University Press, New York, New York, 2005.

7. Lateer, J.W., *The Three Barons, The Organizational Chart of the Kennedy Assassination*, Walterville, Oregon, Trine Day, 2017.

8. Caufield, *General Walker and the Murder of President Kennedy, The Extensive New Evidence of a Radical-Right Conspiracy*.

9. Fried, *Nightmare in Red, The McCarthy Era in Perspective*.

10. Caufield, *General Walker and the Murder of President Kennedy, The Extensive New Evidence of a Radical-Right Conspiracy*.

11. Ibid.

12. Ibid.

13. Fairclough, Adam, *Race and Democracy: The Civil Rights Struggle in Louisiana, 1915-1972*, University of Georgia Press, Athens, Georgia, 1995.

14. Summers, Anthony, *Conspiracy*, New York, New York, McGraw-Hill Book Company, 1980.

15. Epstein, Edward Jay, *Legend, The Secret World of Lee Harvey Oswald*, New York, New York, McGraw-Hill Book Company, 1978.

16. Ibid.

17. Voebel, Edward, testimony of, *Hearings Before the President's Commission on the Assassination of President Kennedy*, Volume VIII, Washington D.C., Government Printing Office, 1964.

18. Caufield, *General Walker and the Murder of President Kennedy, The Extensive New Evidence of a Radical-Right Conspiracy*.

19. Ibid.

20. Ibid.

21. Botelho, James, affidavit from, *Hearings Before the President's Commission on the Assassination of President Kennedy*, , Washington D.C., Government Printing Office, 1964, from History-matters.com/archive/jfk/wc/wcvols/wh8/pdf/WH8_Botelho_aff.pdf.

22. Allaboutphilosophy.org/what-is-marxism-faq.htm

23. Russell, Dick, *The Man Who Knew Too Much*, New York, New York, Carroll & Graf Publishers/Richard Gallen, 1992.

24. Romerstein, Herbert, and Breindel, Eric, *The Venona Secrets, Exposing Soviet Espionage and America's Traitors*, Washington, D.C., Regency Publishing, Inc., 2000.

25. Russell, *The Man Who Knew Too Much.*

26. Caufield, *General Walker and the Murder of President Kennedy, The Extensive New Evidence of a Radical-Right Conspiracy.*

27. Ibid.

28. Summers, *Conspiracy.*

29. *Report of the House Select Committee on Assassinations* – Appendix to Hearings, Volumes IX & X, Washington D.C., United States Government Printing Office, 1979.

30. Caufield, *General Walker and the Murder of President Kennedy, The Extensive New Evidence of a Radical-Right Conspiracy.*

31. Epstein, *Legend, The Secret World of Lee Harvey Oswald.*

32. Summers, *Conspiracy.*

33. Caufield, *General Walker and the Murder of President Kennedy, The Extensive New Evidence of a Radical-Right Conspiracy.*

34. Ibid., and Mellen, *A Farewell to Justice, Jim Garrison, JFK's Assassination, and the Case That Should Have Changed History.*

35. Summers, *Conspiracy.*

36. North, Mark, *Act of Treason, The Role of J. Edgar Hoover in the Assassination of President Kennedy,* New York, New York, Carroll & Graf Publishers, 1991.

37. Epstein, *Legend, The Secret World of Lee Harvey Oswald.*

38. Albarelli, H.P. Jr., *A Secret Order, Investigating the High Strangeness and Synchronicity in the JFK Assassination,* Walterville, Oregon, Trine Day, 2013.

39. Russell, Dick, *On the Trail of the JFK Assassins, A Groundbreaking look at America's Most Infamous Conspiracy,* New York, New York, Skyhorse Publishing, 2008.

40. Albarelli, *A Secret Order, Investigating the High Strangeness and Synchronicity in the JFK Assassination.*

41. Russell, *On the Trail of the JFK Assassins, A Groundbreaking look at America's Most Infamous Conspiracy.*

42. Heath, Dr. Robert, https://en.wikipedia.org/wiki/Robert_Galbraith_Heath

43. Russell, Dick, *On the Trail of the JFK Assassins, A Groundbreaking look at America's Most Infamous Conspiracy.*

44. Albarelli, *A Secret Order, Investigating the High Strangeness and Synchronicity in the JFK Assassination.*

45. Ibid.

46. Ibid.

47. Carpenter, Donald H., *Man of a Million Fragments, The True Story of Clay Shaw,* Nashville, Tennessee, published by Donald Carpenter, 2014, and Mellen, *A Farewell to Justice, Jim Garrison, JFK's Assassination, and the Case That Should Have Changed History.*

48. Carrozza, Anthony R., *William D. Pawley, The Extraordinary Life of the Adventurer, Entrepreneur, and Diplomat Who Cofounded the Flying Tigers,* Washington D.C., Potomac Books, 2012

49. Carpenter, *Man of a Million Fragments, The True Story of Clay Shaw.*

50. Ibid.

51. Summers, *Conspiracy.*

52. Albarelli, *A Secret Order, Investigating the High Strangeness and Synchronicity in the JFK Assassination.*

53. Summers, *Conspiracy.*

54. Mellen, *A Farewell to Justice, Jim Garrison, JFK's Assassination, and the Case That Should Have Changed History.*

55. Caufield, *General Walker and the Murder of President Kennedy, The Extensive New Evidence of a Radical-Right Conspiracy.*

56. Carpenter, *Man of a Million Fragments, The True Story of Clay Shaw.*

57. Mellen, *A Farewell to Justice, Jim Garrison, JFK's Assassination, and the Case That Should Have Changed History.*

58. Ibid.

59. Ibid.

60. Ibid.

61. Carpenter, *Man of a Million Fragments, The True Story of Clay Shaw.*

62. Haslam, Edward T., *Dr. Mary's Monkey, How the unsolved murder of a doctor, a secret laboratory in New Orleans and cancer-causing monkey viruses are linked to Lee Harvey Oswald, the JFK assassination and emerging global epidemics,* Walterville, Oregon, Trine Day, 2007.

63. Ibid.

64. Ibid.

65. Carpenter, *Man of a Million Fragments, The True Story of Clay Shaw.*

66. Ibid.

67. DiEugenio, James, *Destiny Betrayed, JFK, Cuba, and the Garrison Case*, New York, New York, Sheridan Square Press, 1992, and Mellen, *A Farewell to Justice, Jim Garrison, JFK's Assassination, and the Case That Should Have Changed History.*

68. Russell, *On the Trail of the JFK Assassins, A Groundbreaking look at America's Most Infamous Conspiracy.*

69. Mellen, *A Farewell to Justice, Jim Garrison, JFK's Assassination, and the Case That Should Have Changed History*, and Haslam, *Dr. Mary's Monkey.*

70. Garrison, Jim, *On the Trail of the Assassins: One Man's Quest to Solve the Murder of President Kennedy*, New York, New York, Warner Books, 1988.

71. Caufield, *General Walker and the Murder of President Kennedy, The Extensive New Evidence of a Radical-Right Conspiracy.*

72. Russell, *The Man Who Knew Too Much.*

73. Newman, John, *Oswald and the CIA*, New York, New York, Carroll & Graf Publishers, Inc., 1995, and Carpenter, *Man of a Million Fragments, The True Story of Clay Shaw.*

Chapter Two: There's Trouble in Paradise

1. Rovner, Eduardo Saenz, *The Cuban Connection, Drug Trafficking, Smuggling, and Gambling in Cuba from the 1920s to the Revolution*, Chapel Hill, North Carolina, The University of North Carolina Press, 2008.

2. Hinckle, Warren, and Turner, William, *The Fish is Red, The Story of the Secret War Against Castro*, New York, New York, Harper & Row Publishers, 1981.

3. Archer, Jules, *Thorn In Our Flesh: Castro's Cuba*, New York, New York, Cowles Book Co., 1970.

4. Marrs, Jim, *Crossfire, The Plot That Killed Kennedy*, New York, New York, Carroll & Graf Publishers, Inc., 1989.

5. Paget, Karen M., *Patriotic Betrayal*, New Haven Connecticut, Yale University Press, 2015.

6. Ibid.

7. Hinckle and Turner, *The Fish is Red, The Story of the Secret War Against Castro.*

8. *Ibid.*

9. Archer, *Thorn In Our Flesh, Castro's Cuba.*

10. Marrs, *Crossfire, The Plot That Killed Kennedy.*

11. Kaiser, David, *The Road to Dallas, The Assassination of John F. Kennedy*, Cambridge, Massachusetts, The Belknap Press of Harvard University Press, 2008.

12. Archer, *Thorn In Our Flesh, Castro's Cuba.*

13. Albarelli, H.P. Jr., *A Secret Order, Investigating the High Strangeness and Synchronicity in the JFK Assassination*, Walterville, Oregon, Trine Day, 2013.

14. Ibid.

15. Albarelli, H.P. Jr., *A Terrible Mistake, The Murder of Frank Olson and the CIA's Secret Cold War Experiments*, Walterville, Oregon, Trine Day, 2009.

16. Ibid.

17. Albarelli, *A Secret Order, Investigating the High Strangeness and Synchronicity in the JFK Assassination.*

18. Ibid.

19. Mellen, Joan, *The Great Game in Cuba, How the CIA Sabotaged Its Own Plot to Unseat Fidel Castro*, New York, New York, Skyhorse Publishing, 2013.

20. English, T.J., *Havana Nocturne, How the Mob Owned Cuba…and Then Lost It to the Revolution*, New York, New York, HarperCollins Publishers, 2008.

21. Hinckle and Turner, *The Fish is Red, The Story of the Secret War Against Castro.*

22. Fursenko, Aleksandr, and Naftali, Timothy, *One Hell of a Gamble, The Secret History of the Cuban Missile Crisis, Khrushchev, Castro & Kennedy, 1958-1964*, New York, New York, W.W. Norton & Company, 1997.

23. Kaiser, *The Road to Dallas, The Assassination of John F. Kennedy.*

24. Carrozza, Anthony R., *William D. Pawley, The Extraordinary Life of the Adventurer, Entrepreneur, and Diplomat Who Cofounded the Flying Tigers*, Washington D.C., Potomac Books, 2012.

25. Ibid.

26. Ibid.

27. Dorschner, John, and Fabricio, Roberto, *The Winds Of December, The Cuban Revolution of 1958, The Dramatic, Behind-the-Scenes Story of Castro's Revolution*, New York, New York, Putnam Publishing Group, 1980.

28. English, *Havana Nocturne, How the Mob Owned Cuba…and Then Lost It to the Revolution.*

29. Russo, Gus, *Live By the Sword, The Secret War Against Castro and the Death of JFK*, Baltimore, Maryland, Bancroft Press, 1998.

30. Kaiser, *The Road to Dallas, The Assassination of John F. Kennedy*, and English, *Havana Nocturne, How the Mob Owned Cuba…and Then Lost It to the Revolution.*

31. Valentine, Douglas, *The Strength of the Wolf, The Secret History of America's War on Drugs*, London, England, Verso, 2004.

32. Ibid.

33. Rovner, *The Cuban Connection, Drug Trafficking, Smuggling, and Gambling in Cuba from the 1920s to the Revolution.*

34. Waldron, Lamar, and Hartmann, Thom, *Ultimate Sacrifice, John and Robert Kennedy, the Plan for a Coup in Cuba, and the Murder of JFK*, New York, New York, Carroll & Graf Publishers, 2005.

35. Waldron, Lamar, *The Hidden History of the JFK Assassination, The Definitive Account of the Most Controversial Crime of the Twentieth Century*, Berkeley, California, Counterpoint, 2013.

36. Waldron and Hartmann, *Ultimate Sacrifice, John and Robert Kennedy, the Plan for a Coup in Cuba, and the Murder of JFK.*

37. Ibid.

38. Ibid.

39. Kaiser, *The Road to Dallas, The Assassination of John F. Kennedy.*

40. Ibid.

41. Marrs, *Crossfire, The Plot That Killed Kennedy.*

42. Weberman, Alan J., and Canfield, Michael, *Coup D' Etat In America, The CIA and the Assassination of John F. Kennedy*, San Francisco, The Third Press, 1975.

43. Waldron and Hartmann, *Ultimate Sacrifice, John and Robert Kennedy, the Plan for a Coup in Cuba, and the Murder of JFK.*

44. Weberman and Canfield, *Coup D' Etat In America, The CIA and the Assassination of John F. Kennedy.*

45. Ibid.

46. Ibid.

47. Ibid.

48. Scheim, David E., *Contract on America, The Mafia Murder of President John F. Kennedy*, New York, New York, Shapolsky Publishers, Inc., 1988; English, *Havana Nocturne, How the Mob Owned Cuba…and Then Lost It to the Revolution*; Kaiser, *The Road to Dallas, The Assassination of John F. Kennedy*; and Summers, *Conspiracy.*

49. Kaiser, *The Road to Dallas, The Assassination of John F. Kennedy.*

50. Cobb, Viola June, testimony of, *Hearings before the Subcommittee to Investigate the Administraiton of the Internal Security Act and other Internal Security Laws of the Committee on the Judiciary*, United States Senate, Eight-Ninth Congress, Second Session, March 30, 1962.

51. Ibid.

52. Ibid., and Russo, Gus, and Molton, Stephen, *Brothers in Arms: The Kennedys, the Castros, and the Politics of Murder*, New York, New York, Bloomsbury USA, 2008.

53. Fonzi, Garton, *The Last Investigation, A former Federal Investigator for the House Select Committee on Assassinations breaks his oath of silence and tells what insiders know about the assassination of John F. Kennedy*, New York, New York, Thunder's Mouth Press, 1993.

54. Newman, John, *Oswald and the CIA*, New York, New York, Carroll & Graf Publishers, Inc., 1995, and Fonzi, *The Last Investigation, A former Federal Investigator for the House Select Committee on Assassinations breaks his oath of silence and tells what insiders know about the assassination of John F. Kennedy.*

55. Fonzi, *The Last Investigation, A former Federal Investigator for the House Select Committee on Assassinations breaks his oath of silence and tells what insiders know about the assassination of John F. Kennedy.*

56. Ibid.

57. Newman, *Oswald and the CIA*.

58. Ibid. and Albarelli, *A Secret Order, Investigating the High Strangeness and Synchronicity in the JFK Assassination*.

59. Albarelli, *A Secret Order, Investigating the High Strangeness and Synchronicity in the JFK Assassination*.

60. Ibid.

61. Newman, *Oswald and the CIA*.

62. Ibid.

63. Fleming, Tim, *JFK and the End of America, Inside the Allen Dulles/LBJ Plot That Killed Kennedy*, Strategic Book Publishing and Rights Co., 2018, and Albarelli, *A Secret Order, Investigating the High Strangeness and Synchronicity in the JFK Assassination*.

64. Weberman, Alan Jules, *The Oswald Code*, Createspace Independent Publishers, 2014, and Albarelli, *A Secret Order, Investigating the High Strangeness and Synchronicity in the JFK Assassination*.

65. Hilts, Philip, "Louis J. West, 74, Psychiatrist Who Studied Extremes, Dies," *The New York Times* article, January 9, 1999.

66. Mirror.co.uk/news/world-news/lee-harvey-oswalds-killer-jack-957093

67. Albarelli, *A Secret Order, Investigating the High Strangeness and Synchronicity in the JFK Assassination*.

68. Ibid.

69. Russo and Molten, *Brothers in Arms: The Kennedys, the Castros, and the Politics of Murder*.

70. Shenon, Philip, *A Cruel and Shocking Act, The Secret History of the Kennedy Assassination*, New York, New York, Henry Holt and Company, 2013.

71. Aravalo, Juan Jose, "The Shark and the Sardines,", *Kirkus*, from Kirkusreviews.com/book-reviews/juan-jose-arevalo/the-shark-and-the-sardines/

Chapter Three: One Good Revolution Deserves Another

1. Rovner, Eduardo Saenz, *The Cuban Connection, Drug Trafficking, Smuggling, and Gambling in Cuba from the 1920s to the Revolution*, Chapel Hill, North Carolina, The University of North Carolina Press, 2008.

2. Ibid.

3. Ibid., and Fursenko, Aleksandr, and Naftali, Timothy, *One Hell of a Gamble, The Secret History of the Cuban Missile Crisis, Khrushchev, Castro & Kennedy, 1958-1964*, New York, New York, W.W. Norton & Company, 1997.

4. Glass, Andrew, "Fidel Castro visits the U.S., April 15, 1959," *Politico*, from www.politico.com/story/2013/04/this-day-in-politics-april-1959-090037

5. Rovner, Eduardo Saenz, *The Cuban Connection, Drug Trafficking, Smuggling, and Gambling in Cuba from the 1920s to the Revolution*.

6. Waldron, Lamar, and Hartmann, Thom, *Ultimate Sacrifice, John and Robert Kennedy, the Plan for a Coup in Cuba, and the Murder of JFK*, New York, New York, Carroll & Graf Publishers, 2005, and English, T.J., *Havana Nocturne, How the Mob Owned Cuba…and Then Lost It to the Revolution*, New York, New York, HarperCollins Publishers, 2008.

7. Waldron and Hartmann, *Ultimate Sacrifice, John and Robert Kennedy, the Plan for a Coup in Cuba*.

8. Ibid.

9. Russo, Gus, *Live By the Sword, The Secret War Against Castro and the Death of JFK*, Baltimore, Maryland, Bancroft Press, 1998.

10. Fonzi, Garton, *The Last Investigation, A former Federal Investigator for the House Select Committee on Assassinations breaks his oath of silence and tells what insiders know about the assassination of John F. Kennedy*, New York, New York, Thunder's Mouth Press, 1993.

11. Ibid.

12. Albarelli, H.P. Jr., *A Secret Order, Investigating the High Strangeness and Synchronicity in the JFK Assassination*, Walterville, Oregon, Trine Day, 2013.

13. Weberman, Alan Jules, *The Oswald Code*, Createspace Independent Publishers, 2014, and *The San Francisco Sunday Examiner* article, June 22, 1975.

14. Kaiser, David, *The Road to Dallas, The Assassination of John F. Kennedy*, Cambridge, Massachusetts, The Belknap Press of Harvard University Press, 2008, and Waldron and Hartmann, *Ultimate Sacrifice, John and Robert Kennedy, the Plan for a Coup in Cuba*.

15. Waldron and Hartmann, *Ultimate Sacrifice, John and Robert Kennedy, the Plan for a Coup in Cuba*, and Albarelli, *A Secret Order, Investigating the High Strangeness and Synchronicity in the JFK Assassination*.

16. Ibid.

17. Russell, Dick, *On the Trail of the JFK Assassins, A Groundbreaking look at America's Most Infamous Conspiracy*, New York, New York, Skyhorse Publishing, 2008; Waldron and Hartmann, *Ultimate Sacrifice, John and Robert Kennedy, the Plan for a Coup in Cuba*; and Albarelli, *A Secret Order, Investigating the High Strangeness and Synchronicity in the JFK Assassination*.

18. Russell, *On the Trail of the JFK Assassins, A Groundbreaking look at America's Most Infamous Conspiracy*.

19. Waldron and Hartmann, *Ultimate Sacrifice, John and Robert Kennedy, the Plan for a Coup in Cuba*.

20. Shaw, Mark, *The Reporter Who Knew Too Much, The Mysterious Death of What's My Line TV Star and Media Icon Dorothy Kilgallen*, New York, New York, Post Hill Press, 2016.

21. Waldron and Hartmann, *Ultimate Sacrifice, John and Robert Kennedy, the Plan for a Coup in Cuba*.

22. *Hearings Before the President's Commission on the Assassination of President Kennedy*, Volume V, Washington D.C., Government Printing Office, 1964.

23. Waldron and Hartmann, *Ultimate Sacrifice, John and Robert Kennedy, the Plan for a Coup in Cuba*.

24. Fonzi, *The Last Investigation, A former Federal Investigator for the House Select Committee on Assassinations breaks his oath of silence and tells what insiders know about the assassination of John F. Kennedy*.

25. Waldron and Hartmann, *Ultimate Sacrifice, John and Robert Kennedy, the Plan for a Coup in Cuba*, and Kaiser, *The Road to Dallas, The Assassination of John F. Kennedy*.

26. Waldron and Hartmann, *Ultimate Sacrifice, John and Robert Kennedy, the Plan for a Coup in Cuba*.

27. Kaiser, *The Road to Dallas, The Assassination of John F. Kennedy*.

28. Mellen, Joan, *The Great Game in Cuba, How the CIA Sabotaged Its Own Plot to Unseat Fidel Castro*, New York, New York, Skyhorse Publishing, 2013, and *The San Francisco Sunday Examiner* article, June 22, 1975

29. Thomas, Evan, *Ike's Bluff, President Eisenhower's Secret Battle to Save the World*, New York, New York, Little, Brown and Company, 2012.

30. Waldron and Hartmann, *Ultimate Sacrifice, John and Robert Kennedy, the Plan for a Coup in Cuba*.

31. Hunt, Howard, deposition dated November 3, 1978, *Report of the House Select Committee on Assassinations*, Washington D.C., United States Government Printing Office, 1979.

32. Mellen, *The Great Game in Cuba, How the CIA Sabotaged Its Own Plot to Unseat Fidel Castro*, and Kaiser, *The Road to Dallas, The Assassination of John F. Kennedy*.

33. Waldron and Hartmann, *Ultimate Sacrifice, John and Robert Kennedy, the Plan for a Coup in Cuba*.

34. Ibid.

35. Ibid.

36. Ibid.

37. Valentine, Douglas, *The Strength of the Wolf, The Secret History of America's War on Drugs*, London, England, Verso, 2004; McCoy, Alfred W., *The Politics of Heroin in Southeast Asia*, New York, New York, Harper and Row, 1972, and Kaiser, *The Road to Dallas, The Assassination of John F. Kennedy*.

38. English, *Havana Nocturne, How the Mob Owned Cuba…and Then Lost It to the Revolution*.

39. Blakey, G. Robert, and Billings, Richard N., *The Plot to Kill the President, Organized Crimed Assassinated J.F.K., The Definitive Story*, New York, New York, Times Books, 1981.

40. Ibid.

41. Ibid.

42. Kantor, Seth, *The Ruby Cover-up*, New York, New York, Kensington Publishing Corp., 1978.

43. Fensterwald, Bernard Jr., *Assassination of JFK by Coincidence or Conspiracy?*, New York, New York, Kensington Publishing Corp., 1977.

44. Marrs, Jim, *Crossfire, The Plot That Killed Kennedy*, New York, New York, Carroll & Graf Publishers, Inc., 1989.

45. Lane, Mark, *Plausible Denial, Was the CIA Involved in the Assassination of JFK?*, New York, New York, Thunder's Mouth Press, 1991.

Chapter Four: Treason is a Deadly Business

1. Osgood, Kenneth, *Total Cold War, Eisenhower's Secret Propaganda Battle at Home and Abroad*, Lawrence, Kansas, University Press of Kansas, 2006.

2. Thomas, Evan, *Ike's Bluff, President Eisenhower's Secret Battle to Save the World*, New York, New York, Little, Brown and Company, 2012.

3. Jacobsen, Annie, *The Pentagon's Brain, An Uncensored History of DARPA, America's Top Secret Military Research Agency*, New York, New York, Little, Brown and Company, 2015.

4. Beschloss, Michael R., *May-Day, Eisenhower, Khrushchev and the U-2 Affair*, New York, New York, Harper & Row Publishers, 1986.

5. Sherrill, Robert, *The Accidental President*, Pyramid Bools, New York, New York, 1968, and North, Mark, *Act of Treason, The Role of J. Edgar Hoover in the Assassination of President Kennedy*, New York, New York, Carroll & Graf Publishers, 1991.

6. Thomas, *Ike's Bluff, President Eisenhower's Secret Battle to Save the World*.

7. Ibid.

8. Ibid., and Gaddis, John Lewis, Strategies of Containment, A Critical Appraisal of Postwar American National Security Policy, New York, New York, Oxford University Press, 1982.

9. Jacobsen, The Pentagon's Brain, An Uncensored History of DARPA, America's Top Secret Military Research Agency.

10. Gaddis, Strategies of Containment, A Critical Appraisal of Postwar American National Security Policy.

11. Thomas, Ike's Bluff, President Eisenhower's Secret Battle to Save the World.

12. Swanson, Michael, *The War State, The Cold War Origins of the Military-Industrial Complex and the Power Elite, 1945-1963*, North Charleston, South Carolina, CreateSpace Independent Publishing Platform, 2013.

13. Binder, L. James, *Lemnitzer, A Soldier for His Time*, Washington, D.C., Brassey's, 1997.

14. Ibid.

15. Osgood, *Total Cold War, Eisenhower's Secret Propaganda Battle at Home and Abroad*.

16. Thomas, *Ike's Bluff, President Eisenhower's Secret Battle to Save the World*.

17. Binder, *Lemnitzer, A Soldier for His Time*.

18. Osgood, *Total Cold War, Eisenhower's Secret Propaganda Battle at Home and Abroad*.

19. Binder, *Lemnitzer, A Soldier for His Time*.

20. Ibid.

21. Lateer, J.W., *The Three Barons, The Organizational Chart of the Kennedy Assassination*, Walterville, Oregon, Trine Day, 2017.

22. Binder, *Lemnitzer, A Soldier for His Time*.

23. Swanson, *The War State, The Cold War Origins of the Military-Industrial Complex and the Power Elite, 1945-1963*.

24. Wyden, Peter, *Bay of Pigs, The Untold Story*, New York, New York, Simon and Schuster, 1979.

25. Rasenberger, Jim, *Brilliant Disaster, JFK, Castro, and America's Doomed Invasion of Cuba's Bay of Pigs*, New York, New York, Scribner, 2011; and
"Alleged Assassination Plots Involving Foreign Leaders," Interim Report of *U.S. Senate Select Committee to Study Governmental Operations,* 1975.

26. Rasenberger, *Brilliant Disaster, JFK, Castro, and America's Doomed Invasion of Cuba's Bay of Pigs*.

27. Ibid.

28. Fursenko, Aleksandr, and Naftali, Timothy, *One Hell of a Gamble, The Secret History of the Cuban Missile Crisis, Khrushchev, Castro & Kennedy, 1958-1964*, New York, New York, W.W. Norton & Company, 1997.

29. Rasenberger, *Brilliant Disaster, JFK, Castro, and America's Doomed Invasion of Cuba's Bay of Pigs*.

30. Newman, John, *Oswald and the CIA*, New York, New York, Carroll & Graf Publishers, Inc., 1995.

31. Fursenko and Naftali, *One Hell of a Gamble, The Secret History of the Cuban Missile Crisis*.

32. Rasenberger, *Brilliant Disaster, JFK, Castro, and America's Doomed Invasion of Cuba's Bay of Pigs*.

33. Ranelagh, John, *The Agency, The Rise and Decline of the CIA*, New York, New York, Simon and Schuster, 1986.

34. Hunt, Howard, *Give Us This Day, The Inside Story of the CIA and the Bay of Pigs Invasion…By One of Its Key Organizers*, New York, New York, Arlington House, 1973.

35. Powers, Thomas, *The Man Who Kept The Secrets, Richard Helms and the CIA*, New York, New York, Alfred A. Knopf, 1979, and Smith, Joseph B., *Portrait of a Cold Warrior: Second Thoughts of a Top CIA Agent*, New York, New York, Ballantine Books, 1976.

36. Newman, *Oswald and the CIA*.

37. Ranelagh, *The Agency, The Rise and Decline of the CIA*.

38. Ibid.

39. Ibid.

40. Ibid.

41. Morrow, Robert, *First Hand Knowledge, How I Participated In The CIA-Mafia Murder Of President Kennedy*, New York, New York, Shapolsky Publishers Inc., 1992.

42. Ibid.

43. Smith, *Portrait of a Cold Warrior: Second Thoughts of a Top CIA Agent*.

44. Weberman, Alan J., and Canfield, Michael, *Coup D' Etat In America*, San Fransisco, The Third Press, 1975.

45. Pawley

46. Weberman, Alan Jules, *The Oswald Code*, New York, New York, Independent Research Associates, 2014.

47. Newman, *Oswald and the CIA*.

48. Newman, *Oswald and the CIA*, and Caufield, M.D., Jeffrey H., *General Walker and the Murder of President Kennedy, The Extensive New Evidence of a Radical-Right Conspiracy*, Moreland Press, 2015.

49. Weberman, *The Oswald Code*.

50. Mellen, *A Farewell to Justice*.

51. Carrozza, Anthony R., *William D. Pawley, The Extraordinary Life of the Adventurer, Entrepreneur, and Diplomat Who Cofounded the Flying Tigers*, Washington D.C., Potomac Books, 2012.

52. Ibid.

53. Ibid.

54. Johnson, Haynes, *The Bay of Pigs, The Leaders' Story of Brigade 2506*, New York, New York, Dell Publishing Co., Inc., 1964.

55. Wise, David, and Ross, Thomas B., *The Invisible Government*, New York, New York, Random House Inc., 1964

56. Johnson, *The Bay of Pigs, The Leaders' Story of Brigade 2506*.

57. Morrow, *First Hand Knowledge, How I Participated In The CIA-MAfia Murder Of President Kennedy*.

58. Ibid.

59. Waldron, Lamar, and Hartmann, Thom, *Ultimate Sacrifice, John and Robert Kennedy, the Plan for a Coup in Cuba, and the Murder of JFK*, New York, New York, Carroll & Graf Publishers, 2005.

60. Weberman, *The Oswald Code*.

61. Hinckle, Warren, and Turner, William, *The Fish is Red, The Story of the Secret War Against Castro*, New York, New York, Harper & Row Publishers, 1981.

62. Ibid.

63. Weberman and Canfield, *Coup D' Etat In America*.

64. Waldron and Hartmann, *Ultimate Sacrifice, John and Robert Kennedy, the Plan for a Coup in Cuba, and the Murder of JFK*.

65. Hinckle and Turner, *The Fish is Red, The Story of the Secret War Against Castro*.

66. Fonzi, Garton, *The Last Investigation, A former Federal Investigator for the House Select Committee on Assassinations breaks his oath of silence and tells what insiders know about the assassination of John F. Kennedy*, New York, New York, Thunder's Mouth Press, 1993.

67. Russell, Dick, *The Man Who Knew Too Much*, New York, New York, Carroll & Graf Publishers/ Richard Gallen, 1992.

Chapter Five: Deadly Liaisons

1. Gentry, Curt, *J.Edgar Hoover, The Man and the Secrets*, New York, New York, W.W. Norton & Company, Inc., 1991.

2. Kennedy, John F., *The Strategy of Peace*, Harper & Row. New York, New York, 1960.

3. Ibid.

4. Corsi, Jerome R., P.H.D., *Who Really Killed Kennedy?, 50 Years Later, Stunning New Revelations about the JFK Assassination*, Washington, D.C., WND Books, 2013.

5. Ibid.

6. Ibid.

7. Ibid.

8. Valentine, Douglas, *The Strength of the Wolf, The Secret History of America's War on Drugs*, London, England, Verso, 2004.

9. Burbank, Jeff, "Robert Kennedy's Crusade Against the Mob: Part 2, *The Mob Museum*," themobmuseum.org/blog/robert-f-kennedys-crusade-mob-part-2/

10. North, Mark, *Betrayal in Dallas, LBJ, The Pearl Street Mafia, and the Murder of President Kennedy*, New York, New York, Skyhorse Publishing, 2011.

11. Trento, Joseph J., *The Secret History of the CIA*, New York, New York, MJF Books, 2001, Burbank, "Robert Kennedy's Crusade Against the Mob: Part 2."

12. Valentine, *The Strength of the Wolf, The Secret History of America's War on Drugs*.

13. Gingeras, Ryan, Heroin, *Organized Crime, & the Making of Modern Turkey*, New York, New York, Oxford University Press, 2014.

14. North, *Betrayal in Dallas, LBJ, The Pearl Street Mafia, and the Murder of President Kennedy*.

15. Ibid.

16. Waldron, Lamar, *The Hidden History of the JFK Assassination, The Definitive Account of the Most Controversial Crime of the Twentieth Century*, Berkeley, California, Counterpoint, 2013.

17. Valentine, *The Strength of the Wolf, The Secret History of America's War on Drugs*.

18. Shaw, Mark, *The Reporter Who Knew Too Much, The Mysterious Death of What's My Line TV Star and Media Icon Dorothy Kilgallen*, New York, New York, Post Hill Press, 2016, and Waldron, *The Hidden History of the JFK Assassination, The Definitive Account of the Most Controversial Crime of the Twentieth Century*.

19. Shaw, Mark, *The Poison Patriarch, How the Betrayals of Joseph P. Kennedy Caused the Assassination of JFK*, New York, New York, Skyhorse Publishing, 2013.

20. Minutaglio, Bill, and Davis, Steven L., *Dallas 1963*, New York, New York, Hachette Book Group, 2013.

21. Valentine, *The Strength of the Wolf, The Secret History of America's War on Drugs*.

22. Ibid.

23. Ibid.

24. Ibid.

25. Williams, Paul L., *Operation Gladio, The Unholy Alliance Between The Vatican, The CIA, And The Mafia*, Amherst, New York, Prometheus Books, 2015.

26. Ibid.

27. Maier, Thomas, *Mafia Spies, The Inside Story of the CIA, Gangsters, JFK, and Castro*, New York, New York, Skyhorse Publishing, 2019.

28. Ibid.

29. Hougan, Jim, *Spooks, The Haunting of America – The Private Use of Secret Agents*, New York, New York, William Morrow and Company, Inc., 1978.

30. Ibid., and Maier, *Mafia Spies, The Inside Story of the CIA, Gangsters, JFK, and Castro*.

31. Albarelli, H.P. Jr., *A Terrible Mistake, The Murder of Frank Olson and the CIA's Secret Cold War Experiments*, Walterville, Oregon, Trine Day, 2009.

32. Hinckle, Warren, and Turner, William, *The Fish is Red, The Story of the Secret War Against Castro*, New York, New York, Harper & Row Publishers, 1981.

33. Maier, *Mafia Spies, The Inside Story of the CIA, Gangsters, JFK, and Castro*.

34. Scheim, David E., *Contract on America, The Mafia Murder of President John F. Kennedy*, New York, New York, Shapolsky Publishers, Inc., 1988.

35. Ibid.

36. Hinckle and Turner, *The Fish is Red, The Story of the Secret War Against Castro*.

37. Maier, *Mafia Spies, The Inside Story of the CIA, Gangsters, JFK, and Castro*.

38. Ibid.

39. "The Nation: The Momo and Cain Connection," *Time Magazine, June 16, 1975*, and Hinckle and Turner, *The Fish is Red, The Story of the Secret War Against Castro*.

40. Ibid.

41. Hougan, *Spooks, The Haunting of America – The Private Use of Secret Agents*.

42. Talbot, David, *Brothers, The Hidden History of the Kennedy Years*, New York, New York, Free Press, 2007.

43. Ibid.

44. Shaw, *The Poison Patriarch, How the Betrayals of Joseph P. Kennedy Caused the Assassination of JFK*.

45. Blakey, G. Robert, and Billings, Richard N., *The Plot to Kill the President, Organized Crime Assassinated J.F.K., The Definitive Story*, New York, New York, Times Books, 1981.

46. Valentine, *The Strength of the Wolf, The Secret History of America's War on Drugs.*

47. Shaw, *The Poison Patriarch, How the Betrayals of Joseph P. Kennedy Caused the Assassination of JFK.*

48. Trento, *The Secret History of the CIA.*

49. Russell, Dick, *The Man Who Knew Too Much*, New York, New York, Carroll & Graf Publishers/ Richard Gallen, 1992.

50. Trento, *The Secret History of the CIA.*

51. Maier, *Mafia Spies, The Inside Story of the CIA, Gangsters, JFK, and Castro*, and Valentine, *The Strength of the Wolf, The Secret History of America's War on Drugs.*

52. "FBI Memorandum, October 20, 1959,", *The Black Vault*, www.theblackvault.com/document archive/.

53. Hougan, *Spooks, The Haunting of America – The Private Use of Secret Agents.*

54. Goodwin, Doris Kearns, *The Fitzgeralds and the Kennedys, An American Saga*, New York, New York, St. Martin's Press, 1987.

55. Lyndon B. Johnson: *The Exercise Of Power*, Rowland Evans and Robert Novak, New York, New York, The New American Library, 1966.

56. Ibid.

57. Russell, *The Man Who Knew Too Much.*

58. Zirbel, Craig I., *The Texas Connection: The Assassination of President John F. Kennedy*, Scarsdale, Arizona, The Texas Connection Co., Publishers, 1991.

59. Ibid.

60. Janney, Peter, *Mary's Mosaic, The CIA Conspiracy to Murder John F. Kennedy, Mary Pinchot Meyer, and Their Vision for World Peace*, New York, New York, Skyhorse Publishing, 2012.

61. Albarelli, H.P. Jr., *A Secret Order, Investigating the High Strangeness and Synchronicity in the JFK Assassination*, Walterville, Oregon, Trine Day, 2013.

62. Ibid.

Chapter Six: No Ordinary Marine Chapter

1. Epstein, Edward Jay, *Legend, The Secret World of Lee Harvey Oswald*, New York, New York, Mc-Graw-Hill Book Company, 1978.

2. Ibid.

3. Russell, Dick, *The Man Who Knew Too Much*, New York, New York, Carroll & Graf Publishers/Richard Gallen, 1992.

4. Ibid., and Summers, Anthony, *Conspiracy*, New York, New York, McGraw-Hill Book Company, 1980.

5. Epstein, *Legend, The Secret World of Lee Harvey Oswald.*

6. Newman, John, *Oswald and the CIA*, New York, New York, Carroll & Graf Publishers, Inc., 1995.

7. Smith, Joseph B., *Portrait of a Cold Warrior*, New York, New York, Ballantine Books, 1976.

8. Douglas, James, W., *JFK and the Unspeakable, Why He Died & Why It Matters*, Maryknoll, New York, Orbis Books, 2008, and Russell, *The Man Who Knew Too Much.*

9. Ibid.

10. Russell, *The Man Who Knew Too Much.*

11. Epstein, *Legend, The Secret World of Lee Harvey Oswald.*

12. Fried, Richard M., *Nightmare in Red, The McCarthy Era in Perspective*, New York, New York, Oxford University Press, 1990.

13. Epstein, *Legend, The Secret World of Lee Harvey Oswald.*

14. Ibid.

15. Russell, *The Man Who Knew Too Much.*

16. Summers, *Conspiracy.*

17. Ibid.

18. Newman, *Oswald and the CIA.*

19. Ibid.

20. Fensterwald, Bernard Jr., *Assassination of JFK by Coincidence or Conspiracy?*, New York, New York,

Kensington Publishing Corp., 1977.

21. Summers, *Conspiracy.*

22. Newman, *Oswald and the CIA.*

23. Ibid.

24. De Gramont, Sanche, *The Secret War*, New York, New York, Dell Publishing, 1962, from Russell, *The Man Who Knew Too Much.*

25. Russell, *The Man Who Knew Too Much.*

26. Epstein, *Legend, The Secret World of Lee Harvey Oswald.*

27. Trento, Joseph J., *The Secret History of the CIA*, New York, New York, MJF Books, 2001.

28. Russell, *The Man Who Knew Too Much.*

29. Epstein, *Legend, The Secret World of Lee Harvey Oswald.*

30. Russell, Dick, *On the Trail of the JFK Assassins, A Groundbreaking look at America's Most Infamous Conspiracy*, New York, New York, Skyhorse Publishing, 2008.

31. Epstein, Legend, *The Secret World of Lee Harvey Oswald.*

32. Ibid.

33. Waldron, Lamar, and Hartmann, Thom, *Ultimate Sacrifice, John and Robert Kennedy, the Plan for a Coup in Cuba, and the Murder of JFK*, New York, New York, Carroll & Graf Publishers, 2005.

34. Epstein, *Legend, The Secret World of Lee Harvey Oswald.*

35. Ibid.

36. Gilbride, Richard, *Maxim for Assassination: The JFK Conspiracy*, Trafford Publishing, Victoria, BC, Canada, 2009

37. Summers, *Conspiracy.*

38. Albarelli, H.P. Jr., *A Secret Order, Investigating the High Strangeness and Synchronicity in the JFK Assassination*, Walterville, Oregon, Trine Day, 2013.

39. Ibid.

40. CIA Internal Memo on the MKULTRA program in the Joint Hearing before the Select Committee on Intelligence and the Subcommittee on Health and Scientific Research of the Committee on Human Resources, United States Senate, 95th Congress, First Session, "Project MKUltra: The CIA's Program of Research in Behavioral Modification," August 3, 1977, from Ranelagh, John, *The Agency, The Rise and Decline of the CIA*, New York, New York, Simon and Schuster, 1986.

41. Ranelagh, *The Agency, The Rise and Decline of the CIA.*

42. Gilbride, *Maxim for Assassination: The JFK Conspiracy.*

43. Ibid.

44. Epstein, Legend, *The Secret World of Lee Harvey Oswald.*

45. Albarelli, H.P. Jr., *A Terrible Mistake, The Murder of Frank Olson and the CIA's Secret Cold War Experiments*, Walterville, Oregon, Trine Day, 2009.

46. Fisher, Seymour, "The Use of Hypnosis in Intelligence and Related Military Situations," Study SSR 177-D, Contract AT 18 (600) 1797, Technical Report No. 4, Washington D.C.: Bureau of Social Science Research, 1958, from Russell, The Man Who Knew Too Much.

47. Ranelagh, The Agency, *The Rise and Decline of the CIA.*

Seven: Give Peace a Chance . . . and Other Fairy Tales

1. Taubman, William, *Khrushchev, The Man and His Era*, New York, New York, W.W. Norton & Company, 2003.

2. Kruse, Kevin M., "How Corporate America Invented Christian America," *Politico*, April 16, 2015.

3. Kruse, Kevin M., *One Nation Under God, How Corporate America Invented Christian America*, New York, New York, Basic Books, 2015.

4. Ibid.

5. Ibid.

6. Ibid.

7. Ibid.

8. Ibid.

9. Ibid.

10. Caufield, M.D., Jeffrey H., *General Walker and the Murder of President Kennedy, The Extensive New*

Evidence of a Radical-Right Conspiracy, Moreland Press, 2015.

11. Minutaglio, Bill, and Davis, Steven L., *Dallas 1963*, New York, New York, Hachette Book Group, 2013.

12. Caufield, *General Walker and the Murder of President Kennedy, The Extensive New Evidence of a Radical-Right Conspiracy.*

13. Minutaglio and Davis, *Dallas 1963.*

14. Caufield, *General Walker and the Murder of President Kennedy, The Extensive New Evidence of a Radical-Right Conspiracy.*

15. Ibid.

16. Ibid.

17. Ibid.

18. Ibid.

19. Ibid.

20. Ibid.

21. Minutaglio and Davis, *Dallas 1963.*

22. Ibid.

23. Ibid.

24. Caufield, *General Walker and the Murder of President Kennedy, The Extensive New Evidence of a Radical-Right Conspiracy.*

25. Minutaglio and Davis, *Dallas 1963.*

26. Marrs, Jim, *Crossfire, The Plot That Killed Kennedy*, New York, New York, Carroll & Graf Publishers, Inc., 1989.

27. Talbot, David, *The Devil's Chessboard, Allen Dulles, the CIA, and the Rise of America's Secret Government*, New York, New York, Harper Collins Publishers, 2015.

28. Schlesinger, Arthur M. Jr., *Robert Kennedy and His Times*, Boston, Massachusetts, Houghton Mifflin Company, 1978.

29. Bernstein, Irving, *Guns or Butter: The Presidency of Lyndon Johnson*, Oxford University Press, New York, New York, 1996.

30. Minutaglio and Davis, Dallas 1963.

31. North, Mark, *Act of Treason, The Role of J. Edgar Hoover in the Assassination of President Kennedy*, New York, New York, Carroll & Graf Publishers, 1991.

32. Carrozza, Anthony R., *William D. Pawley, The Extraordinary Life of the Adventurer, Entrepreneur, and Diplomat Who Cofounded the Flying Tigers*, Washington D.C., Potomac Books, 2012.

33. Manchester, William, *The Death of a President, November 20 – November 25, 1963*, New York, New York, Harper & Row, Publishers, 1967.

Chapter Eight: The Defector Who Wasn't

1. Russell, Dick, *The Man Who Knew Too Much*, New York, New York, Carroll & Graf Publishers/Richard Gallen, 1992.

2. *The Warren Commission Report, The Official Report of the President's Commission on the Assassination of President John F. Kennedy*, New York, New York, Associated Press, 1964.

3. Epstein, Edward Jay, *Legend: The Secret World of Lee Harvey Oswald*, New York, McGraw- Hill Book Company, 1978.

4. *The Warren Commission Report, The Official Report of the President's Commission on the Assassination of President John F. Kennedy.*

5. Douglas, James, W., *JFK and the Unspeakable, Why He Died & Why It Matters*, Maryknoll, New York, Orbis Books, 2008.

6. Botelho, James, testimony, *Hearings Before the President's Commission on the Assassination of President Kennedy*, Volume VIII, Washington D.C., Government Printing Office, 1964, from www.Jfkassassination.net/russ/testimony/Botelho.htm.

7. Donovan, John E., testimony, *Hearings Before the President's Commission on the Assassination of President Kennedy*, Volume VIII, Washington D.C., Government Printing Office, 1964, from www.Histoymatter.com/archive/jfk/wc/wcvols/wh8/pdf/WH*_Donovan.pdf.

8. Mellen, Joan, *A Farewell to Justice, Jim Garrison, JFK's Assassination, and the Case That Should Have*

Changed History, New York, New York, Skyhorse Publishing, 2013.

9. Ibid.

10. Fensterwald, Bernard Jr., *Assassination of JFK by Coincidence or Conspiracy?*, New York, New York, Kensington Publishing Corp., 1977.

11. Ibid.

12. Mellen, *A Farewell to Justice, Jim Garrison, JFK's Assassination, and the Case That Should Have Changed History.*

13. Caufield, M.D., Jeffrey H., *General Walker and the Murder of President Kennedy, The Extensive New Evidence of a Radical-Right Conspiracy*, Moreland Press, 2015.

14. Botelho, James, testimony, *Hearings Before the President's Commission on the Assassination of President Kennedy*, Volume VIII, Washington D.C., Government Printing Office, 1964, from History matters.com/archive/jfk/wc/wcvols/wh8/pdf/WH8_Botelho_aff.pdf.

15. Garrison, Jim, *On the Trail of the Assassins*, New York, New York, Warner Books, 1988.

16. Epstein, *Legend: The Secret World of Lee Harvey Oswald.*

17. Summers, Anthony, *Conspiracy*, New York, McGraw-Hill Book Company, 1980.

18. Garrison, *On the Trail of the JFK Assassins.*

19. Waldron, Lamar, and Hartmann, Thom, *Legacy of Secrecy, The Long Shadow of the JFK Assassination: Robert Kennedy, National Security, the Mafia, and the Assassination of Martin Luther King*, Berkeley, California, Counterpoint, 2008.

20. Donovan, John E., testimony, *Hearings Before the President's Commission on the Assassination of President Kennedy*, Volume VIII, Washington D.C., Government Printing Office, 1964, from www.Histoymatter.com/archive/jfk/wc/wcvols/wh8/pdf/WH*_Donovan.pdf.

21. Ibid.

22. Jones, Harry J. Jr., *The Minutemen*, Garden City, New York, Doubleday & Company, Inc., 1968.

23. Delgado, Nelson, testimony on April 16, 1964, *Hearings Before the President's Commission on the Assassination of President Kennedy*, Volume VIII, Washington D.C., Government Printing Office, 1964.

24. Ibid.

25. Epstein, *Legend: The Secret World of Lee Harvey Oswald*

26. "Jack London," from https://en.wikipedia.org/wiki/Jack_London.

27. Phillips-Fein, Kim, *Invisible Hands, The Making of the Conservative Movement from the New Deal to Reagan*, New York, New York, W.W. Norton & Company, Inc., 2009.

28. Earhart, David C., *Certain Victory: Images of World War II in the Japanese Media:*, New York, New York, Rutledge, 2008.

29. "Norman Vincent Peale," from https://biography.yourdictionary.com/norman-vincent-peale.

30. *The Warren Commission Report, The Official Report of the President's Commission on the Assassination of President John F. Kennedy*, New York, New York, Associated Press, 1964.

31. Evica, George Michael, *A Certain Arrogance; The Sacrificing of Lee Harvey Oswald and the Cold War Manipulation of Religious Groups by US Intelligence*, Walterville, Oregon, TrineDay, 2011.

32. Ibid.

33. Eddis, Charles W., *Stephen Fritchman: The American Unitarians and Communism,* Morrisville, North Carolina, Lulu Press Publishing Company, 2011.

34. Evica, *A Certain Arrogance; The Sacrificing of Lee Harvey Oswald and the Cold War Manipulation of Religious Groups by US Intelligence.*

35. Thornley, Kerry Wendell, testimony, *Hearings Before the President's Commission on the Assassination of President Kennedy*, Volume XI, Washington D.C., Government Printing Office, 1964, from www.Histoymatter.com/archive/contents/wc/contents/wh11.htm.

36. Ibid.

37. Evica, *A Certain Arrogance; The Sacrificing of Lee Harvey Oswald and the Cold War Manipulation of Religious Groups by US Intelligence.*

38. Eddis, *Stephen Fritchman: The American Unitarians and Communism, and Evica, A Certain Arrogance; The Sacrificing of Lee Harvey Oswald and the Cold War Manipulation of Religious Groups by US Intelligence.*

39. Evica, *A Certain Arrogance; The Sacrificing of Lee Harvey Oswald and the Cold War Manipulation of Religious Groups by US Intelligence.*

40. Eddis, Stephen *Fritchman: The American Unitarians and Communism,* and Evica, *A Certain Arrogance; The Sacrificing of Lee Harvey Oswald and the Cold War Manipulation of Religious Groups by US*

Intelligence.

41. Eddis, Charles W., *Unitarian Universalist History & Heritage Society* article, June 20, 2012.

42. Eddis, *Stephen Fritchman: The American Unitarians and Communism,* and Evica, *A Certain Arrogance; The Sacrificing of Lee Harvey Oswald and the Cold War Manipulation of Religious Groups by US Intelligence.*

43. Ibid.

44. Ibid.

45. Evica, *A Certain Arrogance; The Sacrificing of Lee Harvey Oswald and the Cold War Manipulation of Religious Groups by US Intelligence.*

46. Ibid.

47. Lateer, J.W., *The Three Barons, The Organizational Chart of the Kennedy Assassination,* Walterville, Oregon, Trine Day, 2017.

48. LaFontaine, Ray and Mary, *Oswald Talked, The New Evidence in the JFK Assassination,* Gretna, Louisiana, Pelican Publishing Company, 1996.

49. Ibid.

50. Ibid.

51. Waldron, Lamar, and Hartmann, Thom, *Ultimate Sacrifice, John and Robert Kennedy, the Plan for a Coup in Cuba, and the Murder of JFK,* New York, New York, Carroll & Graf Publishers, 2005.

52. Ibid.

53. Douglas, James, W., *JFK and the Unspeakable, Why He Died & Why It Matters,* Maryknoll, New York, Orbis Books, 2008.

54. Mellen, *A Farewell to Justice, Jim Garrison, JFK's Assassination, and the Case That Should Have Changed History.*

55. LaFontaine, *Oswald Talked, The New Evidence in the JFK Assassination.*

56. Ibid.

57. Summers, *Conspiracy.*

58. Epstein, *Legend: The Secret World of Lee Harvey Oswald.*

59. Russell, *The Man Who Knew Too Much.*

60. Summers, *Conspiracy.*

Chapter Nine: Double Trouble from Moscow

1. Allen Dulles interview, *U.S. News and World Report,* March 19, 1954.

2. Ranelagh, John, *The Agency, The Rise And Decline Of The CIA,* New York, New York, Simon and Schuster, 1986.

3. Ibid.

4. De Gramont, Sanche, *The Secret War,* New York, New York, Dell Publishing Co., Inc., 1962.

5. Paget, Karen M., *Patriotic Betrayal,* New Haven Connecticut, Yale University Press, 2015.

6. Ibid.

7. Ibid.

8. Bird, Kai, *The Chairman, John McCloy The Making of the American Establishment,* New York, New York, Simon & Schuster, 1992.

9. Leffler, Melvyn P., *For the Soul of Mankind, The United States, the Soviet Union, and The Cold War,* New York, New York, Hill and Wang, 2007.

10. Bird, *The Chairman, John McCloy The Making of the American Establishment.*

11. Paget, *Patriotic Betrayal.*

12. Summers, Anthony, *Conspiracy,* New York, New York, McGraw-Hill Book Company, 1980; Mellen, Joan, *A Farewell to Justice, Jim Garrison, JFK's Assassination, and the Case That Should Have Changed History,* New York, New York, Skyhorse Publishing, 2013; and Evica, George Michael, *A Certain Arrogance; The Sacrificing of Lee Harvey Oswald and the Cold War Manipulation of Religious Groups by US Intelligence,* Walterville, Oregon, TrineDay, 2011.

13. Ibid.

14. Epstein, Edward Jay, *Legend, The Secret World of Lee Harvey Oswald,* New York, New York, McGraw-Hill Book Company, 1978, and Summers, *Conspiracy.*

15. *The Warren Commission Report, The Official Report of the President's Commission on the Assassination of President John F. Kennedy,* Exhibit No. 941, Vol. XVIII, Washington D.C., Government Printing Office,

1964.

16. *The Warren Commission Report, The Official Report of the President's Commission on the Assassination of President John F. Kennedy*, Exhibit No. 909, Vol. XVIII, Washington D.C., Government Printing Office, 1964.

17. Newman, John, *Oswald and the CIA*, New York, New York, Carroll & Graf Publishers, Inc., 1995, and Carpenter, Donald H., *Man of a Million Fragments, The True Story of Clay Shaw*, Nashville, Tennessee, published by Donald Carpenter, 2014.

18. Ibid.

19. Johnson, Priscilla, testimony on July 25, 1964, *Hearings Before the President's Commission on the Assassination of President Kennedy*, Volume XI, Washington D.C., Government Printing Office, 1964.

20. McMillan, Priscilla Johnson, *Marina and Lee*, New York, New York, Harper & Row, 1977.

21. Ibid.

22. Mellen, Joan, *Our Man in Haiti, George de Mohrenschildt and the CIA in the Nightmare Republic*, Walterville, Oregon, Trine Day, 2012.

23. Newman, *Oswald and the CIA*.

24. Ibid.

25. Ibid.

26. Saunders, Frances Stonor, *The Cultural Cold War: The CIA and the World of Arts and Letters*, The New Press, 1999, and Heilbrunn, Jacob, *They Knew They Were Right: The Rise of the Neocons*, New York, New York, Random House, 2009.

27. Newman, *Oswald and the CIA*.

28. Marrs, Jim, *Crossfire*, New York, New York, Carroll & Graf Publishers, Inc., 1989, and Lane, Mark, *Plausible Denial, Was the CIA Involved in the Assassination of JFK?*, New York, New York, Thunder's Mouth Press, 1991.

29. *The Twenty-Fifth Yearbook for Brooklyn Institute of Arts and Sciences*, 1912-1913, and *The Bulletin of the Brooklyn Institute of Arts and Sciences, Brooklyn*, New York City January 21, 1911.

30. "Finding aid for the Mary (Mollie) Garfield-Stanley-Brown Papers," *Western Reserve Historical Society, from* http://catalog.wrhs.org/collections/view?docId=ead/MS4571.xml;query=;brand=default,

31. Feis, Herbert, from https://en.wikipedia.org/wiki/Herbert_Feis

32. "Finding aid for the Mary (Mollie) Garfield-Stanley-Brown Papers," *Western Reserve Historical Society, from* http://catalog.wrhs.org/collections/view?docId=ead/MS4571.xml;query=;brand=default,

33. Lane, Plausible Denial, *Was the CIA Involved in the Assassination of JFK?*

34. Ibid.

35. Mellen, Joan, *Our Man in Haiti, George de Mohrenschildt and the CIA in the Nightmare Republic.*

36. Ibid.

37. Eddowes, Michael, *The Oswald File*, New York, New York, Clarkson N. Potter, Inc., 1977.

38. Ibid.

39. *The Warren Commission Report, The Official Report of the President's Commission on the Assassination of President John F. Kennedy*, Vol. XVI, 64, V 112,242, Washington D.C., Government Printing Office, 1964.

40. Russell, Dick, *On the Trail of the JFK Assassins, A Groundbreaking look at America's Most Infamous Conspiracy*, New York, New York, Skyhorse Publishing, 2008.

41. Ibid.

42. Hosty, James P., *Assignment Oswald*, New York, New York, Arcade Publishing, 1996.

43. Corsi, Jerome R., P.H.D., *Who Really Killed Kennedy?, 50 Years Later, Stunning New Revelations about the JFK Assassination*, Washington, D.C., WND Books, 2013.

Chapter Ten: What's Wrong With U-2?

1. Schlesinger, Arthur M. Jr., *Robert Kennedy And His Times*, Boston, Massachusetts, Houghton Mifflin Company, 1978.

2. Newman, John, *Oswald And The CIA*, New York, New York, Carroll & Graf Publishers, Inc., 1995.

3. Bird, Kai, *The Chairman, John McCloy The Making of the American Establishment*, New York, New York, Simon & Schuster, 1992.

4. Jacobsen, Annie, *The Pentagon's Brain, An Uncensored History of DARPA, America's Top Secret Military Research Agency*, New York, New York, Little, Brown and Company, 2015.

5. Bird, *The Chairman, John McCloy The Making of the American Establishment*.

6. Ibid., and Osgood, Kenneth, *Total Cold War, Eisenhower's Secret Propaganda Battle at Home and Abroad*, Lawrence, Kansas, University Press of Kansas, 2006.

7. Jacobsen, *The Pentagon's Brain, An Uncensored History of DARPA, America's Top Secret Military Research Agency*, and Bird, *The Chairman, John McCloy The Making of the American Establishment*.

8. Osgood, *Total Cold War, Eisenhower's Secret Propaganda Battle at Home and Abroad*, and Schlesinger, *Robert Kennedy and His Times*.

9. Thomas, Evan, *Ike's Bluff, President Eisenhower's Secret Battle to Save the World*, New York, New York, Little, Brown and Company, 2012.

10. Fursenko, Aleksandr, and Naftali, Timothy, *Khrushchev's Cold War, The Inside Story of an American Adversary*, New York, New York, W.W. Norton & Company, 2006.

11. Ibid.

12. Gaddis, John Lewis, *Strategies of Containment, A Critical Appraisal of Postwar American National Security Policy*, New York, New York, Oxford University Press, 1982.

13. Thomas, *Ike's Bluff, President Eisenhower's Secret Battle to Save the World*.

14. Ibid., and Beschloss, Michael R., *May-Day, Eisenhower, Khrushchev and the U-2 Affair*, New York, New York, Harper & Row Publishers, 1986.

15. Bamford, James, *Body of Secrets, Anatomy of the Ultra-Secret National Security Agency, From the Cold War Through the Dawn of a New Century*, New York, New York, Doubleday, 2001.

16. Ibid.

17. Nichols, David, A., *Ike and McCarthy, Dwight Eisenhower's Secret Campaign Against Joseph McCarthy*, New York, New York, Simon & Schuster, 2017, and Fursenko, and Naftali, *Khrushchev's Cold War, The Inside Story of an American Adversary*.

18. Thomas, *Ike's Bluff, President Eisenhower's Secret Battle to Save the World*.

19. Fursenko, and Naftali, *Khrushchev's Cold War, The Inside Story of an American Adversary*.

20. Beschloss, *May-Day, Eisenhower, Khrushchev and the U-2 Affair*.

21. Fursenko, and Naftali, *Khrushchev's Cold War, The Inside Story of an American Adversary*.

22. Ibid.

23. Ibid.; Bird, *The Chairman, John McCloy The Making of the American Establishment*; Prouty, L. Fletcher, *The Secret Team, The CIA and Its Allies in Control of the United States and the World*, New York, New York, Skyhorse Publishing, 2011; and Taubman, William, *Khrushchev, The Man and His Era*, New York, New York, W.W. Norton & Company, 2003.

24. Newman, *Oswald and the CIA*.

25. Fursenko, and Naftali, *Khrushchev's Cold War, The Inside Story of an American Adversary*.

26. Ibid.

27. Ibid.

28. Thomas, *Ike's Bluff, President Eisenhower's Secret Battle to Save the World*.

29. Parmet, *Herbert S., Eisenhower and the American Crusades*, New York, New York, The MacMillan Co., 1972.

30. Coffin, Tristram, *The Passion of the Hawks, Militarism in Modern America*, New York, New York, The MacMillan Company, 1964.

31. Bird, *The Chairman, John McCloy The Making of the American Establishment*.

32. Russell, Dick, *The Man Who Knew Too Much*, New York, New York, Carroll & Graf Publishers/ Richard Gallen, 1992.

33. McVicar, John, testimony, *Hearings Before the President's Commission on the Assassination of President Kennedy*, Volume V, Washington D.C., Government Printing Office, 1964.

34. Newman, *Oswald & the CIA*.

35. Riebling, Mark, *Wedge, The Secret War Between the FBI and CIA*, New York, New York, Alfred A. Knopf, 1994.

36. Ibid., and Newman, *Oswald and the CIA*.

37. Riebling, *Wedge, The Secret War Between the FBI and CIA*.

38. Martin, David C., *Wilderness of Mirrors*, New York, New York, Harper Collins Publishers, Inc., 1980.

39. Riebling, *Wedge, The Secret War Between the FBI and CIA*.

40. De Gramont, Sanche, *The Secret War*, New York, Dell Publishing Co., 1962.

41. Ibid.

42. Newman, *Oswald and the CIA*.

43. McMillan, Priscilla Johnson, *Marina and Lee*, New York, New York, Harper & Row, 1977.

44. Newman, *Oswald and the CIA*.

45. Eddowes, Michael, *The Oswald File*, New York, New York, Clarkson N. Potter, Inc., 1977.

46. Ibid.

47. Kempe, Frederick, *Berlin 1961, Kennedy, Khrushchev, and the Most Dangerous Place on Earth*, New York, New York, G.P Putnam's Sons, 2011.

48. Russell, Dick, *The Man Who Knew Too Much*, New York, New York, Carroll & Graf Publishers/ Richard Gallen, 1992.

49. Beschloss, *May-Day, Eisenhower, Khrushchev and the U-2 Affair*.

50. Bamford, *Body of Secrets, Anatomy of the Ultra-Secret National Security Agency, From the Cold War Through the Dawn of a New Century*.

51. Taubman, *Khrushchev, The Man and His Era*.

52. Beschloss, *May-Day, Eisenhower, Khrushchev and the U-2 Affair*.

53. Jacobsen, *The Pentagon's Brain, An Uncensored History of DARPA, America's Top Secret Military Research Agency*.

54. Russell, *The Man Who Knew Too Much*.

55. Prouty, *The Secret Team, The CIA and Its Allies in Control of the United States and the World*.

56. Ibid.

57. Donovan, John E., testimony, *Hearings Before the President's Commission on the Assassination of President Kennedy*, Volume VIII, Washington D.C., Government Printing Office, 1964.

58. Marrs, Jim, *Crossfire, The Plot That Killed Kennedy*, New York, New york, Carroll & Graf Publishers Inc., 1989.

59. Fursenko, and Naftali, *Khrushchev's Cold War, The Inside Story of an American Adversary*.

60. Beschloss, *May-Day, Eisenhower, Khrushchev and the U-2 Affair*.

61. Ibid.

62. Ibid.

63. Ibid.

64. Fursenko, and Naftali, *Khrushchev's Cold War, The Inside Story of an American Adversary*.

65. Beschloss, *May-Day, Eisenhower, Khrushchev and the U-2 Affair*.

66. Ibid.

67. Ibid.

68. Ibid.

Chapter Eleven: Epilogue

1. Schlesinger, Arthur M. Jr., *Robert Kennedy and His Times*, Boston, Massachusetts, Houghton Mifflin Company, 1978.

2. Evica, George Michael, *A Certain Arrogance; The Sacrificing of Lee Harvey Oswald and the Cold War Manipulation of Religious Groups by US Intelligence*, Walterville, Oregon, TrineDay, 2011, and Ganis, Major Ralph P., USAF, Ret., *The Skorzeny Papers, Evidence for the Plot to Kill JFK*, New York, New York, Skyhorse Publishing, 2018.

3. Russell, Dick, *The Man Who Knew Too Much*, New York, New York, Carroll & Graf Publishers/Richard Gallen, 1992.

Index

A

Abbes, Johnny, 55
Ablard, Charles D., 15
Abrams, George, 220, 221
Abramson, Harold A., 31
Adenauer, Conrad, 268
Adzhubei, Alexei, 263
Aleman, Jose, 120, 125
Alexander, Bill, 111, 112
Alger, Bruce, 186
Alliluyeva, Svetlana, 232
Almeida, Juan, 60
Alpha 64, 75, 281
American Civil Liberties Union
   (ACLU), 9
America First Party, 182
American Nazi Party, ix, 7, 20,
   181–82, 184
AM/WORLD, See OMEGA Plan
Anastasia, Albert, 69, 107, 112,
   124
Anderson, Robert, 85
Andrews, Dean, 136
Angleton, James, 25, 46, 61,
   123–26, 129–30, 139–40,
   143, 227, 262, 278
 and Oswald's defection, 256,
   258,
Anikeeff, Nicholas, 279
Ansan Group, 120
Anslinger, Harry, 37, 113
Anti-Communist League of the
   Caribbean, 22, 56
Arango, Aureliano Sanchez, 91
Arcacha Smith, Sergio, 16, 19, 40,
   93, 95, 97, 281
Arevalo, Juan, 50–51
Artime, Manuel, 60–61, 68, 91,
   96–98
Attwood, William, 65
Atzenhoffer, Anthony, 15
Ayers, A.G., 206–207

B

Badeaux, Hubert, 5, 9, 178
Baker, Bobby, 22, 30, 65, 127,
   186, 279
Baldwin, David G., 20
Balletti, Arthur J., 122

Banister, Guy, 4–5, 12, 17, 19,
   20–22, 24, 40, 46, 100, 133,
   193–194
 and racist groups, 5, 20, 46, 178,
   180–81, 184
 Anti-Communist, 4–5, 9, 22,
   25, 213, 261
 and Lee Harvey Oswald, 6–7,
   10, 13–14, 16, 18, 19–21,
   25, 96, 193, 195, 282
Bannerman, Robert, L., 139–140
Barker, Bernard, 60, 68, 75, 87,
   280–81
Barnes, Tracy, 24, 44, 58, 75,
   87–90, 96–97, 101, 126,
   280–81
Barnett, Ross, 178, 180
Barr, Candy, 38, 110–12
Barrett, Bob, 243
Bartes, Frank, 92–93, 100
Bartone, Dominick, 59–60, 97,
   108
Batista, Fulgencio, 27–30, 34–42,
   54–57, 59–60, 62–65,
   67–68, 72, 75–76, 84–85,
   88, 90–91, 93–96, 98, 101,
   120, 124, 130, 196–97, 221,
   272, 280
Bauer, Alice, 233–34, 283
Bauer, Raymond, 233–34, 283
Beauboef, Al, 11
Beckham, Thomas, 7
Beck, Dave, 106
Belli, Melvin, 110–12
Beidas, Youseff, 114
Belmont, August, 65
Belsito, Frank J., 59
Benitez, jose A., 95
Benitez, Manuel, 64
Bethel, Paul, 64–65, 280
Biderman, Albert, 153
Billnitzer, Martin, 19
Bissell, Richard, 77, 85, 87–90,
   95–96, 113, 116–17, 119,
   123, 126, 130–31, 139–40,
   249
Bochelman, Herman, 24
Boggs, Hale, 127
Bonanno, Joe, 113, 115
Bonnano, Bill, 124

Bonsal, Philip, 55, 68, 85
Borenstein, Lorenzo, 73
Bortin, Sylvia, 200
Bosch, Orlando, 73–74
Botelho, James, 1, 8, 192, 195
Boylston, Bob, 213
Braden, Tom, 219
Brady, Surell, 210
Brady, Tom, 3, 178
Braga, George, 65
Braga, Ronny, 65
Brandsetter, Frank, 59
Brent, Theodore, 17
Bringuier, Carlos, 100, 138
Brod, Mario, 123–25
Broglie, Warren, 31–33, 50
Browder, Eddie, 40, 42
Brown, Joe, 111–12
Brown, Joseph Stanley, 230–31
Brown, Mary (Mollie) Garfield,
   Stanley, 230–31
Brown, Ruth, 231
Brundage, Percival Flack, 199,
   202–204
   Century Club member, 204
Bucknell, David, 143–44
Bundy, McGeorge, 89
Burke, Arleigh, 86–87
Burns, Van, 213
Byrd, David Harold, 47, 279

C

Cabell, Charles, 96
Cain, Richard, 186–87
Calo, John, 176
Camarata, Donald, 209, 268
Campbell, Allen, 195
Campbell, Judith, 120–21,
   123–24
Camper, Frank, 146–47
Canete, Ricardo, 125
Carbajal, Ruben, 58
Cardona, Jose Miro, 54, 91, 96
Carrillo, Justo, 139, 91
Carter, Tom, 238, 243
Casasin, Thomas, 218
Cassisi, Peter, 152
Castro, Fidel, 13–14, 17–18,
   26, 33, 39–40, 43–46, 49,
   53–77, 81, 84–99, 102,

110, 116–26, 128–31, 188, 196–97, 200–201, 206, 223, 242, 271–72, 274, 278–81, 285
Pre-takeover of Cuba, 27–30, 33–38, 40–42
Castro, Raul, 34, 55, 57, 66, 69–70, 86, 88, 272
Cellini, Dino, 55, 69
Central Intelligence Agency (CIA), x—xi, 3, 17–18, 20–25, 27, 29, 32, 34–35, 39–40, 44–46, 48, 50, 72–74, 79, 84, 87–88, 90–91, 94–103, 105, 131, 199, 202, 204, 216–24
Attempted coup in Cuba in 1959, 26, 53, 56–66, 74–76
Castro assassination plot, 77, 85–90
Interest in Oswald, 132, 134–40, 148–49, 212
Mafia/CIA Assassination plots, 33, 116–30, 179–82, 185–86, 193, 202
Mind altering drug experiments and hypnosis, 14–16, 31, 47–49, 51, 86, 132–33, 152–54, 201
Plot to defect enlisted men behind the Iron Curtain, 139–142
Reaction to Oswald's defection, 255–259
and organized crime, 36–38, 40–42, 55–56, 60, 70, 110, 113–16
Sabotage of U-2 spy plane, 263–269, 274
U-2 spy plane, 133–134, 143, 248–53, 255, 262–64
Centro Mondiale Commerciale, 24, 100, 279
Charles, Clemard, 279
Cheasty, John Cye, 107
Cherami, Rose, 19
Cheramie, Albert, Paul, 14
Chesler, Louis A., 114
Citizen's Committee to Free Cuba, 64
Civil Air Transport (CAT), 35
Civello, Joseph, 33, 38, 108–10, 112
Clements, Manning, C., 210–11, 241
Cobb, Alvin, 20

Cobb, June, x–xi, 26, 30–33, 38, 42–52, 75, 98, 130–31, 213, 227, 281, 283
Involvement in 1959 Havana coup, 45, 56–60, 68, 87, 126, 280
Cobb, Lloyd J., 20
Cohen, Mickey, 38, 110–12, 123
Colby, William, 219, 275
Congress of Racial Equality (CORE), 178–80
Connally, John, 111, 137, 176
Cordova, Juan Orta, 120, 130
Core, Jesse, 20, 23
Costello, Frank, 38, 107, 110, 115
Cotroni, Pepe, 37
Courtney, Kent, 179
Courtney, Phoebe, 179
Cowles, Gardner, 174
Crichton, Jack, 22, 231, 234, 279–80
Criswell, W.A., 183–84
Croce, Jean, 37
Crocket, Frederick, 275
Crosby, Bing, 175
Crouchet, Erick, 16, 19
Crusade of Revolutionaries Against Communism (CRAC), 65
Cuban Revolutionary Council (CRC), 96–98
Cuban Revolutionary Front (FRD), 12, 91
Cuban Student Directorate (DRE), 27–29, 64, 99, 100–101
Cubela, Rolando, 28
Cumming, Hugh, 139
Cuneo, Ernest, 227
Curington, John, 128
Curry, Jesse, 212
Cusack, John, 37, 108

D

D'Agostino, Antoine, 109, 112
Dallin, Alexander, 221
Daniel, Price, 108–109
Dante, Ronald, 32, 50
Darwin, Charles, 197–98
Davidson, F. Trubee, 229
Davidson, Irv, 22, 30, 65
Davis, Bruce, 140, 256–57
Davis, Louis P., 179–80, 192–93
Davis, Thomas, Eli, 48–49, 112, 278–79, 283
Deageano, Peter, 192

De Bayle, Henri, 22
Decker, R.L., 173, 177
DeCourcy, John, 24
De Gaulle, Charles, 24, 56, 98, 100
Dejanovich, Owen, 154
Delgado, Nelson, 196–97
del Valle, Eladio, 95, 281
del Valle, Pedro, 180–81, 184
De Mohrenschildt, George, 22, 25, 101, 205, 216, 234, 275, 279, 283
DePugh, Robert, 196
Dexter, Robert, 202
Diaz, Lanz, Pedro Luis, 42, 68, 74
Di Giorgio, Giuseppe, 55
Dio, Johnny, 105
Disney, Walt, 174–75
Donovan, Bill, 23, 33, 37, 39, 64, 87, 98, 113–15, 202, 277–80, 282
Donovan, Edna, 123
Donovan, John E., 190–92, 195–97, 265
Doolittle, James, 251
Doughty, George, 243
Dowell, Doris, 193
Dubois, Edward, 188
Dubois, Rene E., 59
Duggan, Laurence, 275
Dulles, Allen, x, 23, 32–35, 37, 48, 51, 64, 78, 84, 94, 98, 113, 126, 202, 204, 216, 223, 249–51, 253, 256, 262–67, 271–72, 274–75, 277–80, 282
And Castro assassination plots, 77, 81, 85–90
Sabotages coup in Cuba, 53, 65–68, 74, 76, 94, 196, 285

Dulles, John Foster, 66, 78, 250
Duran, Sylvia, 32, 50
Dureau, George, 23
Dutkanicz, Joseph, 140–42, 144
Duvalier, Francois, 48, 279

E

Eastland, James, 3–4, 46, 178, 180, 184
Echeverria, Antonio, 27–28
Edwards, Sheffield, 117–19, 122, 128, 131, 227, 256
Egerter, Ann, 258–59
Eisenhower, Dwight, x–xi, 2, 28, 35, 51, 53–54, 56, 67,

79, 81, 85–86, 89, 93–95,
101, 103–104, 174, 176,
204, 220, 222, 246–53, 257,
262–63, 266–69, 274–75
Massive retaliation policy,
78–79, 81–84
Military reaction to U-2 affair,
268–69
Missile Gap, 246–48, 250,
252–54
Nuclear test ban treaty, 245, 251,
253–55, 269–70, 274
Treasonous acts against, 77, 80,
82–84, 245, 250–51, 254–55
Elkins, Jim, 105–106, 108
Ellender, Allen, 22
Eroshkin, Nikolai G., 142,
144–46, 214
Ervin, Sam, 108
Esterline, Jake, 88, 131
Evans, Medford, 179, 184

F

Fain, John, 238, 260
Federal Bureau of Investigation
(FBI), x, 4–5, 9, 12–13,
18–20, 22, 29–31, 33, 37–38,
40–42, 44–46, 48–50, 52,
56, 59, 63–65, 70–73, 84,
92–93, 100, 105, 107, 110,
112, 117–123, 125, 129–31,
138–39, 146, 151, 180–82,
187–90, 198–99, 203–204,
207, 210–12, 216, 221,
227–28, 230–33, 238–43,
255–56, 259–62, 283
Feis, Herbert, 231
Feldman, Ike, 196
Feller, Abraham, 275
Fernandez, Alberto, 66
Fernandez, Mario Fernandez y, 55
Ferrie, David, ix, 11–25, 40, 47,
50, 90, 95, 100, 136, 150,
281–83
Background, 10–11
Civil Air Patrol (CAP), 10,
14–16, 19, 133, 193–94,
213, 282
Field, Noel, 202–203
Fifield, James, 198
Fisher, Seymour, 153
FitzGerald, Desmond, 28
Fletcher, Martha, 203
Flomer, Claude, 26
Foreman, Percy, 112
Forrestal, James, 275

Fox, Martin, 61, 71–72
Fox, Pedro, 71–72
Francisci, Marcel, 114
Franco, Francisco, 401
Franco, Joe, 39
Friedman, Allen, 38–39
Friends of a Democratic Cuba,
12–13, 25, 213, 261
Fritchman, Stephen, 199–200,
203–204
Fruge, Francis, 19
Fullbright, William, 262
Furguson, Margaret, 31

G

Gaither, H. Rowan, 79, 246
Galagher, Cornelius E., 113
Galante, Carmine, 37, 113, 115
Gale, William Potter, 181–82
Gambino, Carlo, 109, 115
Gammons. Steve, 207
Gardner, Arthur, 28
Garner, John Nance, 127
Garrison, Jim, 11, 16–17, 20–21,
23, 95, 100, 193
Garrity, Thomas, 223
Garro, Elano, 50
Garro, Helena, 50
Garthoff, Raymond, 221
Gates, Thomas, 253
Gatlin, Maurice, 24, 56–57, 100
Gaudet, William, 18–19, 23,
39, 73

Gavin, James, 83
Gaynor, Paul, 140
Gehlen, Reinhard, 278
Genco, Giuseppe, 115
Gener, Rafael "Macho," 130
Genovese, Vito, 22, 107, 114–15,
278
Giancana, Sam, 32, 43, 108–109,
116, 129, 275
CIA/Mafia Castro Assassina-
tion plot, 33, 118–22, 126,
128–31, 278
Illegal activity in 1960 election,
123–24
Judith Campbell, 121, 123
Phyllis McGuire, 122–23, 125
Gibson, Richard, 46
Gigante, Vincent, 107
Gill, G. Wray, 40
Gillin, Edward G., 150, 194,
201, 283
Gittinger, John, 49

Gleichauf, Justin, 59
Goldsborough, Laird Shields, 275
Goodpaster, Andrew, 78, 93, 263
Goodwin, Richard, 97
Gordon, Abe, 109
Gottleib, Sidney, 151
Graham, Billy, 176
Graham, Phillip, 397
Granello, Sal, 57
Gray, Gordon, 85
Greenlee, Richard, 114
Gremillion, Jack P. F., 20
Groves, Wallace, 114
Guerrero, Deva, 50
Guevara, Che, 36, 54, 56–57,
86, 272
Gutierrez Menoyo, Eloy, 56,
63–65, 67–68, 99

H

Hack, Jeanne,, 193
Haley, Evetts, 180, 184
Hall Cliff, 192
Hall, Loren, 48–49, 69, 283
Hallet, Joan, 224–25
Hambro, Sir Jocelyn, 115–16
Harriman, Averil, 67
Harris, Roy V., 180
Harvey, William, 48, 59, 64, 75,
97, 115, 125, 129–30, 256,
278–80
Heath, Robert, 15–16, 19, 93
Hebert, F. Edward, 79
Hecksher, Henry, 60–61, 68, 75,
87, 126, 130, 280
Heindel, John, 152
Helliwell, Paul, 113–16, 202,
204, 277
Helms, Richard, 72, 88, 241
Hemming, Gerry Patrick, 45, 59,
63, 73–74, 92, 97, 122
Herran Olozaga, Rafael, 30–33,
38, 43
Herran Olozaga, Tomas, 31–33,
38, 43
Hermsdorf, Harry, 44–46
Herter, Christian, 54, 87, 93– 94,
250, 260, 267–268
Hickey, Edward J., 260–261
Hilton, Conrad, 32, 175
Hobbing, Enno, 130
Hoffa, Jimmy, 22, 30, 38–39, 65,
70, 75, 105–10, 124, 275,
280
Hoke, John, 204
Hoover, Herbert, 175, 231

Hoover, J. Edgar, 40, 49, 59, 65,
    112, 119, 121, 123–24, 188,
    216, 240, 242, 256, 260
Hopkins, Lewis, E., 213
Hosty, James, 243
Hughes, Allan, 129
Hughes, Howard, 118, 123, 129
Hunt, E. Howard, 58, 60, 67,
    74–75, 87–88, 91, 95–97,
    126, 280–81
Hunt, George W. P., 106
Hunt, H.L., 128, 180, 183–84,
    186, 279
Hunt, St. Jean, 75
Hurt, John, 209
Hyde, Carol, 204
Hyde, William Avery, 204

I

Ignacio, Jose, 91
Information Council of the
    Americas (INCA), 23
Irion, John, 14–15
Irwin, Emmett, 179–80
Isaacs, Harold, 232–34, 283

J

Jackson, C.D., 222–23
Jehan, Jean, 37–38

Jenkins, Walter, 127
John Birch Society, 5, 179, 181,
    184
Johnson, Blaney Mack, 40–42
Johnson, Kelly, 248
Johnson, Lady Bird, 22
Johnson, Lyndon, 22, 65, 75, 79,
    89, 103, 108, 111, 126–28,
    140, 173, 176, 184–87, 189,
    248, 273
Johnson, Manning, 3
Johnson, Priscilla, 7, 226–27,
    230–31, 233–36, 238, 259,
    263, 283
    CIA affiliation, 216, 227–30,
    232
    Post-assassination relationship to
    Marina, 216, 226, 231–34
Johnston, Roger E. Jr., 21
Jones, John Roland, 32–33
Junta Of National Liberation, 97

K

Kail, Samuel G., 59,
Kasem-Beg, Alexander, 257
Kennan, George, 253, 273

Kennedy, David, M., 115
Kennedy, Ethel,, 106
Kennedy, John F., 83–84, 89,
    94–96, 99, 101, 103–105,
    176, 178–79, 188, 246, 248,
    270–74, 277, 284, 286
    Assassination attempts against as
    candidate, 187
    Discontent of radical right, 186,
    276–77, 285–86
    Judith Campbell, 120–21, 123
    1960 election, 123–28, 185,
    187–88
    Racial views, 185–86
Kennedy, Joseph, 105, 107
    and Lyndon Johnson, 126–28
    Organized crime involvement,
    123–25, 271
Kennedy, Robert F., 53, 75, 96,
    102, 123, 126–27
    McClellan Committee, 103,
    105–109, 114
Kent, Morton, 275
Khrushchev, Nikita, 66–67, 81,
    84, 187, 249–52, 253, 255,
    262–64
    Blames U.S. militarists for U-2
    affair, 245, 266–69
    Trip to U.S. in 1959, 173–75
Kilgallen, Dorothy, 62, 110, 275
Kilgore, Joe, 127
Killian, James R. Jr., 203, 232–33,
    248, 283
King, J.C., 84–88, 93–94
King, Martin Luther, 11, 64,
    185–86
Kirkpatrick, Lyman, B., 18, 28, 34
Kishi, Nobusuke, 268
Kissinger, Henry, 246
Kleberg, Robert J. Jr., 65–66
Klein, Frank, 100
Knight, Francis, 232
Knights of the White Camellia, 20
Knights of the White Christians,
    20
Kohly, Mario Garcia, 90–91,
    95–98, 272, 281
Korengold, Robert J., 225
Kostikov, Valeriy, 240
Kronthal, James, 275
Ku Klux Klan, 2, 20, 181

L

Lafitte, Jean-Pierre, 17, 20, 37–38,
    48, 60, 109, 129, 278–79,
    281–82

Land, Edwin H., 248
Landry, Al, 14
Lansky, Jake, 55, 69, 125
Lansky, Meyer, 27, 36, 38, 55, 57,
    63, 107, 114, 116, 120, 129
Lanusa, Jose, 100
Lawford, Peter, 123
LeMay, Curtis, 249, 255
Lemnitzer, Lyman, 82–83, 105
Levine, Isaac Don, 231, 234, 280
Levinson, Ed, 22
Lewallen, Jim, 21
Lief, Harold, 21
Lobo, Julio, 65
Lodge, Henry Cabot, 174
Logan, Mae, 47
London, Jack, 197, 198
Long, Huey, 274
Long, Russell, 20
Lorenz, Marita, 44–45, 73–75,
    101, 122, 281
Luby, Elliot, 49
Luce, Clare Boothe, 99–100,
    219, 247
Luce, Henry, 99–100, 113, 175,
    223
Luciano, Lucky, 33, 38, 107,
    114–16, 278
Lumumba, Patrice, 46

M

MacArthur, Douglas, 142,
    176–77, 180–82, 245, 274,
    278, 284
Macedo, Joseph D., 148
Maceo, Antonio, 96
Maddox, Al, 48
Maheu, Robert, 113, 116–20,
    122–23, 128–31
Makinen, William, 218
Malik, Jacob, 78
Malone, Jack, 65–66
Mamantov, Ilya, 231, 234, 280
Mannarino, Gabriel, 36–37, 57
Mannarino, Salvatore, 37, 57
Mannarino, Sam, 36–37, 57
Marcello, Carlos, 22, 30, 32–33,
    37–40, 43, 65, 73, 75, 100,
    108–10, 112–13, 123, 278,
    280, 282
Marchetti, Victor, 23, 139, 210
Marcinkus, Monsignor Paul,
    115–16
Marsh, Lawrence, 14
Marshall, George, 17–18, 51
Martello, Francis L., 200

Martin, Dean, 123
Martin, Jack, 17, 20–21, 38, 49, 282
Martin, William Hamilton, 369
Martino, John, 59–60, 62, 69, 75, 87, 100, 278, 280–81
Marx, Karl, 7
Masferrer, Rolando, 34, 40, 96, 281
Massachusetts Institute of Technology (MIT), 203, 232–34, 283
Mathiessen, Francis Otto, 275
McBride, Palmer E., 6–7
McCarthy, Joseph, 103–105, 137
McCloy, John, 222–23, 246
McClellan Committee, 105, 107–10, 115, 118–19, 121, 124
McCone, John, 255
McDonough, Sue, 211
McElroy, Neil, 81, 250
McGuire, E. Perkins, 204
McGuire, Phyllis, 122
McInerney, Tim, 127
McKeown, Robert Ray, 29–30, 38, 40–41, 119
McMillan, George Edwin, 234
McVickar, John 216, 225, 255
McWillie, Lewis, 32–33, 61–63, 70–73, 281
Medalie, Richard, 220–21
Medaris, John Bruce, 83
Melton, Maurice, 32
Meltzer, Harold, 130–31
Menderes, Adnan, 268
Mertz, Michael, 38, 278–79
Meyer, Cord, 75, 216, 219, 222–24, 227, 229–34, 283
Mikoyan, Anastas, 85
Milteer, Joseph, 180–82, 184
Minutemen, 5, 184, 196, 248
Mitchell, Bernon F., 257
MKULTRA, 47–48, 146, 151
Mondoloni, Paul, 33, 37–38, 41, 43, 55, 109–10, 112, 278–79
Montgomery, John, 275
Montini, Giovanni (Pope Paul VI), 115
Moore, J. Walton, 101, 205
Morales, David, 53, 57–60, 68, 76, 87, 97–98, 126, 130–31, 280
Moreel, Ben, 175
Morgan, William, 45, 63–70, 126, 196, 271, 274, 285

Morrison, de Lesseps, 4, 179
Morrow, Robert, 24, 90, 96–98, 101, 104
Mosby, Aline, 7, 225–26, 235–36, 238
Movement of Revolutionary Recovery (MRR), 91
Murchison, Clint, 22–23, 30, 65, 279
Murphy, Paul, 146
Murret, Marilyn Dorothea, 32, 232–34, 283
Murrow, Edward R., 106
Mynier, Elaine, 71

N

Nagell, Richard, Case, 49, 102, 142, 144–45, 194, 215, 281–82
Nagy, Ferenc, 24
National Students Association (NSA), 28, 218–23
Nichols, Alice, 71
Nixon, Richard, 54, 75, 84–87, 89–91, 94–96, 114, 176, 186–88, 269, 271–72
Noll, Carl, 37
Norstad, Lauris, 67

O

OAS, 23–24, 56, 98, 100, 278
Ochsner, Alton, 21–23
O'Connell, Jim, 117–19
Olson, Frank, 31, 43, 101, 129, 275
OMEGA Plan, 60, 99, 102, 284–85
Operation 40, 77, 96–99, 101, 272, 281
Orlov, Lawrence, 205, 234, 283
Ormento, John, 109–10
Osborn, Frederick Jr., 204–205
Osborn, Frederick Henry Sr., 289
Osborn, Henry Fairfield, 205
Osborn, Nancy, 204–205
Osborne, Mack, 191
Oswald, Audrey Marina Rachel, 8
Oswald, John Pic, 11
Oswald, Lee Harvey, ix–xi, 1, 4, 6, 8, 10, 12, 14–21, 23, 25, 27, 31–32, 39, 41, 49, 64, 72–73, 92–93, 95, 97, 99–100, 102, 110–12, 177, 222, 224, 230, 275, 279, 281–82
A.J Hidell alias, 17, 38, 210–12, 242–44, 281–82, 285

Applies to Albert Schweitzer College, 197–99
at Atsugi, Japan, 133–36
CIA interest in, 25, 101, 135–37, 209–10, 255–59
Conflicting documentation on leaving Marines, 206–12
Defection, 137–43, 206, 218, 232–35, 282–83
Early Marine service, 132–33
at El Toro Marine Corps Air Station, 190, 192, 265–66
Fascist tendencies, 8, 11, 14, 182, 234, 277
Height discrepancy after leaving Marines, 235–42
in Moscow, 7, 214–15, 224–30, 259–60
Interest in Cuba, 196–97
June Cobb connection, 30, 46–52
and Kerry Thornley, 192–95, 199–201
Lorenz caravan, 74–75
Marxist views, 1, 7–9, 11, 192
Military Intelligence possible connection, 217–19
Possible drug experimentation at Atsugi, 146–54, 283
Possible impostor, 216, 239–45, 261–62
Pro-Russian behavior in Marines, 154–55, 191, 195–96
Queen Bee/Eroshkin incident, 142–46
Reading habits, 50, 133–34, 194, 197–98, 201
Teenage years in New Orleans, 6–7, 10–13, 47
Travels to Russia, 212–14
Unitarian Church, 199–206
U.S. response to defection, 270
Oswald, Marguerite, ix, 11, 25, 140, 141, 259, 260
Oswald, Marina, 7–8, 10, 196, 204–205, 216, 226, 231–34, 238, 240, 242, 280
Oswald, Robert, 259
Oswald, Victor, 48, 278, 281
Otepka, Otto, 139–40
Owens, Calvin "Bud," 243

P

Padilla, Antonio Rubio, 91–92
Paget, Mariano, 34
Paine, George, Lyman, 204

Paine, Michael, 204, 227–28, 233–34
Paine, Ruth, 204–205, 228, 233–34, 240, 242, 283
Paine, Ruth Forbes, 204, 227
Panitz, Meyer, 71
Partin, Edward, 39
Papich, Sam, 255
Pash, Boris, 130
Pavlick, Richard Paul, 187
Pawley, William, 17–18, 22, 35–36, 58, 64, 90–95, 99–101, 113–14, 188, 272, 279–80
Peale, Norman Vincent, 197–98
Pelletier, Jesus Yanez, 44
Perez, Leander, 3, 5, 20, 46, 178–81, 183–84
Permindex, 24, 100, 279
Peron, Juan, 22
Philbrick, Herbert, 9–10, 177, 203
Phillips, David Atlee, 50, 58–60, 64, 66, 68, 75, 87, 126, 217, 280–81
Piedra, Orland, 38, 97
Pierson, Jean T., 59
Pinchback, Glenn, 11
Pitts, Gerry E., 152
Pope, Lawrence, 274
Poulson, Norris, 174
Powers, Daniel, 152–53, 191, 195
Powers, Francis Gary, 143, 257, 262–66, 268, 274
Powers, Thomas, S., 254
Price, C.J., 241
Prio, Carlos, 27, 29, 35, 38, 40–43, 54, 56, 68, 91, 101, 120, 275
Priziola, John, 109
Proctor, Thomas G, 48, 278, 281
Project Artichoke, 151
Project Bluebird, 118, 153
Project Troy, 203, 232–33, 283
Prouty, Fletcher, 133, 264, 266
Pullman, John, 114

Q
QJWIN, 48, 278
Quasarano, Rafael, 109
Quintero, Rafael "Chi", 61
Quiroga, Carlos, 100

R
Radford, Arthur, 81, 255
Ragano, Frank, 36, 70, 123

Rankin, Lee, 40, 196
Rainach, Willie, 5, 9, 178, 181
Ray, Manuel, 91, 96
Rayburn, Sam, 176, 185
Reagan, Ronald, 175
Rebozo, Bebe, 114
Reid, Barbara, 192
Reuther, Walter, 178
Reyes, Gustavo de los, 66–68
Rhodes, Charles, 133, 148
Ricciardelli, Libero, 140
Richardson, Sid, 176, 185, 279
Richter, James, 78
Ridgeway, Mathew, 83
Rivard, Lucian, 37, 55
Roa, Raul, 68
Robert E. Lee Patriots, 20
Roberts, Delphine, 10, 14, 178–79, 181
Roache, Wendall, 12
Rockefeller, Nelson, 65, 189, 205
Roman, Jane, 46
Roosevelt, Franklin (FDR), 176, 204–205, 231, 274
Rorke, Alexander, 44–45, 56, 122
Rose, Earl, 241–42
Roselli, John, 57–58, 73, 128–31, 275, 278, 280
CIA/Mafia Castro Assassination plot, 118–20, 122–23, 125
Rothman, Norman, 36–38, 40–43, 57, 62
Rowan, Dan, 122, 125
Ruby, Jack, 19, 26, 30, 32–33, 38–39, 43, 47–48, 61, 236–237, 240, 244, 275, 282, 285
Attempt to get Trafficante out of a Cuba jail, 70–73, 103, 119, 278, 281
Arms trafficking and involvement in 1959 Havana coup attempt, 38–42, 63–64, 110, 278
Jack LaRue alias, 110
Lorenz caravan, 73–74
Mickey Cohen and Candy Barr, 38, 110–12
Ruggles, Lucy, 23
Rusk, Dean, 50, 96, 216, 261
Russell, Richard, 253
Russian Research Center, 232–34, 283
Russo, Don Giuseppe Genco, 115

S
Saavedra, Henry, 32–33, 50, 125
Sanchez, Celia, 43
Schacht, Hjalmar, 24, 278
Schacht, Robert, 199
Schrand, Martin, 136, 147–49
Schlesinger, Arthur Jr., 97, 229, 276
Schwarz, Fred, 176–77
Second National Front of the Escambray (SNFE), 56, 63–64, 99
Seiferheld, David, 202
Sforza, Tony, 58–59, 280
Shackley, Ted, 130
Shamma, Geraldine, 59–60, 65–66, 68
Shaw, Clay, 16–18, 20,–25, 40, 92, 95, 100, 136, 140, 213, 282
Shimon, Joe, 129–30
Shimon, Toni, 129
Shirokova, Rima, 214
Sichel, Peter, 61
Siegel, bugsy, 110
Silva, Frank, 15–16, 19, 92–93
Sinatra, Frank, 120–23
Sindona, Michael, 114–16
Singelmann, George, 5
Siragusa, Charles, 48, 60, 125, 131, 278
Skorzeny, Otto, 278
Slawson, David W., 242
Sloboda, Vladimir, 140–42
Smith, Earl, 35
Smith, Gerald L.K., 182
Smith, Joseph B., 132, 135, 138
Smith, W. Marvin, 275
Smoot, Dan, 180, 184
Snyder, Richard, 224–25, 230, 255–56, 259
Somersett, Willie, 180–82
Somoza, Anastasio, 22, 49
Sorensen, Theodore, 127
Spada, Prince Massimo, 115
Spadaforo, Gutierrez di, 24
Speller, Jon, 45
Spellman, Francis Cardinal, 65
Spiritual Mobilization, 175, 188, 198
and the Committee to Proclaim Liberty, 175–76
Starbird, Alfred, 263
Steinem, Gloria, 222–23
Stevens, Marguerite, 25, 140–41, 218, 256–57

Stevenson, Adlai, 246
St. George, Andrew, 41
Stout, Sergeant, 206
Stout, Zack, 133
Sturgis (Fiorini), Frank, 40,
    42, 44–45, 49, 56–57, 59,
    62–63, 68–69, 73–75, 87,
    92, 97–98, 100–101, 122,
    280–81
Suarez, Alfred, 59
Sucharov, Bert, 72
Suite 8F Group, 22, 188, 279–80,
    282, 284
Sukarno, Kusno, 117, 274
Surrey, Robert, 184
Sweeney Louise, 209
Swift, Wesley, 181–82
Symington, Stuart, 247–48

T

Taylor, Maxwell, 81–84, 105
Teeter, John W., 122
Tejada, Alfredo, 18
Teller, Edward, 263–64
Thomas, Charles, William, 50,
    275, 279
Thompson, Llewellyn 259, 263
Thompson, Dolores, 41
Thompson, Mary, 40–41
Thornley, Kerry, x, 190, 192–93,
    195, 204, 213, 234, 283
    CIA connection, 194
    Unitarian Church, 199,
        200–201, 233
    with Oswald in New Orleans
        182, 193–94, 205, 282
Tippit, J.D., 243, 285
Tourine, Charles, Jr, 55, 57
Trafficante, Santo Jr., 32–33,
    36–39, 42–43, 49–50,
    54–55, 57, 59–63, 69–71,
    112–13, 118, 126, 129, 278
    280–82

Castro agent, 36, 70, 72–73, 75,
    87, 95, 103, 107–109, 121,
    124–25
CIA/Mafia Castro Assassination
    plot, 118–20, 122, 129–31,
    278
Trail William K., 151–52
Treon, Alveeta, 209
Trotsky, Leon, 9, 232
Trujillo, Rafael, 35, 55–57, 63,
    70, 94, 113, 117, 206, 280
Truman, Harry S., 181, 274–75
Twining, Nathan, 67, 83, 249,
    253
Tyler, Linscott, 203

U

Unitarian Church, x, 199–201,
    203–204, 207, 233–34
United Klans of America, 20
Urrutia, Manual, 54, 62

V

Varona, Tony, 68, 91, 96–97,
    120–22, 130
Veciana, Antonio, 75, 281
Venturi, Dominick, 37
Voebel, Edward, 7
von Braun, Werner, 130

W

Wade, Henry, 64, 95, 111
Wagner, Herb, 21
Wagner, Robert, 174
Walker, Edwin, 2, 180, 184
Walton, Bob, 58
Warren, Earl, 2, 176
Webster, Robert E., 140
Welch, Robert, 179, 181
West, Louis, 47–49
Westbrook, W.R., 243
White Citizens Councils, 2, 3, 5,
    179–81, 184

White, George, Hunter, 17, 19,
    38, 48, 60, 86, 150, 228, 282
    Possible connection to CIA/
        Mafia assassination plot,
        128–29, 131, 278
    Connection to June Cobb, 32,
        48
White, Harry Dexter, 275
Wieland, William, 35, 90–91
Wiesner, Jerome, 79–80
Wilcott, Elsie, 135–36
Wilcott, James, 135–36, 138, 150,
    215, 258
Williams, Garland, 131
Williams, Robert F., 46
Williams, Harry, 32
Williamson, Earl, 60
Willoughby, Charles, 23, 142, 278
Wilson, Benton, 21
Wilson, John, 72–73
Wisner, Frank, 24, 218–19, 280
Woodring, Harry H., 205
Woodward, James, 41
Woolam, Paul F., 57
World Commerce Corporation
    (WCC), 33, 48, 114, 116,
    277–80, 282
Wright, Jim, 260
Wright, Skelly, 178
Wulf, William, Eugene, 6–7
Wurms, Ike, 109

Y

Yazbeck, Hanna, 130
York, Herb, 79
Young, Ruth Forbes Paine, 204

Z

Zicarelli, Joseph, 113, 117
Zigiotti, Giuseppi, 24
ZR/AWARD, 130
ZR/RIFLE, 48, 59, 130, 278

About the Author

WALTER HERBST has been researching the assassination of President John F. Kennedy for thirty-eight years and is passionate about uncovering the truth behind the greatest crime in American history. Through the years, his investigation expanded to include related topics, such as America's role in assassinations and government overthrows around the world, the hidden history of the U.S. military and CIA, anti-communism, the civil rights movement, and the rise of the radical right throughout the twentieth century.

He enjoys writing books that reveal the truth about America's secret past, for, like most Americans, he cares deeply about fairness. As a result, his works will appeal to readers who are unwilling to accept the sanitized version of American history and want to know the truth about the nation's sometimes checkered past. Walter lives with his wife Margaret in Mahwah, NJ.

Learn more at herbstbooks.com.

Printed in Great Britain
by Amazon